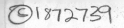

C++

Problem Solving and Programming

C++

Problem Solving and Programming

KENNETH A. BARCLAY
Department of Computer Studies
Napier University, Edinburgh

and

BRIAN J. GORDON
Information and Statistics Division
Scottish Health Services, Edinburgh

Prentice Hall
New York London Toronto Sydney Tokyo Singapore

First published 1994 by
Prentice Hall International (UK) Limited
Campus 400, Maylands Avenue
Hemel Hempstead
Hertfordshire, HP2 7EZ
A division of
Simon & Schuster International Group

Typeset in 10/12 pt Plantin
by Columns Typesetting of Reading

Printed and bound in Great Britain by
Redwood Books, Towbridge, Wiltshire

Library of Congress Cataloging-in-Publication Data

Barclay, Kenneth A.
C++ problem solving and programming / K. Barclay, B. Gordon.
p. cm.
Includes bibliographical references and index.
1. C++ (Computer program language) I. Gordon, B. II. Title.
QA76.73.C153B347 1994
005.13'3–dc20 93–44647
CIP

British Library Cataloguing in Publication Data

A catalogue record for this book is available from the British Library

ISBN 0–13–126673–X

1 2 3 4 5 98 97 96 95 94

Contents

Preface

This book provides a comprehensive introduction to the C++ programming language. It is suitable for both novice and experienced programmers.

The C++ programming language [Str86, Str91] was originally developed as an evolution of the C programming language [Ker88]. The extensions include *strong typing*, and support for *data abstraction* and *object oriented programming*. These changes are sufficiently significant to warrant considering C++ as a completely new language. As a consequence, this text is presented exclusively in terms of a new programming language without reference to C.

By the early 1990s the maturity of the C++ programming language dictated the need for a language standard. The American National Standard Institute (ANSI) formed a standardization committee to provide a definition for the language. The initial work is based on the book *The Annotated C++ Reference Manual* [Ell90]. Every effort has been made to ensure the programs and the text comply with this evolving standard.

Considerable effort has been taken to present the language topics in a clear, structured and concise manner. To achieve these aims the book has been divided into two sections. Part I introduces fundamental language constructs (Chapters 1 to 8). The experienced C programmer may omit this material but language specifics (such as Chapter 4, and Sections 5.9–5.12) will need to be reviewed.

Part II (from Chapter 9 on) introduces those distinguishing object oriented features of the language, including *class structuring* with data and function members, *operator overloading*, *inheritance*, *polymorphism* and *dynamic binding*.

Structure of this book

Chapters 3, 4 and 6 present fundamental aspects of programming: *data types*, *operators, arithmetic expressions, input/output* and *program flow control*. Chapter 3 examines the issues involved in forming computational expressions using the fundamental data types and the arithmetic operators. Chapter 4 demonstrates some basic input/output capabilities so our programs can receive data and deliver results. In Chapter 6 we describe the control flow mechanisms of sequence, selection and iteration and through them extend our computational capabilities.

Chapters 5 and 7 focus on the support provided by the language for *procedural abstraction*. In particular, Chapter 5 provides a detailed exposition of the function in C++, including value, pointer and reference argument passing. The function is one of the pivotal abstraction concepts in the language. For this reason it is introduced early in the text and is reinforced through constant use thereafter.

Chapter 7 addresses the problem of 'programming in the large', using the concept of a *program unit* to maintain a clear separation of the definition and use of a resource from its implementation. These divisions are supported by the storage classes and scope rules of the language.

In Chapter 5 we introduce complete programs, all reproduced from the computer. Each should execute correctly on any machine supporting a standard C++ compiler. A particular feature of the book is the inclusion of a number of major case studies illustrating features not otherwise achievable with small programs.

Chapters 9 and 10 introduce the class mechanism. Here we investigate the language support for the design and implementation of *abstract data types*. A user-defined data type can be defined to model elements of the application. Programs are easier to design, implement and maintain if we can construct entities within the program which imitate those in the problem space.

In Chapter 11 we introduce the object oriented features of C++, namely, inheritance, polymorphism and dynamic binding. Through inheritance we can evolve new classes from existing classes. The new class will share the features of the old class as well as having its own distinctive set. The resulting class hierarchy is reminiscent of taxonomies used in other fields of study where each classification is a specialized kind of some other general classification.

Through polymorphism and dynamic binding some abstract task may be defined over a number of classes related by inheritance. This task may then be applied to any object instance of these classes and the object itself will determine how to achieve it.

Chapter 12 and subsequent chapters then exploit the object oriented constructs of the language by developing a large class library and using it to implement solutions to the case studies.

TYPOGRAPHICAL NOTE

The C++ programming language uses the ellipsis "..." as a syntactic token of the language. To distinguish between the C++ language usage and the standard elipsis which indicates missing items or a range, the latter has been presented throughout the book as ".....".

ACKNOWLEDGEMENTS

Whilst the names of the authors appear on this book, we wish to thank the many individuals who made it possible.

We are grateful to our respective employers for their motivating influences and support. Without their organizational support we could not have written this book. My (KB) gratitude goes to the Department of Computer Studies, Napier University. I wish to thank the students of the Department, particularly the postgraduate students and professional short course students who, as recipients of a course based on this text, directly and indirectly contributed. In particular, special mention is given to the postgraduate students Gerry Dawson, Ian Rae, Calum Taylor and Colin Thomson who worked on the development of the container class library illustrated in the text. I am also indebted to the programming support staff who quietly and effectively made operational the resources of the Department. I (BG) would wish to mention Audrey Stacey and Mary Smalls at the Information Statistics Division of the Health Services in Scotland who regularly gave support and encouragement.

The authors are indebted to Jim Murray of Napier University who scrutinized the many drafts of each chapter. His experience of programming practice contributed significantly to the material. Thanks also to colleague Dr John Savage who offered many stimulating discussions on the object model and object oriented programming.

The encouragement and support of the staff at Edinburgh Portable Compilers is much appreciated. The authors' experience of sharing with a team involved in C++ compiler developments was most beneficial. In particular, we would wish to mention John Murison and Athol Hay.

We acknowledge the permission granted by Elsevier Science Publishers B. V. for allowing us to reproduce Figure 3.5 (from which Figures 3.6, 3.8, 5.3, 5.4, 5.5 and 5.7 are derived) from their publication *Informal Introduction to ALGOL 68.*

Thanks also to Helen Martin and her team at Prentice Hall who gave support when needed, and flexibility with the schedule when it proved necessary.

Finally, I (KB) thank my wife Irene, and children Dawn, Ria and Kim for their love and patience while this book was in preparation. Perhaps now, the absent father can return some time to them. I (BG) gratefully acknowledge the support of Jan, Claire and Jonathan Warner, family and friends, particularly Claire Jones.

K. Barclay
B. Gordon

Part I

1
Programming Paradigms

Computer technology has developed extremely quickly since its inception. Today, computer-based systems affect our lives in many spheres including banking systems, medical systems, flight reservation systems, and educational and military systems. All these systems are distinguished by having large amounts of software at their core. The capabilities of these systems are derived from the complex computer programs which control them.

Whilst we understand the process of developing computer software better, we still deliver systems late, and over budget. Often they fail to do what the user requires and they are difficult to maintain and modify. These clichéd remarks have always applied to the computer software industry, and whilst we have improved the technologies to support the development process, this has not fully matched the size and complexity of contemporary systems.

Computer software was originally developed as an unstructured, monolithic entity. All the data upon which a program performed its processing actions was accessible across the whole system making it very difficult for the developer to isolate any changes. Program flow of control was also undisciplined, with a program's logic explained by code which jumped from one part to another. Little language support was provided by the programming languages whereby the programmer could impose some control over the program logic and its data items.

1.1 Procedural abstraction

A revolution occurred with the introduction of *structured programming* techniques. Essentially this involves decomposing software systems into ever increasing levels of detail. The decomposition is organized around the processing actions required by the software. Structured programs form a hierarchy of processing tasks realized as programming language *procedures* (or *functions*). Each procedure is supported by one or more subordinate procedures in the system hierarchy. Procedures transmit information to other procedures through *parameter* (or *argument*) lists. Procedures process these parameter values in conjunction with local procedure data items to produce the desired effect.

The outcome is that procedures become independent processing tasks. Their behaviour is described fully in terms of their parameters and local data values.

This isolation reduces the dependence of one procedure upon another making it easier to develop maintainable code. Changes to one procedure need not affect any other procedure.

A consequence of these developments is that a procedure may be viewed in terms of *what* it does and not *how* it does it. To achieve some effect it is only necessary to know how to call the procedure. This separation of the what and the how we refer to as *abstraction* and is the basis of structured techniques. *Procedural abstraction* in which we abstract some task into a procedure is the cornerstone of structured programming (see Chapters 5, 6 and 7).

1.2 Data abstraction

More recently we have come to realize that the data structures manipulated by a program are as important as the processing tasks performed on them. In structured programming these structures are encapsulated into *data types* and passed as procedure parameters and used as local data items of that type. When changes occur in these data types then expensive modifications must be made to those procedures that act on the representation of these structures.

Data abstraction is the counterpart of procedural abstraction. An *abstract data type* emphasizes the *what* the data type represents in the problem domain at the expense of the *how* it is implemented. This is achieved by encapsulating the exact implementation of the data type so that it is not directly accessible to any client procedure. The behavioural characteristic of the data type is described by a set of public *operations* applicable to the data type. An application program operates through the public interface and not through the private representation of the data type. This way, changes to the data type representation can be achieved without extensive modifications being necessary across the applications that use the data type. This forces a clear separation between the specification which documents the *what*, and the implementation which defines the *how* (see Chapters 9 and 10).

1.3 Object orientation

It is generally agreed that data abstraction is a major step in gaining leverage over the problem and is the focus for the structuring of our programming systems. The importance of data abstraction is that it is the entry point into object oriented computing.

The fundamental idea of object oriented programming is to model the world of the application in terms of *objects*. One object can direct another object through invoking one of that object's operations.

Objects belong to a *class*. Two or more objects from the same class have the same behaviour. For example, if `Person` is a class describing ordinary people then typical operations on such a class might include asking a `Person` object for their name or age, or an operation which changes the name of a `Person`. All instances of class `Person` will share this behaviour.

Again, the class concept is a form of abstraction. The class `Person`, for example, describes the operations applicable to people. It need only be specified once and can then be applied to any number of `Person` instances.

Probably the most distinguishing feature of object orientation is the use of *inheritance*. Through inheritance a new class can be developed from an existing class. The new class is called the *derived* class and inherits the representation and operations of the original class, known as the *base* class. The derived class shares the behaviour of the base class since it supports the same operations of its base. The derived class may add further representational data items and new operations to those that it inherits from its base class. The derived class may also modify the behaviour of an inherited operation.

A computer program for a personnel record system might introduce a class `Employee`. An `Employee` has a name, an age, a job title and a salary. Rather than develop a new class for `Employee` we might recognize that an `Employee` is like a `Person` but with additional features, e.g. job title and salary. By introducing `Employee` as a class derived from `Person` we inherit, without producing any new code the operations to ask an `Employee` for his name and age and the operation to change the name of that `Employee`.

Through inheritance we have not had to modify the class `Person` to make it into an `Employee`. Programs dependent upon `Person` remain unchanged. This is important if we are to ensure that existing programs do not have to be modified. Further, the code to compute a person's age is *reused* by class `Employee`. Inheritance adds support for the evolution and reuse of code.

Suppose we now have an object instance of class `Employee`. Assuming an appropriate operation, we might ask that instance for its job title. This operation will be provided by the specialized class `Employee`. However, when we ask that `Employee` instance for its age, the actual operation is provided by the base class `Person`. A consequence of this behaviour is that it is necessary to locate the implementation for the operation applied to the object instance. Since class `Employee` does not provide an implementation for obtaining an employee's name, the system selects the most specific by searching back through the base classes until one is found.

Consider also a student record system which introduces the class `Student`. Once again we view a `Student` as a specialized kind of `Person`. A `Student` additionally includes its own unique characteristics such as enrolment number and course name. Again, only those new features of class `Student` need be introduced.

Through inheritance we also introduce another object oriented feature, namely, *polymorphism*. Polymorphism represents a programming shift toward many implementations associated with an operation rather than a single implementation as found in conventional programming languages. Polymorphism enhances abstraction by allowing operations to be defined and redefined over a number of classes related by inheritance. The concern is then with what operation an object supports and not how it is implemented. The implementation may be at any level in the inheritance hierarchy.

To illustrate, consider that class `Person` has an operation `print` which displays the name and date of birth. Class `Employee` also supports this operation but prints the employee's name and job title. Finally, class `Student` prints the name, enrolment number and course name of instances of this class. A file containing a mixture of `Employee` and `Student` objects might exist. We could iterate across the file extracting each object and requesting them to perform their `print` operation. In traditional programming languages we would require the programmer to develop code to determine the type of each item from the file before calling the correct `print` procedure. In object oriented programming languages, objects are responsible for their own behaviour and all that would be necessary is to request that the object taken from the file `print` itself. The code would determine if the actual object was an `Employee` or a `Student` and execute the correct implementation.

The flexibility resulting from the concepts of inheritance and polymorphism provides a framework for a new approach to software development and is introduced in Chapters 11 and 12.

2

Essentials of a C++ Program

The features of C++ introduced in this chapter are covered in greater depth later in this book. Here, details, formal specifications, exceptions and so on, are deliberately avoided. This way we concentrate on the structure of a C++ program without being overwhelmed by the volume of technical detail. Armed with these essentials, we may progress to later chapters and explore the fine detail.

In no sense are the example programs of any real value or use. They are technically complete, however, and will compile and execute on a computer supporting a C++ compiler.

2.1 A first program

We start by considering a very modest program to display on the computer terminal the message `"My first program."`. In C++, the program to print this message is:

PROGRAM 2.1(a)

```
#include <iostream.h>

int main()

{
  cout << "My first program.";
  return (0);
}
```

In the C++ programming language, use is made of both upper case and lower case letters to name program objects. The name `main` in the above program must appear as shown. The names `MAIN` and `Main`, for example, would be interpreted as different names from their lower case form.

C++ programs are described as free-format. This means that the language places few restrictions on the appearance of a program, and that it is the programmer's responsibility to choose the layout of the program. This programmer freedom may be used or abused. The following two versions of the original program are equally acceptable to the C++ compiler. They each achieve the same result. The new variants are, however, very difficult to read and are of doubtful quality. Certain stylistic conventions have been adopted by the C++ programming community and they are noted below and in subsequent programming examples.

PROGRAM 2.1(b)

```
#include <iostream.h>

int main() { cout << "My first program."; return (0); }
```

PROGRAM 2.1(c)

```
#include <iostream.h>

int
main()
{
cout
<<
"My first program."
;
return
(0);
}
```

A C++ program is composed of one or more *functions*. Each function specifies the computation to be performed by that piece of code. Each function in C++ is identified by its name. The name of the function is chosen by the programmer. The exception to this rule is that there must exist one and only one function called `main` in any given program. A program starts executing from the first instruction in the function `main`. Upon completion, control is returned to the program's operating environment through the `return` statement with the value zero as the value of the program. Typically, the return value zero denotes program success and a non-zero value indicates some form of program failure.

The function `main` executes instructions and invokes other functions to perform their operations. The instructions are given as program *statements*. The other functions may be part of the same program or be members of *libraries* of previously developed functions. The standard library is a collection of C++ functions designed to provide, amongst other things, standard input/output facilities. Programs which confine themselves to the facilities of the standard library will be portable and can be moved between computer systems.

The program statement:

```
cout << "My first program.";
```

delivers output to the user's terminal. Output is directed to the user's terminal, referred to as the *standard output,* and associates with the predefined `iostream` (input/output stream) `cout`. The standard output `cout` is defined in the *header file* `iostream.h`. The `#include` line is a *pre-processor directive,* and causes the content of the named file to be read into the program text file when it is compiled, from which we obtain the details about `cout`. The output operator (`<<`), referred to as *insertion,* is implemented as a standard library function.

Finally, the braces `{` and `}` enclose the statements that constitute the function `main`. The statement or statements enclosed within the braces is the *function body.* In C++, the semicolon is the statement terminator, rather like the full stop in natural language. Every C++ statement must have a terminating semicolon. Program 2.2 extends our first program by including another statement with associated semicolon.

PROGRAM 2.2(a)

```
#include <iostream.h>

int main()
{
  cout << "My first program.\n";
  cout << "It is wonderful.\n";
  return (0);
}
```

In this program two stylistic conventions are being followed. First, each statement appears on separate lines. This is not essential but it does improve program readability. Second, the three statements are indented a number of character places from the left margin using blank or space characters. This helps to identify the program structure under consideration, particularly when dealing with large multi-function programs.

The sequence `\n` is the C++ notation for a newline symbol. When a new line is printed, all subsequent output starts from the left margin of the next line. Thus the output from the last program is:

```
My first program.
It is wonderful.
```

Note that two output statements do not imply two separate lines of output. Consider a second version of this program:

PROGRAM 2.2(b)

```
#include <iostream.h>

int main()
```

```
{
  cout << "My first program.";
  cout << "It is wonderful.\n";
  return (0);
}
```

Without the explicit newline symbol appearing in the first character string, the output from this program is:

```
My first program.It is wonderful.
```

In these first examples, the output statement was used to display a character string. It is also capable of displaying the value of *expressions* and *variables*. Consider the following program employing these two new concepts.

PROGRAM 2.3

```
#include <iostream.h>

int main()
{
  int sum;

  sum = 10 + 20;
  cout << "The sum of 10 and 20 is " << sum << "\n";
  return (0);
}
```

The first line of this function body is an example of a *variable definition*. In common with many other programming languages, C++ requires that all variables be defined before they are used. A variable is a name for a region of memory in which a value may be stored. The variable `sum` is declared to be of type `int` (integer), that is, a variable which represents numbers without fractional parts.

The second statement causes the *integer constants* 10 and 20 to be summed and the resulting value placed in the memory location known as `sum`. This is an example of the C++ *assignment*. The *expression* `10 + 20` to the right of the equal symbol (=) is evaluated and the result assigned to the variable on the left. The integer constants are separated by a plus symbol (+). This is an example of a C++ *operator* which informs the computer that the two values are to be added together.

Finally, the output statement has three arguments: a character string, the variable `sum`, and another character string. The second argument is an example of an expression, the value of which is to be printed. In this case, the expression value is that of the variable `sum`, namely `30`, which is printed together with the character strings. The program output is thus:

```
The sum of 10 and 20 is 30
```

Punctuation is used in C++ to define program parts and to separate constituent parts. In Program 2.3 a number of common punctuation symbols are present. We have already noted that blank space is used to form indentation. To heighten readability a blank line has been placed between the definitions and the statements of function `main`. Blank spaces, line separators and tab characters are collectively known as *whitespace* characters and are used extensively in C++ programs to improve their readability.

Besides whitespace characters, Program 2.3 uses a variety of punctuation symbols. Braces `{` and `}` have been noted as function body delimiters. Character strings are delimited by double quote (") characters. The semicolon is the statement terminator. Other punctuation symbols used with C++ programs are the comma (to separate items in a list), and parentheses `(` and `)` to bracket one or more items.

The final program we look at introduces the *comment*. A comment is used by the programmer to annotate the program code. A comment is ignored by the C++ compiler. Comments enhance a program's readability and provide a useful documentation tool. Proper documentation is an essential programming habit. Comments serve to inform the reader of the program – the original program author or the programmer responsible for its maintenance – of the intended logic. Comments can be applied to the overall program, to individual functions, or to a particular sequence of statements.

Comments can be presented with a pair of leading `//` symbols. The remainder of the line following the `//` is considered comment and is ignored by the compiler. The comment symbols can appear anywhere in a program and are often appended to a program statement.

```
//
//      A block of commenting over a number of lines
//      highlights a piece of program code.
//

int sum;        // program statement commenting
```

A second comment style is any sequence of characters enclosed between `/*` and `*/`. There should be no embedded spaces in `/*` and `*/`. A comment may appear anywhere that white space is permitted in a program. An example of this style of comment is:

```
/*
**   This comment extends over seven lines in total.
**   The first and last lines are simply the opening
**   and closing comment symbols. All other lines
**   are marked with a leading pair of asterisks. They
**   are used to emphasize a unit of commenting.
*/
```

Program 2.4 repeats the last problem but includes embedded comments. The two programs are otherwise identical. The comments clarify the program's operation and improve its readability.

PROGRAM 2.4

```
//
//      This program assigns the sum of two integer
//      constants to an integer variable, then displays
//      the result along with some annotation.
//

#include <iostream.h>

int main ()
{
  int sum;              // declare variable, .....

  sum = 10 + 20;        // ..... then assign value, and .....
                        // ..... display the result.
  cout << "The sum of 10 and 20 is " << sum << "\n";
  return (0);
}
```

It is a good habit to insert comments into a program as it is being prepared. There are a number of reasons for this. First, it is easier to document the program when the logic is established. This saves having to return to the coding to insert appropriate commenting. Second, it is frequently the case that comments are not included once the program is operational. Given that a program is written once but read many times, comments can aid the programmer in reading the text and facilitate debugging during development.

2.2 Compiling and running

Before a program can be compiled and run, the source text must first be placed in a file. Generally, this is achieved with a text editor. The file containing the program text is identified by its *filename*. Most C++ compilers require that a source filename has a suffix or extension `.cpp`, as in the filename `example.cpp`. On some systems the suffix is `.C` or `.cxx`.

The source program may then be *compiled* to create an *executable* image of the program. Compilation procedures differ considerably between compilers. If there are no program errors in the source code, an executable program file is created, and the program is ready for execution.

The compilation process consists of translating a program in the high level language C++ into the equivalent sequence of machine code instructions. During the translation process, the compiler may detect errors in the programming language usage, for example, a missing comma or semicolon. The compiler reports these errors in a printout identifying the source and nature of the error. These are known as *compile time* errors.

The executable program file is produced by combining or *linking* the compiled image of the program with any parts required from libraries. If any necessary parts are not found in the libraries then a *link error* occurs.

If the program compiles and links correctly, it can be executed. When running this executable program, further situations, known as *run time* errors may occur. These cause programs to terminate abnormally during execution, and arise from executing perfectly plausible instructions but with erroneous data. For example, division of one number by another is perfectly acceptable providing the second number is not zero, otherwise the answer is infinity. Protection against run time errors to improve program robustness is discussed in later chapters.

A program that is free of both compile time and run time errors may still not produce the correct results. These errors, known as *logical errors*, arise from an incorrect specification of the program solution. A methodical approach to programming, as emphasized in the text, can significantly reduce this type of problem.

2.3 Summary

1. A simple program consists of the function `main`. The body of the function consists of definitions and statements enclosed within the braces `{` and `}`.

2. Every C++ statement and definition concludes with a terminating semicolon.

3. C++ programs are free-format. Certain stylistic guidelines have, however, been adopted. Generally, have no more than one program statement per line. Indent to highlight the program structure and use whitespace characters to separate the program tokens.

4. Comments are written between `/*` and `*/`, or follow `//` to the line end. They are vital to good program documentation. Comments should assist the reader to understand the program logic.

5. The compiler translates a C++ program into its equivalent machine instructions. The input to the compiler is the source C++ program and the output is the executable program image.

6. Programs can exhibit compile time, link time, run time and logic errors, all of which must be corrected to produce an operational program.

2.4 Exercises

1. Explain the meaning of the following terms:

   (a) function (b) standard library
   (c) instruction (d) variable definition
   (e) statement (f) variable

(g) expression (h) literal constant
(i) assignment (j) compile time error
(k) run time error (l) logic error

2. Carefully enter Program 2.1(a) into a file with an editor or word processor then compile it and run it to ensure it produces the required output.

3. What output would you expect from the following program?

```
#include <iostream.h>

int main()
{
  cout << "One.....";
  cout << "Two.....";
  cout << "Three\n";
  return (0);
}
```

4. Write a program which divides the value 47 by the value 12 and displays the result with an appropriate message. The division operator is denoted by the slash symbol (/).

5. The following program contains a run time error. Carefully enter it into a file, and check that it compiles without any errors. What happens when you run the program? What messages, if any, are produced. Consult a local expert or compiler documentation to obtain an explanation.

```
#include <iostream.h>

int main()
{
  int first, second;

  first = 0;
  second = 27 / first;
  cout << "second is " << second << "\n";
  return (0);
}
```

3

Types, Operators and Expressions

A C++ program describes the computational processes to be carried out on items of data. It is necessary in a C++ program to classify each and every item of data according to its *type*. In C++, an infinite number of distinct types is possible, classified as either *fundamental types* or *derived types*. The derived types are constructed from the fundamental types as, for example, *arrays* (see Chapter 8), *functions* (see Chapter 5), or *classes* (see Chapter 9). There are several fundamental types, essentially different kinds of *integral* types and *floating* types, collectively called the *arithmetic* types. For these simple types there are *denotations* or *constants*, i.e. a sequence of symbols possessing a specific value of a particular type. Constants are the subject of Sections 3.1–3.4 of this chapter.

The data items manipulated by a program may be divided into two groups – those whose values remain fixed during execution of a program, and those whose values change. The former are the *literal constants* in a program. The latter are known as *variables*, since the values possessed by such objects is allowed to vary during the program run. Items of both groups share the properties of the type as described above. Variables must be given a type explicitly by the programmer. Variables are considered in Sections 3.5–3.7.

An *expression* is a rule by which a value may be computed. It consists of one or more *operands* (or values) combined with *operators*. C++ has an unusually rich set of operators which provide access to most of the operations implemented by the underlying computer hardware. The full complement of available operators naturally divide into a number of groups. The arithmetic operators, such as addition, are discussed fully in this chapter. The other operators are introduced in the chapters in which they are applied.

3.1 Integer constants

An *integer constant* is a whole number which may be positive, zero or negative (strictly, a negative integer is obtained by applying the unary negative operator to a positive integer; see Section 3.8). Integer constants may be specified in either the decimal, octal or hexadecimal notation.

A *decimal integer constant* is written as a sequence of decimal digits (`0` to `9`), the first of which is not `0` (zero). The values:

```
1234    255    10    9999
```

are all valid examples of decimal integer constants. No embedded spaces or commas are permitted between the digits. The value 10,000, for example, is not a decimal integer constant because of the comma; it must be expressed as `10000`.

A computer can only represent a finite subset of all possible integers. The precision of an integer depends on the amount of storage allocated by the compiler. Integers normally have a size suggested by the machine architecture and may differ across different computer systems. For instance, on the IBM PC[1] an integer is held using a 16-bit 2's complement notation. An integer can, therefore, assume values from `-32768` to `+32767` inclusive.

An *octal integer constant* is written as a sequence of *octal digits* (`0` to `7`) starting with a zero (`0`). The values:

```
0377    0177    00000    01
```

are all valid examples of octal integer constants.

A *hexadecimal integer constant* is a sequence of hexadecimal digits starting with `0x` or `0X`. The hexadecimal digits include `0` to `9`, and the letters `A` to `F` (or `a` to `f`). The letters represent the values `10` to `15` respectively. Examples of valid hexadecimal integer constants include:

```
0XFF    0x4B    0x1f    0XfF
```

To improve readability we shall choose to capitalize the hexadecimal digits following a lower case `'x'`:

```
0xFF    0x4B    0x1F    0xFF
```

Octal and hexadecimal constants frequently find their way into system programming applications. Examples of their use will appear later in this book.

The precision of an integer constant can also be *qualified*. A decimal, octal or hexadecimal integer constant immediately followed by the letter `L` (or letter `l`) is an explicit `long` integer constant. On DEC VAX[2] hardware, long integers employ 32-bits, and can thus express values in the range `-2147483648` to `+2147483647` inclusive. Valid explicit long integer constants are:

```
123L    04774771    0XFFL
```

Note how in the second example using the lower case letter `'l'` can easily be confused for the digit `'1'`. For that reason we will always use an upper case letter `'L'` when denoting a long integer.

Integer constants which exceed the single precision range are also implicitly long integers (examples are for a 16-bit integer):

```
32768    0100000    0X4FFF
```

[1] IBM is a registered trademark of International Business Machines Corporation
[2] DEC is a registered trademark of Digital Equipment Corporation

If the value of an integer constant exceeds the largest representable value, the result is unpredictable. Most compilers generally warn the programmer of the problem.

To illustrate some C++ integer constants, consider the IBM PC implementation. In Table 3.1 some integer constants, their true mathematical value, and their type and values are presented.

Table 3.1

C++ constant	*True value*	*C++ type*	*C++ value*
`0`	0	`int`	`0`
`32767`	$2^{15} - 1$	`int`	`32767`
`077777`	$2^{15} - 1$	`int`	`32767`
`32768`	2^{15}	`long`	`32768`
`0x10000`	2^{16}	`long`	`65536`
`2147483647`	$2^{31} - 1$	`long`	`2147483647`
`2147483648`	2^{32}		undefined

The ISO (International Standards Organization) C standard header files `<limits.h>` contains symbolic constants for the sizes of the integral data types. For example, on an IBM PC the maximum value for an `int` and the maximum value for a `long` might be given as:

```
INT_MAX      32767
LONG_MAX     2147483647
```

For some further details on number representation for a range of computer hardware and sample values for `<limits.h>` see Appendix A.

3.2 Floating point constants

Numbers with fractional parts may be represented as *floating point constants.* If there is a preceding minus sign attached to the number, it is taken to be the unary negation operator applied to the value, and not part of the literal itself (see Section 3.8). Floating point constants may be written in two different forms. The first, and simplest, is a sequence of decimal digits including the decimal point. Valid examples include:

```
3.1415926    12.0    0.1    0.00001
```

Note that the decimal point need not necessarily be embedded, allowing both leading and trailing decimal point forms. The second and third examples above might also be shown as:

```
12.    .1
```

It is recommended, however, that the readability is improved if the former notation is used.

In the second form, a floating point constant is expressed as an integer or as a floating point constant as defined above, multiplied by some integer power of ten. This power is shown as the letter E (or letter e) followed by an optionally signed integer constant. Examples of this form include:

```
1.0E2 (= 100.0)      12.34e-3 (= 0.01234)
1E-2  (= 0.01)       1E+3     (= 1000.0)
```

This latter representation is frequently referred to as *scientific notation*.

Like integers, the range of floating point constants permitted by implementations is restricted. Further, whereas integers are held exactly, floating point constants are held as an (close) approximation. The type of a floating point constant is always `double`. On the DEC VAX a double precision floating point constant has a 64-bit representation, with a magnitude between about `10E-38` and `10E+38`, and an accuracy of approximately 17 decimal digits.

A single precision representation for floating point values is also available with the same range as doubles but with only some 7 significant decimal digits. These values are of type `float`. These are distinguished by the qualifying suffix `f` or `F` as in:

```
1.234F    98.76f
```

Finally, we may qualify a floating point constant with the suffix `l` or `L` to denote a `long double`. A long double further extends the accuracy of a double.

If the magnitude of a floating point constant is too great to be represented, the result is unpredictable. Most compilers generate an appropriate error message in this case. If the magnitude of a floating point constant is below `10E-38`, zero is substituted. The ISO C standard header file `<float.h>` contains symbolic constants for the sizes of these data types (see Appendix A).

3.3 Character constants

A *character constant* is a single character written within single quotes (apostrophe) as in `'X'`. The value of a character constant is the integer numeric value of the character in the machine's character set. Character constants have type `char`. C++ programmers must be aware of the character set of the target computer. The two most commonly used character sets are EBCDIC (Extended Binary Coded Decimal Interchange Code) and ASCII (American Standard Code for Information Interchange). The two sets are not the same. In the ASCII character set, the character `'X'` has decimal encoding 88, whilst the EBCDIC encoding is 231. The full ASCII character set is given in Appendix B.

Escape sequences can be used to represent characters that would be awkward or impossible to enter in a source program directly. An escape sequence consists of the backslash symbol (\) followed by a single character. The two symbols taken together represent the single required character. The characters which may follow the backslash, and their meanings are listed below:

alarm bell	`\a`
newline	`\n`
horizontal tab	`\t`
vertical tab	`\v`
backspace	`\b`
carriage return	`\r`
formfeed	`\f`
single quote	`\'`
double quote	`\"`
backslash	`\\`
question mark	`\?`

Thus the character constant to represent the formfeed symbol in a program is `'\f'`, and the character constant for a backslash is `'\\'`.

The escape sequence may appear as a backslash symbol followed by one, two or three octal digits, or as a backslash symbol followed by the letter `x` and one or more hexadecimal digits. The resulting octal (hexadecimal) value is taken as the octal (hexadecimal) number of the character from the machine's character set. The character constant `'X'` (with ASCII encoding octal 130 and hexadecimal 58) may be represented as `'\130'` (`'\x58'`). More generally, this representation is used for non-printing characters. The ASCII character ACK (acknowledge) would be represented by `'\006'` (`'\x6'`). The first of the ASCII collating sequence is the character NUL and is shown as `'\0'`. This symbol is reserved for a particular role in C++ and is discussed fully later.

If the character following the backslash is neither an octal digit nor one of the character escape codes listed above, the result is considered unpredictable. Commonly, the effect is simply to ignore the backslash.

3.4 String constants

A *string constant* is a possibly empty sequence of characters enclosed in double quotes. The same escape mechanism provided for character constants can also be used in string constants. Examples of string constants include:

```
"Hello world"
"The C++ Programming Language"
""
"She said \"Good morning\""
"This string terminates with a newline\n"
```

A string is allowed to extend over one or more lines provided each line terminates with a backslash character followed immediately by a newline symbol. In this case, the backslash and the newline symbols are ignored.

```
    "This string extends \
over two lines."
```

and is textually equivalent to:

```
"This string extends over two lines."
```

Two adjacent string constants are concatenated at compile time into a single string. For example:

```
"This " "string"
```

is converted into:

```
"This string"
```

This concatenation is convenient for splitting long strings across several source lines.

For each string constant of N characters, there is a block of N+1 consecutive characters whose first N are initialized with the characters from the string, and whose last character is the ASCII NUL character `'\0'`. Thus the string:

```
"hello"
```

is stored as shown in Figure 3.1. As we shall discover later, the NUL character is used to delimit the end of all strings.

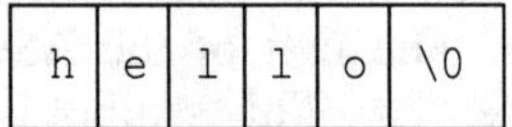

Figure 3.1

Care must be taken to recognize that the character `'X'` and the string `"X"` are not the same. On the majority of computers the character `'X'` is a single character 8-bit byte (see Figure 3.2) whilst the string `"X"` is two character bytes (see Figure 3.3).

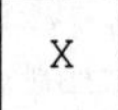

Figure 3.2

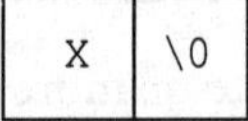

Figure 3.3

Strings and characters are thus distinct, and must on no account be operated upon as if they were the same.

3.5 Identifiers

The C++ programming language requires that various quantities used in a program be given names by which they can then be referenced. These names are known as *identifiers* and are created by the programmer.

An identifier is created according to the following rule:

> An identifier is a combination of letters and digits the first of which must be a letter. The underscore symbol (_) is permitted in an identifier and is considered to be a letter.

From this, the following are valid examples of identifiers:

```
time      day_of_the_week      BUFFER
x         unit_cost            program_name
_MAX      h2o                  AVeryLongIdentifier
```

Two identifiers are the same when they have the same spelling, including the case of all letters. The identifiers `abcd` and `abcD` are thus considered distinct.

A C++ program may reference objects defined elsewhere. These are known as *external objects*. For example, the function `strlen` (string length) is a member of the standard ISO C library and is defined external to the program containing its use. Identifiers in a C++ program which refer to external objects are often subject to restrictions. These identifiers have to be processed by software other than compilers. Software tools such as *linkers* and *librarian managers* may have their own limitations on the length of identifiers. They may further not distinguish between the case of letters.

Notwithstanding these restrictions, the programmer is encouraged to use meaningful identifiers. The name of the identifier should reflect the purpose of the object in a C++ program. If a program operates on, say, a time of day, then the identifiers `hours`, `minutes` and `seconds` are superior to the shorter and less obvious `h`, `m` and `s`.

Certain identifiers are reserved for use as *language keywords* in a C++ program. A complete list of the C++ keywords is given below (and repeated in Appendix C). They may not be used as programmer-defined identifiers.

```
asm         else        private     throw
auto        enum        protected   try
break       extern      public      register
case        float       register    union
catch       for         return      unsigned
char        friend      short       virtual
class       goto        signed      void
const       if          size of     volatile
continue    inline      static      wchar_t
default     int         struct      while
delete      long        switch
do          new         template
double      operator    this
```

In addition, identifiers containing leading pairs of underscores (such as __MAX) are reserved for use by C++ implementations and standard libraries and must be avoided by users.

3.6 Variable definitions

Variables are data items whose values vary during execution of a program. Variables in a C++ program are made to possess one of the fundamental types. Variables must have their type indicated so that the compiler can record all the necessary information about them, and generate the appropriate code during translation. This is done by means of a *variable definition*. A definition has the form:

```
type-specifier list-of-variables;
```

The list-of-variables is a comma separated list of identifiers representing the program variables. Each named variable possesses a fundamental type as given by the type-specifier. The type specifiers for the four fundamental types are introduced by the reserved keywords:

`int`	(integer)
`char`	(character)
`float`	(single precision floating point)
`double`	(double precision floating point)

A complete variable definition is then:

```
int hours, minutes, seconds;
```

Thereafter, the variables `hours`, `minutes` and `seconds` may assume any legal integer value. Integer values may be assigned to these variables, and the integer value associated with a variable may be used in a program statement.

A sequence of variable definitions may appear with the semicolon symbol as the terminator. For improved readability, each definition appears on separate lines:

```
int  day, month, year;
float  centigrade, fahrenheit;
char initial;
double epsilon;
```

Variable definitions may employ the same type specifier as in:

```
int day, month, year;
int hours, minutes, seconds;
```

This facility is often employed to bracket together related variables. In the first definition, the variables are concerned with a calendar date. In the second, the variables are used to represent a time. Because C++ is free-format, we are, of course, free to extend a definition over one or more lines. It is perfectly acceptable to write:

```
int  day, month, year,
  hours, minutes, seconds;
```

where the six variables are defined in the single definition.

A variable may not be redefined in a second definition. Such definitions would cause the C++ compiler to issue an appropriate error message. In the following the variable `time` is defined as an `int` and as a `float`.

```
int   time, interval, period;
float time;
```

The compiler would be unable to determine the correct type for the variable `time`. The compiler message would report that in the second definition, variable `time` has been redefined.

The definition of variables can also be accompanied by *initialization*. A variable is initialized to some value by appending an equal symbol (=) and an expression (see Section 3.8). For example:

```
int sum = 0;
float fahrenheit = 32.0F;
```

Before any statement changes the values of these variables, they are guaranteed to possess the given initial values. An uninitialized variable has no reliable value and must be given one with an appropriate statement before its value is used.

Later, we must fully appreciate variable definitions since they are not as innocent as they might first appear. Each variable in a program has three relevant attributes:

1. It is of some type.
2. It is a particular instance of a value of that type.
3. It has some location.

The *type* specifies how the object or variable is internally represented. Each object is to be found in memory at some *location* (or *memory address*). The variable identifiers in our programs *possess* the address given to them when the program executes.

Consider the definition:

```
int x = 27;
```

Our understanding of such a definition is that an area of memory is set aside sufficient to accommodate an integer value. This area of memory is referenced in the program by the identifier `x`. At the machine level, this memory area has an address (say 5678). The area of memory is initialized with the binary pattern representing decimal 27. Pictorially we have Figure 3.4.

Alternatively, following the notation of [Lin71], we may show this relationship as in Figure 3.5. A program variable possesses an internal memory address and is depicted in the diagram by a line from the variable identifier to the address (represented by a hexagonal box). The relation 'to refer' relates the address to the value at that address. This is shown by an arrow to the memory cell containing the value of the variable. The relation 'to refer' is strictly between two *internal objects*, namely, the memory address and the value. The internals are 'possessed' by an *external object* – the program identifier. The internal address (sometimes known as its *name*) we shall discover is an object of another related type which we can also manipulate in our programs (see Section 3.17).

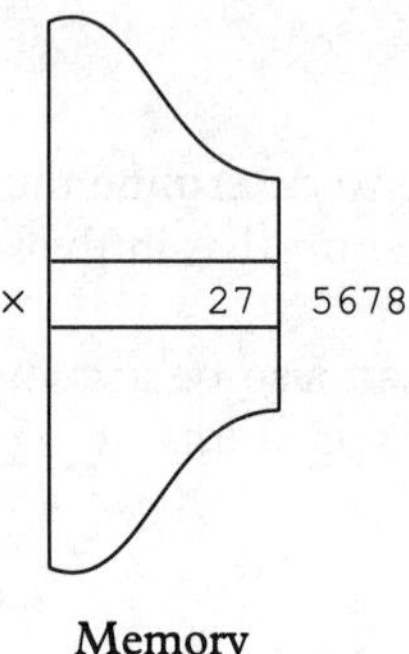

Figure 3.4

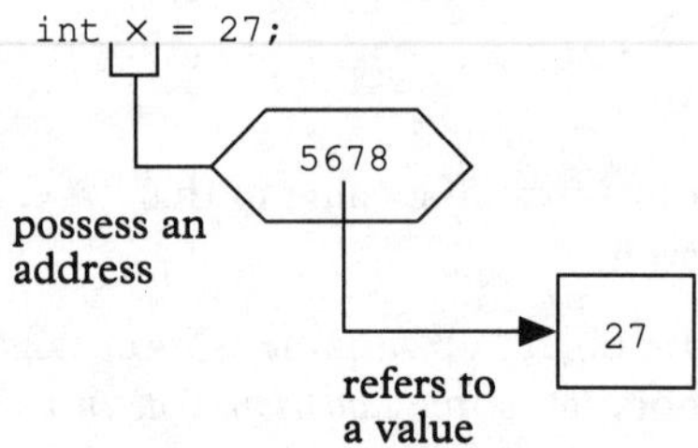

Figure 3.5

3.7 Qualifiers

In the same way that the accuracy of a variable containing a floating point number may be extended by defining it to be of type `double`, so it is possible to control the range of an integer variable.

If the *qualifier* `long` is placed before the type specifier `int` in a definition, then the integer variables will have extended range. Long integer variables provide the largest range of signed integer values. An example of a long definition is:

```
long int memory_address, factorial;
```

On the IBM PC the range of values that may be stored in a long integer variable is that for long integer constants (see Section 3.1 and Appendix A). Operations on objects of type `long` are sometimes slower than the same operations on objects of type `int`, depending upon the implementation.

The qualifier `short` placed ahead of the type specifier `int` in a variable definition specifies that the named variables are used to represent a limited range of signed integer values. The motivation for using short integer variables is primarily one of conservation of memory space. An appropriate definition is:

```
short int day_of_week, week_of_year;
```

In both the examples above, the specifier `int` is optional, and the definitions may be alternatively presented as:

```
long  memory_address, factorial;
short day_of_week, week_of_year;
```

Strictly, C++ does not specify the exact number of bits used to represent `int`, `long` and `short` variables. These quantities are implementation dependent, and determined by the underlying hardware.

The qualifier `unsigned` may also precede `int` (and `char`) in a variable definition. This restricts the integer (character) variables to be positive values. On the IBM PC an unsigned integer (character) variable is represented in 16-bits (8-bits) and can assume values from `0` to `65535` (0–255) inclusive. Examples of these definitions are:

```
unsigned int        natural;
unsigned            record_number;
```

In the last example, the optional `int` is omitted.

An unsigned quantity is denoted with the suffix `U` or `u`. An unsigned integer construct is shown as `123U`. An unsigned long integer is expressed as `123UL`.

All arithmetic operations on unsigned integers behave according to the values of *modulo arithmetic*. If the number of bits in an unsigned integer is N, the arithmetic is modulo 2^N. This amounts to computing the N low-order bits of the true 2's complement result.

Suppose all `unsigned int` is represented using 16 bits. The range of possible values is `0` to `65535` inclusive. The arithmetic is then modulo `65536` (2^{16}). Adding `1` to the largest unsigned value is guaranteed to produce `0`. Subtracting the unsigned value `9` from the unsigned value `6` produces the unsigned value `65533`, that is `65536 −3` since this is modulus `65536` to the true arithmetical value `-3`.

The type `long double` specifies extended precision floating point variables. Along with integers, the sizes of floating point objects are implementation defined. The types `float`, `double` and `long double` could represent up to three distinct sizes.

The qualifier `signed` may be applied to `char` or to any size of `int`. This qualifier is permissible but redundant when used with integral types. The `signed` specifier is useful for forcing `char` objects to have a sign. So, for example, if characters are 8-bit bytes, then `unsigned char` variables have values `0-255` inclusive, while signed chars have values between -128 and 127 in a 2's complement machine. Whether plain char variables (without any qualifier) are signed or unsigned is implementation dependent. Printable characters are, however, guaranteed to be positive.

The qualifier const can be applied to the declaration of any variable to specify that its value will not be changed. Such an object may not be used on the left side of an assignment (see Section 3.10), or have its value modified in any manner whatsoever. An implementation is then free to place const objects in read-only memory, and perform any desirable optimizations. When introducing const objects we must also initialize it to the required value.

```
const double pi = 3.1415926;
const int dozen = 12;
```

Without the initializing value it would be a mistake to write:

```
const double pi;
```

We have not given pi a value and because it is const we cannot later assign a value to it. Such a definition elicits a compiler error.

3.8 Arithmetic expressions

The C++ programming language supports the normal *arithmetic operators*: addition (+), subtraction (-), multiplication (*) and division (/). Also provided is the modulus operator, denoted by the percent symbol (%), used to compute the remainder on dividing two integer values. These are the *binary arithmetic operators* which apply to two operands. The unary negation operator, - (and unary plus operator, +) is also available and is applied to a single operand to produce the arithmetic negative (arithmetic value) of its operand.

Examples of expressions involving such operators are:

```
12 * feet
-1023
3.1415926 * radius * radius
60 * hours + minutes
distance / time
cents % 100
```

For example, in the first illustration the integer constant 12 is multiplied by the current value of the variable feet. In the second example, the integer constant 1023 is made negative using the unary negation operator.

As with normal arithmetic expressions, a C++ expression is evaluated according to the *precedence* of its operators. The precedence or priority of an operator dictates the order of evaluation in an arithmetic expression. An extract of the full table of precedences for all C++ operators is given in Table 3.2 below. The full table is given in Appendix E.

Table 3.2 Precedence and associativity of the arithmetic operators

Operator	*Description*	*Associativity*
+	Unary plus	Right to left
-	Unary minus	Right to left
*	Multiplication	Left to right
/	Division	Left to right
%	Modulus	Left to right
+	Addition	Left to right
-	Subtraction	Left to right

From Table 3.2, unary minus and unary plus are shown to have the highest precedence, whilst addition and subtraction have the lowest equal precedence. The multiplication, division and modulus operators have intermediate precedence. From this, an expression involving a mixture of these operators will first perform all unary minus and plus operations, then any multiplication, division and modulus operations, and then finally, addition and subtraction. Thus,

```
2 + 3 * 4
```

yields 14, since 3 is first multiplied by 4 giving 12, and then 2 is added producing 14.

An expression involving operators of equal precedence is resolved by reference to the column labelled *associativity* in Table 3.2. Associativity refers to the order (or direction) in which operators possessing the same precedence are executed. The expression 2 + 3 * 4 + 5 is evaluated in the following way. Multiplication has the highest precedence of the three operators and is evaluated first. The expression now reduces to 2 + 12 + 5. The two addition operators have equal precedence, and associate left to right. Thus, the 2 and 12 are first added to give 14, before finally the 14 and 5 are summed producing 19 as the final result.

If, in the expression 2 + 3 * 4 + 5, it is required to perform both the additions before executing the multiplication, then this is indicated by employing the *parentheses* (and) around the subexpressions. The expression would then be written as (2 + 3) * (4 + 5), and evaluate to 5 * 9, or 45.

The division operator functions normally, except in situations where both operands are of type integer. For two integer operands, the division operator determines the quotient with any fractional remainder truncated. Thus:

```
13.0 / 5    evaluates to 2.6
13 / 5.0    evaluates to 2.6
13 / 5      evaluates to 2
```

When two positive integers are divided, truncation is always toward zero. If either operand is negative, however, the truncation is machine dependent. Usually, the quotient is positive if the signs of both operands are the same, negative otherwise. Thus:

```
-13 /  5  evaluates to -2
 13 / -5  evaluates to -2
-13 / -5  evaluates to 2
```

The modulus operator (`%`) yields the integer remainder from the division of two integer operands. Therefore:

```
13 % 5    evaluates to 3
15 % 5    evaluates to 0
```

If either operand is negative, the remainder usually has the same sign as the dividend. Thus:

```
-13 %  5  evaluates to -3
 13 % -5  evaluates to 3
```

Irrespective of the particular implementation, it is always true that:

```
a % b     evaluates to a - (a/b) * b
```

where `a` and `b` are integer values and `b` is not zero. This is shown in Table 3.3.

Table 3.3

a	b	a/b	(a/b)*b	a%b	(a/b)*b+a%b
13	5	2	10	3	13
-13	5	-2	-10	-3	-13
13	-5	-2	10	3	13
-13	-5	2	-10	-3	-13

3.9 Type conversions

All integer arithmetic is performed with at least the range of an `int`. As a consequence, a character or short integer appearing in an expression is first converted to `int`. This process is called *integral promotion*. The promotion results in an `int`, if an `int` can hold all of the values of the original type, otherwise the conversion will be to `unsigned int`.

We know that whether plain characters are signed or unsigned is implementation dependent. As a result, on some machines a `char` will be converted to a negative integer by a process of *sign extension* where the leftmost bit of that `char` is a `1`. On other machines, a `char` is promoted to a positive `int` by prepending zeros to the left of the character bit pattern.

The promotion of a `short` is to either an `int` or to an `unsigned int`. If, for example, a `short` has the same number of bits as an `int`, then the value is converted to an `int`; an `unsigned short` would be converted to an `unsigned int`. However, if a short used fewer bits than an `int`, then both a `short` and an `unsigned short` are converted to an `int`.

With the following definitions:

```
char            pc;    // plain char
short           ps;    // assume shorts have same .....
unsigned short  us;    // ..... size as int
int             pi;    // plain int
```

we can list some expressions and show how the operands are first promoted (see Table 3.4).

Table 3.4

C++ expression	*Original types*	*Promoted types*
`pc - pi * ps`	`char - int * short`	`int - int * int`
`3 * us - pi`	`int * unsigned short - int`	`int * unsigned int - int`

The promotion of operands of type `char` to type `int` means that it is sensible to perform arithmetic operations on data objects of type `char`. From the ASCII character set `'D'` is represented by decimal `68`; `'A'` by `65`; `'z'` by `122` and `'a'` by `97`. Thus:

```
'D' - 'A'          evaluates to: 68 - 65 = 3
'z' - 'a' + 1      evaluates to: 122 - 97 + 1 = 26
```

If `ch` is a variable of type char and currently represents any upper case letter in the ASCII character set, then the expression:

```
ch - 'A' + 'a'
```

evaluates to the integer value with the ASCII code that represents the equivalent lower case letter. For example, if variable `ch` represents the character `'D'`, then using decimal representation of the ASCII encodings of the characters, the expression evaluates to:

$$68 - 65 + 97 = 100$$

and the corresponding ASCII character is `'d'`.

An arithmetic expression such as `a + b` computes a value of some type. For example, if both `a` and `b` are of type `int`, then the value of `a + b` is also of type `int`. However, if `a` and `b` are of different types, then `a + b` is a *mixed expression*, and we require rules to establish the type of the result itself.

In a mixed expression *arithmetic conversions* determine whether and how operands are converted before a binary operation is performed. When two values are to be operated upon in combination, they are first converted to a single common type. The result after applying the operation is also of that same common type.

The conversion is performed according to a hierarchy of types. Operands of *lower type* are converted to that of the *higher type* before executing the operator. The implicit arithmetic conversions operate much as expected. In the absence of `unsigned` quantities the following rules apply:

If either operand is `long double`, convert the other to `long double`.

If either operand is `double`, convert the other to `double`.

If either operand is `float`, convert the other to `float`.

Perform the integral promotions.

If either operand is `long`, convert the other to `long`.

Otherwise, both operands are of type `int`.

In the context of the following definitions:

```
int   i = 32;
short s = 10;
```

consider the evaluation of the mixed expression:

```
3.0 * i + s
```

with types:

```
double * int + short
```

Since multiplication has higher precedence than addition, it is evaluated first. The left operand to the multiplier operation is a `double`. Therefore, the right operand is also promoted to type `double` if it is not already one. The expression is now:

```
double * double + short
```

The integer value `32` undergoes a representation change to the equivalent double precision floating point value:

```
3.0 * 32.0 + 10
```

Following execution of the multiplying operator, we have:

```
96.0 + 10
```

and the types involved in the expression are now:

```
double + short
```

Following the same argument, the `short (10)` is promoted to type `double (10.0)` before performing the addition. The final result is of type `double` and has the value:

```
106.0
```

These implicit arithmetic conversions operate much as expected. The programmer is cautioned, however, to be fully aware of the conversions. Without a full understanding, some unexpected results are possible.

Some pitfalls surround the use of unsigned integral quantities in expressions. The full set of rules for arithmetic conversions is:

If either operand is `long double`, convert the other to `long double`.

If either operand is `double`, convert the other to `double`.

If either operand is `float`, convert the other to `float`.

Perform the integral promotions on both operands and:

> if either operand is `unsigned long int`, convert the other to `unsigned long int`. If one operand is `long int` and the other is `unsigned int`, then if a `long int` can represent all values of an `unsigned int` then the latter is converted to a `long int`; if not, both are converted to an `unsigned long int`.
>
> If either operand is `long int`, convert the other to `long int`.
>
> If either operand is `unsigned int`, convert the other to `unsigned int`.
>
> Otherwise, both operands are of type `int`.

The conversion rules are complicated by the introduction of unsigned operands. For example, consider the definitions:

```
unsigned int ui = 10U;   // note the suffix
         int pi = -7;
```

and the expression:

```
ui + pi
```

Here we are mixing signed and unsigned quantities. By the rules of arithmetic we must convert `pi` to `unsigned int`. Unsigned integers obey the laws of arithmetic modulo 2^N where N is the number of bits in the representation. Arithmetic on unsigned quantities can never produce overflow. For N = 16, an `unsigned int` has a range of `0 - 65535` inclusive. Converting the signed value `-7` to `unsigned int` involves adding `65536` producing the result `65529`. The final expression value is `10 + 65529`, the `unsigned int` value `3`.

Similarly, given the definitions:

```
long int     li = -1L;
unsigned int ui = 1U;
```

then the expression:

```
li + ui
```

involves mixing a `signed long int` with an `unsigned int`. Suppose that a standard sized `int` is 16 bits and a `long` is 32 bits. Then since a `long int` can represent all the values of an `unsigned int`, `ui` is converted to `long int` and this is the type of the expression. If, however, both `int` and `long` are 32 bits, then a `long int` cannot represent all the values of an `unsigned int` and both operands are converted to `unsigned long int` (the result type).

The moral is to avoid unsigned quantities in programs. Where they are present, one must be especially careful when they are mixed with signed quantities.

For certain operations in C++, it may be that the true mathematical result of the operation cannot be represented as a value of the expected result type (as determined by the usual conversion rules). This condition is referred to as *overflow*. For example, multiplication of two `ints` result in an `int`. But if, as on the IBM PC `ints` are held as 2's complement 16-bit values, with largest integer representation of 32767, then multiplying 700 by 800 produces the true mathematical value 560000 which is not representable as an `int`. Another example is attempted division by zero, where the result is infinity.

Generally, C++ does not specify the consequences of overflow. A number of possibilities may arise. One is that an incorrect value of the correct type is generated. Another possibility is that the program is prematurely terminated with or without some appropriate error message. A third possibility is to trap the exception within the program and take the appropriate action. In all cases, the programmer must guard against these occurrences and, where possible, handle them within the program. A program that terminates prematurely is not a good program.

3.10 The assignment operator

The *assignment operator* allows the assignment of some new value to a program variable. The simplest form of the assignment operator is:

```
variable = expression
```

The effect of the operator is to evaluate the expression to the right of the assignment operator (=), and the resulting value is then assigned to the variable on the left. If both operands of the assignment operator are arithmetic, the type of the expression is converted to the type of the variable on the left before executing the assignment. Examples of assignments are:

```
(a)  interest  = principal * rate * time / 100
(b)  speed     = distance / time
(c)  total_min = 60 * hours + minutes
(d)  count     = count + 1
```

Since the assignment mechanism in C++ is implemented as an (binary) operator, like all other operators it has a precedence (very low), an associativity (right to left), and indulges in automatic type conversions. The precedence and associativity are given in Appendix E. The low priority of the assignment operator guarantees that the right hand expression is first evaluated before the assignment is performed.

In the same way that `operand1 + operand2` evaluates to the arithmetic addition of the two operands, the assignment:

```
variable = expression
```

also evaluates to a value. That is, after evaluation of the expression and assigning it to the variable on the left, a value is delivered. The type and value is that of the variable, and may be discarded or used in multiple assignment expressions:

$$\texttt{variable}_1 = \texttt{variable}_2 = \ldots\ \texttt{variable}_k = \texttt{expression}$$

The right to left associativity of the assignment operator means that the expression is evaluated, assigned to $\texttt{variable}_k$; the value of this variable is then the delivered value, which in turn is assigned to $\texttt{variable}_{k-1}$, and so on. Thus the expression:

```
x = y = z = p + q
```

is interpreted as:

```
x = (y = (z = p + q))
```

Implicit type conversions also occur across the assignment operator. For example, in an expression in which the left operand is a `double` and the right operand is an `int` as in:

```
double = int
```

the value of the integer expression will be converted to a double before performing the assignment. The integer is automatically promoted to type `double`. A promotion or *widening* is normally well behaved, but *narrowing* or *demotion* such as in:

```
int = double
```

can result in the loss of information. Precisely what happens in each case is implementation dependent. In this example if the `double` were to evaluate to, say, `12.345`, then we should reasonably expect the integer value `12` to be assigned after discarding the fractional part. The behaviour of the conversion is undefined if the `double` value cannot be represented as an integer. For example, the magnitude of the `double` may be too large to be represented as an integer, or if a negative `double` is assigned to an unsigned integer. Questions of rounding versus truncation are also left to the discretion of the implementor. Again, the reader is advised to seek out the appropriate local documentation.

Some possible assignments and the likely effects are as follows:

Assignment	*Effect*
`int = int`	no conversion
`float = double`	truncate (possibly round) the double
`int = long`	implemented by truncation
`char = int`	implemented by truncation

Care must be taken when employing the multiple assignment. If `iii` is a variable of type integer, then in the assignment:

```
iii = 12.34
```

the floating point constant `12.34` will normally be truncated to integer `12` before assigning to the integer variable. The value of this integer variable is then the value delivered by this operation. Then in the multiple assignment:

```
fff = iii = 12.34
```

with variable `fff` of type `float`, the expression to the right of:

```
fff = .....
```

is of type `integer`, with value `12`. The integer is converted back to a floating point representation `(12.0)` before assignment. One must not therefore read that the value `12.34` is assigned to both `iii` (after truncation) and to `fff` (without conversion).

3.11 The compound assignment operators

Assignments of the form:

```
count = count + 2
```

occur repeatedly in programming problems. The effect is to take the current value of the variable `count` and to it add the literal value `2`. The resulting value is then assigned back to the variable `count`. Overall, the value of the variable `count` is increased by two. Such an assignment may also be represented in C++ by:

```
count += 2
```

In fact, this *compound assignment operator* is applicable to all five binary arithmetic operators. Thus we may have:

```
count += 2
stock -= 1
power *= 2.71828
divisor /= 10.0
remainder %= 10
```

In all cases, except the modulus operator assignment (`%=`), the two operands may be of any arithmetic type. For the operator `%=` the two operands must have integral types.

All these new operators have the same precedence level as the simple assignment and associate right to left (see Appendix E).

If `op=` is a generalized denotation for the compound assignment operators, then the semantics of the expression:

```
variable op= expression
```

is specified by:

```
variable = variable op (expression)
```

Note the parenthesized subexpression is evaluated before applying the operator `op`. Thus the expression:

```
sum /= 3 + 7
```

is equivalent to:

```
sum = sum / (3 + 7)
```

Multiple assignments employing both the simple assignment and the compound assignment are possible. Again, some care is required in their interpretation. If variable `iii` is of type integer and value `12`, and variable `fff` is of type `float` and value `1.234`, then the assignment:

```
fff = iii *= fff
```

operates as:

```
fff = ( iii = iii * fff)
```

with `iii` assigned the value `14 (12 * 1.234 = 14.808`, truncated) and `fff` is assigned the value `14.0`.

3.12 The increment and decrement operators

In the previous section, the compound assignment operators were introduced. With these operators, simple assignments of the form:

```
x = x + 1
```

may be represented by:

```
x += 1
```

In fact, incrementing by one is such a commonly occurring operation in a program that C++ supports two forms of unary increment operator. They are known as the *preincrement operator* and the *postincrement operator*. The preincrement expression has the form:

```
++ variable
```

whilst the postincrement expression appears as:

```
variable ++
```

In both cases the constant `1` is added to the arithmetic operand. The usual arithmetic conversions are performed on the operand and the constant `1` before addition is performed, and the usual assignment conversion is performed when storing the arithmetic sum back into the variable.

Both increment operators produce a side effect. In addition to incrementing the value of the variable operand, a value is delivered. In the case of the preincrement operator, the delivered value is the new (incremented) value of the variable. The type of value delivered is the same as the type of the operand. Given two integer variables called `sum` and `count`, then the effect of the assignment:

```
sum += ++count
```

is two-fold. First, the value of the variable `count` is increased by `1`. Second, this new value of `count` is added to the current value of the variable `sum`.

The postincrement operator also delivers a value, but this time it is the old value of the variable before it was incremented. The assignment:

```
sum += count++
```

again increments the value of the variable `count` by `1`, and then adds the original value of `count` (before the incrementing took place) to the variable `sum`. Thus if the initial values of `sum` and `count` are `10` and `20` respectively, then evaluation of this last expression is two-fold:

1. Variable `count` is postincremented to produce `21`.
2. Variable `sum` is incremented by the original value of variable count and evaluates to `30`.

Instead of incrementing a variable value by `1` we can also decrement its value by `1`. This is achieved by the predecrement and postdecrement operators. The former has the form:

```
-- variable
```

whilst the latter appears as:

```
variable --
```

In both cases the constant `1` is subtracted from the operand. Again, the usual arithmetic conversions apply. The same side effect also applies, with a value delivered after decrementing. The value delivered by the predecrement operator is the new variable value after decrementing. The value delivered by the postdecrement operator is the original value of the variable before decrementing.

The precedence and associativity of the increment and decrement operators are shown in the table in Appendix E.

3.13 The type cast operator

In addition to implicit type conversions which can occur across the assignment operator and in mixed expressions, there is an explicit type conversion called a *cast*. The standard way to explicitly convert the type of a value is to apply a pseudo-function of the required type name. If variable `date` is an `int`, then:

```
double(date)
```

will cast or coerce the value of `date` so that the resulting expression value has type `double`.

A cast is implemented as an operator. It possesses both a precedence and an associativity. Its relation to other operators is shown in Appendix E.

Some examples of the use of the cast operator are:

```
char(x)
int(d1) + d2
```

Note how in the last example, the type cast `int` applies only to the operand `d1`. This is because the type cast operator has higher precedence than binary addition. To apply the cast to the result obtained by adding `d1` and `d2`, parentheses are required:

```
int(d1 + d2)
```

The cast operator is a specialized explicit type conversion operator. We shall discuss its use and application in later chapters.

A second way to present an explicit cast consists of a left parenthesis, a type specifier, a right parenthesis and an operand expression:

```
(type-specifier) expression
```

The examples shown above may also appear as:

```
(double) date
(char) x
(int) d1 + d2
(int) (d1 + d2)
```

3.14 The comma operator

The *comma operator* finds applications in a number of specialized areas. For completeness, we discuss it here, since it is an operator. Use of this operator will appear in later chapters.

The comma operator consists of two expressions separated by a comma symbol:

```
expression , expression
```

Of all the C++ operators, the comma operator has lowest precedence, and associates left to right (see Appendix E).

In the comma expression:

```
expression1 , expression2
```

`expression1` is fully evaluated first. It need not produce a value but if it does that value is discarded. The second expression is then evaluated. The type and value of the comma operator is that of the final expression.

An example of the comma operator is:

```
sum = 0, k = 1
```

If variable `k` has been declared an `int`, then this comma expression has value `1` and type `int`. Additionally, variable `sum` has been set to the value zero. In the comma expression:

```
s = (t = 2, t + 3)
```

variable `t` is assigned the value `2`, and the value of the comma expression is `5` (the result of `t + 3`). The value `5` is then assigned to the variable `s`. This effect is achieved only through use of the parentheses, since the comma operator has lower precedence than the assignment operator. Without the parentheses:

```
s = t = 2, t + 3
```

then both s and t would be assigned the value 2, then the comma operator discards the residual value 2 and the result of the expression is 5. Depending upon the context of this comma expression, the result value may or not be discarded.

3.15 Derived types

From the fundamental types other types can be derived using the *declaration operators*. For example, the fundamental types combined with the *function* declaration operators ( ) produce the function. A function describes a computational process to be performed. A function declaration appears as:

```
int sum(int, int);
```

and declares a function called sum with two int arguments returning an int result. The function is the subject of Chapter 5.

Arrays are introduced with the declarator operators [ ]. Strictly, the string constants of Section 3.4 are examples of derived types, namely, array of char. For example, we can initialize a string with:

```
char message[6] = "hello";
```

or:

```
char message[] = "hello";
```

where the variable message is of type char[6] – an array of 6 characters. Note that when the size of the array is given it must account for the NUL character. Other array examples include:

```
int      table[8];              // array of 8 integers
float    temperatures[100];     // array of 100 floating point values
```

Arrays are introduced in Chapter 8.

The array is an example of an aggregate type – a collection of values all of the same type. The fundamental types of various kinds can be gathered together to form another aggregate type called the *class*. A class is an aggregate of possibly different types. The class is the principal means whereby a programmer-defined data type may be introduced into a program. This new type is then used in a manner similar to that for the fundamental types. Classes are the subject of Chapters 9, 10 and 11.

Two further declaration operators introduce the reference and pointer types and are the subject of the next two sections.

These declaration operators can be combined in a variety of ways to provide a wide range of types. For example, classes can be the argument or return type from a function. Arrays may hold pointers to any type (fundamental or derived). Classes can themselves be members of another class. These type construction mechanisms give C++ a wonderfully rich environment for developing types which reflect the kinds of real-world things we are modelling in our computer programs.

3.16 Reference types

A *reference* is an alternative name, or *alias*, for an object which is currently in scope. One principal use for a reference type is as an argument or return type of a function, particularly when used with user defined class types (see Chapter 9).

When a variable is defined to be an `int&` (say), as in:

```
int& b ..... ;
```

the notation `int&` means `b` is a reference to type `int`. A reference must be initialized so that the reference object may be a synonym for an existing object. For example:

```
int k = 5;              // normal definition
int& b = k;             // k and b now refer to the same int
int m = b;              // m is 5
b = 12;                 // k is 12
```

In the third line, the integer variable `m` is defined and initialized with the value of `b`. Since `b` refers to the same `int` as `k` with value `5`, then `m` is set to this value. In the final line, the `int` object to which `b` refers (namely, `k`) is assigned the value `12`.

The value of a reference cannot be changed after initialization. Following the initialization, the reference is permanent. In:

```
int k;
int& b = k;             // k and b now refer to the same int
b = 5;                  // k is 5
b++;                    // k is incremented to 6
```

the fourth line applies the post increment operator to the `int` to which `b` refers. Observe, that `b++` does not increment the reference `b`.

Consider the definition:

```
int& b = k;
```

The result of the elaboration is that the two identifiers `b` and `k` both refer to the same integer object. As we have demonstrated, assigning to `b` or to `k` has the same result; different identifiers but the same value. In some programming languages this phenomenon is known as *equivalencing*.

Figure 3.6 describes the effect of the above definition. In particular, note how the initializing value must be another variable to effect the equivalence.

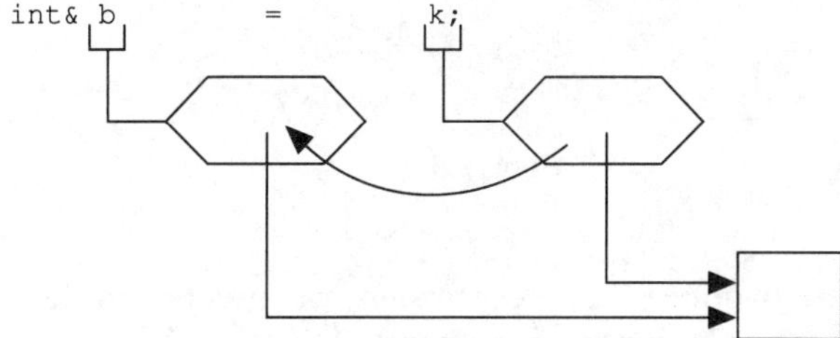

Figure 3.6

The `const` qualifier may also prepend a reference type to emphasize that the object may not be changed through the reference. For example, in:

```
int k = 5;
const int& b = k;
k = 10;                     // ok, k is variable
b = 12;                     // error, b is constant
```

no value may be assigned through `b` due to the constancy associated with it.

3.17 Pointer types

Our normal understanding of a variable (such as `var`) is that it represents a location in memory which has a unique address (5678 in the example), the content of which is a representation of some value currently assigned to the variable.

A *pointer*, however, is a variable which contains the address of some other object. If a pointer is a variable itself, then like all other variables it must occupy an area of memory which will have an address. The content of that area of memory is the address of some other variable. If `pVar` is a variable capable of addressing the integer variable `var`, and if `pVar` resides at memory location 1234, then the arrangement is shown in Figure 3.7. The unary operator `&`, known as the *address operator*, is applied to some variable and gives the address of that object. The assignment

```
pVar = &var;
```

assigns the address of `var` to the pointer variable.

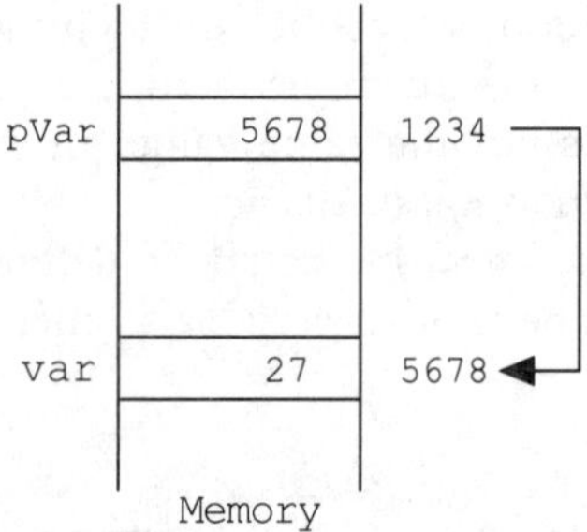

Figure 3.7

If variable `var` were to appear in an expression, we understand that the value of `var` is required. For example, in the assignment:

```
temp = var;
```

for some integer variable `temp`. The value of the integer variable `var`, namely 27, is assigned to `temp`. Equally, if the variable `pVar` were to appear on the right of an assignment operator, the value of `pVar` is required (5678 in this example):

```
..... = pVar;
```

The unary *indirection operator* `*` is applied to some pointer variable, such as `pVar`, and accesses the value referred to by that address:

```
temp = *pVar;
```

Now `pVar` points to `var` and so `temp` is assigned the value of `var` (that is, 27). The expression to the right of the assignment operator is evaluated in two stages. First, the value of `pVar` is obtained (namely, 5678). This is interpreted as the address of an integer object. The unary indirection operator then delivers the value of the integer at this address (namely, 27).

The pointer variable `pVar` is introduced with the declaration

```
int* pVar;
```

Here, the *pointer declarator* `*` is appended to the type specifier `int`, and denotes that the variable `pVar` is an `int` pointer.

Figure 3.8 presents a pictorial representation for the initialized definition:

```
int* pVar = &var;
```

As usual, the variable `pVar` possesses an address. The difference, however, is the value to which the address refers is itself an address (the address of `var`). As shown earlier, the value of the expression `pVar` is the address to which it refers, whilst the value of the expression `*pVar` is the object to which `pVar` points.

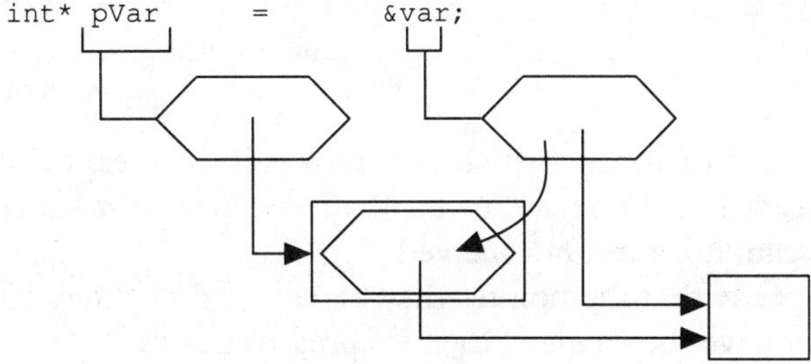

Figure 3.8

Since `*pVar` represents an `int` object, then we may employ `*pVar` as we would `var`:

```
temp = *pVar + 1;         // set temp to 1 + var
cout << *pVar;            // print var
*pVar = 10;               // set var to 10
```

If only pVar appears in an expression then the pointer value is involved. For example:

```
int* qVar = pVar;              // copy pointer into qVar
pVar++;                        // increment pointer (see Chapter 8)
```

In the last statement, the pointer variable pVar is incremented. We shall have to wait until Chapter 8 to discover the meaning of an incremented pointer.

Strictly, when we define pVar as, say, a pointer to an integer variable as above, then we are constraining that pointer to point to a particular kind of object (int in this case). Given the definition:

```
double z;
```

it is illegal to execute the assignment:

```
pVar = &z;
```

We know that the adjective const can be applied to a definition to yield a type that is the same as the original except that the value of the object cannot be changed. As a consequence, we cannot take the address of a const object, because if that were permitted we could assign a value to the object indirectly via its pointer. Thus the following is illegal:

```
const int june = 6;
int* p = &june;                // error
```

We may also specify that the pointer is constant rather than the object referred to by the pointer. This we do with the declarator `* const`:

```
int june = 6, august = 8;      // normal
int* const p = &june;          // constant pointer
// ....."
*p = 7;                        // ok, june is now the value 7
p = &august;                   // error, the pointer cannot change
```

Variable p is a pointer to an int, which is what would be meant if the const were omitted. The presence of the const means that p cannot be modified. The object to which p points can, however, be changed.

If we want to specify that the pointer may be changed but the object referenced by the pointer may never be changed then we present this as:

```
int june = 6, august = 8;
const int* p = &june;          // modifiable pointer to
                               // ..... constant object
                               // ..... but not pointed object
p = &august;                   // ok, p may be changed
*p = 10;                       // error, object cannot be changed
```

and to define that both the pointer and the referenced object cannot be modified:

```
int june = 6, august = 8;
const int* const p = &june;
.....
*p = 7;                 // error, cannot change object
p = &august;            // error, cannot change pointer
```

3.18 Enumeration types

The `const` qualifier of Section 3.7 gives a method for introducing named constants. For example, writing:

```
const int SUN = 0;
const int MON = 1;
// .....
const int SAT = 6;
```

in a program then allows us to use the names `SUN`, `MON`, etc. to represent the days of the week rather than having to work with the codes `0`, `1`, etc. An alternative method for introducing named constants is:

```
enum { SUN, MON, TUE, WED, THU, FRI, SAT };
```

in which seven enumeration constants associate with values which begin at zero and increase by one as we move rightward through the list. The latter is an example of a enumerated type.

The keyword `enum` is used to declare enumerated types. The enumeration type provides a means of naming (or enumerating) the elements of a finite set, and of declaring variables that take values which are elements of that set. The set of values is represented by identifiers called *enumeration constants*. For example, the declaration:

```
enum Day { SUN, MON, TUE, WED, THU, FRI, SAT} d1, d2, d3;
```

creates a new enumeration type `enum Day`, whose values are `SUN, MON, ....., SAT`. It also declares three variables `d1`, `d2` and `d3` of the enumeration type `enum Day`. These variables may be assigned values which are elements of the set:

```
d1 = MON;
```

We may also test the values of enumerated variables:

```
if (d1 == d2) .....
```

or

```
if ( !(d2 == SUN || d2 == SAT) ) .....
```

The *enumeration tag* name `Day` appearing in the declaration above is optional. The declaration is then equivalent to:

```
enum {SUN, MON, TUE, WED, THU, FRI, SAT} d1, d2, d3;
```

The enumeration tag `Day`, however, allows an enumeration type to be referenced after its definition. The single declaration:

```
enum Day {SUN, MON, TUE, WED, THU, FRI, SAT} d1, d2, d3;
```

is exactly equivalent to the declarations:

```
enum Day {SUN, MON, TUE, WED, THU, FRI, SAT};
Day d1, d2, d3;
```

The first declaration does not allocate any storage, but a template is set up for the type `enum Day`. This type may be used, as shown, in any subsequent declaration (including function argument declarations and function type specifiers).

An enumeration without a tag name and without any associated variables is used to introduce to the program the enumeration constants. For example, we may use the names `FALSE` and `TRUE` following the declaration:

```
enum {FALSE, TRUE};
```

Strictly, the C++ compiler assigns an int value starting with 0 to each enumeration constant in a set. In the example:

```
enum Day {SUN, MON, TUE, WED, THU, FRI, SAT};
```

`SUN` has value `0`, `MON` has value `1`, ... and `SAT` has value `6`. These default assignations may be altered by assigning an explicit constant to an enumeration constant in the list. Successive elements from the list are then assigned subsequent values. Consider:

```
enum Navigate {NORTH, EAST = 90, SOUTH = 180, WEST = 270};
```

The enumeration constant `NORTH` has default value `0`; `EAST` has explicit value `90`; `SOUTH` and `WEST` are respectively `180` and `270`.

When an enumerator or variable with an enumeration type is used in an expression, the value is implicitly converted by integral promotion to type `int`. This means that the arithmetic operators may be applied directly to enumeration types.

When writing programs with enumerated type variables, one should not rely on the fact that the enumeration constants are treated as integer constants. Instead these variables should be treated as distinct variable types. The motive behind this segregation deals with one of the main strengths of the enumerated type, namely, safety. It is more difficult accidentally to assign a variable the wrong value if proper mnemonics are used.

If it does prove necessary to mix enumerated types and, say, integer values, casts may be employed:

```
Day today = FRI;
Day tomorrow = Day(int(today) + 1) % 7);
```

We must be careful in our use of explicit casts to an enumerated type. Consider:

```
Day never = Day(27);
```

The outcome is implementation dependent, since there is no guarantee that the result is one of the legal enumerators.

3.19 The typedef statement

The C++ programming language supports a number of fundamental data types such as `char` and `int`. A variable declaration for the fundamental types employs the *type specifiers* `char`, `int`, etc. The declaration:

```
int hours, minutes;
```

specifies that the variables `hours` and `minutes` are of type `int`. The C++ language also provides the *typedef declaration*, which allows a type to be explicitly associated with an identifier. The statement:

```
typedef int    Time;
```

defines the type name `Time` to be equivalent to the C++ data type `int`. The named identifier can be used later to declare a variable or function in the usual way. The declaration:

```
Time hours, minutes;
```

declares the variables `hours` and `minutes` to be of type `Time`, equivalent to the type `int`.

The principal advantage of the use of the `typedef` in the above example is the added readability that it lends to the definition of the variables. The declaration additionally incorporates the intended purpose of these variables in the program. Declaring them to be of type `int` in the normal way would not have made the intended use of these variables clear. A second advantage is that it allows abbreviations for long declarations. This will be made apparent when arrays and function declarations are introduced.

To define a new type name, the following procedure is applied. Firstly, write a declaration as if a variable of the desired type were being declared. For example, to declare a variable `var` of type `int`, the declaration is:

```
int        var;
```

Secondly, substitute the variable name with the new type name:

```
int        Time;
```

Finally, prefix the statement with the reserve keyword `typedef`:

```
typedef int    Time;
```

A common use for the `typedef` statement is to introduce type names for reference and pointer types. For example, instead of the declarations:

```
int*           ptri;
double         d = 0;
double&        dr = d;
```

we might have:

```
typedef int*            Pint;
typedef double&         Rdouble;
Pint                    ptri;
double                  d = 0;
Rdouble                 dr = d;
```

in which the type names `Pint` and `Rdouble` have been introduced to emphasize pointer and reference types.

3.20 Summary

1. The four fundamental types are `char`, `int`, `float` and `double`. `float` and `double` provide two precisions for decimal numbers. The qualifiers `short`, `long` and `unsigned` offer several sizes for integral types. `Long doubles` also feature.

2. Denotations or constants represent specific instances of a particular type. Integer constants preceded with `0` and `0X` (or `0x`) designate octal and hexadecimal integer constants respectively. Integer constants of type long are appended with an `L` (or `l`). Unsigned integer constants are appended `U` or `u`. A constant with a decimal fraction is implicitly of type `double`. A floating point constant may be appended with either `F` or `f` for constants of type `float`, or with `L` or `l` for constants of type `long double`.

3. A character value is delimited by single quotes (`'`). A string value is delimited by double quotes (`"`). Both may involve escape sequences.

4. Identifiers are used to name objects in a program. An identifier is a letter/digit sequence starting with a letter. The underscore symbol (_) is considered to be a letter. Good mnemonic names should always be chosen to improve program clarity.

5. The three types of identifiers are reserved words, standard identifiers and user-defined identifiers. Reserved identifiers (keywords) have a special predefined meaning to the C++ compiler and cannot be redefined by the programmer.

6. A definition contains the names and types of the variables used in a program.

7. An expression is a combination of operators and operands. The operators determine the computation to be performed. The precedence and associativity of operators determines the order of evaluation in an expression. Assignment is an operator and can occur as part of an expression.

8. When evaluating mixed mode expressions, automatic type conversions apply. Integral conversions promote integer data values of a lower type to one of a higher type. Arithmetic conversions apply to operands before performing a binary operation.

9. The comma operator is used for sequential evaluation of a sequence of expressions. The value of the final expression is the value of the entire expression.

10. From the four fundamental types other types can be introduced using the function, array, reference, pointer declarators and the class declaration. New

derived types may then be further combined to produce structures which reflect the real-world entities we model in software.

11. The `typedef` statement associates a programmer defined identifier with an existing type or with a programmer defined type. Programmer defined type names are used to abbreviate longer type specifiers and to incorporate the intended purpose of the variables or functions in declarations.

12. An enumeration data type is defined by listing the identifiers by which the values of the type are to be denoted. In most cases it is preferable to separate the type definition from the variable declaration, in which case the former does not allocate storage but simply acts as a template for the type. Unless integer values are explicitly assigned, the compiler assigns successive integer values to each enumeration constant starting with zero.

3.21 Exercises

1. Which of the following are valid C++ constants? For those which are valid, identify their type. If invalid, state why.

   (a) `-123` (b) `.123` (c) `10E-4`
   (d) `'4'` (e) `'four'` (f) `'\z'`
   (g) 10^6

2. Which of the following are invalid identifiers in C++ and explain why.

   (a) `June` (b) `int` (c) `BBC_1`
   (d) `b` (e) `a$` (f) `X-RAY`
   (g) `_Z` (h) `_12_`

3. Given the following definitions and initial assignments:

```
int   i, j, m, n;
float f, g;
char  c;

i = j = 2;
m = n = 5;
f = 1.2;
g = 3.4;
c = 'X';
```

   use the rules of precedence and associativity of the operators to evaluate the following expressions, showing any conversions which take place and the type of the result.

   (a) `12 * m` (b) `m / j`
   (c) `n % j` (d) `m / j * j`

(e) `(f + 10) * 20` **(f)** `(i++) * n`
(g) `i++ * n` **(h)** `-12L * (g - f)`
(i) `2 + c` **(j)** `(n++), (n++)`
(k) `m = n = -j` **(l)** `(int) f`
(m) `(double) m` **(n)** `double(m) + 10`
(o) `(double)(m + 10)`

4. **Find the errors in the following series of definitions:**

```
int        kilometres, metres;
float      metres;
integer    weeks;
int        fm, medium, long;
short      char, tiny;
```

5. **Using the diagramming notation of Figures 3.6 and 3.8, describe the following definitions.**

(a)
```
int k = 5;
int& b = k;
int& c = b;
```

(b)
```
int k = 5;
int& b = k;
int* p = &b;
```

6. **Prepare enumeration data type declarations for (a) the suits in a pack of cards, (b) the colours of the rainbow, (c) monetary denominations, and (d) the integer binary operators supported by C++.**

4

Simple Input and Output

Strictly, *input* and *output* facilities are not part of the C++ language. Nonetheless, real programs do communicate with their environment. In this chapter we will describe a subset of the standard C++ I/O (input/output) library, consisting of a set of operations designed to provide a standard facility for performing input and output.

We will not attempt to describe the entire I/O library here. We restrict our discussion to a small number of operations which communicate with the user's terminal. This will be sufficient to permit us to write programs involving input/output. In Chapter 15 we will revisit input/output and consider programs which operate on data held in computer files. Appendix F4 provides a reference section for those I/O operations of the standard library.

4.1 Access to the standard C++ library

Whenever a C++ program executes, four *streams* are automatically opened by the operating system environment for use by that program. Two of these streams are known as the *standard input* and the *standard output*. It is intended that normal input by the program will be read from the standard input stream. In an interactive environment the standard input normally associates with the user's terminal (keyboard). Similarly, normal output is written to the standard output which, again, is the user terminal (screen).

In this chapter we are concerned only with programs that operate with the standard input and standard output streams. In Chapter 15 where input/output through files is discussed, we consider more fully the standard input, standard output and the other program streams.

The library described here, referred to as the *iostream library*, is distributed with Release 2.0 of the AT&T C++ Language system. The iostream library defines a set of operations for reading and writing of the basic types. The iostream library provides a standard facility for input/output, facilitating the portability of C++ programs.

All source program files which refer to a standard I/O stream library function must contain the line:

```
#include <iostream.h>
```

near the beginning of the file. A detailed description of this `#include` statement is reserved until the next chapter. Suffice it to say that a *header file* called `iostream.h` defines certain items required by the standard I/O library. For example, the standard input and standard output streams are defined here. These details are incorporated or 'included' into the application program from this header file.

4.2 Unformatted output

Input and output operations are supported by the `istream` (*input stream*) and `ostream` (*output stream*) classes (see Chapter 9). The `ostream` output operation is denoted by the double chevron symbol << and is known as the *insertion operator*. We can visualize this operator as one which points in the direction of its data movement. For example:

```
<< x
```

moves data item `x` toward the output stream. Using the predefined standard output stream `cout` (defined in `iostream.h`), we can direct the value of the data item `x` toward the user's terminal with:

```
cout << x;
```

The insertion operator is, like all C++ operators, subject to precedence and associativity. We must be conscious then of the interplay with other operators, as well as understanding the value delivered by such an operator. Since the operator has lower precedence than the arithmetic operators, then statements like:

```
cout << x + y;
```

achieve the desired effect, namely, to output the sum of the variables `x` and `y`.

The insertion operator delivers a value which is a reference to the output stream for which it was called. Since the << operator associates left to right, we can use it to concatenate the output of a number of items to the output stream:

```
cout << "The sum of " << x << " and " << y << " is " << x+y;
```

First, the string `"The sum of "` is output; the value of that insertion is a reference to the stream `cout`. This is then used in conjunction with the value of the variable `x`; and so on.

4.3 Unformatted input

The *extraction operator* complements the insertion operator. It fetches data from a specified input stream. The `istream` extraction operator is denoted by the double chevron symbol >>. Again, the operator symbol suggests the flow of data. For example:

```
>> x
```

moves the input data into the data item `x`. Using the predefined input stream `cin`, we can direct the input from the user keyboard to the variable `x`:

```
cin >> x;
```

The extraction operator has the same precedence and associativity as the insertion operator. The value associated with this operator is a reference to the input stream for which it was called. Therefore, the extraction operator can be concatenated, as in:

```
cout << "Please enter two numbers: ";
cin >> first >> second;
```

The extraction operator supports all the fundamental C++ types. By default, the extractor for a fundamental type skips leading white space in the input stream, then reads the characters appropriate to the given type. In the last example, if variables first and second are of type `int`, then the input:

```
123            456AB
```

reads the value `123` for the variable `first`, skips the separating white space, then assigns the value `456` to the variable `second`. The input stops on the character `"A"`, awaiting further input statements.

4.4 Output manipulators

The stream library provides a number of ways to format the output from a program. The facilities are provided through a number of routes. Those discussed here are called *manipulators*. These and other mechanisms are more fully discussed in Chapter 15. Here, we provide a simple mechanism to control the format of the output. They are presented as part of the output statement. They produce no output but have the side effect of altering the default style of output.

The simple usage:

```
int dozen = 12;
cout << "[" << dozen << "]";
```

produces the output:

```
[12]
```

The value of the variable `dozen` is printed in a field width large enough to display its value. However, the example:

```
cout << "[" << setw(4) << dozen << "]";
```

produces:

```
[  12]
```

in which the parameterized manipulator `setw` instructs the output stream to display the next value in a field of four character positions.

By default, a decimal value is printed with six decimal digits. The manipulator `setprecision`:

```
double pi = 3.1415926;
cout << setprecision(4) << pi;
```

writes the value of the variable `pi` with four digits following the decimal point:

```
3.1416
```

To use these manipulators in a program we must include the header file `<iomanip.h>`:

```
#include <iostream.h>
#include <iomanip.h>
```

4.5 The functions get and put

Two simple facilities are provided for single character input and output: `get` and `put`. The function `put` takes a single character argument and prints it on the named standard output stream. To output the value of the character variable `ch`, we use:

```
cout.put(ch);
```

To output a single newline character we could use:

```
cout.put('\n');
```

The notation `cout.put(ch)` applies the function `put` with the argument `ch` to the ostream variable `cout`. The actual notation used here is part of the discussion of *classes* in Chapter 13. For the present we need not concern ourselves with this detail and simply be prepared to use this construction when required.

The function `get` reads the next character from the standard input stream and stores it in the character variable given as the function argument.

```
char ch;
cin.get(ch);
```

4.6 Summary

1. Input/output facilities in C++ are provided by a suite of functions from the standard I/O stream library.

2. When using input/output constructs, the system header file `<iostream.h>` should be included in a program by means of the `#include` control line.

3. Formatted output is provided by manipulators. Formatting is the process of controlling the layout of the printed output.

4. Single character transfers are accomplished with the library functions `get` and `put`.

4.7 Exercises

1. Produce the following two lines of output:

```
PROGRAMMING IN C++
IS FUN
```

using (a) two insertion operators
(b) one insertion operator.

2. Given the integer variable `staffno` and the floating variable `salary`, write output statement(s) to produce:

```
STAFF               PAY
ddd                 ddd.dd
```

where each "d" represents a decimal digit.

3. Write program statements which read a sum of money in the form `ddd.dd`, increases it by 10 per cent, and prints out the increased sum. If the input was of the form `ddd:dd`, how would the program have to be modified?

4. In the context of the variable definitions:

```
int   j, k;
float x, y, z;
char  c;
```

and the three lines of program input data:

```
12.34           56.7
      -89E10
0.012
```

what is the effect of executing each of the following sequences of input statements:

```
(a)  cin >> x >> y >> z;
(b)  cin >> x;
     cin >> y >> z;
(c)  cin >> x >> y >> z;
     cin >> j;
(d)  cin >> j >> c >> k >> x;
```

5

Program Structure

In Chapter 2 we explored the fundamentals of a C++ program. In particular, a number of complete examples were presented. No attempt was made to specify the exact construction of a program. In this chapter we will define the exact composition of a C++ program. In later chapters, where we introduce additional language constructs, extensions to this basic form are given.

A C++ program may be developed around any of the programming paradigms introduced in Chapter 1. Using the procedural abstraction, a C++ program is developed in terms of one or more functions. Functions within C++ facilitate partitioning large programs into smaller, manageable units, thus simplifying the programming task. In addition, functions developed in one program may be incorporated into others, saving the need to reprogram them.

With the object oriented paradigm a program revolves around a number of interacting objects, each sending instructions to receiving objects to perform some operation. The operation is expressed as a C++ function. Hence the function is one of the central aspects of a C++ program and is the subject of this chapter.

5.1 The structure of a function

A C++ function describes the computational processes to be carried out on its data. The function must thus describe both its data objects (variable definitions) and its processing actions (statements). The simplest form of function definition reflects this minimum requirement:

```
type-specifier function-name()
{
  definition-and-statement-list
}
```

The *function-name* is the programmer-defined name (identifier) for that function. Function names must be unique otherwise the compiler is unable to distinguish between two distinct functions bearing the same name. We shall relax the rule concerning the uniqueness of function names in a later section where we introduce *function overloading*. A function name is constructed according to the rule for identifiers. The type-specifier indicates the value associated with the function (see p. 67). The unit of text surrounded by and including the braces

`{` and `}`, is called a *compound statement* and also a *block*. A block consists of a (possibly empty) sequence of variable definitions and statements. Individual definitions and statements are terminated by semicolon (`;`) symbols. The definitions identify the data items and the statements specify the processing actions.

All the programs introduced in Chapter 2 conform to this structure. Program 2.1(a), and repeated as Program 5.1(a), consists of the single function `main`. As noted in Chapter 2, all complete C++ programs must have a function called `main`. A program starts executing from the first statement in function `main`.

PROGRAM 5.1(a)

```
//
//  A program to display a simple message to
//      the operator's console.
//

#include <iostream.h>

int main()
{
  cout << "My first program.\n";
  return (0);
}
```

The function `main` has no variable definitions but does have two statements. The first statement is an output statement. `cout` is the output's destination, and is the user's terminal. << is the insertion operator, sending the given string to the terminal. The statement is terminated with a semicolon symbol.

A program which uses input/output functions from the standard C++ library must also have a `#include` statement as shown. This statement supplies the C++ compiler with details relating to the standard input/output operations used by the program.

Program 5.1(a) might alternatively have been written as in Program 5.1(b).

PROGRAM 5.1(b)

```
//
//  This program displays a simple message through
//      three separate output calls.
//      The output is the same as that of Program 5.1(a).
//

#include <iostream.h>

int main()
{
```

```
    cout << "My ";
    cout << "first ";
    cout << "program.\n";
    return (0);
}
```

This time the function main employs three output statements. Again, no variable definitions are present. To assist with program readability, each statement appears on a separate line. This does not, however, imply that the output appears on separate lines. Output onto separate lines is governed by the arguments to << and not by the program layout. Indentation and alignment are used to emphasize the structure of the program. The program output is:

```
My first program.
```

A function need not have any variable definitions, as in the examples above, or any statements. For example, Program 5.2 is a perfectly valid C++ program. The function main, and hence the program, does no real processing. Such a program has no real practical value, yet a null function, other than main, can sometimes prove useful as a place holder during program development for a function not yet programmed.

PROGRAM 5.2

```
//
//  A program to do nothing !
//

#include <iostream.h>

int main()
{
  return (0);
}
```

Consider now a program which includes variable definitions. The program is required to read two integer data values and to print them in reverse order. To achieve this the function main must include a definition for two integer variables which will be the repositories for the two data values.

PROGRAM 5.3

```
//
//  This program accepts two integer data values
//      and displays them in reverse order.
//

#include <iostream.h>
```

```
int main()
{
  int first, second;          // variables to capture data values

  cout << "Enter two integer values: ";
  cin >> first >> second;
  cout << "Reversed data: " << second << ", " <<  first << "\n";
  return (0);
}
```

Program 5.4 is similar to the last example. It reads some data, processes it, then displays the result of its computations. The processing this time involves some arithmetic operations. The program reads three integer data values representing a time expressed as hours, minutes and seconds. The time is converted into a total number of seconds, then printed.

PROGRAM 5.4

```
//
//  This program accepts as input a time measured
//      in hours, minutes and seconds. The time is then
//      converted to the equivalent number of seconds.
//

#include <iostream.h>

int main()
{
  int  hours, minutes, seconds;  // variables to capture data values

  cout << "Enter the time to be converted: ";
  cin >> hours >> minutes >> seconds;

  long time = (60L * hours + minutes) * 60L + seconds;
  cout << "The original time of:\n";
  cout << hours << " hours, " << minutes << " minutes, "
       << seconds << " seconds\n";
  cout << "converts to " << time << " seconds\n";
  return (0);
}
```

The last two programs incorporate a prompt to the user before reading the data values. For interactive programs this is good practice since the user then knows when data is required to be entered (on some systems the output for the prompt may have to be 'flushed', see Chapter 15). Without a prompt, the program hangs awaiting input from the user, which might be misconstrued that the program has, in some way, failed.

Observe how we are permitted to mix statements and variable definitions in a function. The only requirement is that we must first define a variable before its use. Hence, hours is defined before it is used to accept an input value into it. Variable time is defined and initialized with the expression involving the data values.

The definition and initialization of the variable time midway through the function and, by comparison, variable hour at the head of the function raises issues of coding standards. Each programmer and programming team will have their own standards. Since we do not have sufficient information to initialize time until part through function main it seems inappropriate to initialize it (by default or explicitly) at the function head then reassign it later:

```
int main()
{
  int hours, ..... ;
  long time = 0L;          // initializer
  // .....
  time = ..... ;           // now compute it
  // .....
}
```

It seems more natural to get it right first time rather than rebuild it a second time with the correct value having first prepared it with some initial value.

How did we arrive at the solution for Program 5.4? It is sufficiently complex to warrant applying some design process prior to its implementation. The technique of designing a system or program in steps that gradually define more and more detail is called *functional decomposition.*

Functional decomposition is a step-by-step process that begins with the most general functional view of what is to be done, breaks the view down into sub-functions, and then repeats the process until all sub-function units are simple enough to be easily understood and small enough to be easily coded. This method of systematically applying *stepwise refinements* is a powerful tool for dealing with the complexity of many related elements.

We express our functional decomposition through a *program design language* or PDL. The PDL is a design description language specifically intended for documenting software designs. It is not a compiled language in the sense of C++. The language has no formal syntax, but is an extensible language which provides constructs to express the necessary program logic.

PDL descriptions may include informally stated actions, intended to be a self-explanatory description of the program. In our PDL we shall reserve upper case for formalizations of the target programming language. We shall see examples of this in later chapters. Material in lower case is an informal description of some action to be performed. The context of this description should be sufficient to make the action clear.

A first level PDL description of Program 5.4 might then be:

```
prompt the user for the data
accept the data
perform the calculations upon the data
print the results
```

Each of these actions is at a level where no further decomposition is required. Each action is directly expressible as C++ code. The second action, for example, is encoded as:

```
cin >> hours >> minutes >> seconds;
```

Applying the same to all other actions we can synthesize a complete program including all the necessary declarations. The result is Program 5.4.

Had any actions required further analysis, then the process of functional decomposition would have been repeated on these. Each action would be further refined and again expressed in our PDL.

As we progress through the remainder of the book introducing new program features, we shall also introduce an appropriate construct in our PDL.

5.2 Multi-function programs

As noted in the previous section, a C++ program may consist of one or more functions. One of the functions must, of course, be called `main`. Functions offer a means of controlling the complexity of large programs. A function provides a convenient way to encapsulate some discrete programming task. When the function is *called* or *invoked*, the task is executed. Consider a function as a named black box. The name given to the box is the means by which we select the box or function to execute. The box has one entry point and one exit point. During execution of the function some action is performed as described by the executable statements in the function body. Pictorially we represent this by Figure 5.1.

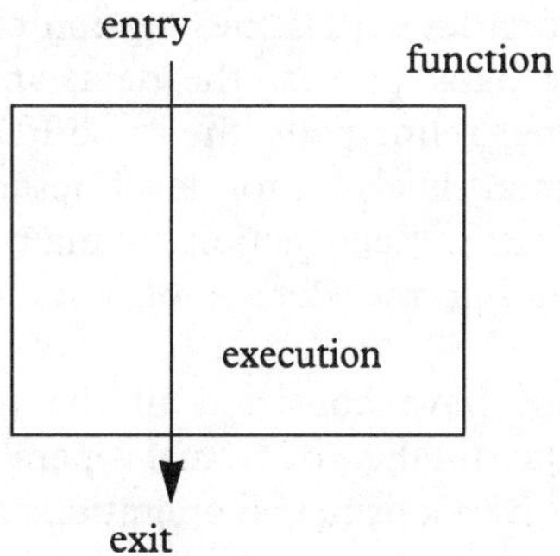

Figure 5.1

Where one function calls a second function, the effect is to temporarily suspend execution of the first function at the *point of call* of the second. The second function is entered (at its entry point), executed and then exited. Upon completion, control returns to the calling function and execution continues with the statement immediately following the point of call. We can express this diagramatically by showing function 1 calling function 2 in Figure 5.2.

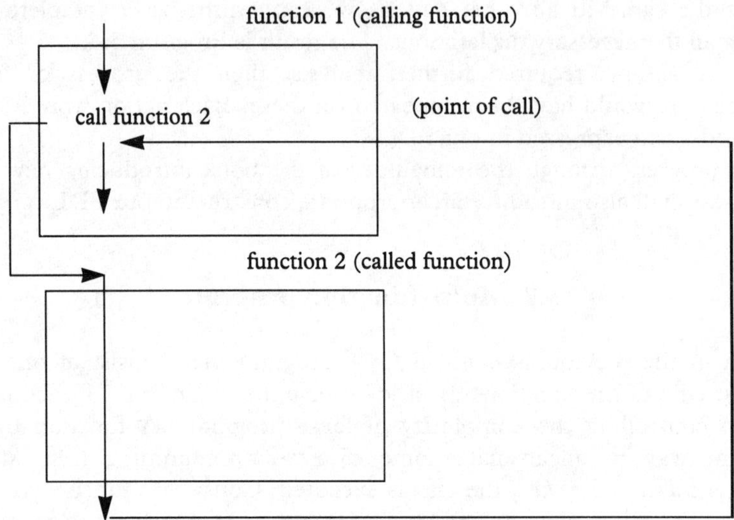

Figure 5.2

Functions can call other functions, building a hierarchical layer of interconnected functions, reflecting the functional decomposition performed during program design. The design can then map directly onto the programming language. For example, a first level PDL description of a program might give rise to three actions: input the data, process the data, and output the results. If all three actions required further refinement, the same PDL analysis may be applied. Since the first level refinement is also a top level description of the problem, it is implemented in function `main`. Each action in main then becomes a call to a subsidiary function containing the details of the corresponding second level refinement.

So far, all our programs have consisted of the single function `main`. Each function `main` specified the totality of actual operations to be performed. In Program 5.4, for example, the six principal operations are:

```
cout << ..... ;
cin >> ..... ;
time = ..... ;
cout << ..... ;
cout << ..... ;
cout << ..... ;
```

Consider now extending this program to operate upon, say, four sets of data. Each data set consists of a time measured in hours, minutes and seconds, and for each set the time is to be converted to its equivalent number of seconds. One possible solution would be to repeat the above six statements a total of four times. This leads to a much larger `main` function, but is, nevertheless, a viable solution.

Further analysis of this programming problem identifies that two sub-tasks are present. The first sub-task is that there are four data sets to be operated upon and that the operations are identical. The second is that for a given data set a distinct series of operations is to be performed. These operations are captured by the six statements outlined above.

Expressed in our PDL, the sub-task to control the processing of four data sets might appear as:

process the first data set
process the second data set
process the third data set
process the fourth data set

Informally, each statement is a description of the required action. They cannot, however, be directly expressed in our chosen programming language. We must further refine the actions. A second level refinement of the operation 'process one data set' is the PDL description we arrived at for Program 5.4, namely:

prompt the user for the data
accept the data
perform the calculations upon the data
print the results

Given that the second level refinements to process the first, second, third and fourth data sets is the same, the implementation is then realized by relegating the second sub-task to a separate function. This function is fully responsible for the operations on a single data set. The function is subordinate to function `main`, which calls or invokes this subsidiary function four times, and in so doing, implements the first sub-task.

PROGRAM 5.5

```
//
//  This program operates on four data sets. Each set
//      consists of a time measured in hours, minutes and
//      seconds. For each set, the time is converted into
//      the equivalent number of seconds and printed.
//

#include <iostream.h>

int main()
{
  void    convert(void);           // prototype declaration
```

```
  convert();            // Four function .....
  convert();            // ..... calls to .....
  convert();            // ..... convert
  convert();
  return (0);
}

//
//  Function convert operates on a single data set,
//      reading, processing and printing.
//

void convert(void)
{
  int  hours, minutes, seconds;   // data values

  cout << "Enter the time to be converted: ";
  cin >> hours >> minutes >> seconds;
  const long time = (60L * hours + minutes) * 60L + seconds;
  cout << "The original time of:\n";
  cout << hours << " hours, " << minutes << " minutes, "
       << seconds << " seconds\n";
  cout << "converts to " << time << " seconds\n\n";
  return;
}
```

The program shown above consists of two functions. The function `main` is, of course, always present. In addition, a function called `convert` is defined. This function contains all the variable definitions and statements required to operate on a single data set. Since it is this function which requires the variable space to hold the data and the computed values, then we define the variables in this function. It would be illegal to define the variables in function `main` and then use them in function `convert`. We shall have more to say on this matter shortly.

Note the definition for function `convert`:

```
void convert(void) { /* ..... */ }
```

The two keywords `void` specify respectively that the function delivers no return value to the calling function `main`, and that no arguments are passed from `main`. Where a function has no arguments then it may also be presented as:

```
void convert() { /* ..... */ }
```

Further, note how in `main` the function header for `convert` is repeated:

```
void convert(void);
```

This is a *prototype declaration* and alerts the compiler that function `main` calls this function before it is properly defined. All functions used in this way must be accompanied with prototypes. The declaration gives sufficient information to the compiler for it to validate the usage of `convert` in `main`. As above, the prototype may also appear as:

```
void convert();
```

Function main now no longer possesses any variable definitions. They are, in this example, unnecessary since no values are processed by this function. Were this not the case, then appropriate variable definitions would also be present in the body of function main. The actual body of function main consists of the statements to control processing the four data sets. This is achieved with four *function calls* to convert:

```
convert();
```

Each such statement causes the named function (convert) to be executed. Each invocation of this subsidiary function processes a single data set. When the function convert is complete, control reverts back to the calling function main. The called function (convert) is said to return control to the calling function (main). This return of control is explicitly specified by the return statement, the last executable statement in convert. Function main then arranges for three further calls to function convert.

The form of the return statement in convert is new. The effect of this statement is described above. The general form of this command is:

```
return;
```

where return is a reserved keyword. If no return statement is present in a called function, then processing continues until the end of the function body, as indicated by the closing brace symbol, }. Upon encountering the function end, control returns to the calling function as if an explicit return had been present. The use of the implicit return is so common that we shall adopt it in all further examples.

The general form of the return statement is:

return expression $_{opt}$;

The optional expression part is omitted for a function with return type void. As noted above, the return statement itself may be omitted then the compiler effectively inserts one before the closing brace (}) of the function body.

A function with a specified return value (such as main) must include a return statement with the expression part present. If no such return statement or one without an associated expression is used the compiler will elicit an error message (see Section 5.4 for details).

The order in which the functions appear in a C++ program text file is unimportant. We might equally well have placed the function convert first. Since normally function main will describe the overall processing, with detail reserved for the subordinate functions, reflecting our functional decomposition of the problem, we will always choose to place function main first.

A principle, present in Program 5.5, is that the program text is an expression of the idea of how the program operates (its *algorithm*). Functional decomposition facilitates expressing this algorithm.

5.3 Automatic variables

In the last section we developed a program with two functions – main and convert. It was noted that the variables in the program were defined in function convert since it is here that data space is required. Also, since no data items are required by function main, then no variable definitions are necessary.

It is known from Chapter 3 that the definition:

```
long time = ..... ;
```

appearing in function convert, introduces a data object called time and is of type long. Strictly, all variables have an attribute in addition to its type and name, which is referred to as its *storage class*. The term refers to the manner in which memory is allocated by the compiler for variables.

The term *scope* refers to the extent of the meaning of a particular variable in a program. Variables defined in a function are said to be *local* to that function and their scope is the block in which they are defined. This means that they have no meaning outside that function. The storage class for such variables is known as *automatic*. Variables defined within a function have storage class auto. This association is implicit. It is quite legal to state this explicitly by the definition:

```
auto long time = ..... ;
```

where auto is a reserved keyword. Since the storage class automatic is implicit because the definition appears in the body of a function, it is normally omitted.

The concept of the scope of a variable is presented by Program 5.6. The variable two defined in the function func is referenced only by this function. However, the variable one is defined in function main, but is illegally referenced by function func. The C++ compiler processing such an illegal reference would generate a compilation error indicating that variable one is not defined in function func.

PROGRAM 5.6

```
//
//      WRONG !
//      The automatic variable "one" is defined in function
//      main. Its scope is the body of function main. It is
//      illegal to reference it outside of main.
//

#include <iostream.h>

int main()
{
    void func(void);     // prototype
    int one;             // scope = main

    one = 1;             // valid reference, within scope
```

```
  func();                // call subordinate function
  return (0);
}

void func(void)
{
  int two;               // has scope of func

  two = one;             // error: variable one undefined here !!
}
```

Automatic variables are only *visible* within the function in which they are defined. Each automatic variable is said to be *local* to its corresponding function. Because of this, variables with the same name appearing in definitions in separate functions are unrelated, except that they are referenced with the same identifier. Operations performed on one automatic variable in one function have no effect whatsoever on an automatic variable with the same name in another function. This is illustrated by the following program. The variable `local` defined in both program functions are quite distinct. This is shown by the program's output.

PROGRAM 5.7

```
//
// A program to illustrate local variables, with the
//     same identifier appearing in two subroutines.
//

#include <iostream.h>

int main()
{
  void    subroutine(void);       // prototype

  int local;                      // this "local" belongs to main

  local = 1;                      // "local" in main set to 1
  cout << "Function main: local = " << local << "\n";  // confirm
  subroutine();                   // call subordinate
  cout << "Function main check: local = " << local << "\n"; //
unchanged
  return (0);
}

void subroutine(void)
{
  int local;             // this "local" belongs to subroutine

  local = 2;             // set subroutine's "local"
  cout << "Function subroutine: local = " << local << "\n";
}
```

The output produced by this program is:

```
Function main: local = 1
Function subroutine: local = 2
Function main check: local = 1
```

The final line of output demonstrates that the two variables called `local` are unrelated and are unaffected by the operations performed upon them in separate functions.

This feature means that the C++ programmer is free to use the same variable name in any number of functions without fear of confusion. It also implies that where functions are written independently by a number of programmers, each has unrestricted use of automatic variable names.

In addition to defining an automatic variable in a function, it is also permissible to assign it an initial value. This process is called *initialization*. A variable is initialized with a value by following its name in the definition with an equal symbol (=) and an expression. For example:

```
int time = 10;
int period = 20 + time;
```

5.4 Function values

Program 5.5 in Section 5.2 employed a subordinate function `convert`, responsible for processing a single data set. The function `main` called `convert` the correct number of times. No data was actually communicated between these functions. The C++ language provides a mechanism whereby the result of a calculation performed by a called function may be transmitted back to the calling function. This is achieved with the return statement. The syntax of this construct is:

```
return expression;
```

To ensure that the returned expression is adequately highlighted from the surrounding program text, it is often presented as a bracketed sub-expression. Thus commonly the statement form is:

```
return (expression);
```

The statement indicates that control is to return immediately from the called function, and that the value of the expression is to be made available to the calling function. The value returned may be 'captured' by the calling function with an appropriate assignment. For example, if `convert` is a function returning an integer value, and `period` is a variable of type `int`, then we may use:

```
period = convert();
```

to record the returned value.

Where a function returns a value, then the type of this returned value must precede the function name in the function definition. Strictly, a function definition now has the extended form:

```
type-specifier function-name(void)
{
  definition-and-statement-list
}
```

The keyword `void` in the argument list is optional. The type-specifier is any of the fundamental types supported by C++, including `void` when the function has no return value. If, for example, function `func` delivers a floating point value through a return statement, then the definition should include:

```
float func(void)
{
  -----
  -----
  return (expression);
}
```

The type of the expression returned must match the type of the function, or be capable of being converted to it as if by assignment (see Section 3.10). For example, the function `func` could contain:

```
return (1);
```

and the integer value will be converted to `float`.

The calling sequence for such a function is now different. Since the function makes available a returned value, a mechanism is required to allow the calling function to capture this value. The assignment operator, or one of its variants is normally used. Assuming a floating point variable called `result`, then function `func` might be called by:

```
result = func();
```

The statement calls function `func` and the returned value is assigned to the variable `result`.

The return value produced by `main` is made available to the operating environment in which the program is executing. This way a C++ program may communicate information to its surroundings.

These ideas are presented in Program 5.8, a variant of Program 5.5. Again we have two functions `main` and `convert`. This time `convert` does not print the result of its computations, but returns with the value computed from processing one data set. Function `main` calls function `convert` four times, and computes and prints a running total of the returned values.

PROGRAM 5.8

```
//
// A program to operate on four data sets each representing
//      a time measured in hours, minutes and seconds. Each set
//      is converted to its equivalent number of seconds.
```

```
//      Additionally, a running total of the number of seconds
//      is maintained.
//

#include <iostream.h>

int main()
{
  long total_time = 0L;         // accumulated total
  long convert(void);           // prototype

  total_time += convert();
  total_time += convert();
  total_time += convert();
  total_time += convert();

  cout << "The total time is " << total_time << " seconds\n\n";
  return (0);
}

long convert(void)
{
  int  hours, minutes, seconds;    // data values

  cout << "Enter the time to be converted: ";
  cin >> hours >> minutes >> seconds;
  const long time = (60L * hours + minutes) * 60L + seconds;
  return (time);
}
```

5.5 Function arguments

The multi-function programs which we have developed either had no data transferred between individual functions, or had a single value returned from the called function by the `return` statement. Many programming problems exist in which functions are required to return more than one item to the calling function. Further, the calling function may wish to transmit values to the called function. We introduce *function arguments* by which values may be conveyed between functions. In this section we restrict the discussion to arguments passed from the calling function to the called function. Passing arguments in the opposite direction is considered in later sections of this chapter.

The means by which a function is invoked has been referred to as the *calling sequence*. The calling sequence in C++ consists of the function name followed by a comma separated list of actual arguments enclosed in parentheses. If any actual argument is an expression, that expression is first evaluated and the value is passed as the argument. This method of argument passing in C++ is known as *pass by value*.

A function definition including arguments has the form:

```
type-specifier function-name(argument-type-list)
{
```

```
    definition-and-statement-list
}
```

The new feature is the *argument type list* appearing within the parentheses. The argument list in a function call is a list of *actual arguments*. The argument type list in a function definition is referred to as the *formal arguments*. The formal and actual arguments should agree in number and type. For every *formal argument*, there should be a corresponding actual argument of the same type in the function call. The type of each formal argument is given in the argument type list of the function definition. These argument declarations have the same basic form as definitions for automatic (local) variables, but with each argument and associated type given individually.

Strictly, we need not name a function argument in the function definition. This is sometimes used with redefined class member functions (see Chapter 11) which has no particular use for the argument. Such a function might appear as:

```
int         fff(int one, int two, int)
{
  // note how the third argument is unnamed
  // and would not be used by the function
}
```

To illustrate, consider a function called `sum` which receives two floating point values as arguments and which delivers their sum through the return statement. One complete definition is:

```
float sum(float first, float second)
{
  float temp;

  temp = first + second;
  return (temp);
}
```

The formal argument list is a comma separated list of argument declarations giving the type and name of a formal argument identifier. These identifiers represent the arguments to be received when the function is called. The behaviour of the function is described fully in terms of these formal arguments and any local variables. The names of arguments and of any local variables must be distinct since they both have the same scope – namely, the function body.

The corresponding function prototype for function `sum` would appear as:

```
float sum(float first, float second);    // prototype declaration
```

and informs the compiler that the function expects two `float` arguments and returns a `float`. Parameter names in a prototype need not necessarily agree with the names in the function definition. Indeed, parameter names may be omitted. They do, however, act as a source of documentation, used to convey the meaning of the variable. Hence, this example may also be presented as:

```
float sum(float arg1, float arg2);    // other names
```

or:

```
float sum(float, float);                    // no names
```

These function prototypes and the function header in the definition proper we sometimes describe as the *function signature*. The function name, its return type and argument types uniquely distinguish it from other functions.

To call function sum we use the assignment mechanism introduced earlier. In addition, we provide two actual arguments. They may be any expression delivering floating point values. Possible uses are:

```
int main()
{
  float result, total, second;       // local data
  float sum(float, float);         // prototype
  // .....
  result = sum(12.3, 17.21);        // = 29.51
  // .....
  total = sum(result, second);
  // .....
  result = sum(total * 3, result - 17.111);
  // .....
}
```

Functions such as these have all been shown with the returned value captured by an assignment. The returned values may equally appear in larger arithmetic expressions. To multiply the returned value from function sum before assigning we may write:

```
result = 3 * sum(total, 10.0)
```

Additionally, we might call the function sum and use its return value as the actual argument to another call on sum:

```
quadratic = sum(x*x, sum(x, 1.04))
```

The first or outer function call to sum has the square of the value for x as its first actual argument. Its second actual argument is the value delivered by the inner call to sum which has arguments x and 1.04. This inner call is executed first. The value delivered then becomes the second actual argument value to the outer call on sum.

Program 5.9 illustrates these features. The integer function hms_time translates its integer arguments representing a time measured in hours, minutes and seconds into a total number of seconds. The actual data values are collected by main and passed as actual arguments to this function. The returned value is then printed.

PROGRAM 5.9

```
//
// Read a time measured in hours, minutes and seconds
//     and convert it to the equivalent number of seconds.
```

```
//

#include <iostream.h>

int main ()
{
  int  hours, minutes, seconds;    // data values
  long hms_time(int, int, int);    // prototype declaration

  cout << "Enter the time: ";
  cin >> hours >> minutes >> seconds;
  long time = hms_time(hours, minutes, seconds);
  cout << "Converted time is " << time << " seconds\n";
  return (0);
}

long hms_time(int h,int  m,int s)
{
  const long t = (60L * h + m) * 60L + s;        // computed time

  return (t);
}
```

Note how function `hms_time` is now responsible for a single task – namely converting a time in hours, minutes and seconds to the equivalent number of seconds. In this form we have a primitive function that may find uses in other applications. We shall strive for this independence in other functions which we shall develop.

When a function is called with expressions for arguments, the value of each actual expression is calculated. The computed values are then matched with the corresponding formal argument. The formal argument within the function body behaves as an initialized local variable (initialized to the value of the actual argument). Thereafter, they may be treated as local variables and have their local copies modified. Only the local copy is changed. The changes do not alter the actual argument. This is demonstrated in Program 5.10.

PROGRAM 5.10

```
//
//  A program to demonstrate that a function argument
//      behaves as an initialized (by the actual argument)
//      local variable, having no effect whatsoever on the
//      actual argument.
//

#include <iostream.h>

int main()
{
  int  actualarg = 20;
  void subroutine(int);     // prototype declaration
```

```
    cout << "Main: actual argument is " << actualarg << "\n";
    subroutine(actualarg);
    cout << "Main check: actual argument is " << actualarg << "\n";
    return (0);
  }

  void subroutine(int formalarg)
  {
    formalarg += 10;              // change (local) value
    cout << "Subroutine: formal argument is " << formalarg << "\n";
  }
```

The output from this program is:

```
Main: actual argument is 20
Subroutine: formal argument is 30
Main check: actual argument is 20
```

The value of the actual argument (`actualarg`) is unchanged even when the local copy in function `subroutine` is modified.

To fully appreciate this argument passing mechanism we remind ourselves of variable definitions as described by Figure 3.5. In Program 5.9, function `main` calls the subordinate function `hms_time`, passing the values of the local variables `hours`, `minutes` and `seconds`. The return value is captured by the assignment to the variable `time`. This is represented by Figure 5.3. The code for the function `hms_time` is depicted by a circle into which the values of the actual arguments are delivered.

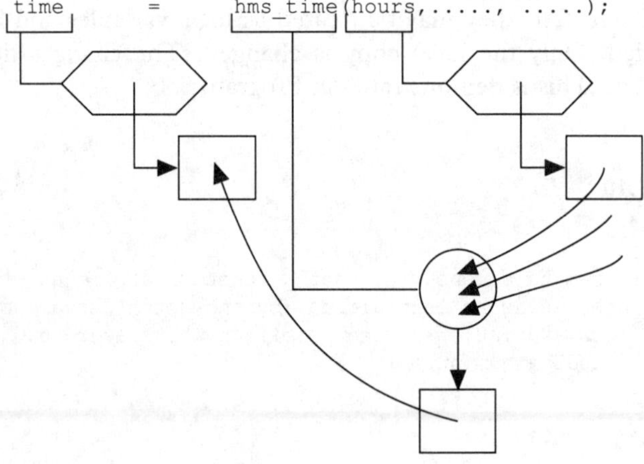

Figure 5.3

The supply of the actual arguments to functions in C++ is through the pass by value mechanism. Our understanding is that the formal argument is treated as an initialized local variable for the called function. The formal argument is initialized with the value of the actual argument expression. Figure 5.4 illustrates how this is achieved for the first argument to function `hms_time`. The figure also confirms the behaviour of Program 5.9. The formal argument `h` is initialized with the actual argument. Thereafter, the formal argument operates as a variable local to `hms_time` and any changes made to `h` apply to the copy and not to the actual argument.

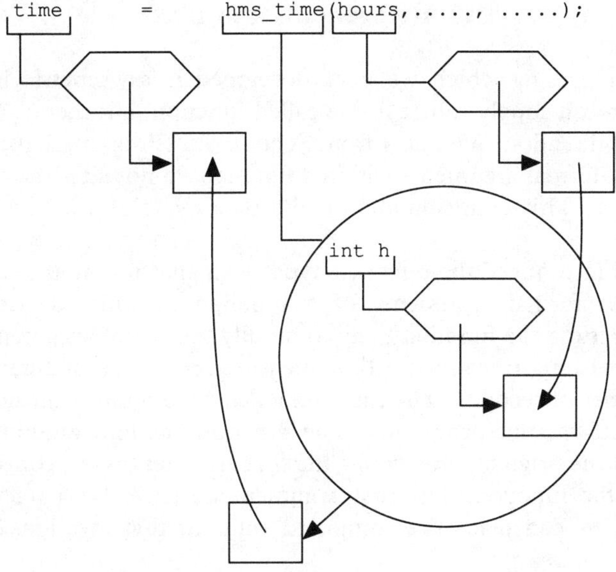

Figure 5.4

5.6 Function argument agreement and conversion

When employing a function with arguments we have stated that the actual and formal arguments must agree in number and type. Because of our insistence that a function prototype be present and in scope, the actual arguments are converted as if by initialization to the types specified in the prototype. Thus in the call to the function `square` in the following fragment, the actual parameter `2` is converted to type `double`:

```
int main()
{
  double answer;
```

```
  double square(double);
  // .....
  answer = square(2);
  // .....
}
double square(double x)
{
  return x * x;
}
```

5.7 Reference arguments

The parameter passing which we have developed is asymmetric insofar as the calling function can supply values to the called function, but there is no equivalent in the opposite direction. We know from Section 5.5 (Program 5.10) that changes to the values of formal arguments within a function do not alter the original actual argument values. This is attributable to the pass by value method of parameter passing in C++.

Section 3.16 introduced the reference type as an alias for another object (Figure 3.6). Reference formal arguments of a function are aliased with the actual argument permitting the function body to modify the actual argument. Consider a function `main` wishing to convert a time measured in hours, minutes and seconds to a total number of seconds. The function `main` will employ a subsidiary function `hms_time` to perform this processing. The function has four arguments: the final three represent the original time, whilst the first argument is the converted seconds computed by the function. The first argument needs to be a reference so that function `hms_time` can place the computed value at that location. The function `main` might then appear:

```
int main()
{
  int  hours, minutes, seconds;
  long time;
  void hms_time(long&, int, int, int);   // note reference argument

  cin >> hours >> minutes >> seconds;
  hms_time(time, hours, minutes, seconds);
  cout << "Converted time is " << time << "\n";
  return (0);
}
```

In the definition for the function `hms_time` we must indicate that the first formal argument is the alias for a long integer supplied in the call to the function. In the function body we need also to assign a value to the integer referenced by the argument. The coding is:

```
void hms_time(long& t, int h, int m, int s)
{
```

```
t = (60L * h + m ) * 60L + s;
}
```

The formal argument `t` is a reference to a long integer. This is shown by:

```
long& t, ....
```

The integer to which `t` refers is assigned a value by:

```
t = ..... ;
```

As a complete example, a program is required to input a time measured as a number of seconds and to convert that value to its equivalent form expressed in hours, minutes and seconds. The program is organized so that function `main` performs all the input and output, and the subordinate function `time_hms` performs the necessary conversions.

PROGRAM 5.11

```
//
//  The program inputs a time measured in seconds
//      and converts it to its equivalent in hours,
//      minutes and seconds.
//

#include <iostream.h>

int main ()
{
  long time;                                // original data value
  int  hours, minutes, seconds;                    // computed values
  void time_hms(long, int&, int&, int&);    // prototype

  cout << "Enter the time in seconds: ";
  cin >> time;
  time_hms(time, hours, minutes, seconds);
  cout << "The time " << time << " seconds\n";
  cout << "converts to " << hours << " hours, "
       << minutes << " minutes and " << seconds << " seconds\n";
  return (0);
}

void time_hms(long t, int& h, int& m, int& s)
{
  const int temp = t / 60;                  // total minutes
  s    = t % 60;                            // number of seconds
  m    = temp % 60;                                // number of minutes
  h    = temp / 60;                                // number of hours
}
```

Figure 5.5 gives the semantics of the call to the subordinate function `time_hms` from function `main`. In particular, the handling of the second actual argument is shown. Observe how, as described above, the variable `hours` local to function `main` is made available to the subordinate function by aliasing it with the formal argument `h`. This function may then place a computed value at that reference, effectively implementing a change in the actual argument. The reference argument `int& h`, for example, is initialized by the corresponding actual argument. The above call results in the initialization:

```
int& h = hours
```

and hence modifications to the argument `h` made in the subordinate function changes the actual argument and not a local copy.

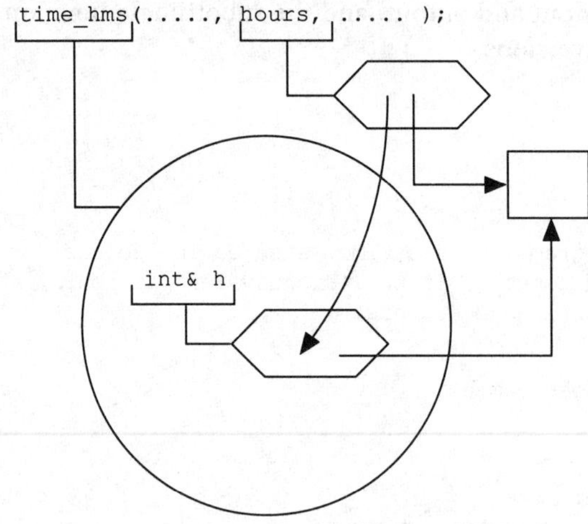

Figure 5.5

Program 5.12 illustrates function `main` controlling the services of subordinate functions. This is typical of how a large program is formed from independent functions with values passed to and from the control function (here, `main`) to the subordinates. The program is a repeat of Program 5.11, and is structured into three subordinate functions: one to read the data, one to process it and one to display the results. The `main` function co-ordinates each, passing and receiving the necessary values.

PROGRAM 5.12

```
//
// Input a time expressed in seconds and convert to
//     the equivalent time in hours, minutes and seconds.
//
```

```
#include <iostream.h>

int main()
{
  long time;                          // original data
  int  hours, minutes, seconds;       // computed results

  void readInput(long&);              // prototype declarations
  void process(long, int&, int&, int&);
  void writeOutput(long, int, int, int);

  readInput(time);
  process(time, hours, minutes, seconds);
  writeOutput(time, hours, minutes, seconds);
  return (0);
}

void readInput(long& t)
{
  cout << "Enter the time in seconds: ";
  cin >> t;
}

void process(long t, int& h, int& m, int& s)
{
  const int mins = t / 60;

  s   = t % 60;
  m   = mins % 60;
  h   = mins / 60;
}

void writeOutput(long t, int h, int m, int s)
{
  cout << "The time " << t << " seconds\n";
  cout << "converts to " << h << " hours, "
       << m << " minutes and " << s << " seconds\n";
}
```

Decomposing the program in this manner allocates separate tasks to separate functions. The generalization of the functions permit their possible use in other programs. Further, the tasks are localized so that changes are readily implemented. If, for example, a new layout of the results is required, only function `writeOutput` need be modified, and this can be done without consideration of the other program elements. This is a consequence of the completeness of the function. The function is independent of its environment, and is described completely in terms of its arguments and its local variables.

This type of function exhibits *functional abstraction*. During program decomposition, we are concerned with what the function does, not *how* it does it. Abstractly we are only interested in the *what*. Pictorially, a function at this level of refinement is a black box. For example, function `process` might be shown as in Figure 5.6, receiving a time in seconds as input and delivering the equivalent time expressed in hours, minutes and seconds. Later during development, the *how* is established by further refinement.

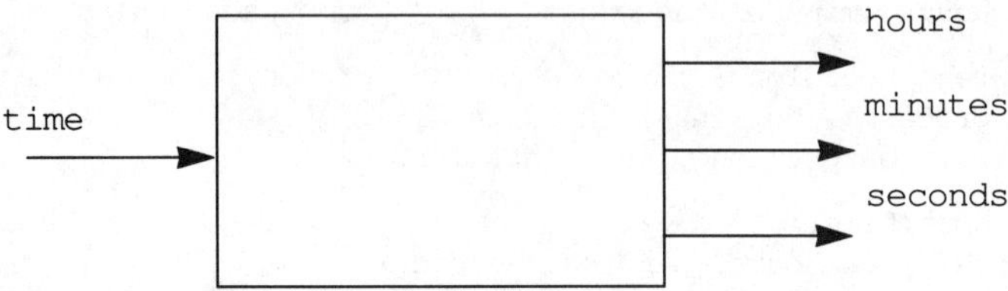

Figure 5.6

Reference arguments can, of course, be used to transmit values into a function and operates as a replacement for pass by value. Consider function `time_hms` from Program 5.11 recast to use pass by reference for the first argument:

```
void time_hms(long& t, int& h, int& m, int& s)
{
  const int temp = t / 60;              // total minutes

  s   = t % 60;                         // number of seconds
  m   = temp % 60;                      // number of minutes
  h   = temp / 60;                      // number of hours
}
```

The danger with this approach is that we may inadvertently include code in `time_hms` which modifies the value for `t` which means the corresponding actual argument is also changed.

From Chapter 3 we know that the adjective `const` can be applied to a declaration to yield a type that is the same as the original except that the value of the object cannot be changed. Applying the qualifier `const` to the formal argument `t` ensures we cannot then write modifying code.

```
void time_hms(const long& t, int& h, int& m, int& s) { /* ..... */ }
```

Call by reference is particularly appropriate when using user defined class objects (see Chapter 9). Under pass by value, large class objects would incur a time penalty where the object is copied with each function call. Qualifying the reference argument as `const` ensures we also avoid any inadvertent attempt to modify the actual argument.

The illustrations have shown the effect when the initializer to a reference variable is some object of the same type. However, the initializer need not be of the same type or another variable. When the initializer is not an object but a constant, as in:

```
const int& b = 5;
```

the compiler generates an anonymous object (whose value is the literal), for which the reference becomes an alias:

```
int anon = 5;
const int& b = anon;
```

Equally, if the initializing value is not of the required type, then a temporary is generated:

```
double pi = 3.1415926;
const int& b = pi;
```

becomes:

```
double pi = 3.1415926;
int anon = int(pi);            // anon has value 3
const int& b = anon;
```

The language permits this kind of initialization only when the reference is a `const` as shown.

Functions may also return references. Anticipating the `if` statement in the next chapter, here is a function which finds the maximum of its two integer arguments:

```
int max(int a, int b)
{
  if(a > b)
    return a;
  else
    return b;
}
```

The function receives the values of its two actual arguments, determines which is the larger, and returns that value. One call to compute the larger of `x` and `y` is:

```
z = max(x, y);
```

The function may also be programmed using references. Superficially, the outcome appears the same. We do, in fact, achieve greater functionality but at the expense of having to be more careful of our understanding of the processes involved. Here is the function written in terms of references:

```
int& max(int& a, int& b)
{
  if(a > b)
    return a;
  else
    return b;
}
```

and two legitimate uses:

```
int main()
{
  int p, q = 10, r = 20;

  p = max(q, r);            // p receives 20
```

```
    // .....
    max(q, r) = 30;            // r set to 30
    return (0);
  }
```

The effect of the first call is as before. The function's return value is a reference to the variable `r` whose value is assigned to `p`. The second use is highly unusual. Here we have an assignment without, apparently, a variable on the left side. Once again, the function's return value is a reference to the variable `r`. This object is assigned the value `30`.

We must be careful with functions returning references. Recalling that local function variables are transient objects, disappearing when the function terminates, means we must be careful not to return a reference to a local. The problem here is that the reference will be to a non-existent object when we return from the function:

```
int& max(void)
{
  int a = 10, b = 20;
  if(a > b)
    return a;
  else
    return b;
}
```

Fortunately, most compilers report this situation as an error.

5.8 Pointers and function arguments

For completeness we introduce the pass by pointer parameter mechanism. Principally, this method is a throwback to C++'s heritage, namely, its development from the C programming language. Pass by pointer is used when processing arrays (see Chapter 8) and functions (see Chapter 14) and would be used, for example, if we wish to exploit some C library function which uses this argument passing mechanism.

To allow a called function access to the value of a variable in the calling function, the latter may supply the *address* of one of its automatic (local) variables. If the called function then has the address of a variable in the calling function, it can arrange to assign a new value at that address.

Consider a function `main` wishing to convert a time measured in hours, minutes and seconds to a total number of seconds. The function `main` will employ a subsidiary function `hms_time` to perform this processing. The function has four arguments: the final three represent the original time, whilst the first argument is the converted seconds computed by the function. The first argument needs to be an address (or pointer) so that function `hms_time` can place the computed value at that location. The function `main` might then appear:

```
int main()
{
  int  hours, minutes, seconds;
  long time;
  void hms_time(long*, int, int, int);

  cin >> hours >> minutes >> seconds;
  hms_time(&time, hours, minutes, seconds);
  cout << "Converted time is " << time << "\n";
  return (0);
}
```

Note how the address of the local variable `time` is given as the actual argument to function `hms_time`.

In the definition for the function `hms_time` we must indicate that the first formal argument is the address of a long integer. In the function body we need also to assign a value to the integer pointed to by the argument. The coding is:

```
void hms_time(long* t, int h, int m, int s)
{
  *t = (60L * h + m ) * 60L + s;
}
```

The formal argument `t` is a pointer to a long integer. This is shown by:

```
long* t, .....
```

The integer to which `t` refers is assigned a value by:

```
*t = ..... ;
```

As a complete example, let us revisit Program 5.11, this time expressed in terms of pointer arguments.

PROGRAM 5.13

```
//
//  The program inputs a time measured in seconds
//      and converts it to its equivalent in hours,
//      minutes and seconds.
//

#include <iostream.h>

int main ()
{
  long time;                                    // original data value
  int  hours, minutes, seconds;                      // computed values

  void time_hms(long, int*, int*, int*);  // prototype

  cout << "Enter the time in seconds: ";
  cin >> time;
  time_hms(time, &hours, &minutes, &seconds);
```

```
  cout << "The time " << time << " seconds\n";
  cout << "converts to " << hours << " hours, "
       << minutes << " minutes and " << seconds << " seconds\n";
  return (0);
}

void time_hms(long t, int* h, int* m, int* s)
{
  const int temp = t / 60;// total minutes

  *s   = t % 60;                    // number of seconds
  *m   = temp % 60;                 // number of minutes
  *h   = temp / 60;                 // number of hours
}
```

Figure 5.7 gives the semantics of the call to the subordinate function `time_hms` from function `main`. In particular, the handling of the second actual argument is shown. Observe how, as described above, the address (internal name) of the variable hours local to function `main` is made available to the subordinate function. This function may then place a computed value at that address, effectively implementing a change in the actual argument.

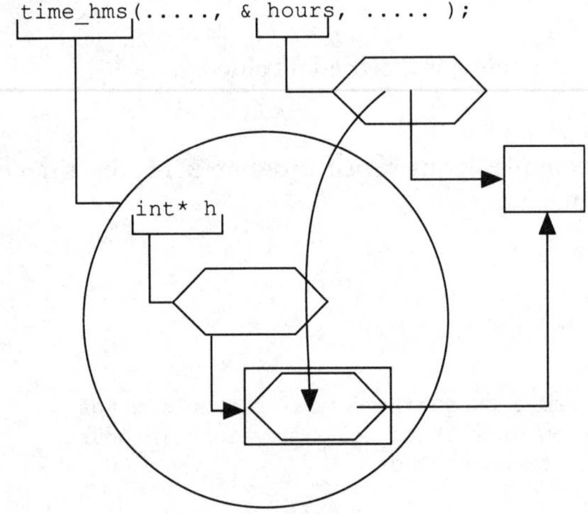

Figure 5.7

To protect against inadvertent modifications we can specify in the function `time_hms` of Program 5.13 that the pointer arguments are not to be modified. This would protect us from code such as `h++` which increments the value of the pointer so that it no longer addresses the required variable. Again we use the qualifier `const`:

```
void time_hms(long t, int* const h, int* const m, int* const s)
{
  const int temp = t / 60;// total minutes
   *s   = t % 60;                // number of seconds
   *m   = temp % 60;             // number of minutes
   *h   = temp / 60;             // number of hours
}
```

5.9 Default arguments

We sometimes meet situations where a function, to be fully general, needs more arguments than is required in the more common examples of its usage. For example, the function `hms_time`, defined as:

```
long hms_time(int h, int m, int s)
{
  return ((h * 60L + m) * 60L + s);
}
```

may be used with the third argument, often the value zero:

```
time = hms_time(hours, minutes, 0);
```

We can, in the function signature, record the default values to be associated with the actual argument using the initializing signature:

```
long hms_time(int h, int m, int s = 0);
```

A function providing default argument initializers can be called with or without the corresponding actual argument. If one is provided, then that actual argument overrides the default. If absent, then the default is employed.

```
time = hms_time(hours, minutes, 35);     //ok, s is 35
time = hms_time(hours, minutes, 0);      // ok, s is 0
time = hms_time(hours, minutes);         //ok, s is implicitly 0
```

A function may specify default initializers for some or all of its arguments. Initialization is given right-to-left amongst the arguments. This means that we cannot provide an initializer for one argument unless all the succeeding arguments also have initializers. Hence:

```
long hms_time(int h, int m = 0, int s = 0);  // ok
long hms_time(int h, int m = 0, int s);      // error
```

This restriction is due to the function call arguments being resolved positionally. If we were to permit the second example above, then in the call:

```
time = hms_time(hours, 35);
```

we cannot resolve whether the `35` is the overriding value for `m` or is the actual value for `s`. Another implication follows from the legal first example. That is, it is impossible to supply an actual overriding value for `s` without also overriding `m`:

```
time = hms_time(hours, 35);          // ok, m = 35, s = 0
time = hms_time(hours, 0, 35);       // ok, m = 0, s = 35
```

A default argument initializer may only be specified once. The prototype declaration:

```
long hms_time(int h, int m, int s = 0);        // prototype
```

establishes the default initializer for the third argument. It is then an error to repeat this information in the definition:

```
long hms_time(int h, int m, int s = 0)           // definition (error)
{
  // ..... others
}
```

It is also permissible to specify additional defaults having first established certain defaults. Given the prototype declaration:

```
long hms_time(int h, int m, int s = 0);
```

we can redeclare `hms_time` in the same scope to provide `m` with a default initializer:

```
long hms_time(int h, int m = 0, int s);
```

Following the first declaration, function `hms_time` can be called with either two or three arguments. The second declaration then overrides the first, allowing `hms_time` to be called with one, two or three arguments. Observe how in the second declaration we appear to be initializing `m` and not `s`. In fact, the initializer for `s` is carried forward. We do not express this as:

```
long hms_time(int h, int m = 0, int s = 0);
```

because this is a respecification of the default for argument `s`.

5.10 Inline functions

Consider the function `sum` that forms the addition of its two integer arguments:

```
inline int sum(int a, int b)
{
  return (a + b);
}
```

The usual benefits accrue from defining such a function and include reuse of the function in one or more applications; full generality through parameterization; localizing the behaviour of the code, and so on. However, every call to this function introduces an overhead at run time. Every (out of line) function call requires saving machine registers, allocating storage space for local function variables, copying the arguments, branching to the out of line code, then undoing all these effects upon return.

```
int total = sum(x, y * z);
```

The expanded code has none of these overheads and is much faster. The run time overhead of making sum a function can be removed with the function specifier `inline`. The keyword `inline` informs the compiler that the function call should be expanded 'inline'. The example above would be expanded during compilation to look like the example:

```
int total = x + y * z;          // expanded code
```

The process of text insertion is conducted with normal type checking.

Strictly, the keyword `inline` informs the compiler that, where possible, the function should be expanded inline. It operates therefore as a recommendation from the programmer of where to optimize the run time code. Inline calls, however, are not generated in all circumstances and can result in out of line function call usage.

Any function may be declared inline, but the optimization of the function call may not always be performed, depending upon how the call is made and the compiler's capabilities. A compiler may, for example, choose not to implement the function inline because the function is too large. The definition of an inline function must precede all uses of the function or the compiler will not inline expand it. For example, if function `sum` appears in the program fragment:

```
int main()
{
  int sum(int, int);
  // .....
  int total = sum(x, y * z);        // no expansion
  // .....
}

inline int sum(int a, int b)
{
  return (a + b);
}
```

an out of line call will be made to initialize `total` since the compiler discovers that the function was to be used inline after the call has been processed.

5.11 Overloaded function names

In a strongly typed language it is possible to support function name overloading. A name is said to be *overloaded* if it has different meaning when used with objects of different type. The arithmetic operators in C++ are overloaded for simple types. The meaning of the expression `a + b` depends on the types of `a` and `b`. The operator `+` means *integer addition* when used with two integer operands, and *floating point addition* when applied to two floating point operands.

In C++, two or more functions may be given the same name providing the *signatures* are distinct, either in the number or the types of its arguments. The signature refers to the types of the function's arguments. For example, given the declarations:

```
void print(int);
void print(double);
```

then the following two calls are resolved as shown:

```
print(12);          // ok, resolves to print(int)
print(3.14159);     // ok, resolves to print(double)
```

There are two aspects to overloaded functions that must be considered. First, we must show how an overloaded function is introduced. Second, we must consider how an overloaded function call is resolved so that the correct function is invoked.

A function name declared more than once in a program may be interpreted as function overloading. However, there are two other possible interpretations. First, if both the return type and function signatures are the same, all but the first are considered as redeclarations. The argument list is referred to as the signature of a function since it is used to distinguish one instance of a function from another. For example:

```
void print(int a, int b);          // first declaration
void print(int p, int q);          // redeclaration!
void print(int, int);              // redeclaration again!
```

Observe how the function argument names are not considered part of the signature. The first two declarations are effectively interpreted by the compiler as the third example.

The return type of a function is not considered when determining whether overloading is used. For example, a second or subsequent declaration of a function is interpreted by the compiler as an erroneous redeclaration of the first when the signatures are identical but the return types differ. Hence, the following will produce a compiler error to this effect:

```
void print(int, int);
int  print(int, int);    // error: erroneous redeclaration!
```

In all other cases, the functions are deemed to be overloaded.

The second issue concerning the use of overloaded functions is how a call to a function is resolved to a particular instance of the set of functions overloaded with the same name. The resolution process is known as *argument matching*, and involves comparing the types of the actual arguments against the types of the formal arguments. This is the reason that all functions must be prototyped before they are used.

The compiler determines the functions whose formal arguments best match the types of the actual arguments. This may, of course, give rise to a set of possible functions. For example, consider the overloaded function f:

```
int  f(int, double);
```

```
int  f(double, int);
int  f(int, int);
```

and the call:

```
i = f(j, k);
```

for some integer objects `i`, `j` and `k`. The first actual argument is of type `int` and the set of possible functions is:

`f(int, double)` **and** `f(int, int)`

For the second actual argument of type `int` the possible functions are:

`f(double, int)` **and** `f(int, int)`

To resolve the overloaded function call the intersection of these sets should result in a single function signature. If the set is empty there is no such function. If the set has two or more members then the call is ambiguous. In both cases the compiler will issue an error message. The intersection of the two sets is:

```
int  f(int, int)
```

to which the call is resolved.

5.12 Template functions

The *template mechanism* of C++ allows the programmer to define a function once which effectively defines a family of functions instantiated from the function template. Consider function `sum` introduced in Section 5.5. The code to sum a pair of `floats` or a pair of `ints` would be identical except for the types. If `TYPE` represents any arbitrary type, then the template version for this function is:

```
template <class TYPE>
TYPE sum(TYPE first, TYPE second)
{
  TYPE total = first + second;
  return total;
}
```

The prefix `template <class TYPE>` indicates that a function template is being introduced and that `TYPE` represents some arbitrary type name. This type name has the function definition which it prefixes as its scope. The following function call of `sum`:

```
int answer = sum(10, 20);
```

determines that the required function has prototype:

```
int sum(int, int);
```

The language implementation is responsible for creating the proper version from the template. Equally, the call:

```
double pi = 3.1415926;
double result = sum(2.71828, pi);
```

should establish a version of the sum function with signature:

```
double sum(double, double);
```

Note that the template for the function must be accessible to the compiler to permit creation of the necessary version. Hence in the programs of this chapter the template function must precede its use.

5.13 Mathematical functions

There are no *mathematical functions* as part of the C++ language. Functions such as:

```
sqrt()        square root
exp()         exponential
sin()         trigonometric
```

occur in the standard C library. Many of these functions take an argument of type `double` and return a value of type `double`. Any program including any of these functions must, therefore, include appropriate prototype declarations, for example:

```
double exp(double);
```

The library header file `<math.h>` is provided and contains all the necessary declarations. They may be incorporated into a program with the statement:

```
#include <math.h>
```

Program 5.14 computes the area of a triangle given by the formula:

```
sqrt(s(s-x)(s-y)(s-z))
```

where:

```
s = (x + y + z)/2
```

and `x`, `y`, `z` are the lengths of the sides of the triangle.

PROGRAM 5.14

```
//
// Determine the area of a triangle given
//     the lengths of its sides.
//

#include <iostream.h>
#include <math.h>

int main()
```

```
{
  float a, b, c;
  float triangle(float, float, float);

  cout << "Enter lengths of sides: ";
  cin >> a >> b >> c;
  cout << "Area of triangle is " << triangle(a, b, c) << "\n";
  return (0);
}

float triangle(float x, float y, float z)
{
  const float s = (x + y + z)/2.0;      // semi-perimeter

  return (sqrt(s * (s-x) * (s-y) * (s-z)));
}
```

5.14 Summary

1. A C++ program consists of one or more *functions*. A complete C++ program has one function called `main`, and processing commences with the first statement in `main`. A function is a named *compound statement* or *block*.

2. A function block may include the definitions for *local* or *automatic* variables. Automatic variables are private to a function and only exist when the function is called, and are deallocated when the function terminates.

3. When a function is called in a *function statement*, program control is passed to the called function. When a return statement is executed explicitly, or implicitly at the function end, control is passed back to the calling function. If the return statement contains an expression, the value of the expression is made available to the calling function.

4. A *function prototype* declaration is required where one function calls another. A function prototype specifies the type of the arguments and return value. A function with no associated value is of type `void`. A function with no arguments has a void formal argument list.

5. *Arguments* are used to communicate data between the calling and the called functions. When a function is called, the *actual arguments* listed replace the *formal arguments*. Argument passing in C++ is implemented as *pass by value*, *pass by reference* or *pass by pointer*. The former two are the principal parameter passing methods used in C++. Pass by pointer is inherited from C.

6. When arguments are passed by value, a copy of the actual argument is used to initialize the formal argument. Thereafter, the formal argument operates

as an initialized local variable to the function, with any changes made to it not affecting the actual argument.

7. In pass by reference the formal argument is an alias for the actual argument. Any changes made to the formal argument in the function body is also a change to the actual argument since they both refer to the same data value.

8. Pass by pointer is the argument passing mechanism inherited from C. Since it is both difficult to apply and dangerous to use then only when it is absolutely necessary (such as referring to a C library function) do we use it.

9. C++ also supports *default argument* passing. The arguments of the function prototype may be specified with a default value, so that when the function is called that particular argument may be omitted. In that case the compiler automatically inserts the default. Strictly, default argument passing is *positional* and operates on a right to left ordering.

10. *Inline functions, overloaded functions and template functions* also feature in C++. The first are particularly useful for small, simple functions since the compiler effectively replaces the function call statement with the function body, saving the run time cost of an out of line function call. The second permits two or more functions to share the same name. This is appropriate when the meaning of the function depends on the type of values being processed. The template function permits one function to be defined over various argument types.

11. *Stepwise refinement* consists of repeatedly decomposing a problem into smaller sub problems. A large program should be written as a collection of functions, each responsible for some identifiable task from the overall problem.

5.15 Exercises

1. Write a program that will convert a length measured in centimetres to its equivalent number of inches. Modify the program to process five data sets.

2. Write a program that reads a data set containing an invoice number, quantity of an item ordered and the unit price of the item. The total price should then be calculated, and the output should appear as follows:

```
INVOICE      QUANTITY     UNIT PRICE     TOTAL
xxx          xxxx         xxxx.xx        xxxxx.xx
```

3. Write a program to determine the number of gallons of paint required to paint a rectangular room. The windows and doors are to be ignored in the

calculation. The width and length of the room and the height of the walls will be entered in feet. A gallon of paint is assumed to cover about 250 square feet.

4. Write a program that will convert a given number of minutes and seconds to the correct fraction of an hour. For example, 37 minutes and 30 seconds is 0.625 of an hour.

5. Assuming that the population of a city is 650,000 and that its rate of growth is 4.5% a year, write a program to calculate the population each year over the next five years.

6. Write a program consisting of the single function `main` which reads two integer values representing the length and breadth of a rectangular figure, and which computes and prints the perimeter length.

   Repeat the same problem, but this time employ a second function called `perimeter` which performs the necessary calculation, given, as arguments, the dimensions of the rectangle. The function header is:

   ```
   int perimeter(int length, int breadth)
   ```

7. Prepare a function called `denominations` which, when supplied with a positive integer argument representing a sum of money expressed in pence less than one pound in value, will print a list of each coin and the quantity required. The function header is to be:

   ```
   void denominations(int money)
   ```

   The sample call:

   ```
   denominations(34);
   ```

   would produce the output:

   ```
   34 pence is:        0 fifty pence
                       3 ten pence
                       0 five pence
                       2 two pence
                       0 one pence
   ```

   Test this function in a program.

8. Predict the output from the following five programs and explain your reasoning.

   (a)
   ```
   #include <iostream.h>
   int main()
   {
     int x;
     void change(void);
     x = 0;
   ```

   (b)
   ```
   #include <iostream.h>
   int main()
   {
     int x;
     void change(int&);
     x = 0;
   ```

```
 change();                        change(x);
 cout << x << "\n";               cout << x << "\n";
 return (0);                      return (0);
}                                }
void change(void)                void change(int& y)
{                                {
 int x;                           y = 1;
 x = 1;                          }
}
```

(c)
```
#include <iostream.h>
int main()
{
 int x;
 void change(int*);
 x = 0;
 change(&x);
 cout << x << "\n";
}
void change(int* y)
{
 *y = 1;
}
```

(d)
```
'#include <iostream.h>
int main()
{
 int thing;
 void cheat(int*, int*)
 thing = 1;
 cheat(&thing, &thing);
 cout << thing << "\n";
 return (0);
}
void cheat(int* hee, int* haw)
{
 *hee = -1;
 *haw = -(*hee);
}
```

(e)
```
#include <iostream.h>
int main()
{
 int thing;
 void untrue(int*, int*);
 thing = 10;
 untrue(&thing, &thing);
 cout << thing << "\n";
 return (0);
}
void untrue(int* hee, int* haw)
{
 *hee = 20 + *haw;
}
```

9. Prepare a function called `swap` which interchanges the values of its two integer arguments. The function header is:

```
void swap(int& x, int& y);
```

Test this function in a program. Rewrite the function in terms of pointer arguments. Rewrite as a template function.

10. The function `min`, defined below, determines the least of its two integer arguments.

```
int min(int a, int b)
{
  return (a < b ? a : b);
}
```

Design and write the corresponding function called `max` which finds the larger of its two integer arguments. Function `max` should make a call to function `min` in determining the correct value.

Similarly, write a function called `min3` which returns the least of its three integer arguments. Use function `min` to determine the result.

11. A time, expressed in terms of the twenty-four hour clock, is provided by three integer values: `hours (0 <= hours <= 23)`, `minutes` and `seconds (0 <= minutes, seconds <= 59)`. Write a function called `hms_time` which converts such a time to a total number of seconds. The function header is:

```
long int hms_time(int hours, int minutes, int seconds);
```

Why is it reasonable to declare the function returning a `long int` rather than an `int`?

Write also the converse function `time_hms` which converts a time in seconds back into its equivalent twenty-four hour clock value. The function header is:

```
void time_hms(long int time, int& hours, int& minutes, int&
seconds);
```

in which the `long int` argument time represents the number of seconds, and the three pointer arguments are the recipient addresses of the converted value.

Prepare a program that checks the execution of both these functions.

Write a function called `add_time_hms` which adds a time in seconds on to a twenty-four hour clock time. The final answer is also expressed as a twenty-four hour clock time, updates the original input values, and ignores any advance of one or more days. This function should be written in terms of the previous two functions. The function header is:

```
void add_time_hms(long int time, int& hours, int& minutes, int&
seconds)
```

Prepare a program to show that:

```
add_time_hms(0L, .....)
```

produces no change of values.

Write a further function called `difference` which finds the number of seconds between two twenty-four hour clock times. It can be assumed that the first time `(hr1, min1, sec1)` is later in the day than the second time `(hr2, min2, sec2)`. The function header is:

```
long int difference(int hr1, int min1, int sec1, int hr2, int
min2, int sec2)
```

Prepare a program to show that:

(a) `difference(hr, min, sec, hr, min, sec)`

is `0L` for some twenty-four hour clock time `(hr, min, sec)`.

(b) `add_time_hms(difference(h1,m1,s1,h2,m2,s2), h2, m2, s2)`

sets the twenty-four hour clock time `(h2, m2, s2)` to the value of `(h1, m1, s1)`.

12. Repeat the last exercise this time using pass by pointer in place of pass by reference. The function signatures are:

```
long int hms_time(int, int, int);
void     time_hms(long int, int*, int*, int*);
void     add_time_hms(long int, int*, int*, int*);
long int difference(int, int, int, int, int, int);
```

13. Write a program to read four decimal values representing the co-ordinates of two points on a plane. Calculate the distance between the points and output the result. Use the formula:

$$distance = sqrt((x2 - x1)^2 + (y2 - y1)^2)$$

14. Determine whether the call:

```
f(1.23, 4.56);
```

is ambiguous in the context of the prototype declarations:

```
void f(int, double);
void f(double, int);
```

15. How would the compiler resolve the call:

```
g(1.23);
```

given the prototype declarations:

```
void g(int&);
void g(const int&);
```

6

Flow of Control

The execution of C++ programming statements causes actions to be performed. The programs that we have developed execute one statement after another in a linear fashion. We can create abstract actions with function definitions and then treat function calls as if they likewise were primitive statements of the language. The simple statements which we have explored can be classified *sequential*, and include the assignment and the function call.

In addition, statements are available to alter the flow of control in a program. The full repertoire of C++ language statements are then classified into one of three control structures:

1. Sequence.
2. Selection.
3. Iteration.

The new program control structures of *selection* and *iteration* permit us to process data with structures other than sequential. Repetitive data items are processed by iteration statements. Alternative data items are processed by selection statements. Through these statements we retain the correspondence between the structure of the problem's data and the program structure.

We shall now examine further C++ statements as instances of the two control structures iteration and selection. A feature of these new statements is the *condition*. A condition determines the *truth* or *falsity* of some expression. We commence this chapter by considering expressions yielding values which are either true or false.

6.1 Relational operators and expressions

The *relational operators* are:

less than :	<
greater than :	>
less than or equal :	<=
greater than or equal :	>=

All four operators are binary. They each take two expressions as operands and yield one of two possible values. Just as with arithmetic operators, the relational operators have rules of precedence and associativity that determine how expressions involving these operators are evaluated. All four operators have the same precedence levels and associate left to right. Their relationship with the other operators is shown in Appendix E.

Some examples of relational expressions include:

```
x < 0.0
ch2 >= 'A'
y * y <= 2 * y + 1
pointer > end_of_list
```

From Appendix E we observe that the relational operators have lower precedence than the arithmetic operators. Expressions like:

```
index <= limit - 1
```

are, therefore, interpreted as:

```
index <= (limit - 1)
```

The greater than or equal and less than or equal operators are described with two symbols. No embedded spaces are allowed, nor can the operators be expressed as equal or greater than or equal or less than. The following are illegal expressions:

```
p <  = q              // imbedded space disallowed
r=> s                 // no such operator
```

Consider the relational expression `a < b`. Intuitively, if the value of `a` is less than the value of `b`, then the expression is true. If the value of `a` is not less than the value of `b`, then the expression is false. In C++, the logical value false is represented by the integer value zero and the logical value true by any non-zero integer value. In particular, the relational operators return either the integer value `0` (for false) or the integer value `1` (for true).

In the context of the following declarations:

```
char c = 'x';
int  i = 1, j = 3, k = -4;
```

Table 6.1 gives a number of expressions involving the relational operators, together with the derived value. For each expression, the parenthesized equivalent is also shown. The logical value upon evaluation of the expression is indicated.

Table 6.1

Expression	*Equivalent expression*	*Logical value*	*Derived value*
`'b' + 1 < c`	`('b' + 1) < c`	true	1
`5 * j >= 12 - k`	`(5 * j ) >= (12 - k)`	false	0
`i + j <= -k`	`(i + j) <= (-k)`	true	1

6.2 Equality operators and expressions

The *equality operators* are:

equal : ==
not equal : !=

These binary operators act on two expressions and yield either of the two logical values true or false. Appendix E shows these two new operators alongside the other operators.

Some valid examples of expressions using these operators include:

```
ch == LTRZ
j + k != t
```

The equality operator works perfectly correctly with integer operands. When used with operands of type floating point (`float` or `double`), some surprising results can arise. This is entirely attributable to the limited precision of the floating point representation. If we were to divide `1.0` by `3.0` and then multiply the result by `3.0`, we might reasonably expect the answer to be `1.0`. If the variable `x` is defined as:

```
float x = 1.0F;
```

then we might assume the expression:

```
x == x / 3.0 * 3.0
```

to evaluate to the logical value true. The mathematical result of the division is `0.33333333 .....` If on some hypothetical computer, floating point values were held with 6 decimal digits of accuracy, then the result is `0.333333`. When we multiply by `3.0` the result is `0.999999`. The expression now reduces to:

```
1.0 == 0.999999
```

which is clearly false.

The equality operator should be avoided when comparing two floating point expressions. The solution is normally not to ask if the two expressions are equal, but if the two expressions are approximately equal. This is expressed by asking if the difference between each expression is small enough to be considered negligible. We will show in a later section how to formulate this.

Care is required not to confuse the equality operator (==) and the assignment operator (=). This is a common programming mistake which can lead to unexpected results. For example, if we wish to determine if the integer variable `a` is equal to `2`, the expression is:

```
a == 2
```

and yields either true or false according to the value of `a`. However, if the expression is mistakenly written as:

```
a = 2
```

then the expression is valid, has the effect of assigning the value 2 to the variable a, and delivers the value 2 interpreted as logical true. The expression is always true, irrespective of the original value of a. Thankfully most compilers warn about assignments used in control flow expressions.

6.3 Logical operators and expressions

The *logical operators* are:

logical and : &&
logical or : ||
(unary) negation : !

The *logical and* and *logical or* operators are binary, both acting on two expressions and yielding either the logical value true or logical value false. Both operators treat their operands as logical values. The *logical negation* operator is a unary operator. The single operand is taken to represent either logical true or logical false. The effect of applying these operators is shown in Table 6.2. The precedence and associativity of these logical operators is given in Appendix E.

Table 6.2

P	*Q*	*P* && *Q*	*P* || *Q*	*P*	! *P*
false	false	false	false	false	true
false	true	false	true	true	false
true	false	false	true		
true	true	true	true		

Some expressions involving the negation operator are:

```
! 5        evaluates to 0
! 0        evaluates to 1
! 't'      evaluates to 0
3 + ! x    evaluates to 3 if x is non-zero, and to 4 if x is zero
! ! 5      evaluates to 1
! ! 0      evaluates to 0
```

The expression !5 evaluates to false since 5 is interpreted by the unary negation operator as the representation for true. The expression !'t' is somewhat unusual but also yields false since the ASCII encoding for character 't' is decimal 116, namely true. The expression !!5 has the equivalent form !(!5). With the integer value 5 interpreted as true, then, as above, !5 is false. Negating this value again delivers true.

In the context of the following definitions:

```
char c = 'x'
int  i = 1, j = 3, k = 4;
```

Table 6.3 shows some example expressions involving the logical operators.

Table 6.3

Expression	*Equivalent expression*	*Logical value*	*Derived value*
`i && j && k`	`(i && j) && k`	true	1
`i && j || !c`	`(i && j) || (!c)`	true	1
`k < i && i < j`	`(k < i) && (i < j)`	false	0
`i == 2 || j == 1`	`(i == 2) || (j == 1)`	false	0
`i > 2 && !j`	`(i > 2) && (!j)`	false	0

There is one subtlety about the *logical and* and the *logical or* operators. In the evaluation of sub expressions that are the operands of the operators `&&` and `||`, the evaluation process stops as soon as the outcome is determinable. Suppose that `expression1` and `expression2` are the expression operands. If `expression1` has value zero (false), then in:

```
expression1 && expression2
```

`expression2` will not be evaluated because the value of the logical expression is already determined to be false. Similarly, if `expression1` has a non-zero value (true), then in:

```
expression1 || expression2
```

`expression2` will not be evaluated since the value of the expression is already determined to be true.

In both instances the second expression may never be evaluated. If the second expression includes a side effect of its evaluation, then this will not be obtained if the expression is not evaluated. For example, using the above declarations, the expression:

```
j < i && k += 2
```

is interpreted as:

```
(j < i) && (k += 2)
```

and since the sub expression `(j < i)` is false, then variable `k` is not incremented. Statements or expressions that employ this kind of side effect can make programs very difficult to correct or to maintain and are actively discouraged.

A useful consequence of enumeration constants (see Section 3.18) having default values `0`, `1`, `2`, ... and implicitly converting to type `int` when required is that we can introduce what is in essence the boolean type:

```
enum Bool { FALSE, TRUE };
```

with `FALSE` having the value `0` and `TRUE` the value `1` as we require. We can then write:

```
Bool       isempty = TRUE;
isempty = FALSE;
// .....
if(isempty) { ..... }      // see later
```

6.4 The conditional operator

For completeness we discuss here the *conditional operator*. Strictly, this is not an operator that delivers a logical value. It does, however, include a logical expression and so we consider it here. The conditional operator consists of three expressions, with the first and second expressions separated by the query symbol (?) and the second and third expressions separated by the colon symbol (:). The form is:

```
expression1 ? expression2 : expression3
```

The first operand is used to determine which of the other two operands should be evaluated. If the first expression delivers logical true (non-zero) then the result of the expression is `expression2`; if the first expression delivers logical false (zero) then the result of the expression is `expression3`.

To determine the least of two values we might use this operator. The minimum of the two values `a` and `b` can be obtained by:

```
min = a < b ? a : b
```

Like all operators, this operator has a precedence and an associativity. This is shown in Appendix E.

In Section 6.2 we noted that equality comparisons on two floating point values is best performed by determining if the two values are approximately equal. Thus instead of testing if:

```
a == b
```

we should test if the absolute difference between `a` and `b` is negligible. Mathematically, we express this as:

```
| a - b | < epsilon
```

where, `epsilon` represents some small value and the notation `|x|` means the positive value of `x`. To achieve this, we require a function to obtain the absolute value of some quantity. This function could be written using the conditional operator:

```
double absolute(double x)
{
  return ( x < 0 ? -x : x );
}
```

With this function, the original expression may be written using:

```
const double EPSILON = 1.0E-4;

absolute(a-b) < EPSILON
```

Note that the functions `abs` and `fabs` are members of the standard C library and respectively obtain the absolute value of an integer and a floating point argument. For details, see Appendix F5.

6.5 The while statement

The fundamental means of constructing iterative clauses in C++ is the *while statement*. The syntax of the while statement is:

```
while (expression)
   statement;
```

where `while` is a reserved keyword.

The while statement is executed by first evaluating the control expression within the parentheses. If the result is non-zero, that is logical value true, then the statement is executed. The entire process is then repeated starting once again with evaluation of the expression. This looping continues until either because of the effect on the expression by execution of the statement or by a side effect of the expression itself, the expression now evaluates to zero. The value zero is the C++ representation for logical false. When the expression is zero, the loop terminates and the program continues execution with the next statement. A flow diagram for the while statement is shown in Figure 6.1.

The principal feature of the while statement is that the control expression is first tested before deciding whether or not to execute the associated statement. This means that if the expression on first evaluation produces zero (logical false) then the loop is never obeyed. Because of this, a while statement is often described as causing the statement under its control to be obeyed none or more times.

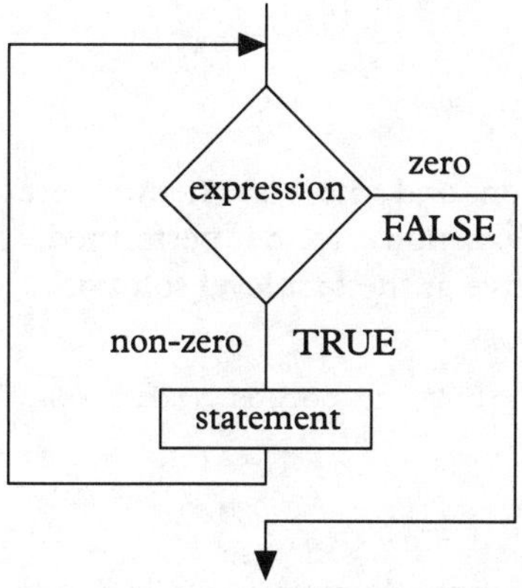

Figure 6.1

Where the logic of a problem requires more than a single statement to be executed under control of the while, a compound statement may be used:

```
while (expression){
  statement 1;
  statement 2;
  // .....
  // .....
}
```

We are now ready to explore programs containing loops. As we shall note, problems with repeating data items give rise to solutions with similar structures. By being able to recognize this, such programs are relatively straightforward to implement. We can then apply the same type of solution to most programs exhibiting this feature.

Program 6.1 reads single characters from the standard input, copying each character as it is read, to the standard output. The copying continues until the first occurrence of a period symbol (.) is encountered in the data. The period is not copied and the program terminates. The use of a distinguishing data item to mark the end of the data set is a common programming device. This *sentinel* guards the end of the data. It is often referred to as the *end of file record.*

The use of an iterative statement in the solution to this program is suggested by the form of the data. The program data is a list or series of single character data items. Where the structure of the program's data has this form, the equivalent program structure is:

```
while(more data items)
  process data item
```

To generate the program design, we first extend our PDL with an iterative clause based on the while statement. The structure is:

```
WHILE some condition DO
  some statement(s)
ENDWHILE
```

As before, both the condition and the statement(s) are expressed as concise informal descriptions of the actions to be performed. Applying this to our programming problem, we arrive at the first level solution:

```
read first character
WHILE this character is not the period symbol DO
  print this character
  read next character
ENDWHILE
```

Each action and expression is directly expressible in C++. No further analysis is therefore necessary. We can immediately encode the solution as Program 6.1.

PROGRAM 6.1

```
//
// Read a sequence of characters from the standard input
//      and echo them to the standard output. Terminate the
//      program upon the first occurrence of a period (.)
//      symbol in the data set.
//

#include <iostream.h>

int main()
{
  const char      PERIOD = '.';
  char            c;                // data item

  cin.get(c);                       // get first character
  while (c != PERIOD){              // test for end of data
    cout.put(c);                    // copy to standard output
    cin.get(c);                     // get next character
  }
  return (0);
}
```

The program operates by first reading the initial data character. The character just read is then compared in the while control expression against the period symbol. Providing it is not the period, the character is copied to the output and the next data character is read. The looping continues until the period terminator appears in the data, at which point the loop and the program terminate. Notice that if the first data character is a period, the loop is never entered. An initial period means that there are no characters to be copied, corresponding to non-execution of the while loop.

This and many other programs involving loops have the same solution pattern. First some initialization is performed before entering the loop. This includes, amongst other things, any initialization associated with the first iteration of the loop. In Program 6.1 the first character is read so that the loop condition can be evaluated. This is known as the *read ahead* mechanism. We must read the first data item otherwise we cannot determine whether or not to obey the loop for the first time. Equally, the read ahead mechanism applies to all subsequent data items.

Second, the condition controlling repetition of the loop is expressed. This determines how the loop will be terminated. In the example program the required condition is that the current character is not the period symbol.

Thirdly, some processing associated with the loop is executed. One or more statements will make up this processing logic. This often consists of processing one or more items of input data or of processing internally generated data. In the example, the processing is trivial. The data character previously read from the standard input is copied to the standard output.

Finally, the necessary actions are taken before determining whether the loop is to continue. This is the side effect which influences continuation of the loop. For our problem, the next data character is read from the input.

The shape of this solution in our PDL is:

```
initialize before entering loop
WHILE condition controlling execution of the loop DO
  processing logic
  set up for next iteration
ENDWHILE
```

We observe the same solution structure in Program 6.2. This program reads a series of positive floating point values. The data set terminates with a negative value sentinel. The program forms the sum of the positive values. The initialization consists of zeroizing the summation and reading the first data item. The condition for loop continuation is that the current data value is positive. The processing logic consists of forming a running total and setting up for another iteration by reading the next data value. Expressed in our PDL we arrive at:

```
initialize the sum to zero
read first number
WHILE this number is positive DO
  add the number to the sum
  read next number
ENDWHILE
print the sum
```

PROGRAM 6.2

```
//
//  Read a series of positive floating point numbers
//      and form their sum. The data is terminated with
//      a unique negative value.
//
#include <iostream.h>

int main()
{
  const float       ZERO = 0.0F;
  float  data,              // data value .....
                    sum = ZERO;  // ..... and running total

  cin >> data;              // get first data item
  while (data >= ZERO){          // data terminator?
    sum += data;            // form the sum
    cin >> data;            // get the next data item
  }
  cout << "The sum is " << sum << "\n";
  return (0);
}
```

This same shape is also readily recognizable in the next program. The program operates on no input data. All the data is generated by the program itself. The program computes the sum of the first twenty integers: 1 + 2 + 3 + ... + 20. Once again the program's data is an iteration of values. This time, they happen to be generated by the program and not provided as input data. The same analysis still applies – the program structure mirrors the data structure.

PROGRAM 6.3(a)

```
//
// Compute the total of the first 20 positive integers.
//     The program requires no data. All data values in the
//     program are self generated.
//
#include <iostream.h>

int main()
{
  const int      INITIAL = 1;
  const int      MAX = 20;
  const int      ZERO = 0;
  int            data, sum = ZERO;      // data and running total

  data = INITIAL;          // initial integer
  while (data <= MAX){         // terminate loop?
    sum += data;           // form running total
    data++;                    // advance to next loop value
  }

  cout << "The sum of the first 20 integers is " << sum << "\n";
  return (0);
}
```

The same result can be achieved by counting downward from 20 to 1. The major difference between the two program versions is the condition to terminate the loop.

PROGRAM 6.3(b)

```
//
// Form the sum of the first 20 positive integers.
//     Self generate the integer sequence 20, 19, ..... ,2, 1
//     and simultaneously sum.
//

#include <iostream.h>

int main()
{
  const int       MAX = 20;
  const int       ZERO = 0;
```

```
    int             data, sum = ZERO;      // data and running total

    data = MAX;                  // first integer value
    while (data > ZERO){             // loop control
      sum += data;               // form running total
      data-;                         // decrement loop control variable
    }

    cout <<"The sum of the first 20 integers is " << sum << "\n";
    return (0);
}
```

It is common practice when writing such fragments of a C++ program to incorporate all or part of the loop control into one place in the program. This unifies these related activities. The program is generally then more readable since control of the loop is no longer scattered amongst other processing statements.

Program 6.1 can be rewritten by incorporating the reading and testing of the single data character into the control expression. The solution is shown in Program 6.4.

PROGRAM 6.4

```
//
//  Copy a character sequence from the standard input
//      to the standard output. The data is terminated by
//      an end-of-file.
//

#include <iostream.h>

int main()
{
  char c;                  // data character

  while(cin.get(c))               // read and test data
    cout.put(c);
  return (0);
}
```

The loop statement:

```
while(cin.get(c)) .....
```

reads a character at a time from the standard input. When end-of-file is encountered (under Unix this is usually control-D, sometimes control-Z), the condition evaluates to false and the loop terminates.

In the program above, the strategy is to perform a combined input and conditional test in a single expression. The assignment is performed first, then the test. A similar approach can be taken when rewriting Program 6.2 as Program 6.5. The assignment is performed through a >> input statement. The condition is then tested. The sequencing of these two actions is achieved this time with the comma operator. The comma operator guarantees sequential execution of each expression. The returned value is that of the last executed expression – the required condition.

PROGRAM 6.5

```
//
//  Sum a sequence of positive floating point values.
//      The series is of indeterminate length, but is
//      terminated with a negative number.
//

#include <iostream.h>

int main()
{
  const float       ZERO = 0.0F;
  float     data, sum = ZERO;        // data and running total

  while (cin >> data, data >= ZERO)        // read and test
    sum += data;                   // processing
  cout << "The sum is " << sum << "\n";
  return (0);
}
```

A final example illustrates how the unary decrement operator combines with the loop condition testing. We remember that the logical value false is represented by the value zero, whilst any non-zero value represents logical true. We can therefore establish a loop which counts downward from some initial positive value, terminating when the count reaches zero. While the count is not zero, the loop continues. In Program 6.6, the data consists of a single positive integer value followed by a series of floating point values. The integer specifies the number of supplied floating point values. The program calculates the mean (average) of the floating point numbers.

PROGRAM 6.6

```
//
//  Compute the mean of a number of floating point values.
//      The program data consists of an integer N, followed
//      by N floats.
//

#include <iostream.h>

int main()
{
```

```
    const float     ZERO = 0.0F;
    int       count, number;          // loop control, number of values
    float     data, sum = ZERO;       // data and running total

    cin >> number;                   // read how many floats
    count = number;                  // initialize loop control
    while (count--){                 // cycle number of times
      cin >> data;                   // read data value
      sum += data;                   // process it
    }
    cout << "Mean is " << sum/number << "\n";
    return (0);
}
```

When developing software, we must endeavour to ensure its *robustness*. A robust program should, under all conditions, terminate in a controlled manner. If this last program was presented with the single data value `0`, then no floating point numbers are to be averaged. The loop is therefore never executed, and the expression printed, i.e. sum/number, is evaluated as `0.0/0`. Upon evaluation, the expression generates an overflow condition and the program abruptly terminates. To ensure that the program is more secure, this condition should be tested. Similarly, if the integer input value is negative, the program loops forever. A negative-valued count is interpreted as logical true. The value remains negative through decrementing. Ultimately negative overflow occurs and the program fails. We introduce the statement to achieve this level of security later in this chapter.

There is no restriction on the statement or statements under control of a while statement. It is permissible to have while statements controlling other while statements. This gives rise to a construct known as nested while loops or simply *nested loops*. The operation of nested while statements is analogous to the hour and minute hands of a clock. The minute hand moves with rapidity from minute to minute. When the minute hand completes a cycle of 60 minutes, the hour hand advances by one hour. The minute hand then repeats the same rapid cycle. Similarly with nested while statements. The outer while statement progresses more slowly than the inner while statement. When the inner while statement completes one cycle, the outer while advances to the next iteration and the inner while restarts with a new inner loop.

Nested loops in a program arise from data sets which exhibit the same nested structure. A bank account program may process the accounts for a number of customers. The initial data analysis reveals that we have a series or iteration on customers. The resulting program outline is then:

```
WHILE more customers DO
  process one customer
ENDWHILE
```

Each customer, in turn, may hold a number of accounts. Again, an iteration on accounts for a given customer. We refine 'process one customer', replacing it with a loop over the customer's accounts:

```
WHILE more customers DO
  WHILE more accounts for this customer DO
    process customer's account
  ENDWHILE
ENDWHILE
```

These ideas are present in the next program, the output from which has a nested iterative structure.

Program 6.7 plots a solid isosceles triangle composed of asterisk (*) symbols. The first line contains a single asterisk. The second line contains three asterisks centred below the first, and so on. The full triangle spans 5 lines. The outer loop controls the number of lines to be displayed. Each line consists of a number of leading blanks and a number of asterisks. The number of blanks and the number of asterisks on any one line is dependent upon which line is being printed. Both the leading blanks and the asterisks are printed by two successive loops contained within the outer loop.

PROGRAM 6.7

```
//
//  Form an isosceles triangle composed of asterisk
//      symbols. The first line contains a single * symbol.
//      The second line contains three asterisks centred
//      below the first, and so on. In all, the figure
//      spans five lines.
//

#include <iostream.h>

int main()
{
  const int       NUMLINES = 5;
  const char      BLANK = ' ';
  const char      ASTERISK = '*';
  const char      NEWLINE = '\n';

  int             line;         // five line counter
  int             leading_blanks;     // left margin counter
  int             stars;        // number of asterisks

  line = 1;           // for each line
  while (line <= NUMLINES){
    leading_blanks = 1;      // margin
    while (leading_blanks++ <= NUMLINES - line)
      cout.put(BLANK);

    stars = 1;          // asterisks
    while (stars++ <= 2 * line - 1)
      cout.put(ASTERISK);

    cout.put(NEWLINE);
    line++;
```

```
    }
    return (0);
}
```

The control expression in a while statement governs whether the loop is to be obeyed or to be terminated. Any non-zero expression value represents logical true and causes the loop to be obeyed one further time. A non-zero integer constant for this expression gives rise to what is known as an infinite loop. An infinite loop cycles indefinitely, never terminating.

```
const int TRUE = 1;

while(TRUE){
  // .....
  // .....
}
```

A program containing such a construct will run forever unless some action is taken to stop it or some statement embedded within the body of the loop is able to break the cycle. Section 6.9 of this chapter introduces the appropriate statement. An infinite loop containing a statement to break the cycle at some prescribed junction can provide a natural way of expressing certain constructs.

6.6 The for statement

The *for statement* is closely related to the while statement. The syntax of the for statement is given by:

```
for(expression1; expression2; expression3)
     statement;
```

with `for` a reserved keyword. Like the while statement, the statement under control of the for may be a single statement or a compound statement. Any of the statements controlled by the for may be another for statement giving rise to nested for loops.

The for statement is semantically equivalent to:

```
expression1;
while(expression2){
  statement;
  expression3;
}
```

The first expression is used to initialize the loop. Then `expression2` is evaluated and if it is non-zero (logical true) then the statement is executed. `Expression3` is evaluated, and control passes back to the loop beginning, to re-evaluate `expression2`. Normally, `expression2` is a logical expression used to control the iteration. Note that if this expression initially evaluates to zero (logical false), the loop is never entered. The third expression is frequently used to update some loop control variable before repeating the loop.

Two examples of the for statement are:

```
for(k = 1; k <= 10; k++)
    cout << "The square of " << k << " is " << k*k << "\n";
```

and

```
sum = 0;
for(i = 1; i <= m; i++)
    sum += i;
```

The first example generates and prints a table of the squares of the first ten integers. In the second example, the sum of the first `m` integers is computed. By employing the comma operator, the initialization of variable `sum` and the control variable `i` may both be accomplished in `expression1`. The second example may then be written as:

```
for(sum = 0, i = 1; i <= m; i++)
    sum += i;
```

The use of the comma operator is equally applicable to all three expressions in the for statement.

Any or all of the three expressions in a for statement may be omitted, but the two semicolon separators and the parentheses are mandatory. If $\texttt{expression}_1$ is missing, no initialization step is performed as part of the for loop. The last example might have been coded:

```
sum = 0;
i = 1;
for( ; i <= m; i++)
    sum += i;
```

Equally, we might have absorbed the increment to variable `i` into the assignment forming the running total for `sum`. In this case, the third expression can also be removed:

```
sum = 0;
i = 1;
for( ; i <= m; )
    sum += i++;
```

When `expression2` is missing, the condition always evaluates to logical true. Thus the loop in the code:

```
for( ; ; ){
  // .....
  // .....
}
```

is the infinite loop. It parallels the infinite while loop shown in the previous section. Again, some appropriate statement is required to break from this loop (see Section 6.9).

The initializing expression of a for statement can also include a declaration to introduce the control variable for the loop. For example, the above illustrations may have been presented as:

```
for(int k = 1; k <= 10; k++) .....
```

We must be careful with the interpretation of the scope of the variable `k`. The appearance of the declaration might suggest that the scope for `k` is bounded by the statements under control of the for loop. In fact, the scope of variable `k` extends to the end of the block which encloses the for loop.

Extending the scope of the control variable to the end of the block prevents subsequent for statements from declaring and using the same control variable. The following is then illegal:

```
for(int k = 0; k < 10; k++){ /* ..... */ }
// .....
for(int k = 0; k < 100; k++){  // error - redefinition of k
  // .....
}
// .....
```

Since the for statement is semantically equivalent to the while statement, it can equally well be used with iterative data structures. In certain instances, the for statement more naturally expresses the iterative processing logic than the while statement. For example, the loop in Program 6.3(a) is better represented by:

```
for(data = INITIAL; data <= MAX; data++) .....
```

when a known number of iterations is required.

We illustrate a simple example of the use of a for statement by repeating Program 6.1. The first and last expressions of the for are unused. The second expression controls the iteration.

PROGRAM 6.8

```
//
//  Read a series of characters from the standard
//      input and echo them to the standard output. The
//      program finishes when the period symbol is
//      encountered in the data.
//

#include <iostream.h>

int main()
{
  const char          PERIOD = '.';
  char                c;

  for(; cin.get(c), c != PERIOD; )
    cout.put(c);
  return (0);
}
```

Working with the same data as Programs 6.1 and 6.8, we can develop a modified version which counts the number of data characters. The terminating period is omitted from the count. The first expression is used to initialize the count. The final expression is empty as nothing is to be done before advancing to the next iteration. The second expression again controls program looping. The statement under control of the loop increments the counter for each character read.

PROGRAM 6.9(a)

```
//
// Count the number of characters read from the standard
//     input. The character stream is terminated with the
//     first occurrence of the period symbol.
//

#include <iostream.h>

int main()
{
  const char        PERIOD = '.';
  char              c;          // data character

  for(int count = 0; cin.get(c), c!= PERIOD; )
    count++;
  cout << "Number of characters is " << count << "\n";
  return (0);
}
```

The third expression could also be the place to perform the increment to the counter. In that case there is now no statement to be controlled by the for statement. The program logic is completely encapsulated by the three for statement expressions. The statement consisting solely of the semicolon symbol is called the *null statement*. As the semicolon is easily 'lost' when reading the code, we annotate it with a comment.

PROGRAM 6.9(b)

```
//
// Count the number of characters read from the standard
//     input. The character stream is terminated with the
//     first occurrence of the period symbol.
//

#include <iostream.h>

int main()
{
```

```
    const char      PERIOD = '.';
    char            c;        // data character

    for(int count = 0; cin.get(c), c != PERIOD; count++)
      /* do nothing */  ;
    cout << "Number of characters is " << count << "\n";
    return (0);
  }
```

By using the comma operator in the three for statement expressions, very dense and cryptic C++ code can be produced. The code is both difficult to read and maintain if modification or correction is required. Because of this, the reader is not encouraged to indulge in this type of coding. This idiomatic C++ coding, however, may be experienced in others' programs. We illustrate with the following example.

A series of positive floating point values is given as data. The data set is terminated with a negative floating point number. Program 6.10 computes the mean of the positive data values. Note how all the processing and loop control logic is compacted into the three for statement expressions.

PROGRAM 6.10

```
//
//  Compute the mean of a number of positive floating
//      point values. The data consists of a series of
//      positive values, terminated with a negative number.
//

#include <iostream.h>

int main()
{
  int    count;      // count the positives
  float data, sum;       // data item, running total

  for (count = 0, sum = 0.0F;
      cin >> data, data >= 0.0F;
      sum += data, count++)
            /* do nothing */  ;
  cout << "The mean is " << sum/count << "\n";
  return (0);
}
```

6.7 The do statement

As previously noted, the while statement tests the condition (expression) prior to obeying the loop. Since the for statement is semantically equivalent to the while, it too tests before entering the loop. In both cases if the condition is initially zero (logical false), then the loop is never obeyed at all.

Normally, iterative constructs are more logically coded using loops with initial condition checking (while and for). In a small number of cases, checking is required at the conclusion of the loop body. In these cases the *do statement* is the appropriate construct.

The do statement has the form:

```
do
  statement;
while(expression)
```

The distinction between this statement and the while and for statements is that the conditional test is performed after executing the loop. The loop body is then guaranteed to be obeyed at least once. After first executing the statement, the expression is evaluated. If it is non-zero (logical true) then control passes back to the beginning of the do statement and the processing repeats. When the expression evaluates to zero (logical false), control passes to the next program statement.

The statement under control of the `do` may be a single statement or a compound statement. In the latter case, the form of the do statement is:

```
do {
  statement 1;
  statement 2;
  // .....
  // .....
} while(expression)
```

Consider a program to read a single positive integer value and to output the digits of that number in reverse sequence. For example, if the input value is `1234`, then the output is `4321`. The logic consists of repeatedly extracting the rightmost digit of the number and printing it. The digit is then removed from the number before continuing. The iteration stops when the number is reduced to zero. The solution, expressed in our extended PDL, is:

```
read the number
REPEAT
  obtain the rightmost digit
  print the digit
  remove the digit from the number
WHILE number is non zero
```

and the program is Program 6.11.

PROGRAM 6.11

```
//
//  Read a single positive integer value and output
//      the digits of that number in reverse sequence. For
//      example, if the input value is 1234, then the output
//      is 4321.
```

```
//

#include <iostream.h>

int main()
{
  int number, digit;            // data value, rightmost digit

  cin >> number;                // input data item
  do {
    digit = number % 10;        // obtain rightmost digit .....
    cout << digit;              // ..... and print it
    number /= 10;               // reduce the number
  } while(number != 0);        // repeat until nothing left
  cout << "\n";
  return (0);
}
```

We might have considered coding the problem with a while statement:

```
cin >> number;
while(number != 0){
  digit = number % 10;
  cout << digit;
  number /= 10;
}
```

The same input number `1234` produces the same output `4321`. However, note what happens if the input value is `0` (zero). Since the do statement is obeyed once, the output is `0`. However, when the solution is in terms of the while statement, which is obeyed none or more times, no output is produced as the loop is never entered. The do statement solution guarantees the display of at least one digit in all cases. This is the better solution since no output from a program can mislead the user into thinking that the program has somehow failed.

CASE STUDY 6.1
Reports

A student class is partitioned into a number of project groups. The number of students in each group is not necessarily always the same. Each student in the class is given an assessment and assigned a raw mark measured out of 80. A report is required showing the assessment for each student, for each group and for the entire class. The report format is shown below.

```
          PROJECT REPORT

PROJECT GROUP 1
          IDENTIFICATION    RAW              PERCENTAGE
          NUMBER            MARK (/80)       MARK
          1234              40               50
          5678              55               68
```

```
     9012                30          37
   GROUP 1 TOTAL                     155

 PROJECT GROUP 2
     IDENTIFICATION      RAW         PERCENTAGE
     NUMBER              MARK (/80)  MARK
     3456                10          12
     7890                20          25
     9876                30          37
     5432                40          50
     1098                50          62
     7654                60          75
     3210                70          87
   GROUP 2 TOTAL                     348

 GRAND TOTAL                         503
```

No account is to be taken of page breaks in the report.

The program input consists of a series of records presented one per line. Each record gives the student's identification number and the raw assessment mark. The records are batched into project groupings with the group number prepended to each record. A trailer record containing all zeros terminates each group, whilst another trailer record containing all nines terminates the data. The sample data set for the illustrated report above is:

```
1  1234   40
1  5678   55
1  9012   30
0  0000   00
2  3456   10
2  7890   20
2  9876   30
2  5432   40
2  1098   50
2  7654   60
2  3210   70
0  0000   00
9  9999   99
```

Analysis of the data indicates that nested iteration is required. Two repeating groups are present in the data – a repetition over the project groups, and a repetition over the students in each group. The outer iteration cycles through each project group, with the inner iteration processing each student in that group. The outline logic for this processing is:

```
initialize grand total
produce class report heading
WHILE read next record; not the end of data record DO
  initialize project group total
  produce project group headings
  REPEAT
    process the current record
```

```
    read the next record
  WHILE not the end of group record
  produce project group summary
  add project group total to grand total
ENDWHILE
produce class report summary
```

The coding for the program is now relatively straightforward. The PDL is sufficiently close to the final version that we can convert to code directly.

```
//
//  A student class is partitioned into a number of project
//      groups, not necessarily of equal sizes. Each student
//      in the class is assigned an assessment mark measured
//      out of 80. Produce a report showing the assessment for
//      each student, for each project group and for the whole
//      class.
//

#include <iostream.h>
#include <iomanip.h>

int main()
{
  const int        GROUP_TRAILER = 0;
  const int        FILE_TRAILER = 9;

  int grand_total;              // percent mark
  int group_total;              // percent mark
  int group_no, current_group_no;    // project groups
  int identification;           // student number
  int raw, percent;             // student assessment mark

  grand_total = 0;
  cout << "\t\t\tPROJECT REPORT\n\n";

  while (cin >> group_no >> identification >> raw,
          group_no != FILE_TRAILER){
    cout << "PROJECT GROUP " << setw(2) << group_no << "\n";
    cout << "\t\tIDENTIFICATION\tRAW\t\tPERCENTAGE\n";
    cout << "\t\tNUMBER\t\tMARK (/80)\tMARK\n";
    current_group_no = group_no;

    group_total = 0;
    do {
      percent = raw * 100 / 80;
      cout << "\t\t" << setw(4) << identification << "\t\t"
           << setw(2) << raw << "\t\t" << setw(3) << percent << "\n";
      group_total += percent;
      cin >> group_no >> identification >> raw;
    } while (group_no != GROUP_TRAILER);
    cout << "\tGROUP " << setw(2) << current_group_no
         << " TOTAL\t\t\t     " << setw(6) << group_total << "\n\n";

    grand_total += group_total;
  }
```

```
  cout << "GRAND TOTAL\t\t\t\t      " << setw(6) << grand_total <<
"\n\n";
  return (0);
}
```

6.8 The if statement

The general form of the *if statement* is:

```
if(expression)
     statement 1;
else
     statement 2;
```

where `if` and `else` are reserved keywords. If the expression evaluates to non-zero (logical value true), `statement 1` is executed and control then passes to the next program statement following the if statement. If the value of the expression is zero (logical false), `statement 2` is executed. Pictorially, the if statement can be described by the flow diagram of Figure 6.2.

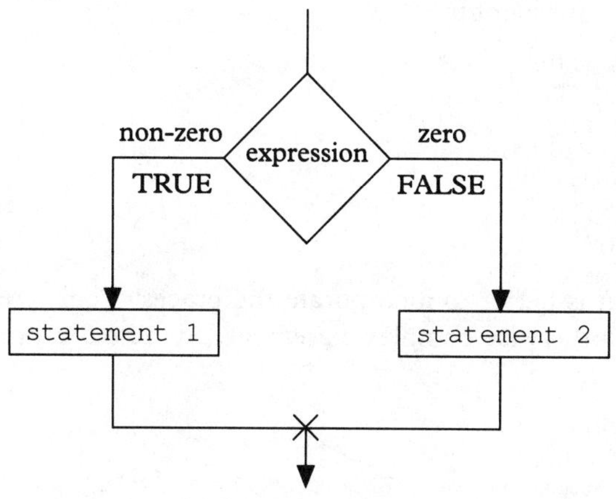

Figure 6.2

Both `statement 1` and `statement 2` may be single statements or compound statements. Some examples of valid if statements are:

(a)
```
if(count == 0)
  cout << "The count is zero\n";
else
  cout << "The count is not zero\n";
```

(b)
```
if(a < b)
  cout << "Originally, a less than b\n";
```

```
else {
  temp = a;
  a = b;
  b = temp;
  cout << "Interchange a and b\n";
}
```

(c)
```
if(ch == ' ' || ch == '\t' || ch == '\n') {
  whitespace++;
  cout << "More whitespace characters\n";
} else
  others++;
```

We may also include another if statement as either or both of the statement parts. This gives rise to what is known as a *nested if statement*. Examples include:

(d)
```
if(expression 1)
  if(expression 2)
    statement 1;
  else
    statement 2;
else
  statement 3;
```

Semantically this is equivalent to:

```
if(expression 1){
  if(expression 2)
    statement 1;
  else
    statement 2;
} else
  statement 3;
```

In many instances it is better to incorporate the braces. Their presence highlights the structure of an otherwise complex statement. An actual example with explicit braces is:

```
if(number > 20){
  if(number < 30)
    cout << "Number between 21 and 29 inclusive\n";
  else
    cout << "Number exceeds 29\n";
} else
  cout << "Number does not exceed 20\n";
```

Similarly, an if statement may be used in the else clause of another if statement:

(e)
```
if(expression 1)
  statement 1;
else
  if(expression 2)
    statement 2;
  else
    statement 3;
```

Semantically, this is equivalent to:

```
if(expression 1)
  statement 1;
else {
  if(expression 2)
    statement 2;
  else
    statement 3;
}
```

Again, the braces are often best included where it is felt the structure needs to be emphasized. An example of this form is:

```
if(ch >= 'a' && ch <= 'z')
     cout << "Lowercase letter\n";
else {
  if(ch >= '0' && ch <= '9')
    cout << "Digit symbol\n";
  else
    cout << "Other symbol\n";
}
```

In the present form the if statement provides a means of selecting one of two distinct logic paths. Sometimes we wish to select whether or not to obey some statement or statements. This is achieved through a shortened version of the if statement:

```
if(expression)
     statement;
```

If the expression evaluates to logical true (non-zero) the statement is obeyed. Having obeyed the statement the program continues with the next instruction following this if statement. If the expression evaluates to logical false (zero) the statement is ignored and the program continues with the next statement. The statement part under control of this if statement may, as before, be a single statement or a compound statement.

When using this last form of if statement, an ambiguous construct can arise where the statement part is itself an if statement:

```
if(expression 1)
  if(expression 2)
    statement 1;
  else
    statement 2;
```

The ambiguity arises from the fact that we are unable to say whether the else part belongs with `if(expression 1)` or with `if(expression 2)`. Two possible interpretations are:

(a)
```
if(expression 1){
  if(expression 2)
    statement 1;
```

(b)
```
if(expression 1){
  if(expression 2)
    statement 1;
```

```
     else                                    } else
        statement 2;                           statement 2;
  }
```

In version (a) the else part associates with `if(expression 2)`. In version (b) the else part associates with `if(expression 1)`. This ambiguity, known as the *dangling else problem*, is resolved by the compiler always associating an else part with the nearest unresolved preceding if. Version (a) is therefore the correct interpretation. Explicit braces as shown in version (a) can often improve the readability of the code.

Various combinations of if statements can occur. The statement associated with the else clause may be another if–else statement. Equally, the next else clause may be yet another if–else statement, and so on. To illustrate, consider a program fragment to read an examination score and to assign a letter grade based on the score. The grading scheme that applies is shown by the following table:

Score	*Grade*
80–100	A
70–79	B
60–69	C
50–59	D
40–49	E
0–39	F

A single nested if statement can describe the necessary processing:

```
if(score >= 80)
  grade = 'A';
else
  if(score >= 70)
    grade = 'B';
  else
    if(score >= 60)
      grade = 'C';
    else
      if(score >= 50)
        grade = 'D';
      else
        if(score >= 40)
          grade = 'E';
        else
          grade = 'F';
```

The whole construct is a single statement forming a cascading chain of if statements. Suppose, for example, that the score is `65`. The first two expressions evaluate to logical false and the corresponding two statements `grade = 'A'` and `grade = 'B'` are skipped. The third expression evaluates to logical true and the statement `grade = 'C'` is executed. Control then passes to the end of this statement.

The proper indentation for such a construct is shown as above. As can be seen, the structure rapidly tracks to the right. To avoid this situation, these statements are generally presented as:

```
if(score >= 80)
  grade = 'A';
else if(score >= 70)
  grade = 'B';
else if(score >= 60)
  grade = 'C';
else if(score >= 50)
  grade = 'D';
else if(score >= 40)
  grade = 'E';
else
  grade = 'F';
```

The if statement is used in programs in which the data offers a selection. If the program data offers a choice between, say, data item 1 and data item 2, then the corresponding program structure (expressed in our PDL) is a conditional:

```
IF data item 1
THEN
  process data item 1
ELSE
  process data item 2
ENDIF
```

Program 6.12 illustrates a simple use of an if statement. The program inputs two floating point numbers and outputs them in ascending order. The program data can either be already ordered or in descending order. These two alternatives are reflected in the solution structure:

```
read the two data values
IF first value less than second
THEN
  print first and second
ELSE
  print second and first
ENDIF
```

PROGRAM 6.12

```
//
// Read two floating point values and display them in
//      ascending order.
//

#include <iostream.h>

int main()
{
```

```
float first, second;          // data items
  cin >> first >> second;
  if (first < second)
    cout << first << " " << second << "\n";
  else
    cout << second << " " << first << "\n";
  return (0);
}
```

The second program of this series operates on a sequence of characters of unknown length. The data set is terminated with a period symbol. The character sequence spans a number of lines and the program determines the number of text lines by enumerating the number of newline symbols. The program employs an if statement with no else part, used to detect the newline characters. The program data is an iteration of single characters. The corresponding program structure is then a loop. The PDL is:

```
WHILE read next character; character is not terminator DO
 process the character
ENDWHILE
```

The character processing is a selection. If the character is a newline symbol, the line counter is incremented. If the character is not a newline symbol it is ignored. The final PDL is:

```
initialize line counter
WHILE read next character; character is not terminator DO
 IF a newline symbol
 THEN
  increment line counter
 ENDIF
ENDWHILE
print final line counter value
```

PROGRAM 6.13

```
//
//  Read a sequence of characters of indeterminate length
//      and count the number of lines of text by enumerating
//      the number of newline symbols. The data is terminated
//      by a period symbol.
//

#include <iostream.h>

int main()
{
  const char       PERIOD = '.';
  const char       NEWLINE = '\n';
```

```
    char           c;            // data character
    int            lines = 0;       // line counter

    while(cin.get(c), c != PERIOD)
      if(c == NEWLINE)
        lines++;
    cout << "Number of lines is " << lines << "\n";
    return (0);
}
```

Operating with the same data as in the program above, we develop a program to count the number of 'words' in the input character sequence. A word is defined to be any character sequence separated by whitespace characters (blanks, tabs and newlines).

Once again the data is a repetition of characters, giving rise to the same initial program structure:

```
WHILE read next character; character not the terminator DO
 process the character
ENDWHILE
```

The character processing must select from a whitespace character or a non-whitespace character. The former indicates that the input is no longer part of a word and a flag is set accordingly. For a non-whitespace character two possibilities exist. If the previous data item was also a non-whitespace character, then we continue to be part of the same word. If the preceding symbol was a whitespace character then we are processing the first character of a new word and the word counter is incremented. The overall PDL is:

```
initialize word count and set the in-word flag
WHILE read next character; character not the terminator DO
 IF a whitespace character
 THEN
  unset the in-word flag
 ELSE
  IF start of new word
  THEN
   increment word count
   set the in-word flag
  ENDIF
 ENDIF
ENDWHILE
print final word count
```

PROGRAM 6.14

```
//
//  A piece of text consists of a character sequence
//      spanning a number of lines and terminated by a period
//      symbol. Count the number of "words" in the text.
```

```
//      A word is defined as any character string delimited
//      by whitespace (blank, tab and newline) symbols.
//

#include <iostream.h>

int main()
{
  const char      PERIOD = '.';
  const char      BLANK = ' ';
  const char      TAB = '\t';
  const char      NEWLINE = '\n';

  enum Bool { FALSE, TRUE };

  char            c;              // data character
  int             words = 0;          // word counter
  Bool            inword = FALSE;         // word indicator

  while(cin.get(c), c != PERIOD)
    if(c == BLANK || c == TAB || c == NEWLINE)
      inword = FALSE;
    else if(! inword){
      inword = TRUE;
      words++;
    }
  cout << "Number of words is " << words << "\n";
  return (0);
}
```

Once more with the same data, we count the number of occurrences of lower case letters, upper case letters, digits and other symbols. A nested if statement provides the necessary logic. The character handling operations are performed with the library macros `islower`, etc. See Appendix F.1 for details.

PROGRAM 6.15

```
//
// Enumerate the number of occurrences of lowercase
//      letters, uppercase letters, digits and other symbols
//      in a data set consisting of a character sequence
//      terminated with a period symbol.
//

#include <iostream.h>
#include <ctype.h>

int main()
{
  const char      PERIOD = '.';

  char            c;                                 // data character
  int             lowercase, uppercase, digits, others;  // counters
```

```
    lowercase = uppercase = digits = others = 0;
    while(cin.get(c), c != PERIOD)
      if(islower(c))
        lowercase++;
      else if(isupper(c))
        uppercase++;
      else if(isdigit(c))
        digits++;
      else
        others++;

    cout << "Number of lowercase letters " << lowercase << "\n";
    cout << "Number of uppercase letters " <<  uppercase << "\n";
    cout << "Number of decimal digits " << digits << "\n";
    cout << "Number of other symbols " << others << "\n";
    return (0);
  }
```

The final program in this section is a multi-function program making extensive use of the conditional if statement. The program accepts as input a date expressed in numerical form and verbalizes it. The input date appears in the international form:

```
DD/MM/YYYY
```

for example:

```
10/12/1985
```

The input date is assumed to be valid. The output from the program (for the above) is:

```
Tuesday 10 December 1985
```

To calculate the day of the week for a given date, Zeller's congruence can be employed. The algorithm computes for any valid date an integer in the range 0 to 6 inclusive, with 0 representing Sunday, 1 is Monday, and so on. The formula for Zeller's congruence is:

$$z = [\frac{26m - 2}{10} + k + D + \frac{D}{4} + \frac{C}{4} - 2C + 77] \bmod 7$$

The square brackets denote 'the greatest integer in', and mod 7 is the remainder (modulus) on dividing by 7. In the formula:

D = the year in the century
C = the century
k = the day of the month
m = month number, with January and February taken as months 11 and 12 respectively of the preceding year. March is then month 1, April is 2, ..., December is 10.

Thus for 10/12/1985, $D = 85$, $C = 19$, $k = 10$ and $m = 10$. For January 1, 1800, $k = 1$, $m = 11$, $C = 17$ and $D = 99$.

The congruence for 10/12/1985 is:

$$z = \left[\frac{26 \star 10 - 2}{10} + 10 + 85 + \frac{85}{4} + \frac{19}{4} - 2 \star 19 + 77 \right] \bmod 7$$

$$z = [25 + 10 + 85 + 21 + 4 - 38 + 77] \bmod 7$$

$$z = 184 \bmod 7$$

$$z = 2$$

which, of course, is Tuesday. The program is as follows:

PROGRAM 6.16

```
//
//  The program accepts as input a single date expressed
//      in the form DD/MM/YYYY and verbalizes it. For example,
//      the date 10/12/1985 produces the output:
//
//              Tuesday 10 December 1985
//
//      The input date is assumed to be valid and no checking
//      is performed.
//

#include <iostream.h>
#include <iomanip.h>

int main()
{
  int  day, month, year;                      // input date
  char ch;                                    // separator

  int  zeller(int, int, int);                 // forward .....
  void day_name(int), month_name(int);        // ..... references

  cout << "Enter the date as DD/MM/YYYY: ";   // get the date
  cin >> day >> ch >> month >> ch >> year;

  const int zell = zeller(day, month, year);  // apply congruence
  day_name(zell);                             // verbalize the day
  cout << setw(2) << day;                     // print the day
  month_name(month);                          // verbalize the month
  cout << setw(4) << year << "\n";            // print the year

  return (0);
}

//
//  Apply Zeller's congruence to a date expressed in
//      the form 21/11/1985. The date given is assumed to
```

```
//      be valid.
//

int zeller(int day, int month, int year)
{
  int m;                          // formula variable

  const int k = day;              // initialize
  int y = year;

  if (month < 3){                 // formula month
    m = month + 10;
    y = year - 1;
  } else
    m = month - 2;

  const int d = y % 100;          // year and .....
  const int c = y / 100;          // ..... century

  const int z = (26 * m - 2)/10 + k + d + (d/4) + (c/4) - 2 * c + 77;
  return (z % 7);
}

//
// Verbalize a day number, encoded according to Zeller's
//      congruence, into a variable length character string
//      surrounded by single blank characters.
//

void day_name(int d)
{
  if (d == 0)
    cout << " Sunday ";
  else if (d == 1)
    cout << " Monday ";
  else if (d == 2)
    cout << " Tuesday ";
  // .....
}

//
// Verbalize a month number in the range 1 to 12 inclusive
//      into a variable length character string surrounded
//      by single blank characters.
//

void month_name(int m)
{
  if (m == 1)
    cout << " January ";
  else if (m == 2)
    cout << " February ";
  else if (m == 3)
    cout << " March ";
  // .....
}
```

CASE STUDY 6.2
Bank statement

A program is required to read details of transactions on a bank account and produce a statement summarizing these transactions. The program input consists of a sequence of integer values. The first value is a positive integer representing the bank account number. The second integer value is the initial balance of the account. The remaining integer values are either positive or negative and represent the transactions. The final transaction is the unique trailer value `0`. A positive transaction represents a deposit (credit transaction) and a negative transaction represents a withdrawal (debit transaction).

For example, given the input data `1234, 847, -150, -35, +30, -249, -172, +55` and `0`, the bank statement produced should appear as shown in Figure 6.3.

Bank Statement

Account number: 1234

Transaction	Credit	Debit	Balance
			847
1		150	697
2		35	662
3	30		692
4		249	443
5		172	271
6	55		326
Totals	85	606	326

Figure 6.3

The first-level design of the bank statement program is relatively straightforward. After the first two data values have been read, the statement headers and the initial balance line may be printed. Successive transactions are read and processed until the end of data trailer record is processed. Finally, the statement summary is generated. In outline, the program is:

```
read account number and initial balance
print statement headers and initial balance
initialize credit and debit totals
read the first transaction
initialize the transaction counter
WHILE not end of data value DO
 process and print this transaction
```

```
  read the next transaction
  increment the transaction counter
ENDWHILE
print the statement summary
```

Given this outline it is possible to be satisfied about its correctness. Using sample test data, such as that above, we can trace the program's behaviour. Only when this implementation has been fully tested do we progress to the next phase and continue with the refinement.

Printing the statement headers and producing the initial balance line is a self contained task that should be isolated to a separate function. For it to operate correctly, the `main` function will need to provide this subsidiary function with the bank account number and the value of the initial balance.

The same analysis applies when we consider the statement summary. It too is programmed as a separate function. The summary is produced from the credit total, the debit total and the final balance. These values are communicated as arguments to the function.

Finally, we consider processing a single transaction. The transaction value is added to the current balance to produce the updated balance value. A positive transaction will increase the value of the balance when added to it. A negative transaction will reduce the value of the balance when added to it. Thus no special processing is required to update the balance other than by adding the transaction value.

If the transaction is positive, the total credit value is changed. If the transaction is negative, the total debit is changed. When all the computations are complete, the transaction print line can be presented. The processing and printing of one transaction is assigned to a secondary function.

From this analysis we can complete the coding of function `main`. Note how even the detailed coding still reflects the original program design. Details concerned with printing headers, processing transactions and printing summaries are not allowed to clutter the simple logic of the `main` function.

```
int main()
{
  int account_number;                  // identification
  int number_of_transaction;           // transaction counter
  int credit_total, debit_total;       // total credits/debits
  int transaction_value;               // value of transaction
  int balance;                         // balance of the account

  void print_headers(int, int),         // prototype declarations
       process_transaction(int, int, int&, int&, int&),
       print_summary(int, int, int);

  credit_total = debit_total = 0;      // initialize totals

  cin >> account_number >> balance;    // initial data
  print_headers(account_number, balance);     // initial headers

  cin >> transaction_value;            // get first transaction
```

```
    number_of_transaction = 1;              // initialize count
    while (transaction_value != 0){         // end of data?
      process_transaction(number_of_transaction, transaction_value,
           credit_total, debit_total, balance);

      cin >> transaction_value;           // next transaction
      number_of_transaction++;            // update count
    }

    print_summary(credit_total, debit_total, balance);
    return (0);
  }
```

Processing and printing one transaction is covered by the function `process_transaction`. This function receives the transaction number and the value of the transaction. The function is also supplied with the addresses of the credit and debit totals and the current balance. Through these addresses the current values can be obtained and new updated values assigned. The new assignations are returned to `main` for transmission to the next processing task.

Coding the functions `print_headers` and `print_summary` is trivial. We leave these for the final program listing. The major sub-problem we must solve is the coding for function `process_transaction`. Like `main`, we start with an outline:

```
add value of transaction to current balance
IF a credit transaction
THEN
 update current credit total
 print a credit statement line
ELSE
 update current debit total
 print a debit statement line
ENDIF
```

A positive transaction (credit) is added to the current credit total. The credit total is initially set to zero and increases positively when a transaction is accumulated. A negative transaction (debit) is subtracted from the debit total. Subtracting a negative value equates to adding a positive value. The debit total, therefore, also increases positively when a transaction is accumulated. Thus, both the credit and debit totals remain positive throughout the program execution, as required.

The format of a transaction statement line is determined by whether the transaction is a credit or a debit. Two prints using different formats selected by the if statement simplify this problem. The function coding is:

```
void process_transaction(int number, int transaction,
        int& credit, int& debit, int& balance)
{
  balance += transaction;
  if (transaction > 0){
    credit += transaction;
    cout << setw(8) << number << "\t"
```

```
            << setw(8) << transaction << "\t\t\t"
            << setw(8) << balance << "\n";
    } else {
      debit -= transaction;
      cout << setw(8) << number << "\t\t\t"
            << setw(8) << -transaction << "\t"
            << setw(8) << balance << "\n";
    }
  }
```

The program listing follows.

```
//
// Read a series of transactions on a bank account and
//      produce a bank statement summarizing these transactions.
//      The program input consists of a sequence of integers.
//      The first value is a positive integer representing
//      the bank account number. The second integer is the
//      initial balance of the account. The remaining data
//      values are either positive or negative. A positive
//      value represents a deposit and a negative value
//      represents a withdrawal. The end-of-data trailer
//      record is the value zero.
//

#include <iostream.h>
#include <iomanip.h>

int main()
{
  // .....
}

//
// Process a single transaction and produce a statement
//      line resulting from this. As a side effect, update
//      the balance and either the credit or debit totals.
//

void process_transaction(int number, int transaction,
        int& credit, int& debit, int& balance)
{
  // .....
}

void print_headers(int number, int balance)
{
  cout << "\t\t\tBank Statement\n\n";
  cout << "Account number: " << setw(6) << number << "\n\n";
  cout << "Transaction     Credit      Debit     Balance\n";
  cout << "-----------------------------------------\n";
  cout << "\t\t\t\t\t\t\t" << setw(8) << balance << "\n";
}

void print_summary(int credit, int debit, int balance)
```

```
    {
      cout << "-------------------------------------------\n";
      cout << "Totals\t\t" << setw(8) << credit
           << "\t" << setw(8) << debit
           << "\t" << setw(8) << balance << "\n";
    }
```

6.9 The switch statement

The if–else statement chain that we encountered in the last section (cf. Program 6.16), where the value of a variable is successively compared against different values, occurs so frequently that a special statement exists for this purpose. This is called the *switch statement*. Its format is:

```
switch(expression){
  case constant-expression-1 :
    statement 1a;
    statement 1b;
    // .....
    // .....
  case constant-expression-2 :
    statement 2a;
    statement 2b;
    // .....
    // .....
    // .....
    // .....
  case constant-expression-N :
    statement Na;
    statement Nb;
    // .....
    // .....
  default :
    statement Da;
    statement Db;
    // .....
    // .....
}
```

where `switch`, `case` and `default` are reserved keywords.

The control expression enclosed within parentheses is evaluated. The result must be of an integral type including `chars`. The constant expressions associated with each case keyword must also resolve to an integer. These expressions, called *case labels*, may be an integer constant, a character constant or an integer constant expression. When evaluated, each constant expression must deliver a unique integer value. Duplicates are not permitted.

During execution of the switch statement, the control expression is first evaluated. The resulting value is then compared with each case label in turn. If a case label value equals the value of the expression, control is passed to the first statement associated with that case label. Execution would then continue through successive statements ignoring any additional case or default labels that are encountered until the end of the switch statement is reached. Generally, however, the switch statement is used as a multi-way selector. After transfer to a case label or to the default label, the group of associated statements is executed, then control is transferred to the end of the switch ignoring all other statement groups. This is achieved by making the last statement in each group the break statement. The break statement is fully discussed in the next section. In the context of a switch statement, the break statement is used to terminate it immediately. Consider now:

```
n = 3;
switch(n){
  case  1 : cout << "One\n";            break;
  case  2 :
  case  3 : cout << "Two or three\n";   break;
  case  4 : cout << "Four\n";           break;
  default : cout << "Default\n"; break;
}
cout << "End of switch\n";
```

which generates the output:

```
Two or three
End of switch
```

While the last break is logically unnecessary, it is a good thing to include it as a matter of style. It will help to prevent errors in the event that a fifth case label is later added to the switch during program maintenance.

The following program illustrates the use of the switch statement. The program operates on a character sequence of indeterminate length, terminated with the period symbol. The program counts the number of blanks, the number of tabs, the number of newline symbols and the number of all other symbols (cf. Program 6.15). The outline processing logic of this program is expressed by the PDL:

```
initialize all counters
WHILE read the next character; not the end of data character DO
 SWITCH this character TO
  WHEN (a blank) increment blank counter
  WHEN (a tab)  increment tab counter
  WHEN (a newline) increment newline counter
  OTHERWISE  increment all other counter
 ENDSWITCH
ENDWHILE
```

PROGRAM 6.17

```
//
// A program to separately count the number of blank,
```

```
//      tab, newline and other characters. The input data
//      consists of a stream of characters terminated
//      by a period symbol.
//
#include <iostream.h>

int main()
{
  const char        PERIOD = '.';
  const char        TAB = '\t';
  const char        NEWLINE = '\n';
  const char        BLANK = ' ';

  int               nblank = 0, ntab = 0, nnewline = 0, nother = 0;
  char              c;

  while(cin.get(c), c  != PERIOD)
    switch(c){
      case BLANK    : nblank++;     break;
      case TAB      : ntab++;       break;
      case NEWLINE  : nnewline++;   break;
      default       : nother++;     break;
    }
  cout << nblank << " " << ntab << " "
       << nnewline << " " << nother << "\n";
  return (0);
}
```

Note the additional PDL construction used in the last example representing a multi-way switch. The structure used is:

```
SWITCH on-some-expression TO
  WHEN (this-value) these-statements
  WHEN ( ..... ) .....
  .....  .....
  .....  .....
  OTHERWISE   .....
ENDSWITCH
```

If the expression evaluates to a value which matches any of the WHEN clauses, the associated statements, and only these, are executed. The switch then terminates and the program logic continues with the following statement. If no match occurs, the escape mechanism is to the statements of the OTHERWISE clause. Note that our PDL avoids the need to specifically incorporate break statements. Our concern at this level is solely with the overall program design. Equally, no restrictions are placed on the expressions or values. We are allowed to say, for example:

```
SWITCH day-of-week TO
  WHEN (Mon, Tue, Wed, Thu, Fri)  working-days
  OTHERWISE                       weekend
ENDSWITCH
```

Program 6.18 also illustrates the use of the switch statement. The program is supplied with a date in the form of two integers representing the day and the month. The year is known not to be a leap year. The program calculates the date (day, month) of the day following the input date.

PROGRAM 6.18

```
//
// Determine tomorrow's date, given the date for
//     today. the year is known not to be a leap year,
//     and so only the day and month is provided as data.
//

#include <iostream.h>

int main()
{
  int               day, month;
  void              tomorrow(int&, int&);

  cout << "Enter today's date: ";
  cin >> day >> month;
  tomorrow(day, month);
  cout << "Tomorrow's date is " << day << " " << month << "\n";
  return (0);
}

                                          // compute tomorrow's date
void tomorrow(int& d, int& m)
{
  const int         JAN = 1;
  const int         FEB = 2;
  const int         APR = 4;
  const int         JUN = 6;
  const int         SEP = 9;
  const int         NOV = 11;
  const int         DEC = 12;

  int               days_in_month;

  switch(m){                                  // which month?
    case APR :
    case JUN :
    case SEP :
    case NOV : days_in_month = 30;  break;
    case FEB : days_in_month = 28;  break;
    default  : days_in_month = 31;  break;
  }

  if(d == days_in_month){                     // end of month?
    d = 1;                                    // yes, first day
    if(m == DEC)                              // end of year?
      m = JAN;
    else
      m++;
```

```
    } else
      d++;
  }
```

CASE STUDY 6.3
Printing bank cheques

Computerized banking systems issue cheques to bank customers. The cheques include, amongst other things, the value of the cheque expressed numerically and as words. For example, the numerical sum of money `123:45` is expressed as:

```
ONE HUNDRED AND TWENTY THREE DOLLARS AND FORTY FIVE CENTS
```

A program is required to accept an indeterminate number of numerical monetary values and to output each value in both its numeric form and in its word equivalent form. Each monetary data value appears on a separate line and is represented by two integers separated by a colon symbol. The first integer is the number of dollars. The second integer is always given as two digits and represents the number of cents. All input values are less than 1000 dollars. The data is terminated with the zero monetary value `0:00`.

The overall program structure is relatively simple. Each data value is read and processed. This iteration continues until the terminator is read. The program then stops. The PDL is:

```
read the first sum of money
WHILE not the terminating monetary value DO
 print the sum of money numerically
 print the sum of money in words
 read the next sum of money
ENDWHILE
```

Only the step `'print the sum of money in words'` causes us any difficulty. Further work is necessary to refine this stage. We can, in the meantime, relegate it to a subordinate function, passing the value of the dollars and cents as arguments. Armed with both these values the function can do its work. The `main` function is then immediately coded as:

```
int main ()
{
  int dollars, cents;           // input data
  char ch;                              // separator
  void do_conversion(int, int);

  cin >> dollars >> ch >> cents;
  while( !(dollars == 0 && cents == 0) ){
    cout << dollars  << ":" << cents << "      ";
    do_conversion(dollars, cents);
    cin >> dollars >> ch >> cents;
  }
  return (0);
}
```

The subordinate function, `do_conversion`, receives the monetary sum as two integer values – the number of dollars and the number of cents. The first value contributes to the first part of the alphabetical output as far as the word DOLLARS:

```
..... DOLLARS .....
```

The second value is responsible for the phrase starting AND:

```
..... AND .....
```

Care must be taken if either case is zero. If there are no dollars, the phrase up to and including the AND is omitted. Similarly, if there are no cents, the output stops at DOLLARS. The design for function `do_conversion` is:

```
IF non zero dollars
THEN
  convert dollars into words
  print "DOLLARS" or "DOLLAR"
ENDIF

IF non zero cents
THEN
  IF non zero dollars
  THEN
    print "AND"
  ENDIF
  convert cents into words
  print "CENTS" or "CENT"
ENDIF
```

and is programmed as:

```
void do_conversion(int dollars, int cents)
{
  void convert_to_words(int);

  if(dollars > 0){
    convert_to_words(dollars);
    if(dollars > 1)
      cout << " DOLLARS";
    else
      cout << " DOLLAR";
  }

  if(cents > 0){
    if(dollars > 0)
      cout << " AND";
    convert_to_words(cents);
    if(cents > 1)
      cout << " CENTS";
    else
      cout << " CENT";
  }
  cout << "\n\n";
}
```

The interesting feature of this function is that converting both the dollars and the cents into words is achieved with the same function (`convert_to_words`). The suffix `DOLLARS` and `CENTS` is the responsibility of the function `do_conversion`. Otherwise, the words produced are the same for both the dollars and the cents. The PDL for function `convert_to_words` is:

```
obtain the number of hundreds in the number
obtain the number of tens in the number
obtain the number of units in the number

IF non zero hundreds
THEN
  convert to words the number of hundreds
  print "HUNDREDS"
ENDIF

IF some tens or some units in the number
THEN
  print "AND"
  IF the tens and units is expressible as teens
  THEN
    convert to words the tens and units
  ELSE
    convert to words the number of tens
    convert to words the number of units
  ENDIF
ENDIF
```

The function `convert_to_words` is then:

```
void convert_to_words(int number)
{
  void do_units(int), do_teens(int), do_tens(int);

  const int hundreds = number / 100;
  const int tens     = (number % 100) / 10;
  const int units    = number % 10;

  if(hundreds > 0){
    do_units(hundreds);
    cout << " HUNDRED";
  }

  if(tens + units > 0){
    if(hundreds > 0)
      cout << " AND";
    if(tens == 1)
      do_teens(units);
    else {
      do_tens(tens);
      do_units(units);
    }
  }
}
```

The completed program is listed below, together with some sample input data and the resulting output.

```
//
// Accept as input an indeterminate number of monetary
//      values each less than 1000 dollars and output the sum
//      both numerically and in words. Each value is expressed
//      in the form PPP:pp, where PPP represents the dollars
//      and pp represents the cents. The data is terminated
//      with the value 0:00.
//

#include <iostream.h>

int main ()
{
  // .....
}

//
// Convert a sum of money into words by first expressing
//      the dollars and then expressing the cents.
//

void do_conversion(int dollars, int cents)
{
  // .....
}

//
// Convert a numerical value into its equivalent expressed
//      in words.
//

void convert_to_words(int number)
{
  // .....
}

//
// Routines to express selected values in words.
//
void do_units(int units)
{
  switch(units){
    case 0 : break;
    case 1 : cout << " ONE";        break;
    case 2 : cout << " TWO";        break;
    case 3 : cout << " THREE";      break;
    // .....
  }
}

void do_teens(int units)
{
```

```
  switch(units){
    case 0 : cout << " TEN";        break;
    case 1 : cout << " ELEVEN";     break;
    case 2 : cout << " TWELVE";     break;
    // .....
  }
}

void do_tens(int tens)
{
  switch(tens){
    case 0 : break;
    case 1 : break;
    case 2 : cout << " TWENTY";     break;
    case 3 : cout << " THIRTY";     break;
    // .....
  }
}
```

Sample data:

```
123:45
1:07
10:00
0:66
0:00
```

Program output:

```
123:45    ONE HUNDRED AND TWENTY THREE DOLLARS AND FORTY FIVE CENTS
  1:07    ONE DOLLAR AND SEVEN CENTS
 10:00    TEN DOLLARS
  0:66    SIXTY SIX CENTS
```

6.10 The break statement

The *break statement* is used to alter the flow of control inside loops and inside switch statements. We have already introduced the break statement in the previous section, where it was used to cause immediate exit from within the nearest enclosing switch statement. The break statement can also be used with while, for and do statements. Execution of a break statement causes immediate termination of the innermost enclosing loop.

A break statement in loops is normally used in conjunction with an if statement. Firstly, a loop is established to repeat some specified number of times or until some expected condition occurs. If, at any time, some abnormal situation occurs, the loop is terminated. The latter is achieved with a combination of if and break statements.

Program 6.19 illustrates this idea. Essentially, the program is a revised version of Program 6.13. An unknown number of single characters up to and including the period symbol are input. The number of lines in the text is enumerated by counting the number of occurrences of the newline symbol.

Instead of iterating until the terminator is discovered in the input, an infinite loop is established. The loop conveys the fact that an iteration is the major program construct. From within the loop we test for the end of data sentinel, and quit from the loop. The PDL is:

```
initialize the line counter
FOREVER DO
 read the next data character
 IF the terminator symbol
 THEN
  quit the loop
 ENDIF

 IF a newline symbol
 THEN
  increment the line counter
 ENDIF
ENDFOREVER
print the result
```

resulting in the program:

PROGRAM 6.19

```
//
// Input a stream of characters from the standard
//     input and count the number of lines of text by
//     enumerating the number of newline symbols. The
//     text is terminated by a period symbol.
//

#include <iostream.h>

int main()
{
  const char      PERIOD = '.';
  const char      NEWLINE = '\n';
  const int       TRUE = 1;

  int             lines = 0;                        // line count
  char            c;                             // data character

  while(TRUE) {
    cin.get(c);
    if(c == PERIOD)
      break;
    if(c == NEWLINE)
      lines++;
  }

  cout << "Number of lines is " << lines << "\n";
```

```
  return (0);
}
```

The break statement can also reduce the complexity of the expression governing repetition of a loop. A simple description of the normal termination of the loop is handled by the loop test itself. The abnormal termination of the loop is the responsibility of a break statement within the loop. Program 6.20(a) illustrates this use for the break statement. The program reads and forms the sum of 100 floating point data values. If at any time a negative floating point value is encountered in the data, the summation terminates. Firstly, the PDL:

```
initialize the running total
FOR 100 times DO
 read the next data value
 IF a negative data item
 THEN
  quit the loop
 ENDIF
 add the data value to the running total
ENDFOR
print the result
```

PROGRAM 6.20(a)

```
//
//  Read and form the sum of at most 100 positive
//      floating point numbers. If at any time a
//      negative value is encountered in the input
//      terminate with the sum thus formed.
//

#include <iostream.h>

int main()
{
  const int        MAX = 100;

  float    data, sum = 0.0;                  // data, running total

  for(int k = 1; k <= MAX; k++){
    cin >> data;
    if(data < 0.0)
      break;
    sum += data;
  }

  cout << "Sum is " << sum << "\n";
  return (0);
}
```

Consider the above solution against the following version, Program 6.20(b). This second attempt is more complex and harder to understand since we have combined the tests for normal and abnormal loop termination. The increased complexity also lessens the likelihood that the program is correct.

PROGRAM 6.20(b)

```
//
// Read and form the sum of at most 100 positive
//     floating point numbers. If at any time a
//     negative value is encountered in the input
//     terminate with the sum thus formed.
//

#include <iostream.h>

int main()
{
  const int       MAX = 100;
  const int       FALSE = 0;
  const int       TRUE = 1;

  float    data, sum = 0.0;                  // data, running total
  int      abort = FALSE;                    // abnormal termination

  for(int k = 1; k <= MAX && !abort; k++){
    cin >> data;
    if(data < 0.0)
      abort = TRUE;
    else
      sum += data;
  }

  cout << "Sum is " << sum << "\n";
  return (0);
}
```

6.11 The continue statement

The *continue statement* complements the break statement. Its use is restricted to while, for and do loops. When a continue statement is executed, control is immediately passed to the test condition of the nearest enclosing loop. All subsequent statements in the body of the loop are ignored for that particular loop iteration. The continue statement, like the break statement, is normally used in conjunction with an if statement. The syntax of the continue statement is simply:

```
continue;
```

The following short program demonstrates an application of the continue statement. The program reads ten floating point numbers, summing only the positive values. Negative data values are ignored by skipping the processing actions of the loop. Firstly, the PDL:

```
initialize the running total
FOR 10 times DO
  read the next data value
  IF a negative data item
  THEN
   skip the loop
  ENDIF
  add data value to running total
ENDFOR
```

Then the program:

PROGRAM 6.21

```
//
//  Input 10 floating point values, summing only
//      those values which are positive.
//

#include <iostream.h>

int main()
{
  const int       MAX = 100;

  float    data, sum = 0.0;              // data, running total

  for(int k = 0; k < MAX; k++){
    cin >> data;
    if(data < 0.0)
      continue;
    sum += data;
  }

  cout << "Sum of positive values is " << sum << "\n";
  return (0);
}
```

6.12 Summary

1. The three principal program control structures are *sequence*, *selection* and *iteration*. The while, do and for statements provide the loop mechanism in C++; selection is provided by the if and switch statements.

2. Logical expressions have an `int` value of `0` or `1`, in which `0` represents logical *false* and `1` represents logical *true*. Further, any non-zero value is interpreted as logical true when evaluating a logical expression. Logical expressions are constructed from the relational operators (`<`, `<=`, etc.) and the logical operators (`&&`, `||`, `!`), as well as the usual arithmetic operators.

3. The *while statement* is the fundamental loop construct in C++. Since the control expression is tested prior to execution of each iteration, the statement(s) under control of the while may be executed zero or more times.

4. The *for statement* is semantically equivalent to the while statement, providing an abbreviated version of the latter. A for loop, therefore, executes zero or more times.

5. The *do statement's* control expression is computed following execution of the statement body. A do loop is therefore guaranteed to be obeyed one or more times.

6. The *if statement* provides a means of choosing whether or not to execute a statement. The if–else statement decides which of two statements to execute. In nested if statements, the compiler always associates an else part with the nearest unresolved preceding if.

7. The *switch statement* is a multiple-alternative control statement. It compares an integer expression against many possible values selected from *case labels*.

8. The *break statement* is used to alter flow of control inside loops and switch statements. The break statement when used with a loop (while, for and do), causes immediate termination of the innermost enclosing loop. When used with a switch statement, the break causes immediate exit from the enclosing switch clause.

9. The *continue statement* is used solely with while, for and do statements, and an execution causes control to pass immediately to the nearest enclosing loop's conditional expression for re-evaluation.

6.13 Exercises

1. Give equivalent logical expressions without using the negation operator:

```
!(a > b)                 !(a <= b + 3)
!(a + 1 == b + 1)        !(a > 2 || b < 5)
!(a < b && c < d)
```

2. In the context of the following initialized declarations:

```
char c = 'X';
int  h = 2, i = -3, j = 7, k = -19;
```

Complete the following table:

Expression	*Equivalent expression*	*Value*
`h && i && j`	`(h && i) && j`	`1 (true)`
`h && i || j`		
`h || i && j`		
`h || i && j || k`		
`!h && !j`		
`!h + !j`		
`h > j`		
`h <= j`		
`(j < k) || h`		
`j < (k || h)`		

3. **What is the difference between the two operators = and == ?**

4. **Is the following statement correct? If not, why?**

```
if (q >= r)
     cout << "q is greater than or equal to r";
     a = b;
else
     cout << "r is less than q";
     x = y;
```

5. **We have already explained that:**

```
while(1){
  .....
}
```

is an infinite loop. What happens when the following program is executed? If you are unsure, try it.

```
#include <iostream.h>
int main()
{
  while(-22.55){
   cout << "run forever, perhaps?";
  }
  return (0);
}
```

6. **What happens when you run the following program on your system? If it does not run as expected, change it so that it does.**

```
#include <iostream.h>
int main()
{
  float x, total = 0.0;

  for(x = 0.0; x != 0.9; x += 0.1){    // bad test
```

```
    total += x;
    cout << "x= " << x
         << ", running total= " << total << "\n";
   }
   return (0);
}
```

7. Input three positive integers representing the sides of a triangle, and determine whether they form a valid triangle. (*Hint:* In a triangle, the sum of any two sides must always be greater than the third side.)

8. Write a program which computes the sum of the first ten integers. Modify the program to compute the sum of the first N integers, where N is given as a data value.

9. Prepare a function `quotient` which finds the quotient of two positive integers using only the operations of addition and subtraction:

```
int quotient(int numerator, int denominator)
```

Employ this function in a program which inputs two integers and outputs their quotient.

10. Prepare a function called `power` which computes `a` to the power `b` for two non-negative integer values `a` and `b`, using repeated multiplication:

```
long int power(int a, int b)
```

Then write a program to tabulate x, x^2, and x^3 for `x = 1, 2, ..... ,10`.

11. Write a program that reads a single positive integer data value and extracts each digit from the integer and displays it as a word. For example, the input value `932` should display:

```
932: nine three two
```

12. Write a program that reads a number, then reads a single digit and determines how many times the digit occurs in the number.

13. Data to a program consists of a sequence of characters of unknown length. The data set is terminated with a unique period symbol. Write a program which counts the number of lines, the number of words and the number of characters in the input. Each input line is terminated by the newline symbol. A word is any sequence of characters that does not contain a blank, tab or newline symbol. The terminating period is not included in any count.

14. Using the data of Question 13, write a program which prints the words in the input one per line.

15. A prime number is one that is divisible only by 1 and by itself. Write a program to input a series of numbers and determine whether they are prime or not. Perhaps the simplest way to determine if a number is prime is to test whether the number is divisible by any value from 2 to one less than the number. The process can be shortened appreciably by performing the test from 2 to some lesser value than that given. How is this value obtained? Use it in your solution.

16. Write a program to display a multiplication table with the format shown below. The range of the table is given as program input.

```
X 1 2  3  4
-----------
1 1 2  3  4
2 2 4  6  8
3 3 6  9 12
4 4 8 12 16
```

17. Write a program to operate on the data of question 13 and to compress repeated characters. The program copies its input to its output, replacing strings of repeating character sequences by `[nX]`, where n is an integer count of the number of repetitions, and `X` is the character. Restrict the input not to include the characters `[`, `]` or digit. For example, the input:

```
ABCCCDEEFFFFG.
```

produces the output:

```
AB[3C]D[2E][4F]G.
```

Prepare a second program to expand the compressed text. Using the output of the first program, this second program should recreate the original input.

18. Input to a program is the monthly sales figures for a sales team. For each salesman, show his identification number, total sales, value of sales, profit (total sales – value of sales), and commission (= 10 per cent of profit). The output to have the format:

NUMBER	TOTAL SALES(A)	VALUE(B)	PROFIT (A-B)	COMMISSION 10%(A-B)
1234	234.56	174.56	60.00	6.00
|	|	|	|	|
|	|	|	|	|
XXXX	XXX.XX	XXX.XX	XXX.XX	XX.XX
TOTALS	XXXX.XX	XXXX.XX	XXXX.XX	XXX.XX

19. Write a program which accepts a time expressed in hours, minutes and seconds and verbalizes that time as suggested by the following outputs:

```
09:10:00       ten past nine
10:45:00       quarter to eleven
11:15:00       quarter past eleven
17:30:00       half past five
19:50:00       ten to eight
06:12:29       just after ten past six
06:12:30       just before quarter past six
00:17:29       just after quarter past midnight
```

7

Program Files

The unit of compilation in C++ is the file. To date all C++ programs have consisted of a single program file. In this chapter we shall describe how a single program can be spread across a number of C++ program files and how they are compiled and linked together to form the executable program. As a consequence of this program structuring we must investigate how separately compiled functions call each other, how they share data, and how declarations used in different program files are kept consistent.

7.1 Types, storage class and scope

An identifier references the region of memory used to hold the object's value (or set of values, see Chapters 8 and 9). In addition to its name, each object has type, storage class and scope attributes. The *type* information determines the correct amount of storage required by the object, how the binary pattern representing the value is interpreted when the object is accessed, and is used by the compiler to perform type checking.

Storage class determines the *duration* or lifetime of the object during execution of the program. The storage class for an object is determined by the position of the declaration in the program source code, by the nature of the declaration, or by a combination of these two forms. For example, we know from Chapter 5 that variables declared in a function block have storage class *auto* and only exist while the function is being executed.

In all, there are three kinds of duration: local duration, static duration, and dynamic duration (see Chapter 12). Local duration objects, also known as automatic objects, have a transient existence. They are allocated storage space when a function block (or enclosing block, see later) is entered, and are deallocated when the program exits that block.

At the start of a program storage space is allocated to static objects. That space remains intact until the conclusion of the program. If the associated variable definitions are in scope for a number of functions, then their values can be accessed by these functions.

Scope and storage class can be combined in a number of ways. For example, variables can be specified with local scope and static duration. Such variables can only be referenced in the block in which they are declared, yet retain their values across exit and re-entry of the block. Equally, functions can be statically scoped to limit their visibility.

In this chapter we shall investigate the implications for these attributes and their combinations.

7.2 Local duration

Function definitions in C++ may not be nested. In a function block the only permissible definitions introduce data items. Variables defined in the body of a function have storage class auto (automatic). Arguments to functions are processed in a similar manner.

A variable defined in a function block is said to have *local scope*. Such a variable may be referenced in program statements from the point of definition in the function to the end of that block. In the function shown below, the variable `temp` has the storage class auto (as do the formal arguments `a` and `b`). The scope of the variable `temp` is the body of the function and cannot be accessed outside of this function.

```
void order(int& a, int& b)
    // arrange a, b into ascending order
{
   int temp;

   if(a > b){
      temp = a;
      a    = b;
      b    = temp;
   }
}
```

The declaration for variable `temp` explicitly specifies the type `int` and implicitly specifies the storage class auto. It is permissible to include the storage class explicitly with the reservered keyword `auto`, as in:

```
auto int temp;
```

though in practice it is usually omitted.

A function body is a *compound statement*, also called a *block*. A compound statement consists of a possibly empty sequence of declarations and statements, all enclosed in braces:

```
{
  definition-.....-and-statement-sequence
}
```

Additionally, a compound statement may appear as a replacement for any single statement. When the compound statement has no declarations, it simply represents a group of statements. In the function `order`, a statement group is used with the `if` statement:

```
if(a > b){
  temp = a;          // compound statement
  a    = b;
  b    = temp;
}
```

When the compound statement includes declarations, it brings into existence a new scope. Recognizing that the variable `temp` is only required within the `if` statement, the function may be rewritten:

```
void order(int& a, int& b)
     // arrange a, b into ascending order
{
   if(a > b){
     const int temp = a;
     a = b;
     b = temp;
   }
}
```

The scope of the variable `temp` is reduced to the inner compound statement which is part of the `if` statement. Any reference to the variable `temp` outside this compound statement is illegal, even within the remainder of the function itself.

Compound statements that are nested may include definitions for identifiers with names the same as those in surrounding blocks. This introduces the concept of *visibility*. In the assignment:

```
b = temp;
```

appearing in the function `order` immediately above, the use of the identifier `temp` is bound to the definition:

```
const int temp = a;
```

in the compound statement in which they both appear. The definition for this identifier is said to be visible since the use of the identifier is associated with that definition.

A definition for an identifier can become temporarily invisible when the definition for an identifier with the same name appears in an enclosing inner compound statement. For example, in Program 7.1 the definition for the integer variable `sum` is hidden by the definition of `sum` as a floating point variable in the inner block. This loss of visibility is temporary. The integer variable `sum` reappears when the inner block terminates.

PROGRAM 7.1

```
//
//  A program to demonstrate the concepts of scope
//      and visibility. Variables in an inner block with
//      the same name as those on an outer block
//      temporarily make invisible those outside the
//      block.
//

#include <iostream.h>

int main()
{
  int sum = 10;                    // sum at the top level

  {                                // inner block
    float sum = 3.1416;           // outer sum hidden
    cout << "Inner sum (float): " <<  sum << "\n";
  }

  cout << "Outer sum (int): " << sum << "\n";
  return (0);
}
```

The output from this program is:

```
Inner sum (float): 3.1416
Outer sum (int): 10
```

The definition of an automatic variable may also be accompanied by an initializer. The initializer is any expression which specifies the initial value a variable may have at the beginning of its lifetime. An automatic variable comes into existence when its definition is encountered in the block in which it is defined. The initial expression may employ any item having a valid run-time value at the point of entry to the block. The following program illustrates these ideas.

PROGRAM 7.2

```
//
//  Initialization of local variables by any known
//      run-time expression.
//

#include <iostream.h>
#include <iomanip.h>

int main ()
{
  void square(int);     // prototype declaration

  square(1);
```

```
    square(2);
    square(3);
    square(4);
    return (0);
}

void square(int d)
{
    int dsquared = d * d;    // initialized expression

    cout << d << " squared is " << setw(3) << dsquared << "\n";
}
```

The automatic variable dsquared defined in the body of the function square, and local to it, has a perfectly valid initializer. The initializer is based on the formal argument d. When the function is executed an actual value for the argument will be available to initialize dsquared. The initialization takes place each time the automatic variable is established; that is, each time the function square is invoked. At each call a different actual argument value is provided and a different initial value computed. The program output is thus:

```
1 squared is   1
2 squared is   4
3 squared is   9
4 squared is  16
```

C++ allows the programmer to define variables anywhere in the scope. This permits one to define a variable immediately before it is used. This is especially important when we define and initialize a variable. For example, the following fragment repeats Program 5.4 with the variable time defined where required.

```
int main()
{
    int hours, minutes, seconds;
    cout << ..... ;
    cin >> ..... ;
    long time = (60L * hours + minutes) * 60L + seconds;
    cout << ..... ;
    // .....
}
```

7.3 Static duration

In the programs that we have developed, it has been assumed that all the program source code resides in a single file. C++ supports the concept of modular programming in that it does not require that all of the code for a program be contained in a single source file. These separate modules equate to the idea of a program file or *program unit*.

To allow one function in one program unit to call another function in a second program unit, an *external referencing declaration* is required. The declaration informs the compiler that a function is to be called separately from its definition, that the function has a particular signature and return type, and that the function's definition is in another program unit. These declarations are simply the prototype declarations of Chapter 5.

Consider an application constructed from two program units `main.cpp` and `time.cpp`. The program determines the difference between two measures of time both expressed as a 24-hour clock time.

The `main` function resides in the program unit `main.cpp`. The problem solution is expressed in terms of the subordinate functions `hms_to_time` and `time_to_hms`. Both these complementary functions are contained in the second program unit. Function `hms_to_time` converts a 24-hour clock time into its equivalent number of seconds. Function `time_to_hms` performs the inverse operation. We represent compileable program units as rectangular figures, annotated with the resources of the unit. Any invisible features remain fully enclosed within the figure. The *exportable resources* are shown in windows, accessible beyond the module. Using this notation, the second program unit is shown by Figure 7.1.

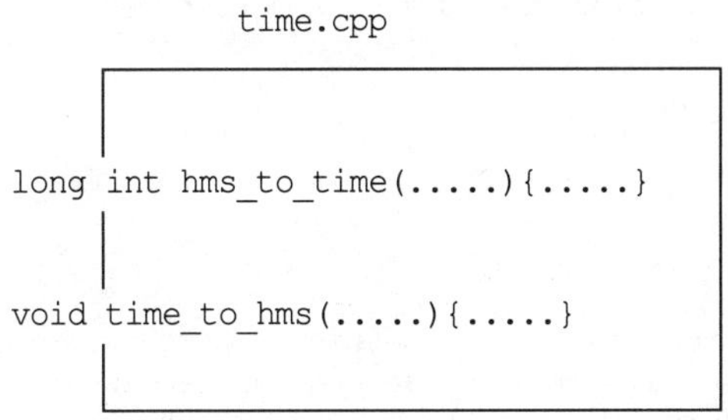

```
                 time.cpp
        ┌──────────────────────────┐
        │                          │
long int hms_to_time(.....){.....} │
        │                          │
void time_to_hms(.....){.....}     │
        │                          │
        └──────────────────────────┘
```

Figure 7.1

Both these functions are exported from this module and imported into the client program unit `main.cpp`. The latter thus contains two external referencing declarations for these subordinate functions. The coding for these two program units is then:

PROGRAM 7.3

```
//
//  File: main.cpp
//
```

```
// Determine the difference between two 24-hour
//     clock times. The input data and the result
//     are all expressed in the same 24-hour format.
//

#include <iostream.h>
#include <stdlib.h>       // prototype for labs

int main()
{
  int      hours1, minutes1, seconds1;   // 1st time
  int      hours2, minutes2, seconds2;   // 2nd time
  int      hours, minutes, seconds;      // result
  long int time1, time2;                 // conversions

                // external prototype declarations
  long int hms_to_time(int, int, int);
  void time_to_hms(long int, int&, int&, int&);

  cin >> hours1 >> minutes1 >> seconds1;
  cin >> hours2 >> minutes2 >> seconds2;

  time1 = hms_to_time(hours1, minutes1, seconds1);
  time2 = hms_to_time(hours2, minutes2, seconds2);

  time_to_hms(labs(time1-time2), hours, minutes, seconds);
  cout << "The difference is " << hours << " "
       << minutes << " " <<  seconds << "\n";
  return (0);
}


//
// File: time.cpp
//
// Two functions to convert between a time measured
//     in a total number of seconds and a time expressed
//     in hours, minutes and seconds. Each function is
//     the complement of the other.
//

const int SECS_IN_MIN    = 60L;
const int MINS_IN_HOUR   = 60L;

void time_to_hms(long int t, int& h, int& m, int& s)
{
  const int mins = t / SECS_IN_MIN;

  s = t % SECS_IN_MIN;
  m = mins % MINS_IN_HOUR;
  h = mins / MINS_IN_HOUR;
}

long int hms_to_time(int h, int m, int s)
{
  return ((h * MINS_IN_HOUR + m) * SECS_IN_MIN + s);
}
```

Further, the C++ programmer who is the author of the program unit `time.cpp` minimizes the burden on the client by providing a header file containing all the necessary external declarations. We extend our notation by showing both the program unit and its associated header file with Figure 7.2. The actual content of this header file would contain:

```
//
// File: time.h
//
// Header file providing the specification of the
//      two time conversion functions.
//

long int hms_to_time(int, int, int);
void time_to_hms(long int, int&, int&, int&);
```

The two external referencing declarations in the application program unit (`main.cpp`) can then be replaced by a preprocessor `#include` statement:

```
#include "time.h"
```

The C++ programming language also supports variables with static duration. Such variables are introduced by defining them outside function blocks. Since they are defined in a program unit at the same level as functions they are said to have *file scope*. File scope identifiers, also known as *globals* have the point of declaration to the end of the program source file as their scope. Any function definition following the point of declaration for a global variable may access that variable by simply referring to its name.

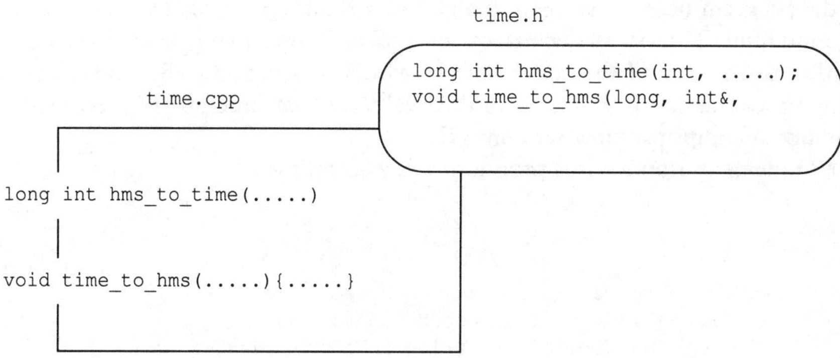

Figure 7.2

We present these ideas by introducing a program unit for pseudo random number generation. The functions in the unit produce an apparently random sequence of integer values. A very simple generator is employed so that we may concentrate on program construction. The sequence begins with an initial value provided as an argument to the function `set_random`. Successive values of the sequence are produced by the integer function `random`. Each new value is computed from the previous value, which must, therefore, exist across successive calls of function `random`. If two functions share data or one function is repeatedly called and uses the previous value of some variable, then that variable must have static duration. The program unit `random.cpp` has the signature shown in Figure 7.3.

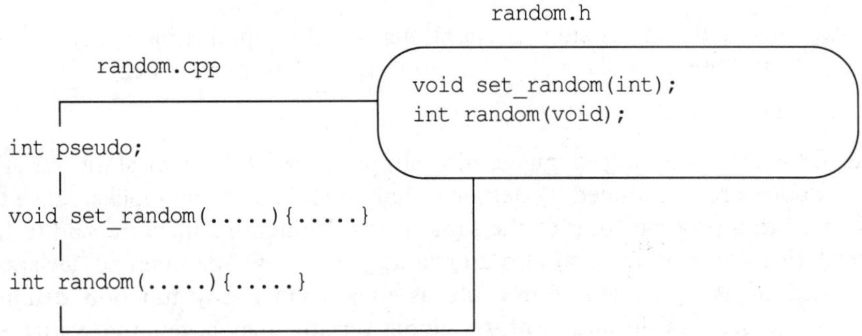

Figure 7.3

In the program unit `random.cpp`, the global variable `pseudo` can be referenced by both functions. This is as a consequence of its scope being from the point of definition to the end of the source file in which it is introduced. Thus, function `set_random` can assign to `pseudo` an initial value, whilst function `random` can use it repeatedly to compute a new random value.

The implementation for this program unit is as follows:

```
//
// File:          random
//
// Package of pseudo random number generating
//      code. Each random is generated from the
//      previous. The initial value is established
//      by the function set_random.
//

const int MULTIPLIER        = 97;
const int MODULUS           = 256;
const int INCREMENT         = 59;
```

```
int pseudo;             // permanent

void set_random(int seed)
{
  pseudo = seed;
}

int random(void)
{
  pseudo = (MULTIPLIER * pseudo + INCREMENT) % MODULUS;
  return (pseudo);
}
```

The associated header file for this program unit is given below. It is incorporated into an application program using an `#include` preprocessor statement, and provides the necessary external referencing declarations.

```
//
// File:          random.h
//
// Specification of the exportable items from
//     the random number package.
//

void set_random(int);
int  random(void);
```

We now complete our application program. A program simulates 100 throws of a die, counting the occurrences of the individual face values.

PROGRAM 7.4

```
//
// Tabulate the number of occurrences of each
//     of the six sides of a die which is thrown
//     100 times.
//

#include <iostream.h>
#include "random.h"

const int SIDES          = 6;
const int SEED           = 17;
const int THROWS  = 100;

int main()
{
  int      one = 0,        two = 0,three = 0,
           four = 0,       five = 0,       six = 0;

  set_random(SEED);

  for(int dicethrow = 1; dicethrow <= THROWS; dicethrow++){
    const int face = random() % SIDES + 1;      // 1 to 6 inclusive
```

```
        switch(face){
          case 1 : one++;     break;
          case 2 : two++;     break;
          case 3 : three++;   break;
          case 4 : four++;    break;
          case 5 : five++;    break;
          case 6 : six++;     break;
        }
      }
      cout << "Distribution of die face:\n";
      cout << one << ", " << two << ", " << three << ", "
           << four << ", " << five << ", " << six << "\n";
      return (0);
    }
```

Note how the header file `random.h` is included at the topmost level. This means that these external references have global scope and can be referenced in any function in the program unit containing their declarations. Hence a function subordinate to `main` and appearing in the same file may also use any of the randomizing functions.

The C++ compiler guarantees to initialize all global data objects to the value zero when no explicit initializer is present. It is generally considered good programming practice, however, to show all initializations explicitly. To avoid any errors caused by the application programmer failing to initialize the random sequence, variable `pseudo` is explicitly initialized to `1` (see Figure 7.4).

The visibility of a global variable may be temporarily obscured by the declaration for an automatic variable within a function having the same name as the external variable. For example, consider Program 7.5.

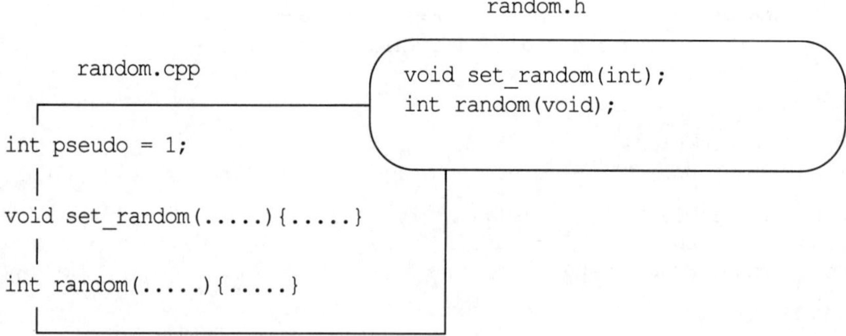

Figure 7.4

PROGRAM 7.5

```
//
// The visibility of external variables may be
//      temporarily obscured by the declaration for an
//      automatic variable in a function. Variable
//      sum in the program exhibits this feature.
//

#include <iostream.h>

int sum;                        // defining declaration .....
                                // ..... for external variable

int main()
{
  void subroutine(void);        // prototype declaration

  sum = 15;                     // the external variable
  subroutine();                 // call the function
  cout << "External sum is " << sum << "\n";
  return (0);
}

void subroutine(void)
{
  float sum = 1.234;            // auto, shields external

  cout << "Local sum is " << sum << "\n";
}
```

The variable `sum` assigned the value `15` in the `main` function binds to the definition for the external variable of type integer. However, within the function `subroutine` the variable `sum` appearing in the output statement associates with the definition for the local of type `float`. Thus the output from the program is:

```
Local sum is 1.234
External sum is 15
```

In Chapter 9 we will introduce a syntax which permits a block to refer to a global variable which is otherwise invisible because of the presence of a local variable bearing the same name.

External variables are initialized at compile time. The initialization is performed once. The initial value may be any constant expression:

```
int sum = 0;
long int memory = 64 * 1024;
char ampersand = '&';
```

7.4 Storage class static

We know that variables may be defined either within a function body or outside the body of a function. We refer to the former as local variables and to the latter as global variables. *Static* variables offer a new class of storage management. *Static* variables may be either local or global.

Local static variables are restricted to the particular block in which they are declared, that is, they have local scope. Unlike automatic variables, static variables remain in existence, they do not come and go each time a block is entered and they retain their values between exit and entry to the block.

Local static variables, like globals, may be initialized with a constant expression. A local static variable is initialized once at the start of program execution. Thereafter, the value of a static variable when leaving a block is the same when the block is next entered. This is demonstrated by the following program.

PROGRAM 7.6

```
//
// Local static variables are initialized once
//      at compile time. Local variables, on the other
//      hand, are initialized each time the function
//      is entered.
//

#include <iostream.h>

int main()
{
  void subroutine(void);       // prototype declaration

  subroutine();
  subroutine();
  subroutine();
  subroutine();
  subroutine();
  return (0);
}

void subroutine(void)
{
  static int static_var = 0;     // performed once
  int        auto_var   = 0;     // for every function call

  cout << "automatic = " << auto_var
       << ", static = " << static_var << "\n";

  auto_var++;                    // redundant operation
  static_var++;                  // carried forward
}
```

The function subroutine contains definitions for two local variables. The variable auto_var is an automatic of type int. The variable is initialized to zero at each function invocation. The increment performed on this variable is lost on function termination. On the other hand, the initialization of the local static variable static_var is performed once at program invocation but the increment is executed on each function call. As a consequence, the output from the program is:

```
automatic = 0, static = 0
automatic = 0, static = 1
automatic = 0, static = 2
automatic = 0, static = 3
automatic = 0, static = 4
```

Storage class static may also be applied to global variables. A global static object may be referenced by any function statement in the same program unit following the point of definition. They may not, however, be accessed from any other program unit.

In the program unit random.cpp introduced in the previous section, the global variable pseudo is used to hold successive values of the sequence of random numbers. The associated header file random.h provides the application program unit with the external references to the two exportable functions. There is nothing, however, to stop the application program from also including an external reference to the variable pseudo. If the application program contains the declaration:

```
extern int pseudo;
```

then this variable may now be referenced in the application program. In particular, it is capable of being erroneously assigned. The effect would be, of course, to corrupt the sequence of pseudo random numbers.

By giving this variable storage class static, it will be global to the functions in the program unit in which it is defined, but not exportable to other program units. Controlled access to this variable is then provided by the exportable functions. Figure 7.5 illustrates how the program unit now reads.

The application's programmer cannot now misuse the variable pseudo. Further, a link error would occur if the client program unit contained an explicit external referencing declaration to variable pseudo. The identifier pseudo may, however, be used in some other different context, for example, as a local or global variable in program unit main.cpp. It is not confused with the private variable with the same name in program unit random.cpp.

The storage class static can also be applied to functions. Static functions are known only within the source file in which they are defined. The concept of privacy equally well applies to functions as well as to static variables. Functions are exportable to other program units, whereas static functions are not. This way the programmer of a module may select which functions in the module are to be accessible in other program units. Static functions can be considered as the building blocks of a module from which higher level functions are constructed.

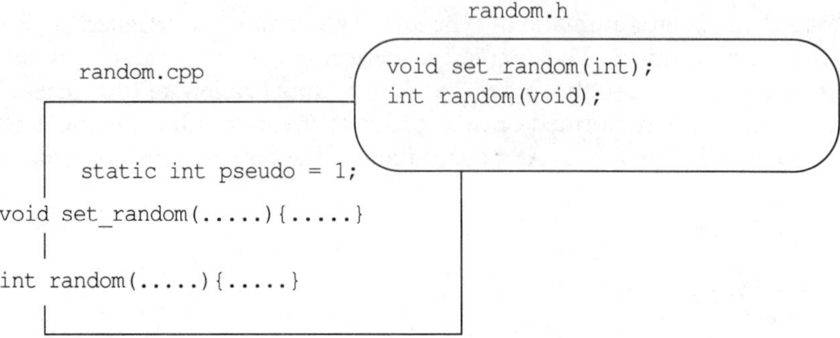

Figure 7.5

These higher level functions are exported to the application program, whilst the lower level static functions remain concealed.

Static globals and static functions support the concept of *information hiding*. The aim of information hiding is to make inaccessible those details which do not concern other parts of the programming system. Information hiding makes programs more secure. Hidden information may not be corrupted by a program unit which is not supposed to have access to that information.

The resulting program portrayed in Figure 7.5 gives rise to the notion of an *abstract data type*. An abstract data type is characterized by its behaviour and not by its representation. In some measure the fundamental data types are abstractions. For example, we have not considered the implementation of floating point types but are aware of the operations we are permitted to apply to instances of such objects. Equally, the program unit `random.cpp` and its associated header file `random.h` give an abstraction for a random number data type. The representation is hidden (using static storage on variable `pseudo`), while the operations upon a random number are specified by the external function declarations in the header file.

Data abstraction is a significant approach to program development. The C++ programming language provides specific language constructs in support of this development style, and is the subject of Chapter 9.

7.5 The C++ pre-processor

The C++ pre-processor is a simple *macro processor* that conceptually processes the source text of a C++ program immediately before the compilation process. In some implementations, the pre-processor is actually a separate program which reads the program source file and produces a new intermediate file that is then used as input to the compiler proper. In other implementations a single program supports both the pre-processing and compiling phases, with no intermediate file produced.

The capabilities of the pre-processor are the same as those for the C programming language [Bar90, Ker88]. However, a number of language constructs in C++ have made redundant some aspects of the pre-processor. For example, the `const` qualifier has all but made the use of the `#define` (see next section) unnecessary. For this reason we shall only concern ourselves with those pre-processor features we require in our C++ programs.

The pre-processor is controlled by pre-processor *command lines* or *directives*, which are lines in the source program text beginning with the character `'#'`. The pre-processor removes all directives from the source file, and makes any necessary transformations to the source, as directed by these commands. The resultant text is then processed by the compiler.

The pre-processor operates on a line-at-a-time basis. The syntax of these pre-processor lines is independent of the other parts of the C++ language. The pre-processor also operates independent of the scope rules of C++. Pre-processor directives like `#define` remain in effect until the end of the program (translation) unit.

Pre-processor commands are program lines that start with a `'#'` symbol optionally preceded by whitespace characters. The `'#'` is followed by an identifier that is the *command name*. For example, `#define` is the command that defines a macro. Whitespace is also permitted between the `'#'` and the command name.

7.6 Macro definitions

A *macro definition* (or simply a *macro*) is an identifier that symbolizes a defined string composed of one or more tokens. The pre-processor statement that establishes this association is the `#define` statement. The pre-processor then guarantees to textually replace occurrences of that identifier appearing in the remainder of the program file with the *token string*. The token string is frequently referred to as the *body* of the macro.

The string of tokens is not a string as defined in Section 3.4, but rather a character sequence terminated by a newline symbol. This character sequence without the newline symbol is the macro body.

There are two different forms for the `#define` statement; one for use in simple string replacement, and the second to perform string replacement with argument passing. A number of macro definitions include the examples:

```
#define BYTESIZE    8
#define WORDSIZE    (BYTESIZE + BYTESIZE)
#define SQUARE(X)   ((X) * (X))
#define DEBUG
```

The first two forms define the macros `BYTESIZE` and `WORDSIZE`, and associate them with the token strings `8` and `(BYTESIZE + BYTESIZE)` respectively. Any subsequent occurrence of these macros is replaced by the pre-processor with the corresponding token strings. For example, the macro `WORDSIZE` is first replaced with `(BYTESIZE + BYTESIZE)` which, in turn, is replaced with `(8 + 8)`. However, both these forms are supported by the use of named constants. We could have achieved the same with:

```
const int BYTESIZE     = 8;
const int WORDSIZE     = (BYTESIZE + BYTESIZE);
```

Further, named constants offer additional features including compiler type checking and program names which remain visible to symbolic debugger tools which is otherwise lost when pre-processed out of the program.

The third macro definition above is notionally equivalent to an inline function (see also template functions in Chapter 5). For example, assuming `X` is an integer argument we may write:

```
inline int SQUARE(int X)
{ return X * X; }
```

The inline function is a much safer alternative. For example, the macro `SQUARE` invoked in the expression:

```
SQUARE(y++)
```

evaluates to:

```
(y++)  *  (y++)
```

whose value is system dependent. In contrast, the inline function respects pass by value semantics and delivers the desired value.

The final macro definition introduces `DEBUG` but does not associate with it any token string. This type of macro definition is the only one we retain from C and combine its use with the conditional compilation facility of the pre-processor (see Section 7.8).

7.7 File inclusion

The `#include` pre-processor statement causes the content of a named text file to be processed as if it had appeared in place of the `#include` command. There are three forms of the command:

```
#include "filename"
#include <filename>
```

and

```
#include token-sequence
```

The first two forms differ in how the specified file is located in the computer's file store. If the filename is surrounded by double quotes then the file is expected in the same directory as the file containing the `#include` command. Generally, this form is used to refer to other files written by the user. If the filename is delimited by diamond brackets < and >, the search for the file takes place in certain standard places. On Unix systems, the files are expected in the directory `/usr/include`. This form is generally used to reference standard system files. In all our programs which perform input/output we have included the standard header `<iostream.h>`.

The final variant is a form of *computed include*. The token sequence is interpreted and expanded by the pre-processor in the normal way. The result then must be one of the two original forms and is processed as described above.

An included file may itself contain other `#include` commands. Nested `#includes` are therefore supported. The depth of nesting is implementation dependent. Nesting to at least five or six levels is not uncommon.

7.8 Conditional compilation

The C++ pre-processor supports a facility known as *conditional compilation.* Conditional compilation features in a number of common programming tasks. It is used to enhance program portability by establishing definitions which are themselves the subject of other definitions. Conditional compilation can also be used to selectively incorporate or omit a series of statements in a program. Commonly this is used to activate or deactivate debugging statements.

The statement we use is:

```
#if constant-expression
     lines-1
#else
     lines-2
#endif
```

The series of lines, denoted `lines-1` and `lines-2`, is any number of lines of program text. The lines may be program declarations, program statements or even other pre-processor statements. The `#else` directive and its associated group of lines is optional and may be omitted. Either series of lines may also contain one or more sets of nested conditional compilation commands.

The pre-processor operates by first evaluating at compile time the constant-expression. If the expression evaluates to `0` (logical false), the first group of lines, `lines-1`, are discarded and the second group are passed on for compilation. If the expression evaluates to other than zero (logical true), `lines-1` is passed on and `lines-2` is discarded. The expression must be capable of being determined at compile time. That is, it may involve C++ operators but only with constants (literal or symbolic). No run time values such as a program variables may be used in these expressions.

This facility may be used to turn on and off debugging statements. When developing a program we might incorporate statements to trace a program's behaviour, for example statements to print messages or the values of program variables. During program development these statements are invaluable for detecting programming errors. When the program is fully operational they are no longer required or even desirable and are compiled out of the code. Consider a function to convert a distance in yards, feet and inches to its equivalent distance in inches. The function behaviour is traced by including additional print statements. This is conditionally compiled into the code:

```
#define DEBUG                1

const int YARDS_TO_FEET      = 3;
const int FEET_TO_INCHES     = 12;

int distance (int yards, int feet, int inches)
{
#if DEBUG
    cout << "function distance\n";
    cout << yards << " yards, " << feet << " feet, " << inches << "
inches\n";
#endif
   return((YARDS_TO_FEET*yards+feet)*FEET_TO_INCHES+inches);
}
```

To turn off the tracing we merely have to redefine `DEBUG` to logical false:

```
#define DEBUG        0
```

Usually the whole operation may be controlled at compile time with a C++ compiler option.

The constant expression in `#if` may take the form:

```
defined identifier
```

or

```
defined ( identifier )
```

or:

```
! defined ( identifier)
```

and are replaced by the integer constant `1` if the identifier is defined to the pre-processor, and by `0` otherwise. The identifier need not be associated with a macro body, but simply be known to the pre-processor. Hence the above illustration may also be expressed by:

```
#define DEBUG
    // .....
#if defined(DEBUG)
    // .....
#endif
```

The pre-processor conditional may also include nested `#if` using the `#elif` directive. The full form for an `#if` statement is then:

```
#if constant-expression-1
     lines-1
#elif constant-expression-2
     lines-2
#elif .....
     // .....
#else
     // .....
#endif
```

Semantically, the control lines:

```
#if defined ( identifier )
#if ! defined ( identifier )
```

are equivalent to:

```
#ifdef identifier
```

and

```
#ifndef identifier
```

respectively.

Since the pre-processor supports nested include files, sequential dependencies lead to interminable conflicts during program integration. Each include file should be included only once during compilation, and if the includes are nested unconditionally, this property becomes hard to control. For example, consider a header file `graphics.h` which provides a number of prototype declarations for a range of graphics routines. A number of functions default their `color` argument the values of which are defined in the header `color.h` (see Figure 7.6). Now some application program may include both header files. This might, after all, be reasonable since one gives access to the graphics functions and one provides definitions for the named constants. When compiling the application program, duplicate definitions for the `color` constants would result from including that header file twice (see Figure 7.7).

To avoid multiple inclusion of the same header file we use the conditional compilation facility described above. The content of each include file tests whether some `#define` symbol has already been defined (see Figure 7.8). Compilation of the application proceeds by first pre-processing the program files. The application first includes the header file `color.h`. Since the macro `COLOR` is unknown to the pre-processor the named color constants are included in the program and the macro `COLOR` is defined to the pre-processor. The application program then includes the header file `graphics.h`. Since the macro `GRAPHICS` has not been defined we first define it to the pre-processor then perform an include of `color.h`. This time the macro `COLOR` is known to the pre-processor and we omit introducing the same definitions for the named color constants.

Notice that with this arrangement the second time that we include `color.h` we first have to open this header file to discover that it is not required. Accessing the

graphics.h
#include "color.h"
void clear(void);
void moveTo(int x, int y);
void drawLine(int x, int x, intcolor = BLACK);
// .....
graphics.cp
#include
void
color.h
const int BLACK = 0;
const int WHITE = 64;
// .....

Figure 7.6

demo.cpp
#include "color.h"
#include "graphics.h"
int main()
{
// .....
}

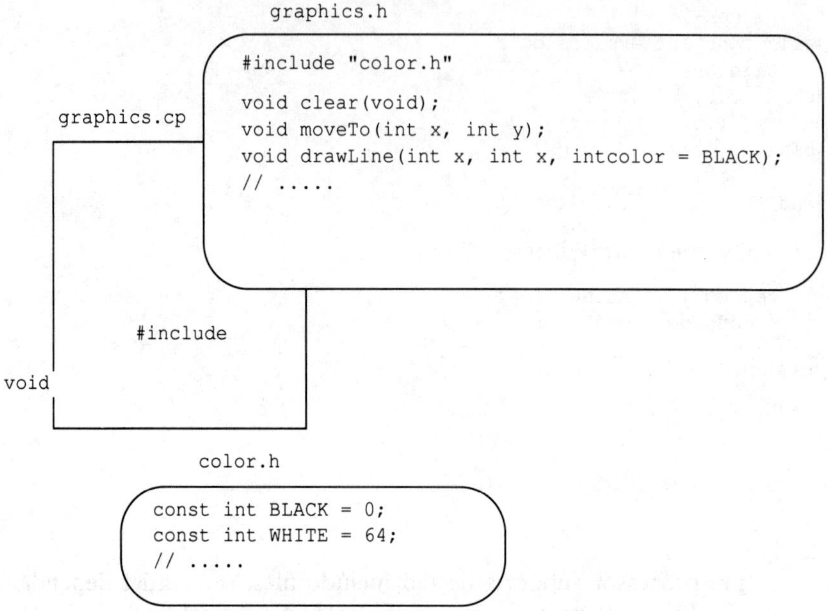

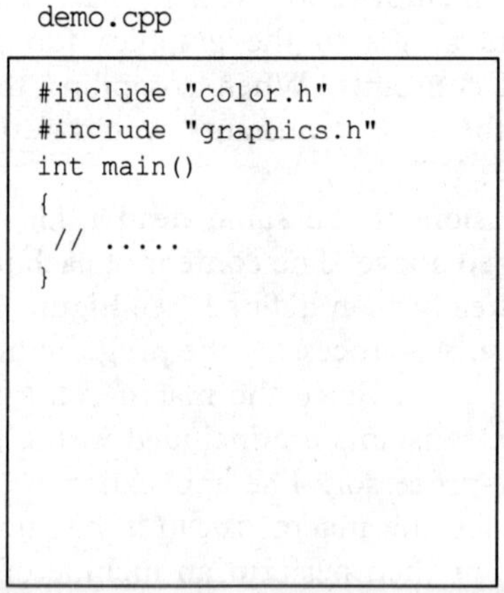

Figure 7.7

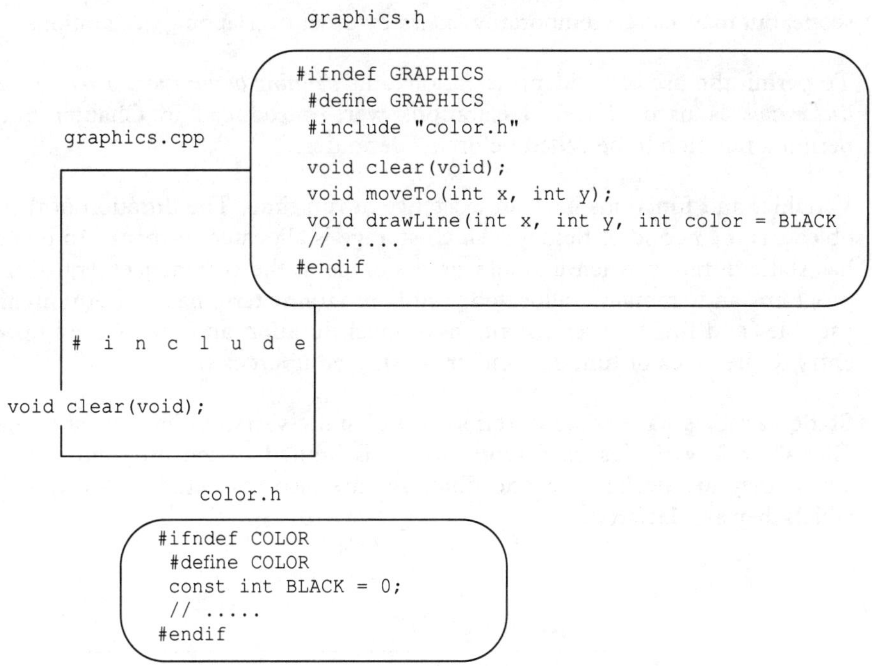

graphics.h

```
#ifndef GRAPHICS
 #define GRAPHICS
 #include "color.h"
 void clear(void);
 void moveTo(int x, int y);
 void drawLine(int x, int y, int color = BLACK
 // .....
#endif
```

graphics.cpp

```
# i n c l u d e

void clear(void);
```

color.h

```
#ifndef COLOR
 #define COLOR
 const int BLACK = 0;
 // .....
#endif
```

Figure 7.8

file store is a relatively slow procedure compared to the rest of the compilation process and we might alternatively arrange the conditional compilation as shown in Figure 7.9. This alternate style of conditional compilation is also required when dealing with mutually recursive class declarations (see Chapter 9).

7.9 Summary

1. Identifiers associate with some C++ object, such as a variable or a function, in a *declaration*. Declarations include both type and storage class. Storage classes may be given implicitly or explicitly in a declaration.

2. Declarations also have *scope* which determines the region of the C++ program over which that declaration is active. An identifier declared in a top-level declaration has a scope that extends from the declaration point to the end of the source program unit. Such objects have external linkage and are described as *global*. Parameter declarations and declarations blocks have storage class `auto`, described as *local*.

3. A declaration is *visible* in some context if the use of the identifier in that context is bound to the declaration. A declaration might be visible throughout its scope, but may also be temporarily *hidden* by other overlapping declarations.

4. To permit the use of an identifier prior to its *defining declaration*, a *referencing declaration* is used. These declarations were introduced in Chapter 5 to permit a function to be called before its definition.

5. Variables and functions have an existence at run time. The duration of these objects is the period of time for which storage is allocated to them. An object has static duration when it is allocated storage at the commencement of the program and remains allocated until program termination. Automatic variables and function arguments have local duration and are created upon entry to the block or function and are destroyed upon exit.

6. Static variables have static duration. Local static variables have local scope. Global static variables have scope which is limited to the program unit in which they are declared. Static functions are also restricted to the unit in which they are declared.

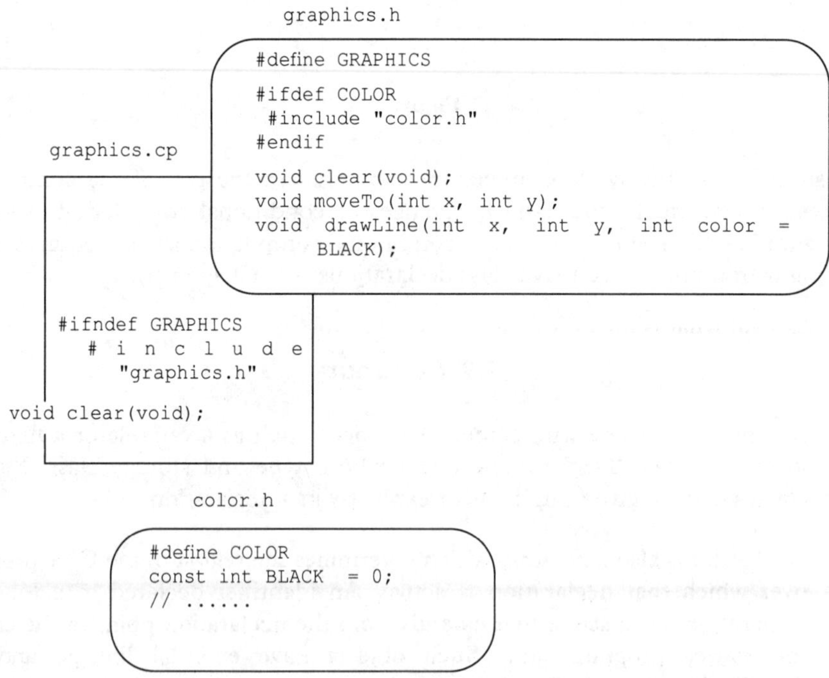

Figure 7.9

7. The declaration of variables may be accompanied by an initializer. Initializers for automatic variables may be arbitrary expressions which are evaluated at run time upon block entry. Variables with static duration can only be initialized with compile time (constant) expressions. Variables with static duration and no explicit initializers are guaranteed to be initialized to zero.

8. The C++ pre-processor is a simple macro processor which conceptually processes the source text of a C++ program prior to compiling. The pre-processor is controlled by command lines, which are lines of the source program beginning with the character `'#'`.

9. The `#define` command introduces a macro definition. A macro is an identifier which symbolizes a token string. The pre-processor replaces occurrences of that identifier with the token string, possibly replacing any formal arguments appearing in the macro body with the actual arguments supplied when the macro is invoked.

10. The `#include` pre-processor command line causes the content of a named file to be processed as if it appeared in place of the command. Two forms of file naming is provided, and differ in how the specified file is located in the computer's file store.

11. Conditional compilation is used to selectively incorporate or omit a series of program statements. The commands used are `#if`, `#ifdef` and `#ifndef`, as well as the associated `#else`, `#elif` and `#endif`. Conditional compilation is used to enhance program portability and to embed debugging statements.

7.10 Exercises

1. Explain what is meant by the following terms:

   (a) abstraction
   (b) program unit
   (c) information hiding
   (d) localization
   (e) exportable
   (f) scope rules
   (g) private
   (h) storage class
   (i) abstract data type

2. Distinguish between defining declarations and referencing declarations.

3. Why would an error occur at link time when the following two files are compiled and linked? Why is there no error at compile time?

```
        file1                       file2
  _________________           ____________________
       .....                        .....
  extern int time;            static int time = 0;
       .....                        .....
```

4. **What output is produced when the following three files are separately compiled then linked and run?**

```
        file1                       file2
  _________________           ____________________

#include <iostream.h>         static int date = 10;
extern int date;
int main()
{
  cout << date << "\n";
  return (0);
}

                file3
         _________________

         int date = 20;
```

5. **A programmer has designed a screen handling program unit, an outline of which is provided below. In the package, a screen is identified as an abstract data type for which a representation and a number of operations are provided.**

```
#include <iostream.h>
static int nrows, ncols;                  // screen dimensions
static int row, col;                      // cursor co-ordinates

static void loadcursor(int ro, int co)    // position cursor
{
   .....
   row = ro;
   col = co;

void home(void)                           // cursor at top left
{
   loadcursor(0, 0);
}

void atsay(int ro, int co, char ch)       // print ch at screen
                                                    position ro, co
{
   loadcursor(ro, co);
   cout.put(ch);
}

// ..... etc.
```

(a) What are the resources in this program unit?
(b) What are the resources that represent the operations on the screen abstraction?
(c) Why do the integer variables `nrows`, `ncols`, `row` and `col` have storage class external static? What was the programmer's reasoning behind this decision?
(d) What are the exportable resources from this unit? What resources are hidden? Provide a suitable interface header file for this package.
(e) Suggest why the function `loadcursor` has storage class static.

6. Rework the problem involving random number generation. The services available for this new version of the data type are initialization (`set_random`), obtain the current random value (`random`), and advance to the next random number in the sequence (`next_random`).

7. Revisit Exercise 11 from Chapter 5 treating a twenty-four hour clock time as an abstract data type. The following services are to be provided on the data type:

```
void set_time(int hours, int minutes, int seconds);
void print_time(void);
long int hms_time(void);
void set_long_time(long int seconds);
void add_to_time(long int seconds);
```

   The function `set_time` establishes a clock time according to the given elements. The function `set_long_time` initializes the clock time according to the number of seconds that have elapsed since midnight. Function `hms_time` determines the number of seconds in a clock time. Function `add_to_time` advances the clock time by a number of seconds. Finally, `print_time` displays the time in the eight character format HH:MM:SS.

8. Define a macro `MIN` that gives the minimum of two integer values, then write a program to test the definition. Recast it as an inline function.

9. Define a macro `MIN3` that gives the minimum of three values. Test the definition in a program. Again, recast as an inline function.

10. Protect the header files of this chapter to avoid multiple inclusion.

8

Arrays and Pointers

In the programs written thus far, a simple scalar variable is associated with a single data value. In this chapter we shall begin the study of *aggregate types* – types involving collections of values. An *array* is an aggregate with all the items of the same type.

The array is a relatively primitive data structuring facility. In this chapter we shall demonstrate how the array is handled, but in subsequent chapters it will be used primarily as a primitive to implement a user-defined data abstraction.

The array is a structure used to store a collection of data items that are all of the same type. By using an array, we can associate a single variable name with an entire collection of data values. To process an individual item we need to specify the array name and indicate which array element is being referenced. Specific elements are distinguished by an *index* or *subscript*.

The motivation behind arrays is illustrated with the following problem. Suppose that we wish to construct a program which reads five integer values and prints them out in reverse order. To do so we might declare and use five integer variables as in:

```
int main()
{
    int first, second, third, fourth, fifth;

    cin >> first >> second >> third >> fourth >> fifth;
    cout << fifth << fourth << third << second << first << "\n";
    return (0);
}
```

If now, instead of five integer values to reverse we had, say, fifty, then manipulating the data by means of unique identifiers is an extraordinarily cumbersome approach.

8.1 Defining and referencing arrays

In C++, an array is defined just like any other variable. The syntax for an array definition is:

```
type-specifier  name[number-of-elements]
```

Type specifier is any of the fundamental types of C++ and the derived types such as pointers or classes. The type `void` is not included in this permissible set. The array size is specified as a constant expression representing the maximum number of elements. The array name is introduced as an identifier. An array called `table` with eight elements of type integer would be given by the definition:

```
int table[8];
```

An array occupies a block of consecutive memory locations. Pictorially, the storage space reserved for the array table might appear as in Figure 8.1.

To process the data stored in an array, we must be able to reference each individual element. The array *subscript* is used to differentiate between different elements of the same array. A *subscripted variable* consists of an array name followed by an integer expression enclosed in square brackets. The subscripted variable `table[0]` refers to the first element of the array `table`, `table[1]` references the second element, and `table[7]` references the last element. Observe how the array definition specifies the number of elements (eight), whilst the elements themselves are referenced by the subscripts `0, 1, 2, 3, 4, 5, 6` and `7`.

A subscripted variable may be used in any expression in which a simple variable of the same type may be used. Examples of expression involving subscripted variables include:

```
sum4 = table[0] + table[1] + table[2] + table[3];

table[7] = 7;

if (table[0] > table[7])
  cout << "First is greater than last\n";
```

The expression used in a subscript is any generalized expression which yields an integer value. Thus we may write for simple integer variables `i, j` and `k`:

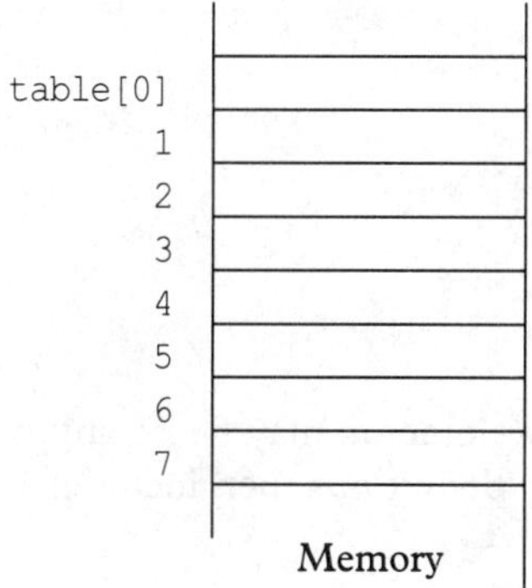

Figure 8.1

```
table[i+j] = 0;
for(int k = 0; k < 8; k++)
 cout << table[k] << "\n";
table[7 - table[j]] = j;
```

C++ does not define support for any array bounds checking. The programmer must be especially diligent to ensure the code does not attempt to access an array element that is not within the bounds of the array definition. In the context of the definition for array `table`, the following statement is syntactically and semantically correct:

```
table[10] = 0;
```

It is anticipated, however, that the statement is not that required by the programmer. Nevertheless, the C++ compiler will accept the statement. The effect is that some area of memory is initialized to zero, possibly with disastrous effects if it is an area of memory assigned to another program variable.

We can now address and reprogram the original problem. Five integer values are read as input and printed in reverse order. An array is used in the solution, as shown in Program 8.1.

PROGRAM 8.1

```
//
//  Read five integers from the standard input and
//      output them in reverse order.
//

#include <iostream.h>

const int SIZE    = 5;

int main()
{
  int k;                              // loop control
  int table[SIZE];                    // data values

  for(k = 0; k < SIZE; k++)
    cin >> table[k];        // data input

  for(k = SIZE - 1; k >= 0; k—)
    cout << table[k] << "\n";                // display results
  return (0);
}
```

It was stated earlier that array elements may be of any of the fundamental and derived types. Further valid array definitions then include:

```
const int ASIZE   = 10;
const int TSIZE   = 20;

int        age[ASIZE];                       // array of integers
```

```
float       temperature[TSIZE + 1];          // array of decimal values

const int NAMESIZE        = 20;
const int ADDRSIZE]       = 30;

char        name[NAMESIZE];                  // character strings
char        address[ADDRSIZE];

const int PSIZE    = 10;
int*        pointers[PSIZE];                 // array of pointers
```

Note especially the declaration for the array `pointers` which is an array of size `10` in which the elements are integer pointers.

The following program performs a simple *bubble sort* on an array of `N` integer values. The algorithm is one of many of the interchange sorts. The inner loop rearranges out of order adjacent pairs on each pass. At the end of the first pass, the largest element has been 'bubbled' to the end of the array, that is, to the element at index position `N-1`. The outer loop repeats the process, each time decreasing by one the number of items to be sorted.

Data to our program consists of a single integer value followed by a number of integer data values. The first integer specifies the number of data items to follow.

PROGRAM 8.2

```
//
//  Input a series of integer values, sort them, and
//      print them out. The ordering of the data into
//      ascending sequence is performed by a simple
//      bubble sort. The data set is preceded with an
//      integer count of the number of data items.
//

#include <iostream.h>

const int TABLESIZE        = 100;

inline void        swap(int& x, int& y)
{ int temp = x; x = y; y = temp; }

int main()
{
  int size;                          // number of data values
  int table[TABLESIZE];              // data set

  cout << "Enter the number of data values: ";
  cin >> size;

  if(size > TABLESIZE)
    cout << "Too many elements, max is " << TABLESIZE << "\n";
  else {
    for(int i = 0; i < size; i++){          // accept data
      cout << "data item " << i << ":";
      cin >> table[i];
```

```
      }
                                          // bubble sort algorithm
      for(i = size - 1; i > 0; i-)
        for(int j = 0; j <= i - 1; j++)
          if(table[j] > table[j+1])
               swap(table[j], table[j+1]);

                                          // print sorted data
      cout << "\nSorted list:\n";
      for(i = 0; i < size; i++)
        cout << "data item " << i << ": " << table[i] << "\n";
    }
    return (0);
  }
```

8.2 Multi-dimensional arrays

Consider a table containing the marks scored by a class of students in each of several examination papers. The marks of one student could be stored in a one-dimensional array:

```
const int NUMBER_OF_PAPERS        = 5;

int student[NUMBER_OF_PAPERS];
```

The complete marks table for all the students could be stored in array of such arrays, that is, in a two-dimensional array:

```
const int NUMBER_OF_PAPERS   = 5;
const int NUMBER_OF_STUDENTS = 50;

int marks[NUMBER_OF_STUDENTS][NUMBER_OF_PAPERS];
```

We can visualize a two-dimensional array as having rows and columns. A row in this example would represent the marks obtained by a single student. A column represents the marks gained by all students in an individual examination paper. The intersection of a given row and column is the mark obtained by one student in a particular examination.

As suggested by the definition for a two-dimensional array, a subscripted variable to reference the mark of an individual student in a single paper is written:

```
marks[row][column];
```

As an example of the use of multi-dimensional arrays, we present a program that measures the frequencies of pairs of adjacent letters in words. The program counts only within-word pairs, so that, given the input 'THE DOG.', it will count `TH`, `HE`, `DO` and `OG`, but not `ED`. The input stream is terminated by a period symbol as shown.

The counters are stored in a two dimensional array whose definition is:

```
const int ALPHABET = 26;
int counter[ALPHABET][ALPHABET];
```

The letter pair `AA` is recorded in `counter[0][0]`, the pair `AZ` in `counter[0][25]`, the pair `ZZ` in `counter[25][25]`, and so on. Note how the letter `A` results in an index value `0`, the letter `B` index value `1`, etc. We must, therefore, translate each letter into the correct index value. If `ch` is the variable representing the input character, then the conversion in an ASCII environment is readily achieved with the expression:

```
ch - 'A'
```

To process the text we use a two character *window*. The window moves through the input stream one character at a time, and whenever both characters in the window are letters, the corresponding element of `counter` is incremented.

PROGRAM 8.3

```
#include <iostream.h>
#include <iomanip.h>
#include <ctype.h>

const int ALPHABET     = 26;

const char BLANK       = ' ';
const char PERIOD      = '.';
const char NEWLINE     = '\n';

int counter[ALPHABET][ALPHABET];

int main()
{
  void initialize(void), process(void),
       display(void);

  initialize();
  process();
  display();
  return (0);
}

void initialize(void)                      // counter array to zero
{
  for(int row = 0; row < ALPHABET; row++)
    for(int col = 0; col < ALPHABET; col++)
      counter[row][col] = 0;
}

void process(void)                         // input stream
{
  char thischar, prevchar;                 // input window
```

```
    prevchar = BLANK;                        // initialize
    cin.get(thischar);
    while (thischar != PERIOD){
      if( ! isspace(thischar)){
        if(isupper(thischar) && isupper(prevchar))
            counter[prevchar-'A'][thischar-'A']++;
        prevchar = thischar;
      }
      cin.get(thischar);
    }
}

void display(void)
{
    for(int row = 0; row < ALPHABET; row++){
      for(int col = 0; col < ALPHABET; col++)
        cout << setw(2) << counter[row][col];
      cout << "\n";
    }
}
```

8.3 Arrays as function arguments

We introduced in Chapter 5 the pass by value argument passing mechanism in which the formal argument is initialized with the value of the actual argument. When an array is passed as an argument to a function, this would suggest that a copy of the actual array argument is passed. For a large array this would prove prohibitively expensive, with large amounts of processor time spent copying the array. What then is actually passed is the location of the beginning of the array. The formal argument is initialized with this address. Individual array elements of the actual parameter are accessed within the function by employing the usual subscripting notation with the formal array argument name.

An array formal argument to a function definition is declared as:

```
void f(float t[ ], ..... ) { /* ..... */ }
```

which specifies that the argument `t` is an array of `floats`. The length of the array is not specified. The notation `t[ ]` indicates that `t` is an array. The actual array dimension will be established by the calling function. The prototype declaration would be presented as:

```
void f(float [ ], ..... );
```

To pass a multi-dimensional array as a function argument we present the size of all but the first dimension. Thus if array `counter` in the last exercise was to be passed as an argument to the subordinate functions, then the declaration for `initialize`, for example, would be:

```
initialize(int counter [ ][ALPHABET]) { ..... }
```

All but the first dimension of a formal array argument is required so that the compiler can determine the correct *storage mapping function*. Effectively, a two-dimensional array such as:

```
int table[3][4];
```

is stored in consecutive storage locations in row-order (Figure 8.2). To access, for example, element `table[1][3]` the storage mapping function determines that it is seven locations relative to the base of the array (element `table[0][0]`). In general, element `table[i][j]` is `4*i+j` locations relative to the array base. The storage mapping `4*i+j` is dependent upon `4`, the number of elements in the second dimension. Hence the need to include this value in a formal array argument.

```
table[0][0]
table[0][1]
table[0][2]
table[0][3]
table[1][0]
table[1][1]
table[1][2]
table[1][3]
table[2][0]
table[2][1]
table[2][2]
table[2][3]
```

Memory

Figure 8.2

Program 8.2 performed a sort on a series of integer values using the bubble sort algorithm. We repeat the same problem on the same data, this time separating the task of reading, sorting and writing the array into three separate functions, passing the array between functions as an argument. Note how the function `writeoutput` qualifies its argument as `const` to emphasize that the elements of the array are unmodified. The generality of the `sort` function is extended by the template mechanism so that any array type can be sorted.

PROGRAM 8.4

```
//
// Input a sequence of integer values and sort them
```

```
//      into ascending order using the bubble sort
//      algorithm. The data set is preceded with an
//      integer count of the number of items.
//

#include <iostream.h>
#include <iomanip.h>

const int TABLESIZE       = 100;

inline void      swap(int& x, int& y)
{ int temp = x; x = y; y = temp; }

template <class TYPE>                          // prototype
void sort(TYPE[], int);

int main()
{
  int  size;                               // number of data items
  int  table[TABLESIZE];          // data values

  int  readinput(int[], int);              // referencing .....
  void writeoutput(const int[], int);      // ..... declarations

  if((size = readinput(table, TABLESIZE)) > TABLESIZE)
    cout << "Too many elements, max is " << TABLESIZE << "\n";
  else {
    sort(table, size);
    writeoutput(table, size);
  }
  return (0);
}

//
// Read a stream of integers from the standard input
//      and record in an array. The user is first prompted
//      for the number of data items. If this values exceeds
//      the maximum permissible value, then the program
//      terminates.
//

int readinput(int table[], int limit)
{
  int size;                       // expected number

  cout << "Enter number of data items: ";
  cin >> size;

  if(size > limit)                // sufficient room?
    return (size);                // no, return error

  for(int k = 0; k < size; k++)
    cin >> table[k];

  return (size);
}
```

```
//
// Sort an array of integers into ascending order
//     by application of the bubble sort algorithm.
//     Out of order pairs are repeatedly exchanged
//     'bubbling' the largest item to the end of the
//     array. The process repeats, with the second
//     largest element displaced into the penultimate
//     entry in the array, and so on.
//

template <class TYPE>
void sort(TYPE table[], int size)
{
  for(int i = size - 1; i > 0; i–)
    for(int j = 0; j < i; j++)
      if(table[j] > table[j+1])
           swap(table[j], table[j+1]);
}

//
// Print the sorted array.
//

void writeoutput(const int table[], int size)
{
  cout << "Sorted list:\n";

  for(int k = 0; k < size; k++)
    cout << setw(5) << table[k] << "\n";
}
```

The main advantage of the bubble sort is its simplicity. Its drawback, a serious one, is that it gets very slow as the number of elements to be sorted rises. Having constructed the program in a modular manner we can readily replace this sort routine with an improved version.

The *Shell sort* is usually much faster for large arrays. A full discussion of the Shell sort method is out of place here, but research has shown that the halving of intervals given in this implementation is not the optimal sequence (see Exercise 6 at the end of this chapter).

```
//
// Sort an array of integers into ascending order
//     by application of the Shell sort algorithm.
//     In the early stages distant elements are
//     compared and, if necessary, exchanged. Gradually
//     the interval between compared elements is
//     reduced until adjacent elements are involved
//     in the comparison.
//

template <class TYPE>
void sort(TYPE table[], int size)
{
```

```
    for(int interval = size/2; interval > 0; interval /= 2)
      for(int i = interval; i < size; i++)
        for(int j = i-interval;
           j >= 0 && table[j] > table[j+interval];
           j -= interval)
        swap(table[j], table[j+interval]);
  }
```

8.4 Array initialization

It is permissible in C++ to initialize arrays with an *array initializer* consisting of a brace-enclosed, comma-separated list of constant expressions. For example, a six element integer array may be initialized by:

```
int array[6] = {0, 1, 2, 3, 4, 5};
```

Strictly, the bounds of the array need not be given explicitly. In this case the compiler counts the number of initializers and determines the array size. The above might also have been written:

```
int array[] = {0, 1, 2, 3, 4, 5};
```

Where the array size is given explicitly and the number of items in the initializer is fewer than the number of elements, then the remaining elements are initialized to zero. The default initializer zero only applies to variables with static duration. For automatic arrays the language leaves undefined the effect. Therefore,

```
static int array[6] = {0, 1, 2, 3};
```

is equivalent to:

```
static int array[6] = {0, 1, 2, 3, 0, 0};
```

If the number of initializers exceed the number of elements in the array definition, then the initializer is in error.

Multi-dimensional arrays may also be initialized. The initialization follows the same pattern. A multi-dimensional array with, say, `N` elements in the first dimension is initialized with an initializer appearing as:

int array[N] ..... [...] = { I_0, I_1, I_2, ... I_{N-1} };

The initializers I_k apply the definition of an initializer recursively for the remaining array dimensions. Thus the two-dimensional integer array `rectangle[3][4]` has an initializer having the form:

int rectangle[3][4] = { I_0, I_1, I_2 };

Each initializer I_k is appropriate to an integer array now reduced to one dimension, having four elements. Such an initializer would appear as:

```
{1, 2, 3, 4}
```

A complete initializer for `rectangle` is then:

```
int rectangle[3][4] =  {  {  1,  2,  3,  4},
                          {  5,  6,  7,  8},
                          {  9, 10, 11, 12}
                       };
```

Again, where there are fewer than the required number of items, remaining elements are initialized to zero (but not automatic arrays). The initialization:

```
int rectangle[3][4] =  {  {1,2,3},
                         {5}
                      };
```

is equivalent to:

```
int rectangle [3][4] = {  {1, 2, 3, 0},
                          {5, 0, 0, 0},
                          {0, 0, 0, 0}
                       };
```

When the array size is not given in an initializer then we have no means of specifying the number of elements in a program. In that case we can use the compiler function `sizeof` which returns the size, in bytes, of its operand. The operand may be either a type name or an expression. For example, `sizeof(int)` is the number of bytes occupied by an integer. When the operand is a variable expression or an array element expression the result is the number of bytes occupied by that object. When applied to an array the result is the number of bytes in the array; an array of size `N` elements occupies `N` times the size of each element. Hence we might have:

```
int main()
{
  int x[ ] = { 0, 1, 4, 9, 16, 25 };
  const int XSIZE = sizeof(x) / sizeof(x[0]);
  for(int k = 0; k < XSIZE; k++)
    cout << x[k] << "\n";
  return (0);
}
```

8.5 Pointers and arrays

Chapter 5 introduced the concept of a pointer. Specifically it was used to pass the address of a variable to a called function enabling that function to obtain the variable's current value and, if necessary, to modify that value.

In Section 8.3 we introduced the fact that an array formal argument is initialized with the location or address of the first array element. Hence in C++ an array is also an address. The address associated with an array name is the initial location in memory in which the array is stored. Since an array name is an address, it is also, therefore, a pointer, but one which is fixed at compile time. Suppose we have the array declaration:

```
const int SIZE    = 8;

int table[SIZE];
```

and that the compiler assigns the base address 400 to the array, then the memory image might appear as illustrated in Figure 8.3. In the figure we are assuming that an integer occupies two storage locations (bytes).

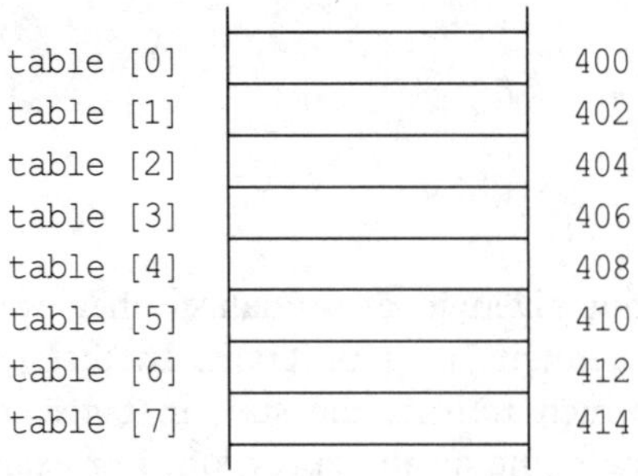

table [0]		400
table [1]		402
table [2]		404
table [3]		406
table [4]		408
table [5]		410
table [6]		412
table [7]		414

Figure 8.3

If `ptr` is a pointer to an integer, defined as in Chapters 3 and 5:

```
int* ptr;
```

then the assignment involving the address operator:

```
ptr = &table[0];
```

sets `ptr` to point to the first element of `table` (see Figure 8.4). Following the discussion in Chapter 3 the assignment:

```
int t = *ptr;
```

copies the content of `table[0]` into `t`. Equally, the assignment;

```
*ptr = 0;
```

sets the value of `table[0]` to zero.

Instead of writing:

```
ptr = &table[0];
```

we may also express it as:

```
ptr = table;
```

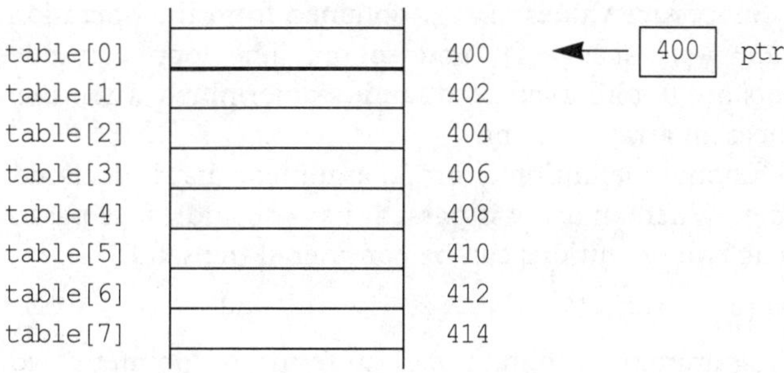

Figure 8.4

since, as we have already noted in Section 8.3, an array name (formal argument) is interpreted as the base address of the array space.

If a pointer into an array is incremented by one then it refers to the next element in the array. Equally, if it is decremented by one then it points to the previous item. Then by using the dereferencing operator we may access the array elements with:

```
cout << *ptr;                // output first item
*(ptr + 1) = 0;              // zeroize second element
*(ptr + i) = 0;              // zeroize table[i]
```

The final example illustrates the interchangeability of subscripted expressions and pointer expressions. Effectively, the compiler converts expressions involving `table[i]` into its pointer equivalent, say:

```
table[i] = 0;                // with the equivalent .....
*(table + i) = 0;
```

Because of this equivalence, either of the last two statements are legal programmer constructions. So too are the following:

```
*(ptr + i) = 0;              // is the same as .....
ptr[i] = 0;
```

To set all the elements of the array table to zero we previously would have used:

```
for(i = 0; i < SIZE; i++)
  table[i] = 0;
```

Knowing that `table[i]` and `*(table + i)` are equivalent, we could also have used:

```
for(i = 0; i < SIZE; i++)
  *(table + i) = 0;
```

Using the pointer variable `ptr`, we express the same logic by:

```
for(ptr = table; ptr < &table[SIZE]; ptr++)
  *ptr = 0;
```

In this loop, the pointer variable `ptr` is initialized to the base address of the array `table`. Successive values of `ptr`, obtained from the operation `ptr++`, are equivalent to `&table[0]`, `&table[1]`, and so on. The loop continues provided the array elements are not all exhausted, and is determined when the pointer `ptr` no longer references an array element.

In a function definition a formal argument that is declared as an array is actually a pointer. When an array is passed, its base address is passed by value. Hence the following two definitions can be considered the same:

```
void f(float t[], ..... )          and          void f(float *t, ..... )
```

Reprogramming Program 8.1 in terms of pointers, we have the alternative solution:

PROGRAM 8.5

```
//
//  Read five integers and output them in reverse
//      order. Use an array to record the values, and
//      a pointer to reference the elements of the array.
//

#include <iostream.h>

const int SIZE    = 5;

int main()
{
  int table[SIZE];            // data values

  for(int *ptr = table; ptr < &table[SIZE]; ptr++)
    cin >> *ptr;

  for(ptr = &table[SIZE-1]; ptr >= table; ptr—)
    cout << *ptr << "\n";
  return (0);
}
```

In Program 8.4, the function `writeoutput` cycles through successive elements of the array argument `table`, printing each value. A revised version expressed in terms of pointers is:

```
//
//      Print the sorted array.
//

void writeoutput(const int* table, int size)
{
  cout << "Sorted list:\n";

  for(int* base = table; table < base+size; table++)
    cout << setw(5) << *table << "\n";
}
```

The important difference between an array name and an array pointer is that the latter is a variable but the former is a constant. It would not make sense to allow us to change the address of the space to which an array name associates. The array name is firmly anchored to the address of the first cell of the array space. Hence expressions like `table = ptr + 1` or `table++` are invalid and caught by the compiler.

Within the body of function `writeoutput` incrementing the formal argument is a legal operation since it is a pointer variable initialized to address the base of the actual array. Note how we emphasized that the elements of the array are not modified through the use of the `const` qualifier.

8.6 Functions returning pointers

A function processing an array and returning an array element can do so by returning the integer value of the array element subscript. Here, it is appropriate to describe the processing logic with subscripts. For example, consider a function called `smallest` that returns the integer index of the smallest item in an array of `floats`:

```
int smallest(float array[], int limit)
{
  int   index = 0;
  float least = array[index];

  for(int subscript = 1; subscript < limit; subscript++)
    if (array[subscript] < least)
      least = array[index = subscript];

  return (index);
}
```

This function might then be invoked in some calling function to find the smallest element in an array `table` with `SIZE` elements:

```
cout << "Smallest is " << table[smallest(table, SIZE)] << "\n";
```

In some applications it is often more appropriate to describe the processing in terms of pointers. To achieve this, C++ supports *functions returning pointers* to data items. Reprogramming the previous function with pointers:

```
float* smallest(float* const array, int limit)
{
  const float* final = array + limit;
  float* index = array;
  float least = *index;

  for(float* subscript = array + 1; subscript < final; subscript++)
    if (*subscript < least)
```

```
        least = *(index = subscript);

    return (index);
  }
```

The definition for function `smallest` now specifies that the returned value is a pointer to a `float`. This is indicated by the notation:

```
  float* smallest( ..... ) .....
```

The corresponding function call is now:

```
  cout << "Smallest is " << *smallest(table, SIZE) << "\n";
```

8.7 External array referencing

We have followed the rule that all objects in a C++ program must be declared before they are used. Where the definition follows a reference to the item, then an explicit referencing declaration appears. This has been used in a number of cases: functions called before they are defined, references to data items declared in other program units, and so on.

The same principle applies to arrays. If a definition for an array appears in a separate file or appears after it is to be referenced, then a referencing declaration must be used. Defining declarations are responsible for having actual storage allocated. For an array, a definition might appear as:

```
  int table[SIZE];
```

Referencing declarations act as compiler directives, informing the compiler of the attributes of the object. No space is allocated. An appropriate referencing declaration for array `table` is:

```
  int table[];
```

indicating that `table` is an array of integers. The number of array elements is given in the corresponding defining declaration. Similar to formal array arguments, multi-dimensional arrays are referenced using declarations containing all but the first dimension. The referencing declaration for a two-dimensional array having four elements in the second dimension is:

```
  float code[][4];
```

8.8 Character strings

Strings are one-dimensional character arrays. Normally, a string in C++ is terminated by an end-of-string sentinel consisting of the null character, `'\0'`. It is useful to think of strings as having variable length, but with a maximum allowable length determined by the size of the character array holding the string. The size of the array must be sufficient to include the end-of-string sentinel. As usual it is the programmer's responsibility to ensure that the array bounds are not exceeded.

String constants were defined in Section 3.4 as a character sequence enclosed in a matching pair of double quotes. The string `"abc"` is implemented as a character array of size four. The final element of the array is the null character (see Figure 8.5). From Section 8.4, a character array may be initialized with these same values using the construct:

```
static char word[] = { 'a', 'b', 'c', '\0' };
```

C++ additionally permits a character array to be initialized with a string constant rather than having to list the individual characters. The above can also be expressed by:

```
static char word[] = "abc";
```

The latter is preferred since it is that much more readable.

A string constant such as:

```
"hello"
```

is an array of characters. The C++ compiler associates a pointer to the first character of the array. A variable defined of type pointer to `char` may be assigned the pointer to such a character string. If variable `greeting` is defined as:

```
char* greeting;
```

then the assignment:

```
greeting = "hello";
```

involves copying the pointer to the character string into the pointer variable `greeting`. The declaration and assignation may be combined into:

```
char *greeting = "hello";
```

Care is required to distinguish between the declaration:

```
char word[] = "hello";
```

and

```
char *greeting = "hello";
```

Superficially, both appear to achieve the same thing. The literal strings are treated

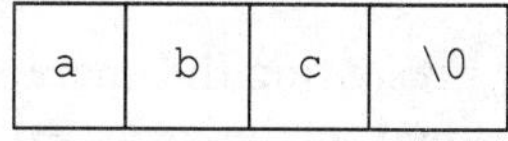

Figure 8.5

as pointers to characters which then associate with the identifiers `word` and `greeting`. The difference is that the former is a constant pointer to a character (see Section 8.5), whilst the latter is a variable of type pointer to a `char`. All array names, such as `word`, are treated as constant pointers. On the other hand, `greeting` is a variable and may be subsequently assigned some new value, as in:

```
greeting = "Good morning";
```

As an illustration of how variable length character strings are used, let us develop a program to count the number of characters in a string. We shall use the function `strlen` from the C library (see Appendix F.2) which determines the length of the character string given as its argument. The function has the prototype:

```
int strlen(const char*);
```

which is made available to the program by including the header file `<string.h>`. The header file includes prototype declarations for a range of string handling functions including string copying, string concatenation, etc. Appendix F.2 gives details of the functions we can expect as part of the library.

PROGRAM 8.6

```
//
// Count the number of characters in a character string.
//      The null character is not included in the count.
//

#include <iostream.h>
#include <string.h>

int main()
{
  static char word[] = { "abc" };
  static char *greeting = "hello";

  int length(const char[]);              // prototype declaration

  cout << "Lengths " << strlen(word) << " and "
                     << strlen(greeting) << "\n";

  return (0);
}
```

8.9 Character string input/output

A character string is output by presenting the character array name to the insertion operator. The characters contained in the array excepting the null terminator are sent to the nominated output stream. For example:

```
char     name[] = "Ken";
char*    message = "Hello";

cout << "My name is: " << name << "\n";
cout << "Greeting is: " << message << "\n";
```

produce the expected values with the strings referred to by `name` and `message` displayed as part of the output.

Character strings are output in a field equal to their length. We can use the manipulator `setw` to control the required width of the field. If the value given to `setw` is greater than the string length then the string is output right justified in the field. If the value is smaller than the string width then the full string is displayed, ensuring no information is lost. Program 8.7 illustrates this.

PROGRAM 8.7

```
//
//  Formatting strings with setw
//

#include <iostream.h>
#include <iomanip.h>

int main()
{
                    // expected output: [               Hello]
  cout << "[" << setw(20) << "Hello" << "]\n";

                    // expected output: [Good Bye]
  cout << "[" << setw(4)  << "Good Bye" << "]\n";

  return (0);
}
```

The standard library extraction operator >> can be used to read a string of characters. The definition and statement:

```
const int MESSAGESIZE    = 20;
char message[MESSAGESIZE];

cin >> message;
```

have the effect of reading a character string from the standard input and storing it in the character array `message`.

If the above input statement were executed and the following characters entered at the terminal:

```
Hello
```

then the null terminated string `"Hello"` is read and stored in the character array `message`. If instead, the following line of text were supplied:

```
Good morning
```

then only the string `"Good"` is stored in the array `message`, since any whitespace character terminates the input. If the same input statement were executed a second time, then the string `"morning"` is stored in the array replacing the previous string.

One problem with this input statement is what happens if a character string greater than the capacity of the array is supplied? Since a character array requires space for the terminating null character then at most only nineteen characters may be recorded in the array. If a character string of length twenty or more is input to the code above we cannot guarantee the program's behaviour since the array bounds will have been exceeded. One solution is to use the manipulator `setw` this time in an input statement:

```
cin >> setw(MESSAGESIZE-1) >> message;
```

which ensures that no more characters than can be recorded in the character array are stored.

Program 8.8 illustrates the use of the string input statement to read three strings.

PROGRAM 8.8

```
//
//  Program to illustrate character string input
//       through use of the standard extraction operator.
//

#include <iostream.h>
#include <iomanip.h>

const int SIZE = 20;

int main()
{
  char word1[SIZE], word2[SIZE], word3[SIZE];

  cout << "Enter the text: ";
  cin >> setw(SIZE-1) >> word1;
  cin >> setw(SIZE-1) >> word2;
  cin >> setw(SIZE-1) >> word3;

  cout << "word1 = " << word1 << "\n";
  cout << "word2 = " << word2 << "\n";
  cout << "word3 = " << word3 << "\n";

  return (0);
}
```

The program operates by first issuing the prompt `"Enter the text: "`. If, in response, the user were to enter two character strings separated by a space, then the first is assigned to variable `word1` and the second to variable `word2`. The space acts as a separator between each string, terminating the first string and discarded as leading whitespace preceding the second string. If the second string is terminated by a newline, it too is discarded when reading the third string.

The program was tested with the following dialogue. User input is italicized to distinguish it from program output.

```
Enter the text: Programming in
C++
word1 = Programming
word2 = in
word3 = C++
```

Running the program for a second time with a very long first word produces the effect:

```
Enter the text: aaaaaaaaaaaaaaaaaaaaaaaaa bbbbb ccccc
word1 = aaaaaaaaaaaaaaaaaaa
word2 = aaaaaa
word3 = bbbbb
```

in which only the first nineteen characters of the first input string is stored as `word1` and the remaining portion as `word2`. The input string `"ccccc"` remains in the input buffer awaiting further input from the program.

Many text processing applications require that an entire line of text be read from the terminal before processing can commence. To use the above statement we would need to know in advance the number of individual strings appearing on a single line. Commonly this is not always available. Lines of text often contain different number of words or strings.

To support line-at-time reading we use the input stream function `getline`:

```
istream&  getline(char* line, int limit, char delim = '\n');
```

which extracts characters into the character array `line` to a maximum of `limit-1` characters or until the third delimeter argument has been read. The character array should be of length `limit`. A terminating null character is placed in the string. The delimeter is not recorded. For example:

```
const int LINESIZE    = 80;
char          buffer[LINESIZE];
cin.getline(buffer, LINESIZE);
```

8.10 Arrays of pointers and pointers to pointers

A C++ array may hold any of the fundamental types or derived types. For example, in the next chapter we shall have arrays of class objects. Equally, from this chapter we may define an array of pointers. In:

```
int* ptr[4];
```

variable `ptr` is an array of four elements of pointers to integers. If `x` and `t` are integer variables, then the assignment:

```
ptr[3] = &x;
```

sets the last element of the array to the address of the variable `x`. By the usual notation, the assignment:

```
t = *ptr[3];
```

copies the content of `x` into the variable `t`.

Equally, any element of the array `ptr` may address any element of an integer array. Given the declarations:

```
int v4[4], v7[7], v2[2], v3[3];
```

we may set the zeroth element of `ptr` to address the first item in integer array `v4` by the assignment:

```
ptr[0] = &v4[0];
```

or, more commonly, by:

```
ptr[0] = v4;
```

If we were to assign successive elements of the array `ptr` to the base address of arrays `v4`, `v7`, `v2` and `v3`, then in effect we have constructed a two-dimensional *jagged array*. The rows of this array have varying number of elements. The array is no longer the conventional rectangular shape. Pictorially, the two-dimensional array may be viewed as shown in Figure 8.6. The necessary assignments are:

```
ptr[0] = v4;
ptr[1] = v7;
ptr[2] = v2;
ptr[3] = v3;
```

The array `v7` may be printed with the function call:

```
printRow(ptr[1], 7);
```

where function `printRow` has been programmed as:

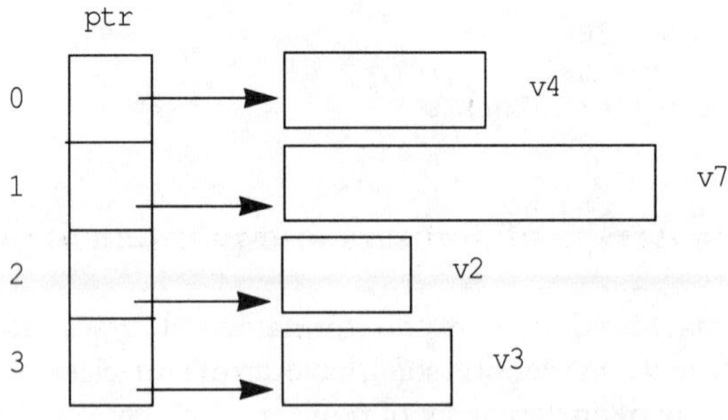

Figure 8.6

```
void printRow(int* pt, int n)
{
  for(int k = 0; k < n; k++)        // for every element
    cout << *pt++ << "\n";          // print and advance
}
```

A formal argument of a function declared to be of type 'array of `T`' where `T` is some arbitrary type, is treated as if it were declared to be of type 'pointer to `T`'. Because of the equivalence of pointers and arrays (see Section 8.3), this change is invisible to the programmer and performed automatically by the C++ compiler. For example, in the function:

```
int sumarray(int a[], int n)
{
  int sum = 0;              // running total

       for(int k = 0; k < n; k++)
         sum += a[k];

       return (sum);
}
```

the argument `a` could have been declared by the programmer as:

```
int* a
```

This is what the C++ compiler effectively does.

Where a function argument is declared to be of type 'array of `T`' and `T` is of type 'pointer to `S`' for some arbitrary type `S`, it is equivalenced to type 'pointer to pointer to `S`'. For example, the function `printLines` which has the definition:

```
void printLines(char* linepointer[], int numlines)
{
  // .....
}
```

is converted to:

```
void printLines(char** linepointer, int numlines)
{
  // .....
}
```

as happened to function `printRow` above.

That is, `linepointer` has as its value the base address for a series of memory locations (i.e. an array), each of which is the address of the first character of a null terminated array of characters (a string). Pictorially the arrangement appears as shown in Figure 8.7. The object referred to as `linepointer` possesses the value that is the address of the array of addresses. The object referred to as `*linepointer` is the first address contained in that array, and is therefore the address of the first character in the first string. The object referred to as `**linepointer` is the first character in the first string.

The precedence and associativity of the indirection operator `*` and the other

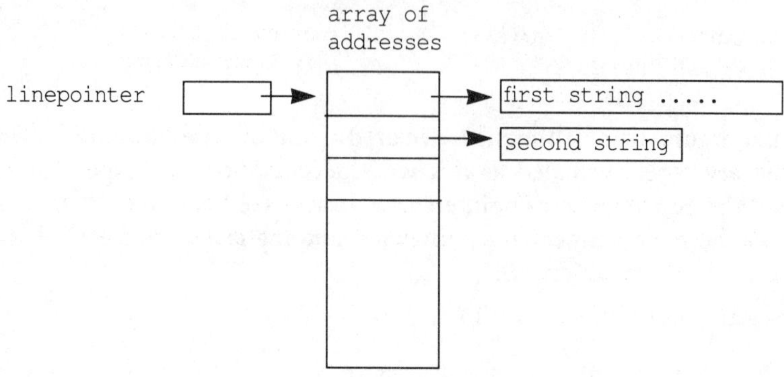

Figure 8.7

operators must be carefully noted. Particular attention should be paid to the operators * (indirection), + + (increment) and – – (decrement), all having equal precedence and all associating right to left. Thus `*(*linepointer+1)` references the second character of the first string; `**linepointer++` references the first character of the first string (and advances `linepointer` by one); whilst `**++linepointer` references the first character of the second string (having first advanced `linepointer` by one). An array of character (string) pointers based on Figure 8.7 is the subject of the next section.

8.11 Command line arguments

Normally a C++ program exists in an environment established by the resident operating system. The environment usually supports passing *command line arguments* to a program when it begins execution. For example, consider a program called `sum` which is invoked with two arguments on the command line. These arguments are an integer pair which are summed and printed by the program. The program might be activated by:

```
sum 123 456
```

The output from the program is, of course, `579`.

Function `main` of a program is often defined with two formal arguments conventionally called `argc` and `argv`. The first argument is the number of command line arguments. Since the program name is always included in the count, `argc` always exceeds `0`. In the example call of program `sum`, `argc` is `3`. The second argument, `argv`, is an array of pointers to `char`, pointers to the first character in the array of characters that represent the argument strings. `argv[0]` is the program name. In the example, `argv[0]`, `argv[1]` and `argv[2]` are respectively `"sum"`, `"123"` and `"456"`. One possible version for this program follows.

PROGRAM 8.9

```
//
// Form the sum of two integers given as command
//      line arguments.
//

#include <iostream.h>
#include <stdlib.h>

int main(int argc, char *argv[])
{
  int first, second;

  if(argc != 3)           // check number of arguments
    cout << "Usage: " << argv[0] << " number number\n";
  else
    cout << atoi(argv[1]) + atoi(argv[2]) << "\n";

  return (0);
}
```

The function `atoi` (see Appendix F.3) converts a character string argument into an integer value.

Many C++ programs are supplied with arguments in this manner. Often, the arguments are the names of files to be processed by the program, permitting the program to be constructed such that these file names are run time arguments. In some instances, these arguments are supplemented with *options* used to further vary the effect of the program. Options are frequently introduced as single characters or as multiple characters preceded by a leading hyphen (-) symbol.

8.12 Initializing pointer arrays

Program 6.16 converted Zeller's congruence value into a name for the day of the week using a selection statement. Alternatively, we may develop a function which returns a pointer (see Section 8.6) to the character string for the day name. The function is:

```
char* day_name(int n)
{
  static char *name[] =
    { "Sunday",   "Monday", "Tuesday", "Wednesday",
      "Thursday", "Friday", "Saturday"

                   6)
                  ]);
    return (name[n]);
}
```

The definition for `name` is a list of character strings.

Care is required when a `const` specifier appears in such a declaration. Given:

```
const char* weekend[] = {"Saturday", "Sunday"};
```

then it is the characters that are constant, not the pointers:

```
weekend[0] = "Monday";      // ok, pointer changed
weekend[0][0] = 'B';       .// error, chars are const
```

Respectively,

```
char* const weekend[] = { ..... };
const char* const weekend[] = { ..... };
```

the pointer is constant, and both the pointer and the characters are constant.

8.13 Caveat

It was noted in the introduction to the chapter that arrays are perceived as relatively primitive data structuring facilities and is a consequence of some of the characteristics of arrays. For example, the array size must be defined at compile time, and if this is insufficient space at run time it leads to array bounds being exceeded without errors being reported. Equally, two arrays cannot be assigned without copying the individual elements (this is exactly the effect of the string copying function `strcpy`).

In subsequent chapters we shall introduce classes which remove most of these restrictions. In the next chapter we shall use a class `String` offering superior string handling capabilities. In Chapter 12 we shall define a number of `Vector` classes which can replace the basic array facility. These and other classes are often part of a C++ library.

8.14 Summary

1. An *array* is an example of an aggregate type in which a collection of data items that are all of the same type are associated with a single name. An array definition includes the type of the elements and the number of elements. Elements of an array are accessed by a *subscripted variable*, where the *subscript* or *index* is an integer expression. It is the programmer's responsibility to ensure that an array index is within bounds.

2. When an array name is passed as a function argument, a copy of the base address of the array is actually passed. In the header to a function definition, the declaration:

   ```
   int table[];
   ```

   is equivalent to:

   ```
   int *table;
   ```

   Within the function body either form can be indexed or used as a pointer

The declaration for a multi-dimensional array in a function definition must have all the dimensions specified with the exception of the first.

3. An array can be initialized with a list of compile time values. If a global or internal static array is not fully initialized, then all the remaining elements are guaranteed to be set to zero for the primitive types, or initialized with the constructor with no parameters for a user-defined type (see next chapter).

4. *Strings* are one dimensional arrays of type `char`. The null character `'\0'` is used to delimit a string. System functions such as `strlen` will only work on properly null terminated strings.

5. Arrays of pointers to type `char` (i.e. pointer to pointers) are used to process lists of strings. The second argument to function `main` is of this type, allowing a program access to its command line arguments.

6. External and static strings may be initialized. Initializations of the form:

```
char s[] = { 'a', 'b', 'c', '\0' };
char s[] = "abc";
```

are considered identical by the compiler. A list of strings can be used to initialize an array of character pointers:

```
char* list[] = { "Programming", "in", "C++" };
```

7. Function main of a program is often defined with two formal arguments conventionally called `argc` and `argv`. The first argument, `argc`, is the number of command line arguments. Since the program name is always included in the count, `argc` always exceeds 0.

8.15 Exercises

1. In the context of the declarations:

```
float table[10];
float *pt, *qt;
```

what is the effect of the following statements:

```
(a) pt = table;                    (b) pt = table + 2;
    *pt = 0;                           qt = pt;
    *(pt + 2) = 3.14;                  *qt = 2.718;

(c) pt = table;                    (d) pt = table;
    qt = table + 10;                   qt = table + 10;
    cout << qt - pt << "\n";           for(; pt < qt; pt++)
                                           *pt = 1.23;
```

2. A firm employs a group of twenty salesmen (with reference numbers 1–20 inclusive) who are paid commission on that portion of their sales which exceeds two-thirds of the average sales of the group. A program is required to read the sales value of each salesman and to print out the reference number of those who qualify for commission, together with their sales.

3. Data to a program consists of a sequence of positive integers terminated by a negative sentinel value. Determine if the number sequence is palindromic, reading the same both forwards and backwards.

4. Assume the number of rooms in a hotel is given by a constant `NMBROFROOMS`. Write (a) an array declaration suitable for keeping track of which rooms are free; and (b) a function to count how many rooms are free, given that appropriate values have been stored in the array.

5. A hospital patient's temperature is recorded four times a day for a week. Construct a program that will input the readings for each day, and:
   (a) output the data in a table as shown below:

```
          SUN  MON  TUE  WED  THU  FRI  SAT
   TEMP 1  X    X    X    X    X    X    X
        2  X    X    X    X    X    X    X
        3  X    X    X    X    X    X    X
        4  X    X    X    X    X    X    X
```

   (b) output the highest and lowest recorded temperatures together with the day and the number of the reading on which they occurred.

6. Modify the Shell sort function of Section 8.3 by having the interval reduce by one third on each pass. Initially the interval is determined from the recurrence relation:

$$\text{interval}_0 = 1$$
$$\text{interval}_{k+1} = 3 * \text{interval}_k + 1$$

   until the value exceeds the number of items to be sorted.

7. (a) Using the abstraction principles introduced in Chapter 7 prepare a program unit which operates as a stack data type. The outline for this structure is given by Figure 8.8. Now use the stack to input a series of integers and to print them in reverse order.
   (b) In a similar manner construct a *queue* abstraction.
   (c) Repeat Exercise 3 above using the stack and queue.

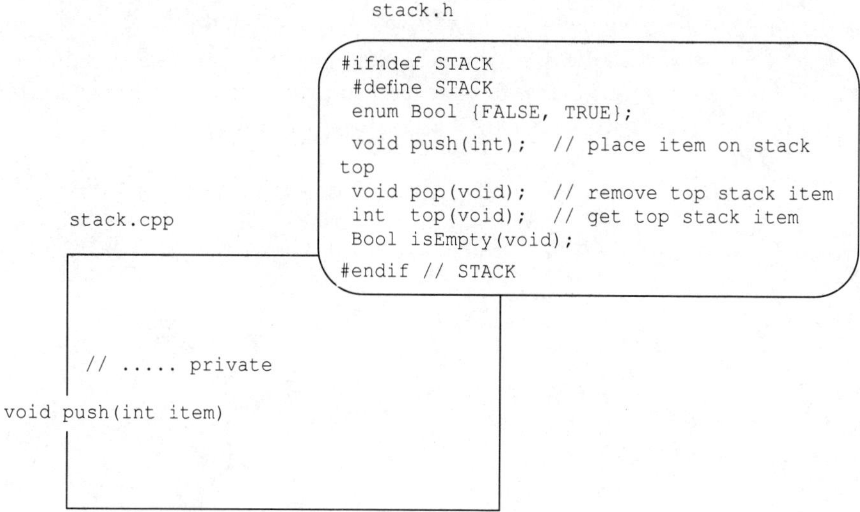

stack.h
#ifndef STACK
#define STACK
enum Bool {FALSE, TRUE};
void push(int); // place item on stack top
void pop(void); // remove top stack item
int top(void); // get top stack item
Bool isEmpty(void);
#endif // STACK
stack.cpp
// ..... private
void push(int item)

Figure 8.8

8. Prepare a function to capitalize every lower case alphabetic character in the string argument `s`. All other characters remain untouched. The function header is:

```
void capitalize(char *s)
```

(*Hint*: use the macros in `ctype.h`.)

9. Prepare a function to shift the characters of its string argument one place to the left, overwriting the original initial character. Develop the complementary function to shift the characters of a string one place to the right, padding with a single blank (space) character on the left.

10. Write a function called `left_rotate` with the following header, to rotate cyclicly the characters of the argument string `s`, `n` character places to the left.

```
void left_rotate(char *s, int n)
```

Write the corresponding function `right_rotate`.

11. Write a function that accepts strings of any length and determines whether they are palindromes. Additionally, allow the function to accept a sentence string containing spaces which are to be ignored when determining if the sentence is palindromic.

Part II

9 Classes

Previous chapters identified *abstraction* as a key concept in contemporary programming language design. It is a weapon against complexity; a vehicle for making software systems manageable. Functions in C++ are *procedural* (or *functional* or *process*) *abstractions*: in a calling program, we are not concerned with the inner operations of a called function, only how to use it. A function call is thus an abstraction of the actual process conducted by the function.

Data abstraction is a more recent development. Like procedural abstraction, it is a software engineering tool to help build reliable software systems. Data abstraction has, in some manner always been present in programming languages. Floating point values are examples of abstract data types. In C++ we can both declare and manipulate objects of this type. We can develop programs using this type without recourse to their internal format. The actual format is normally hidden from the user, or is, at least, of little concern to the user.

Information hiding is a key concept in data abstraction. Hidden information makes programs more secure – hidden information may not be corrupted by an application program. Information hiding can also facilitate *data independence* – the data representation may be changed without normally affecting application programs which use it. For example, we have in some sense considered the fundamental data type `double` as an abstract data type. We may define objects of this type and are provided with a range of applicable operators. In many cases we are able to ignore the representation, even when it may be different across various computer architectures.

A user-defined abstract data type should provide the same characteristics, namely, a type definition that permits programs to declare objects of that type, and a set of operations for manipulating objects of that type. The *class* concept in C++ provides the programmer with a means of creating new types that can be used as conveniently as the fundamental types.

9.1 Class types

Abstract data types provide a way of organizing and designing programs. The essential idea behind an abstract data type is that it consists of a set of operations and a representation. The former is visible and hence available to the user or client, whilst the latter is hidden. To use the data type it is not necessary to know the actual implementation. Strictly, the crucial aspect of data abstraction is that knowledge about the implementation is not used in any user program.

The C++ programming language supports an aggregate type known as a *class*. The class is a composite of components which are distinct. The components of an aggregate class type can be both data items and functions.

Classes allow groups of objects to be created which share the same behaviour. This we achieve by providing class definitions for the creation of objects in the application. The class is a definition for the operations (functions) on objects of the class, and the representation. Generally, the representation is hidden from the user of objects of the class. Access to an object is controlled through an external interface of operations.

Consider the following problem in which we introduce and define a class and utilize it in the subsequent solution. Data to a program consists of a series of dates with some unique terminator. The second and subsequent date is compared against the first. Each date more than two weeks after the first is displayed by the program.

The input dates are presented in the international form `DD/MM/YYYY`. The terminator we arbitrarily select as the first day of the next century, `1/1/2000`. Each printed date is displayed in the form:

```
Friday 27 September 1991
```

The first step in analyzing the requirements of the problem is to construct an *object model*. The model identifies the data objects of the problem domain which we organize into classes. Problem domain objects include both physical items such as employees, students, cars, as well as more abstract concepts such as dates.

From the problem statement we can formulate the expected behaviour of the class objects. In this program an input data set is used to properly initialize date objects. To present a date in the required output format we must interrogate the date object to obtain the day and year number, the month number from which we can get the month name, and Zeller's congruence of the date from which we can determine the day name. Finally, we must determine the number of days between two dates so that we may choose those dates to be printed. This same operation can also be used to compare an input date with the terminator. If they are the same date then the difference will evaluate to zero.

Using a notation similar to that of Chapter 7 we have the *class diagram* (see Figure 9.1) for the principal data objects in the problem, namely, `Date` values. A soft box represents the class types in the problem domain. The upper region of the box names the class types which it represents. The middle region publicizes the available operations on objects of that class type. In a manner similar to that of Chapter 7, since these operations are available to users of the class, they project from the right margin of the box. The third region documents how the class is represented. By placing the implementation for the class within the boundary we are informed that it is inaccessible to clients of the class.

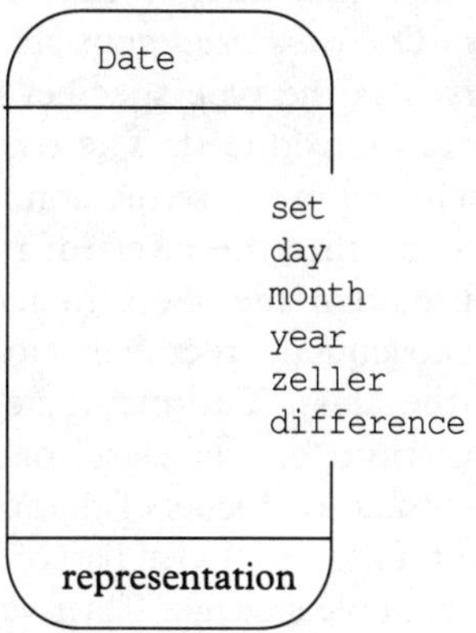

Figure 9.1

The `set` operation is used to initialize the representation part of a `Date` object. To do so the operation is parameterized with the day, month and year values. The operation `day` (`month` and `year`) interrogates a `Date` object to obtain the constituent part. Operation `zeller` applies Zeller's congruence (see Program 6.16) to the `Date` object. Operation `difference` finds the number of days between the `Date` argument of the operation and the object itself. In C++ the operations are presented as functions and the parameters are delivered as function arguments.

We can now part-declare a class `Date` with the specified operations as follows:

```
// ———————— FILE: date01.h ————————

#ifndef DATE
  #define DATE

  class Date{
  public:
    void          set(int aDay, int aMonth, int aYear); // initialize
                                                               values
    int           day(void);                            // access
                                                           components
    int           month(void);
    int           year(void);
    int           zeller(void);                         // congruence
                                                                value
    int           difference(const Date& aDate);        // days apart
  private:
    // .....
  };      // Date

  // .....

#endif    // DATE

// ———————— END: date01.h ————————
```

The reserved keyword `class` introduces a class declaration consisting of the class head and the class body. The *class head* consists of the keyword and the *class tag name*. The tag name serves as the type specifier for the user-defined class. Here, the tag name `Date` has been introduced. The *class body* is enclosed with a pair of matching braces and followed by a semicolon. The class body introduces the *members* of the class and specifies the levels of information hiding. The keyword `public:` declares the subsequent members to have public access. The keyword `private:` declares the subsequent members to be private to that class and inaccessible to users of the class. The members of the class can be either data members – the representation for the class, or function members – the set of operations that may be applied to objects of that class.

A class declaration not followed by a list of variables (such as the example above) does not allocate variable storage. Class variables are defined by employing the class tag name as a type specifier followed by a list of variables as in:

```
Date  birthday, today;
Date  holiday;
```

The type specifier `Date` may also be used to specify function return values or function arguments. For example:

```
int         isLeap(const Date& d) {  .....  }
Date        tomorrow(Date d) {  .....  }
void        advance(Date* d) {  .....  }
```

Note how the class `Date` describes the structure of a possibly infinite set of objects. All such objects are called *class instances* (or simply, instances) of the class. All instances of class `Date` will have the same representation and identical behaviour as specified by the named operations.

A class, as we have shown, describes a type. Instances of that type are the objects which exist at execution time. The class declaration presents the features that are common to all such instances. To apply an operation to a class object, the object name is qualified by the member function name in a *member access operator* (.) construction of the form:

```
object-name.member-function-name(actual-arguments)
```

For example, the statement:

```
if(birthday.year() == 1989) .....
```

determines if the `Date` object `birthday` has year component 1989.

The class body also controls the visibility of member names. Information hiding is the mechanism for controlling user access to the members of a class. This is specified by the labels `public:` and `private:`. Members declared in the public section are accessible to users of the class. Those declared private are not accessible to the class user.

A class declaration may contain any number of sections labelled with the *access specifiers* `public:` and `private:`. A section extends until the occurrence of another access specifier which may be the same as the preceding level or the closing right brace of the class body. If no access specifier immediately follows the open left brace for a class body, then the named members are implicitly private. By convention, we shall present the public class members first since they are the only significant members for a user of a class.

These discussions are incorporated into the problem solution presented as Program 9.1. The class specification is given in the header file `date01.h`. The code for the member functions is given in the corresponding program unit file.

PROGRAM 9.1

```
// ————— FILE: p01.cpp —————

#include <iostream.h>
#include "date01.h"

void      printDate(Date);// prototypes
void      printDay(int);
void      printMonth(int);

int main()
{
  Date    sentinel, first, other;
  int     day, month, year;
  char    separator;

  sentinel.set(1, 1, 2000);              // terminator

  cout << "Enter data values:\n";
  cin >> day >> separator >> month >> separator >> year;
  first.set(day, month, year);

  cin >> day >> separator >> month >> separator >> year;
  other.set(day, month, year);
  while(other.difference(sentinel) != 0){
    if(other.difference(first) > 14)
      printDate(other);
    cin >> day >> separator >> month >> separator >> year;
    other.set(day, month, year);
  }
  return (0);
}

void      printDate(Date aDate)
{
  printDay(aDate.zeller());
  cout << " " << aDate.day() << " ";
  printMonth(aDate.month());
  cout << " " << aDate.year() << "\n";
}

void      printDay(int d)
{
```

```
  switch(d){
    case 0:
      cout << "Sunday";
      break;
    case 1:
      cout << "Monday";
      break;
    // ..... others
  }
}

void        printMonth(int m)
{
  switch(m){
    case 1:
      cout << "January";
      break;
    case 2:
      cout << "February";
      break;
  // ..... others
  }
}

// ———————— END: p01.cpp ————————
```

Now we may consider the representation for `Date` objects. One obvious representation is to use three integers for the day, month and year and to program the functions in terms of these:

```
class Date{
public:
  // .....
private:
  int             theDay;
  int             theMonth;
  int             theYear;
};        // Date
```

An alternative would be to combine the day and month values into a day-in-the-year value which together with the year would provide the representation. If this was considered more appropriate then it could replace the above and the functions could be reprogrammed. Significantly, we would not have to alter the application program because of its reliance solely on the functions as the interface to the class.

A further representation would have been to realize a `Date` by a single long integer representing the number of days that have elapsed since some epoch. This we call a `julian` value. It makes `Date` arithmetic, such as `difference`, easy to implement. In our following solution we use an intermediate julian value to implement function `difference`.

Using the international triple as the chosen representation we may now program the functions. The member functions of a class can be defined in one of two places: either within the class declaration itself or separate from it. For example:

```
// ———————— FILE: date01.h ————————

#ifndef DATE
  #define DATE

  class Date{
  public:
    int          day(void)
          { return theDay; }
    int          month(void)
          { return theMonth; }
    // .....
  private:
    int          theDay;
    int          theMonth;
    int          theYear;
  };        // Date

  // .....

#endif    // DATE

// ———————— END: date01.h ————————
```

Because, for example, function `day` is defined as part of the class body it is processed by the compiler as an inline function.

Note how, because of their simplicity, it is appropriate to program the functions `day`, `month` and `year` as inline functions. As noted, this is implied if they are defined in the class body. Equally, if they are defined separate from the class body and qualified as `inline`, then the definitions must appear in the header file:

```
// ———————— FILE: date01.h ————————

#ifndef DATE
  #define DATE

  enum Bool { FALSE, TRUE };

  class Date{
  public:
    void  set(int aDay, int aMonth, int aYear);
    int          day(void);
    int          month(void);
    int          year(void);
    int          zeller(void);
    int          difference(const Date& aDate);
  private:
    int          theDay;                   // representation
    int          theMonth;
    int          theYear;

    long  julian(int, int, int);           // support functions
    Bool  isLeap(int y);
    int          daysInMonth(int aMonth, int aYear);
    int          dayOfYear(int aDay, int aMonth, int aYear);
  };        // Date
```

```
  // .....

  inline int      Date::day(void)
          { return theDay; }

  inline int      Date::month(void)
          { return theMonth; }

  inline int      Date::year(void)
          { return theYear; }

#endif    // DATE
// ———————— END: date01.h ————————
```

This approach has the usual advantage of inlining functions whilst at the same time removing the function body from the class declaration which otherwise distorts the appearance of the latter making it difficult to see what member functions are supported by the class.

Member functions of greater complexity than that of `Date` member function `day` are defined in an associated program unit (see Chapter 7). Since C++ permits different classes to have member functions overloaded with the same name, it is necessary to specify the class of a member function when defining it outside the class declaration. The *scope resolution operator* (`::`) is used to select a class member. Here is the definition of function `set` from class `Date` (inlined and included in the header file):

```
inline void       Date::set(int aDay, int aMonth, int aYear)
{
  theDay          = aDay;
  theMonth        = aMonth;
  theYear         = aYear;
}
```

Member function definitions are within the scope of their class. As a consequence, the data members of the class object on which a member function is operating can be referenced without the member access operator. Member function `set`, for example, refers to `theDay` without qualification.

Structurally, the program organization is the same as that of Chapter 7. The header file `date01.h` contains the class declaration and the definition for any inline functions. The file content is protected from multiple inclusion through the usual conditional compilation arrangements. The program unit `date01.cpp` is the code file for the non-inline member functions. The arrangement is as shown in Figure 9.2.

```
// ———————— FILE: date01.cpp ————————

#include "date01.h"

int         Date::zeller(void)
{
  const int k = theDay;           // day and .....
  int y = theYear;                // year number
```

date01.h
#ifndef DATE
#define DATE
enum Bool {FALSE, TRUE};
class Date {
public:
void set(int, int, int);
// .....
};
inline void Date::set(.....){.....}
// .....
#endif // Date
date01.h
#include "date01.h"
int Date::zeller(.....){.....}

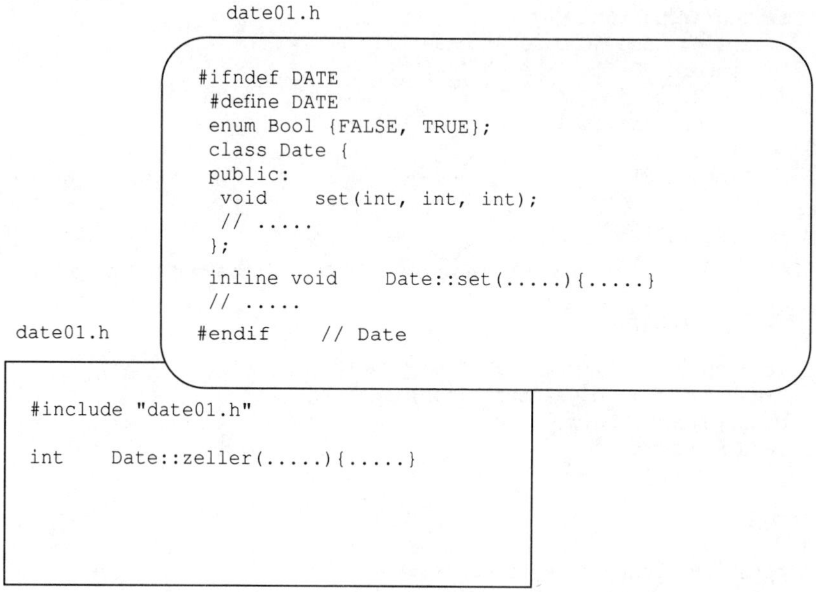

Figure 9.2

```
  int m;                  // month number
  if(theMonth < 3){
    m = theMonth + 10;
    y = theYear - 1;
  } else
    m = theMonth - 2;

  const int d = y % 100;  // year and .....
  const int c = y / 100;  // century

  int z = (26*m - 2)/10 + k + d + (d/4) + (c/4) - 2*c + 77;
  return (z % 7);
}
int       Date::difference(const Date& aDate)
{
  const long thisJulian = julian(theDay, theMonth, theYear);
  const long thatJulian = julian(aDate.theDay, aDate.theMonth,
                                                 aDate.theYear);
  return thisJulian - thatJulian;
}

inline Bool       Date::isLeap(int y)
{
  return (y % 4 == 0 && y % 100 != 0 || y % 400 == 0) ? TRUE : FALSE;
}

int               Date::daysInMonth(int aMonth, int aYear)
```

```
{
  switch(aMonth){
    case 4: case 6: case 9: case 11:
      return 30;
    case 2:
      return (isLeap(aYear) == TRUE) ? 29 : 28;
    default:
      return 31;
  }
}

int               Date::dayOfYear(int aDay, int aMonth, int aYear)
{
  int dayofyear = 0;

  for(int mon = 1; mon < aMonth; mon++)
    dayofyear += daysInMonth(mon, aYear);
  dayofyear += aDay;
  return dayofyear;
}

long              Date::julian(int aDay, int aMonth, int aYear)
{
  const int leapyear = isLeap(aYear);
  const int dayofyear = dayOfYear(aDay, aMonth, aYear);
  int leapyears = aYear/4 - aYear/100 + aYear/400;
  if(leapyear == FALSE)
    leapyears++;
  return 365L * aYear + leapyears + dayofyear;
}

// ———————— END: date01.cpp ————————
```

Observe how functions such as `set` and `difference` form the public interface to the class and represent the collection of publicized operations that may be used by a client. The other functions, such as `julian`, provide support for these principal operations but otherwise play no part in the interface and are declared in the private section.

The success of a class is often determined by the range of services that it supports through its public member functions. The class should be designed so that it can be used in many applications. For example, in our version of class `Date` the only public services are those necessary to solve the given problem. The design of the class should reflect a desire to build one of general applicability. For example, the member `isLeap` has been placed in the private section since in this problem it only has a supportive role, yet for some other application we may wish to know if a date represents a leap year. Therefore, we might expect a `Date` class to have `isLeap` and other date services as part of its public interface. A more useful `Date` class is part of a class library we develop in later chapters, and is often provided by the compiler vendor or other third party software developers.

Class member functions, like normal functions, can have default arguments. For example, the member function `set` of class `Date`, denoted `Date::set()`, would use the default values for January 1, 1990 if no arguments were passed to it. The revised function declaration is:

```
class Date{
public:
  void    set(int aDay = 1, int aMonth = 1, int aYear = 1990);
  // .....
};          // Date
```

Default argument initializers are only provided in the function declaration. They do not appear, or reappear, in the function definition.

Note how for every call of the member function `difference` the actual `Date` argument is transmitted to the function using pass by reference. We might equally have considered using pass by value but the overhead would be slightly greater since the actual value is copied. However, for classes with large representations, using pass by value would prove very expensive and to avoid this unnecessary copying we should declare such functions to take class reference arguments. Further, where the arguments are not modified by the function they should be qualified as `const` as in function `difference`.

9.2 Calling other member functions

Member functions are not like the ordinary functions of Chapter 5 – they can only be called in association with a class object. If, however, the definition of one member function involves calling another member function, then no object needs to be explicitly referenced. The subordinate function is called as if it were an ordinary function. The member function being defined will, of course, be associated with an object when called. This object is effectively carried forward in the call of the subordinate function.

Consider the class `Date` above. The member function `difference` uses a subordinate function `julian` to convert a `Date` value into a number of days elapsed since some epoch.

```
class Date{
public:
   int            difference(Date&);    // note, const has been
                                               removed (see section 9.7)!
  // .....
private:
  int             theDay;
  int             theMonth;
  int             theYear;

  long            julian(void);
  // .....
};
```

The function has no arguments since it operates on the representation of the `Date` object for which it is called. The public function difference is programmed as:

```
int  Date::difference(Date& aDate)
{
  const long thisJulian = julian();              // no object named!!
  const long thatJulian = aDate.julian();
  return (thisJulian - thatJulian);
}
```

The second call to julian applies the function to the Date class argument aDate. This is the conventional use of a member function applied to a class instance. The first call has no explicit class object named. In this case the class object for which member function difference is called is considered the object reference for function julian (see Section 9.11).

9.3 Class constructors and class initialization

Program 9.1 provides the function Date::set() to initialize objects of class Date. Of course, it is not obligatory for the programmer to call this function. Failure to do so results in uninitialized values – a source of many, difficult kinds of programming problems. A safer approach is to provide, for every class, a function for initializing objects when they are created. A special class member function, called a *constructor*, is invoked implicitly by the compiler whenever a class object is established. The name constructor reflects the function usage – to construct properly initialized values of the class type.

A constructor function is a user-defined initialization function given the tag name of the class. For example:

```
class Date {
public:
  Date(int aDay, int aMonth, int aYear = 1990);    // constructor
  // .....
private:
  int     theDay;
  int     theMonth;
  int     theYear;
};

inline Date::Date(int aDay, int aMonth, int aYear)
{
  theDay = aDay;
  theMonth = aMonth;
  theYear = aYear;
}
```

The constructor function does not specify a return type or return a value. In this example the constructor for Date requires two or three arguments of type int. The default for the third argument is the year 1990. A constructor can be used to create objects of this type, using the syntax:

```
constructor-name(actual-argument-list)
```

and used as an initializer as in:

```
Date hogmanay = Date(31, 12, 1989);
```

The abbreviated form, more commonly employed, is:

```
Date hogmanay(31, 12, 1989);
```

(Hogmanay is a Scots word of uncertain origin used to denote the last day of the year – December 31. It is a time when people forget their woes, slake their thirst, and look to the future.)

Since the definition of a class object implicitly calls the constructor function, compile time type checking is performed on the definition. Several further examples of the definition of `Date` objects using this constructor are:

```
int decade = 1990;

Date newyearday(1, 1);              // ok, default year 1990
Date birthday;                      // error: no arguments
Date xmas(25, 12, 1989, 1989);      // error: four arguments
Date epoch(&decade);                // error: bad type: int*
```

It is quite common to provide several ways to initialize a class object. A collection of alternative initializations is provided by overloading the constructor. For example:

```
class Date {
public:
     Date(int, int, int);          // day, month, year
     Date(int, int);               // day number, year
     Date(long int);               // julian day
     Date(int, char*, int);        // day, month name, year
     // .....
};
```

The compiler selects the correct constructor function according to the actual arguments:

```
Date xmas(25, 12, 1989);            // December 25, 1989
Date hogmanay(365, 1989);           // December 31, 1989
Date christian(1L);                 // first day of epoch
Date newyear(1, "January", 1990);   // first day of 1990
```

It is also useful to permit the definition of a `Date` object without the need to supply an argument list. For example, we may wish to declare objects as:

```
Date today;
```

This can be achieved by defaulting all the arguments for one of the previous constructors, or by supplying a *default constructor*. A default constructor has an empty argument list:

```
class Date {
public:
     Date(void);     // default constructor
     // .....
};
```

The implementation of the default constructor for the `Date` class might obtain the computer system date using the appropriate library functions (see Appendix F.11). In the presence of this constructor, the following are both correct definitions of the variable `now` as a `Date` class object:

```
Date     now;               // abbreviated form
Date     now = Date();      // explicit form
```

By providing appropriate checks, the constructor function can be made to ensure that a class object is properly initialized. For example, the `Date` constructor:

```
class Date {
public:
     Date(int aDayNumber, int aYear);        // constructor, day-in-
                                                         year and year
     // .....
};
```

can ensure that the initializing arguments `aDayNumber` and `aYear` represent a legal date. Here we would require that `aDayNumber` >= 1, `aYear` >= 0, and `aDayNumber` <= 366 for a leap year and `aDayNumber` <= 365 for a non-leap year. Failing this, the constructor might report an error, terminate, give predefined defaults, or some combination of these actions. This is demonstrated in Program 9.2 which reports an error, then terminates using the library function `exit` declared in the header file `<stdlib.h>`.

PROGRAM 9.2

```
// ———————— FILE: p02.cpp ————————

#include "date02.h"

int main()
{
  Date     hogmanay(365, 1990);          // ok
  Date     newyeareve(366, 1992);        // ok
  Date     bad(366, 1990);               // error: non-existent date

  // ..... others
  return (0);
}

// ———————— END: p02.cpp ————————

// ———————— FILE: date02.h ————————
```

```
#ifndef DATE
  #define DATE

  enum Bool { FALSE, TRUE };

  class Date {
  public:
    Date(int aDayNumber = 1, int aYear = 0);      // constructor
  private:
    int          theDayNumber;           // representation
    int          theYear;

    Bool         isLeap(void);           // hidden operation
  };

  inline Bool Date::isLeap(void)
  {
    return (theYear % 4 == 0 && theYear % 100 != 0
    || theYear % 400 == 0) ? TRUE : FALSE;
  }

#endif    // DATE

// ——————— END: date02.h ———————

// ——————— FILE: date02.cpp ———————

#include <iostream.h>
#include <stdlib.h>
#include "date02.h"

Date::Date(int aDayNumber, int aYear)
{
  if(aYear < 0){
    cout << "Error: Date(....., " << aYear << ")\n";
    exit(EXIT_FAILURE);
  }

  theYear = aYear;
  const int daysinyear = isLeap() ? 366 : 365;

  if(aDayNumber < 0 || aDayNumber > daysinyear){
    cout << "Error: Date(" << aDayNumber << ", .....)\n";
    exit(EXIT_FAILURE);
  }

  theDayNumber = aDayNumber;
}

// ——————— END: date02.cpp ———————
```

Earlier we noted that the definition:

```
Date      hogmanay(31, 12, 1989);
```

was an abbreviation for:

```
Date       hogmanay = Date(31, 12, 1989);
```

and that both described the initialization of the `Date` object `hogmanay`. Effectively, the data members of the `Date` object `hogmanay` are given the corresponding values of the `Date` object created by the constructor `Date(13, 12, 1989)`. Hence we may interpret such a constructor as a means of producing a `Date` literal. This means that if we wish to assign a new `Date` value to `hogmanay` we may write:

```
hogmanay = Date(31, 12, 1993);
```

Recall from Chapters 3 and 5 that `const` and `reference` data items may only be given a value once as part of the defining initializer. Thereafter, the values cannot be changed by assignment. Following the allocation of the necessary storage, a class constructor provides the inaugural values for the data members defined for the class. The values are given by assignments in the body of the constructor functions.

Clearly, where the class data members are `const` or `reference` items, the assignment cannot be used as the initialization mechanism. Strictly, the execution of any constructor consists of two phases, namely, *initialization* and *assignment.* The constructors shown have all used the assignment phase to establish the original values for the class data members. The assignment phase is always associated with the class constructor body.

The initialization phase is specified in the definition of the constructor. It is represented by a *member initialization list* consisting of a comma-separated list of member names and initial argument expressions. The list is set off from the constructor function header by a colon symbol. The initial argument expression appears within parentheses following the member name with which it associates. For example, the member initialization list may be used to initialize the data members `theDay` and `theMonth` in class `Date` with the following:

```
class Date {
public:
     Date(int aDay, int aMonth, int aYear);        // constructor
     // .....
private:
  int        theDay;
  int        theMonth;
  int        theYear;
};

inline Date::Date(int aDay, int aMonth, int aYear)
     : theDay(aDay),                  // initialization phase
       theMonth(aMonth)
{
  theYear = aYear;                     // assignment phase
}
```

Equally in this example there need be no assignment phase, and all the initial values are given by the member initialization list. In this case the body of the constructor is null.

```
inline Date::Date(int aDay, int aMonth, int aYear)
      : theDay(aDay),          // initialization phase
        theMonth(aMonth),
        theYear(aYear)
{ /* empty */ }              // assignment phase, null
```

At this stage there is no distinction between initialization and assignment. However, `const` and `reference` data members can only employ the member initialization list mechanism to initialize them. For example:

```
class Demo {
public:
  Demo(int ip);        // constructor, integer parameter
    // .....
private:
  int       iv;        // integer variable
  const int ic;        // integer constant
};

inline Demo::Demo(int ip)
     : ic(ip)          // initialization, necessary
{
  iv = ip;             // assignment, or by initialization
}
```

Since the effect is the same, the data member `iv` could alternatively have been assigned in the member initialization list. However, the following constructor is illegal:

```
inline Demo::Demo(int ip)
{                     // assignment phase:
  iv = ip;            // ok
  ic = ip;            // error: cannot assign a constant data member
}
```

The problem is that initialization of `const` (and `reference`) data members must already have been established before the body of the constructor (the assignment phase) is executed.

In Program 9.3 we have the solution for Program 9.1 expressed in terms of constructors which establish properly initialized `Date` objects.

PROGRAM 9.3

```
// ———————— FILE: p03.cpp ————————

#include <iostream.h>
#include "date03.h"

void      printDate(Date);// prototypes
void      printDay(int);
void      printMonth(int);

int main()
```

```
{
  int      day, month, year;
  char     separator;
  Date     sentinel(1, 1, 2000);

  cout << "Enter data values:\n";
  cin >> day >> separator >> month >> separator >> year;
  Date     first(day, month, year);

  cin >> day >> separator >> month >> separator >> year;
  Date     other(day, month, year);
  while(other.difference(sentinel) != 0){
    if(other.difference(first) > 14)
      printDate(other);
    cin >> day >> separator >> month >> separator >> year;
    other = Date(day, month, year);
  }
  return (0);
}

void       printDate(Date aDate)
{
  // ..... as before
}

void       printDay(int d)
{
  // ..... as before
}

void       printMonth(int m)
{
  // ..... as before
}

// ————————— END: p03.cpp —————————

// ————————— FILE: date03.h —————————

#ifndef DATE
  #define DATE

  enum Bool { FALSE, TRUE };

  class Date{
  public:
    Date(int aDay, int aMonth, int aYear);
    int            day(void);
    int            month(void);
    int            year(void);
    int            zeller(void);
    int            difference(Date aDate);
  private:
    int            theDay;                  // representation
    int            theMonth;
    int            theYear;
```

```
    long          julian(int, int, int); // support functions
    Bool          isLeap(int y);
    int           daysInMonth(int aMonth, int aYear);
    int           dayOfYear(int aDay, int aMonth, int aYear);
  };      // Date

  inline Date::Date(int aDay, int aMonth, int aYear)
  {
    theDay        = aDay;
    theMonth      = aMonth;
    theYear       = aYear;
  }

  inline int        Date::day(void)
   { return theDay; }

  inline int        Date::month(void)
   { return theMonth; }

  inline int        Date::year(void)
   { return theYear; }

  inline Bool     Date::isLeap(int y)
   { return (y % 4 == 0 && y % 100 != 0 || y % 400 == 0) ? TRUE :
                                                              FALSE; }

#endif    // DATE

// ---------- END: date03.h ----------
```

We may initialize an object of some class with another object of the same class. For example, the second definition below, initializes variable `newyeareve` with the value of the variable `hogmanay`:

```
Date hogmanay(31, 12, 1990);
Date newyeareve = hogmanay;
```

The initialization is performed by initializing the values of the data members of `hogmanay` to the corresponding data members of `newyeareve`.

A constructor that is invoked with an argument with the type of its own class specifies how to initialize an object with another of the same class. Such a constructor, known as the *copy constructor*, is presented with a single argument of type reference to the class for which it is a member. For some class `X`, the copy constructor has the signature `X(const X&)`. In the second definition above, the copy constructor is called to effect the initialization. The example is an abbreviation for:

```
Date newyeareve(hogmanay);
```

in which we explicitly present the invocation of the copy constructor. Defining an `X(const X&)` constructor for a class emphasizes that the copying of objects of class `X` requires special control. If no copy constructor is given, then by default the compiler generates such a function. In Chapter 12 we shall meet examples where we must take control of the copying process.

The initialization of `newyeareve` is performed by copying the data members of `hogmanay` into the corresponding members of `newyeareve`. This is referred to as ***memberwise initialization***, in which the compiler implicitly defines the copy constructor like:

```
class Date {
public:
  Date(const Date& aDate)   // copy constructor
  {
    theDay        = aDate.theDay;
    theMonth      = aDate.theMonth;
    theYear       = aDate.theYear;
  }
  // .....
private:
  int     theDay;
  int     theMonth;
  int     theYear;
};
```

In addition to that described above, there are two further program situations where there is initialization of one class object with another of the same class. The full list is:

1. One class object is explicitly initialized with an object of the same class. This has been illustrated above with the declaration for `Date` class objects `hogmanay` and `newyeareve`.
2. A class object is passed by value as the argument to a function. For example, a non-member function `isWeekend` with prototype declaration:

   ```
   Bool isWeekend(Date d);
   ```

   expects an actual argument of class `Date`. The function call:

   ```
   if(isWeekend(hogmanay)) .....
   ```

   results in the local instance of the formal parameter `d` initialized with the actual argument `hogmanay`.
3. A class object is the return value of a function. For example, the non-member function `tomorrow` with prototype declaration:

   ```
   Date tomorrow(Date d);
   ```

   and the call:

   ```
   holiday = tomorrow(hogmanay);
   ```

In situation 2, it is the local copy of the class object that causes the object initialization. This, of course, is because of the nature of pass by value.

Note how the copy constructor's argument is of type `const X&` for some class `X`. This signature is used for two reasons. First, if we used call by value, then a copy of the actual argument would be passed, which if the class represented a large object, would prove expensive (worse, a recursive call to the same function would result as in situation 2 above). Instead, the reference argument aliases the formal argument with the actual argument. Second, to ensure the function does not modify the value of the actual argument we declare the parameter as `const`.

We shall demonstrate in later chapters how, under certain circumstances, the default memberwise initialization is inadequate. A class can take additional responsibility by defining an explicit version of the `X::X(const X&)` constructor. This explicitly defined constructor is then called to initialize one class object with another.

We demonstrate the use of an explicit initializing constructor in Program 9.4. As shown we trace the existence and behaviour of this constructor with suitable print statements. The program output is:

```
Date(31, 12, 1991)
Date(31, 12, 1991)
Date(1, 1, 1992)
Tomorrow's date: 1/1/1992
```

and demonstrates the three implicit calls to the initialization constructor `Date::Date(const Date&)`.

PROGRAM 9.4

```
// ────────── FILE: p04.cpp ──────────

#include <iostream.h>
#include "date04.h"

int main()
{
  Date    today(31, 12, 1991);
  Date    now = today;              // call Date(const Date&) for
                                                     intialization
  Date    tomorrow(Date);                  // prototype

                                    // call Date(const Date&) for
                                                          argument
  Date nextday = tomorrow(today);

  cout << "Tomorrow\'s date: "
       << nextday.day()
       << "/" << nextday.month()
       << "/" << nextday.year() << "\n";

  return (0);
}

Date      tomorrow(Date aDate)
{
  Date nextday(1 + aDate.julian());
  return nextday;                   // and Date(const Date&) for result
}
```

```
// ———————— END: p04.cpp ————————

// ———————— FILE: date04.h ————————

#ifndef DATE
  #define DATE

  class Date{
  public:
    Date(int aDay, int aMonth, int aYear);// basic constructors
    Date(long aJulian);
    Date(const Date& aDate);                     // copy constructor

    int            day(void);
    int            month(void);
    int            year(void);
    int            zeller(void);
    long           julian(void);
    int            difference(Date aDate);
  private:
    int            theDay;                      // representation
    int            theMonth;
    int            theYear;

    int            dayOfYear(int aDay, int aMonth, int aYear);
    int            daysInMonth(int aMonth, int aYear);
  };      // Date

  inline Date::Date(int aDay, int aMonth, int aYear)
  {
    theDay         = aDay;
    theMonth       = aMonth;
    theYear        = aYear;
  }

  inline int      Date::day(void)
   { return theDay; }

  inline int      Date::month(void)
   { return theMonth; }

  inline int      Date::year(void)
   { return theYear; }

#endif    // DATE

// ———————— END: date04.h ————————


// ———————— FILE: date04.cpp ————————

#include <iostream.h>
#include "date04.h"

enum Bool { FALSE, TRUE };
```

```
inline Bool       isLeap(int aYear)
{
  return (aYear % 4 == 0 && aYear % 100 != 0 || aYear % 400 ==0) ?
          TRUE : FALSE;
}

Date::Date(const Date& aDate)
{
  cout << "Date(" << aDate.theDay << ", " << aDate.theMonth
      << ", " << aDate.theYear << ")\n";
  theDay          = aDate.theDay;
  theMonth        = aDate.theMonth;
  theYear         = aDate.theYear;
}

Date::Date(long aJulian)
{
  int estyear = aJulian/365;
  int leapyears = estyear/4 - estyear/100 + estyear/400;
  Bool leapyear = isLeap(estyear);
  int remdays = aJulian - leapyears - 365L * estyear;
  if(leapyear == FALSE)
    remdays--;

  while(remdays <= 0){
    estyear--;
    leapyears = estyear/4 - estyear/100 + estyear/400;
    leapyear = isLeap(estyear) ? TRUE : FALSE;
    remdays = aJulian - leapyears - 365L * estyear;
    if(leapyear == FALSE)
      remdays--;
  }

  for(int mon = 1; mon <= 12; mon++){    // Jan to Dec
    const int dayofyear = dayOfYear(1, mon, estyear);
    if(remdays < dayofyear){
      theYear = estyear;
      theMonth = mon - 1;
      theDay = remdays - dayOfYear(1, mon-1, estyear) + 1;
      return;
    }
  }
  theYear = estyear;
  theMonth = 12;               // December
  theDay = remdays - dayOfYear(1, 12, estyear) + 1;
}

int        Date::zeller(void)
{
  // .....
}

int        Date::difference(Date aDate)
{
  // .....
```

```
}

long        Date::julian(void)
{
  // .....
}

int         Date::daysInMonth(int aMonth, int aYear)
{
  // .....
}

int         Date::dayOfYear(int aDay, int aMonth, int aYear)
{
  // .....
}

// ———————— END: date04.cpp ————————
```

From Chapter 7 we know that global variables or local variables declared as `static` are initialized once at the commencement of the program. By the same token, C++ calls the necessary constructors to initialize static or global class objects. If, for example, we write:

```
Date epoch(1, 1, 1900);

int main()
{
  // .....
}
```

the constructor to initialize `epoch` is called before any other C++ statements are executed. Hence the first executable statement obeyed in a program is either the first statement in `main`, the first constructor called from `main` to initialize a class object, or the statements for the constructors for any global or static class objects.

9.4 Arrays and class objects

The data members of a user-defined class may be any of the fundamental types or any derived type such as an array or another class type (see Section 9.8). For example, a *stack* is a data type in which the last item added to the stack is the first to be removed. A stack is an unbounded ordered collection of items into which new items may be inserted and from which items may be deleted. Both insertion and deletion take place at one end of the stack called the *stack top*. The stack may be realized using an array for its representation.

From the definition, a single end of the stack must be designated as the stack top. New items may be put on top of the stack (in which case the top of the stack moves upward to correspond to the new element), or the item at the top of the stack may be removed (and the stack top moves downward). See Figure 9.3.

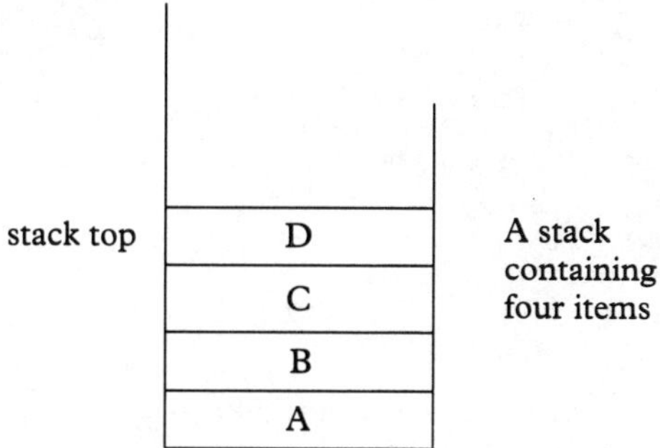

Figure 9.3

The three primitive operations that can be applied to a stack are given special names. When an item is added to the stack, it is `pushed` on to the stack. Given a stack `s` and an item `i`, performing the operation `s.push(i)` is defined as adding the item to the top of the stack.

The operation `s.pop()` removes the top element from the stack `s`. The operation `s.top()` delivers a copy of the topmost element in stack `s`, the stack remaining unchanged. If a stack contains a single item and the stack is popped, the resulting stack contains no items and the stack is called the empty stack. The `top` and the `pop` operations cannot be applied to the empty stack because such a stack has no element to deliver or remove. Therefore, before applying such operations we must ensure that the stack is not empty. The operation `isEmpty` determines whether or not a stack is empty.

Theoretically, there is no upper limit on the number of items that may be kept in a stack. A simple implementation is to use an array to hold the items, which bounds the stack according to the array size. The stack top is maintained by an array subscript which indexes the topmost item of the stack. When a new item is pushed on the stack the index is increased by one and the item stored at that position in the array. Equally, when the stack is popped the index is reduced by one.

Program 9.5 reads a series of positive integers of unknown number (with a negative terminator) and prints the values in reverse order. The problem solution is to push each data value on to the stack until the sentinel is reached. The sentinel is not recorded on the stack. The data items are then repeatedly popped off the stack and printed until the stack is empty.

PROGRAM 9.5

```
// ———————— FILE: p05.cpp ————————

#include <iostream.h>
#include "intstack.h"
```

```
int main()
{
  int            data;
  IntStack       stack;

  cout << "Start entering the data:\n";
  cin >> data;
  while(data >= 0){
    stack.push(data);
    cin >> data;
  }

  cout << "\nReversed data values:\n";
  while( ! stack.isEmpty()){
    data = stack.top();
    cout << data << "\n";
    stack.pop();
  }
  return (0);
}
// ———— END: p05.cpp ————

// ———— FILE: intstack.h ————
#ifndef INTSTACK
  #define INTSTACK

  enum Bool { FALSE, TRUE };

  class IntStack {
  public:
    IntStack(void);                 // basic constructor

    void  push(int item);           // add item to stack top
    void  pop(void);                // remove item from stack top
    int   top(void);                // copy of top stack item

    Bool  isEmpty(void);            // is stack empty?
    int   depth(void);              // number of items in stack
    void  reverse(void);            // reorder stack items (unusual)
  private:
    int         stack[100];         // array representation
    int         stackTop;           // stack top
  };

  inline IntStack::IntStack(void)
   { stackTop = -1; }

  inline void     IntStack::push(int item)
   { stack[++stackTop] = item; }

  inline void     IntStack::pop(void)
   { stackTop—; }

  inline int      IntStack::top(void)
   { return stack[stackTop]; }
```

```
    inline Bool      IntStack::isEmpty(void)
     { return (stackTop < 0) ? TRUE : FALSE; }

    inline int       IntStack::depth(void)
     { return 1 + stackTop; }

#endif     // INTSTACK

// ————— END: intstack.h —————

// ————— FILE: intstack.cpp —————

#include "intstack.h"

void       IntStack::reverse(void)
{
  if(stackTop > 0){
    const int middle = (1 + stackTop) / 2;
    int ktop = stackTop;
    for(int k = 0; k < middle; k++, ktop--){
      const int temp = stack[k];
      stack[k] = stack[ktop];
      stack[ktop] = temp;
    }
  }
}

// ————— END: intstack.cpp —————
```

The class `IntStack` has been provided with two further operations. They are used in an exercise in this chapter. Function `depth` determines the number of items in the stack. Function `reverse` is an unusual stack operation since it disturbs the order of the items in the stack. The function fully reverses the order of the elements in the stack with the topmost now at the bottom, the second from top now second from bottom, and so on. Of course, applying the `reverse` operation twice to the same stack will reinstate the original configuration.

In the previous chapter we saw how to define an array. The elements of the array we said can be any fundamental or derived type, including pointers and user-defined class types. Given a `Date` class we might expect to be able to define:

```
const int ALLOWANCE = 40;
Date      holidays[ALLOWANCE];
```

However, the compiler will only accept such a definition if the `Date` class has either:

(a) No constructor (see Program 9.1), or
(b) A constructor with no formal arguments, i.e. a default constructor or a constructor in which all the formal arguments have a default initializer value.

This arrangement is necessary because the compiler insists on calling a constructor to initialize all the `Date` items of the array. This is not unreasonable since, after all, we introduced constructors to properly initialize objects of a user-defined class type, and an array is simply an aggregate of such types.

The `Date` class:

```
class Date {
public:
  Date(int aDay, int aMonth, int aYear = 1900);
  // .....
};
```

will result in a compile time error in the definition for the array `holidays`. The class would have to initialize all three arguments of the constructor or provide a default constructor:

```
class Date {
public:
  Date(void);                          // default constructor
  Date(int aDay, int aMonth, int aYear = 1900);
  // .....
};
```

We can also use an explicit initializer list for the elements of an array of class objects. Again, for example, we can write:

```
Date special[2]    = { Date(25, 12, 1992), Date(31, 12, 1992) };
date bank[]        = { Date(31, 5, 1993), Date(30, 8, 1993) };
const int BANKHOLIDAYS = sizeof(bank) / sizeof(bank[0]);
```

with the second example using the compiler to determine the number of items in the array.

If the array size is given explicitly and the number of items in the initializer exceeds this value then, as in the previous chapter, a compiler error is reported. If there are fewer items in the list then, as above, a default constructor or one with all arguments defaulted is required, and this constructor will be called to initialize the missing array elements. Using the `Date` class above:

```
Date       holidays[5]    = { Date(10, 7, 1993), Date(27, 9, 1993) };
```

the final three array elements are initialized with the default constructor. If no such default constructor is available then the user must fully complete the initializer list.

An individual element of an array is, of course, referred to with a subscripted variable. For example, to assign the tenth element of the array `holidays` to some `Date` object we might have:

```
Date       today;            // default constructor
today = holidays[9];         // assignment of two Date objects
```

Since the expression `holidays[9]` references the tenth element of the array which is a `Date` object then we may apply any of the `Date` class member functions to this object with the member access operator:

```
int todayMonth = holidays[9].month();
```

The following program illustrates the issues associated with arrays of class objects. The program initializes an array of holiday dates then prints them in the manner of Program 9.1.

PROGRAM 9.6

```
// ———————— FILE: p06.cpp ————————

#include <iostream.h>
#include "date04.h"

char*     dayNames[] = {
  "Sunday", "Monday", "Tuesday", "Wednesday",
  "Thursday", "Friday", "Saturday"
};

char*     monthNames[] = {
  "January", "February", "March", "April",
  "May", "June", "July", "August",
  "September", "October", "November", "December"
};

int main()
{
  Date     holidays[] = { Date(31, 5, 1993), Date(27, 7, 1993),
                  Date(25, 12, 1993), Date(31, 12, 1993)
                };
  const int HOLIDAYS = sizeof(holidays) / sizeof(holidays[0]);

  cout << "Holidays:\n";
  for(int k = 0; k < HOLIDAYS; k++)
    cout << dayNames[holidays[k].zeller()] << " "
   << holidays[k].day() << " "
   << monthNames[holidays[k].month()-1] << " "
   << holidays[k].year() << "\n";

  return (0);
}

// ———————— END: p06.cpp ————————
```

9.5 Destructors

When a class object is defined, storage space for its data members is allocated and the constructor is called. The constructor is responsible for any additional installation procedures associated with the object. For example, the constructor for class `Date` is concerned with storage initialization.

Whenever an object of a class goes out of scope, its storage space is deallocated. A user-defined class may include a special member function which is called when an object of that class is deallocated. This member function, called the *destructor*, is used to define any clean up operations associated with objects of the class.

```
int main()
{
  Date    today(27, 9, 1990); // constructor call here
  // .....
}                         // destructor call here
```

Presently, we have no practical use for destructors. Unlike our constructors, destructors have no corresponding de-initialization duties to perform. In later chapters we shall find a proper role for these member functions. For completeness, however, we introduce them here.

A member function is introduced as the class destructor by giving it the class tag name prefixed with the tilde (~) symbol. This unusual member function name is intended to connote the complement of the constructor. Like its constructor counterpart, a destructor does not specify a return type nor include an explicit return value.

The `Date` class destructor has no explicit de-initialization to perform. The correct definition for the `Date` class destructor then is an empty function body:

```
class Date {
public:
     ~Date(void);                  // destructor
     // .....
};

inline Date::~Date(void) { }       // do nothing
```

Destructors can perform any operations required prior to the class object going out of scope. In Program 9.7 the destructor and its constructor have been augmented with print statements. The constructor prints its initialization arguments, whilst the destructor displays the value of its data members prior to deallocation of the class object. The program output is:

```
Date(31, 12, 1989)
Date(1, 1, 1990)
Date(25, 12, 1990)
~Date(25, 12, 1990)
~Date(1, 1, 1990)
~Date(31, 12, 1989)
```

and demonstrates that the global variable `hogmanay` has file scope and exists until the program end. The local (automatic) variables `newyear` and `xmas` have the body of function `main` as their scope. The class `Date` objects `xmas` and `newyear` go out of scope on return from function `main` in that order. The compiler guarantees that destructors will be called in the opposite order to that for constructors, as shown by the output.

PROGRAM 9.7

```
// ———————— FILE: p07.cpp ————————

//
// Program to demonstrate the scope of variables
//         in a C++ program. The behaviour of the program
//         is examined by tracing the constructors and the
//         destructors for class Date.
//

#include "date07.h"

Date       hogmanay(31, 12, 1989);                // global variable

int main()
{
  Date     newyear(1, 1, 1990);         // local variables
  Date     xmas(25, 12, 1990);

  // ..... others
  return (0);
}                // xmas and newyear out of scope here
          // hogmanay out of scope here

// ———————— END: p07.cpp ————————

// ———————— FILE: date07.h ————————

//
// Definition file for class Date in which the
//         constructor and destructor calls are
//         highlighted in the program with print
//         statements.
//

#ifndef DATE
  #define DATE

  #include <iostream.h>

  class Date {
  public:
    Date(int aDay, int aMonth, int aYear);// constructor
    ~Date(void);                         // destructor
  private:
    int         theDay;              // representation
    int         theMonth;
    int         theYear;
  };

  inline Date::Date(int aDay, int aMonth, int aYear)
  {
    cout << "Date(" << aDay << ", " << aMonth << ", "
              << aYear << ")\n";
    theDay = aDay;
```

```
    theMonth = aMonth;
    theYear = aYear;
  }

  inline Date::~Date(void)
  {
    cout << "~Date(" << theDay << ", " << theMonth << ", "
              << theYear << ")\n";
  }

#endif     // DATE

// ———————— END: date07.h ————————
```

9.6 Class scoping rules

The scope rules for identifiers introduced in Chapters 5 and 7 must be augmented with class scope rules. From Section 9.1 we know that all class member functions are within the scope of their associated class, and that a class member can be freely referenced within the function definition without qualification. For example, constructor function `Date` references the class data member `theDay` even when the function definition is separate from the class declaration:

```
class Date {
public:
     Date(int aDay, int aMonth, int aYear = 1990);
     // .....
private:
  int       theDay;
  int       theMonth;
  int       theYear;
};


inline Date::Date(int aDay, int aMonth, int aYear)
{
  theDay   = aDay;          // no further qualification
  theMonth= aMonth;         // required for class data members
  theYear  = aYear;
}
```

Since member functions are within the scope of their class we require rules for locating identifiers with the same name appearing as local variables in member functions, as class member objects and as global objects. An identifier used within a member function is resolved by first associating it with a declaration in the current block or any enclosing block. Next, the enclosing scope is the class, otherwise file scope is used. For example:

```
class X {
public:
  int f(void);
```

```
private:
  int x;                   // class scope
};

int  x;                    // file scope

int X::f(void) { int x = 27; return x; }  // function scope
```

The member function `f` returns the value of the local variable `x`. This would be the same if `x` were an argument to function `f` rather than a local variable. Using the scope resolution operator, this function may be made to return the class data member `x`:

```
int X::f(void) { int x = 27; return X::x; }
```

and the global variable `x` with the special syntax:

```
int X::f(void) { int x = 27; return ::x; }
```

9.7 Constant member functions

In Chapter 3 the `const` qualifier was introduced. The qualifier specifies that the named object cannot have its value changed. The compiler reports an error if any attempt is made to modify a `const` object.

Class objects may also be specified as `const`. A `const` class object is one in which the data members are never modified following initialization. For example:

```
const Date hogmanay(31, 12, 1989);
```

The data members of class objects are normally modified through the provision of a set of public member functions. To ensure that the data members of a `const` class object remain constant, the compiler must distinguish between member functions that do and those that do not enforce the constancy of the data members.

The class member functions which respect the integrity of the data members are specified as `const`. For example:

```
class Date {
public:
  Date(int aDay, int aMonth, int aYear);
  int       year(void) const { return theYear; }
  // .....
private:
  int       theDay;
  int       theMonth;
  int       theYear;
};
```

The `const` keyword is placed as shown. A member function defined separate from the class body must include the `const` keyword in both places. For example:

```
class Date {
public:
  Date(int aDay, int aMonth, int aYear);
  int      year(void) const;
  // .....
};

inline int Date::year(void) const
    { return theYear; }
```

Member functions specified as `const` can be applied to a `const` class object. For example:

```
if(hogmanay.year() == 1989) .....     // permissible
hogmanay.set(31, 12, 1990);           // disallowed
```

A member function declared as `const` may not modify a data member. A compile-time error is reported if any attempt is made to violate this rule. For example:

```
class Date {
public:
  Date(int aDay, int aMonth, int aYear);
  void      setYear(int aYear) const
    { theYear = aYear; }                  // error
  // .....
};
```

9.8 Class member objects

It is possible to define classes that contain other class objects as one or more members. An application might, for instance, process details of the book stock held in a library. For each book the following information is maintained: the book title, the author, the publication and accession date and the library catalog number. The date of publication is readily implemented using a `Date` class as previously illustrated. The title and author are obviously character strings for which an array of characters may be employed. However, as observed in Chapter 8, arrays of `char` are a somewhat primitive arrangement for strings. We might then consider developing and using a `String` class for this purpose:

```
class String {
public:
  String(char* str = "");          // constructor
  String(const String& str);       // copy constructor
  // .....
};
```

The default constructor shown expects a literal string as defined in Chapter 3 to initialize a `String` object. If absent, an empty character string is used. Hence we can define `String` objects as:

```
String   ken("Barclay");
```

Thus we might have the declaration:

```
class Book {
public:
  Book(const String& aTitle, const String& anAuthor,
          const Date& aPublication, const Date& anAccession,
                  int aCatalog);
  // .....
private:
  String          theTitle;         // representation
  String          theAuthor;
  Date            thePublication;
  Date            theAccession;
  int             theCatalog;
};
```

Five constructors must now be activated for every `Book` object – the constructor for the `Book` object itself, the constructors for the two `String` members `theTitle` and `theAuthor`, and for the two `Date` class member named `thePublication` and `theAccession`. In Section 9.4 we noted that generally, there is no distinction between initialization and assignment when establishing a class constructor. However, in this example the member initialization list is the only correct means of initializing the `String` class members `theTitle`, `theAuthor` and the `Date` class members `thePublication` and `theAccession`. Here is the `Book` constructor:

```
Book::Book(const String& aTitle, const String& anAuthor,
                  const Date& aPublication, const Date& anAccession,
                          int aCatalog)
    : theTitle(aTitle),               // initialization phase
      theAuthor(anAuthor),
      thePublication(aPublication),
      theAccession(anAccession)
{
  theCatalog = aCatalog;            // or as part of initialization phase
}
```

We might have considered using the assignment phase of the `Book` constructor to initialize its data members as in:

```
Book::Book(const String& aTitle, const String& anAuthor,
                  const Date& aPublication, const Date& anAccession,
                          int aCatalog)
{
  theTitle          = aTitle;               // assignment phase
  theAuthor         = anAuthor;
  thePublication    = aPublication;
  theAccession      = anAccession;
  theCatalog        = aCatalog;
}
```

However, this would be incorrect for two reasons. First, when we enter the assignment phase for the constructor the data members will have already been initialized. In the case of class data members this assumes that a default constructor or one with all arguments defaulted is available. If no such constructor has been defined then a compiler error will be generated. Second, if such a constructor exists, then the data member is initialized with the constructor then subsequently assigned the correct value during the assignment phase. This is obviously an expensive process requiring both an initialization and assignment. Better that we initialize the member immediately with the required value.

A class member object such as `thePublication` must appear in the member initialization list for constructor `Book`, since the `Date` constructor requires an argument list. If a `Date` constructor has the empty list:

```
class Date {
public:
    Date(void);          // default constructor
    // .....
};
```

then no explicit initialization of member `thePublication` would be necessary. It would, of course, be initialized by the actions of `Date::Date()`, which might, for example, obtain the computer system date.

The question that arises from having five constructors called is what is the order of constructor invocation? To answer it let us first consider Program 9.8, which is a development of the above. The constructors and destructors have been annotated with print statements to monitor their invocation.

PROGRAM 9.8

```
// ——————— FILE: p08.cpp ———————

#include <iostream.h>
#include "cstring.h"
#include "date07.h"
#include "book.h"

int main()
{
  String  title("C Problem Solving and Programming");
  String  author("Barclay");
  Date          publication(1, 1, 1989);
  Date          accession(1, 7, 1989);

  Book    mine(title, author, publication, accession, 12345);

  // ..... others

  return (0);
}
```

```
// ———————— END: p08.cpp ————————

// ———————— FILE: book.h ————————

#ifndef BOOK
  #define BOOK

  #include "cstring.h"
  #include "date07.h"

  class Book {
  public:
    Book(const String& aTitle, const String& anAuthor,
         const Date& aPublication, const Date& anAccession,
         int aCatalog);
    ~Book(void);
  private:
    String       theTitle;        // representation
    String       theAuthor;
    Date         thePublication;  // note order of .....
    Date         theAccession;    // ..... these two
    int          theCatalog;
  };

  inline Book::Book(const String& aTitle, const String& anAuthor,
                    const Date& aPublication, const Date& anAccession,
                    int aCatalog)
              : theTitle(aTitle),
                theAuthor(anAuthor),
                theAccession(anAccession),        // note order of .....
                thePublication(aPublication)      // ..... these two
  {
    cout << "Book(" << aCatalog << ", .....)\n";
    theCatalog = aCatalog;
  }

  inline Book::~Book(void)
   { cout << "~Book(.....)\n"; }

#endif    // BOOK

// ———————— END: book.h ————————
```

When the program is executed the following output is produced (the last two lines of output are the destructors for the variables `accession` **and** `publication` **respectively):**

```
Date(1, 1, 1989)
Date(1, 7, 1989)
Book(12345, .....)
~Book(.....)
~Date(1, 7, 1989)
~Date(1, 1, 1989)
~Date(1, 7, 1989)
~Date(1, 1, 1989)
```

The class object mine, containing a class member object such as the Date member thePublication, recursively applies the constructor ordering rules. In this rule, the class object members are initialized through their constructors before the body of the containing class constructor is executed. The destructors are called in the reverse sequence, with the destructor for the enclosing class called before that for the member class. If, as in this example, there are multiple class members, then the order of invocation of the constructors for the members is the class declaration order, and not the order of appearance in the member initialization list. Hence the constructor for the Date member thePublication is called before the constructor for theAccession.

As shown by this example, a class object may be declared as a data member of another class object. Strictly, this is only permitted if the class definition for the data member has already occurred. A forward declaration (consisting of the keyword class and the class tag name) may precede the definition proper. A forward declaration allows only pointers and references to objects of the class to appear as data members of another class. For example:

```
class Date;                  // forward declaration

class Book {
  // ..... others
private:
  long           theCatalog;
  int            theClassification;
  Date&          thePublication;          // ok, but NOT: Date
thePublication
};

class Date {
  // ..... definition proper
};
```

Only pointers and references are allowed because their storage requirements are not dependent on the class of the object they address.

CASE STUDY 9.1
Geometry

A line segment in a two-dimensional plane is defined by the coordinates of two points P and Q on the line (see Figure 9.4). An individual point is specified by its Cartesian coordinate pair (x, y) in the X and Y axes. For example, in Figure 9.4 point P has coordinates (2, 3).

A line segment has a number of geometrical properties. The *slope* of the line is the angle subtended by the line and the X axis. The slope is portrayed as the angle θ in the figure. If P and Q were the end points of the line segment, then we may compute the *length* of the line. Finally, for two such line segments we may wish to

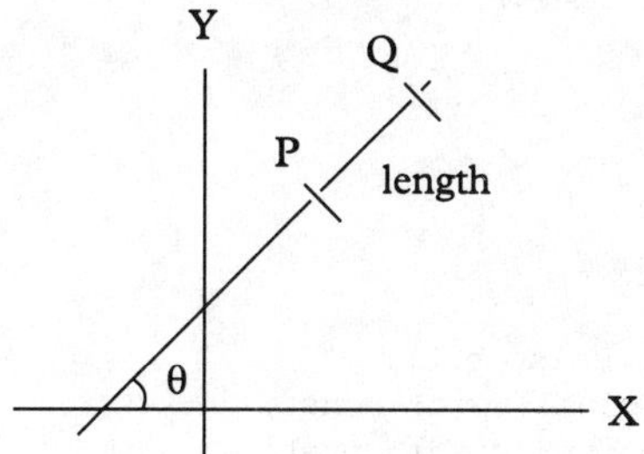

Figure 9.4

determine the coordinates of the point of *intersection*. We assume here that the lines are not parallel.

An individual point defined by its cartesian coordinates may be declared by class `Point`:

```
// ———— FILE: point.h ————

#ifndef POINT
  #define POINT

  class Point {             // Cartesian coordinate pair
  public:
    Point(double xc, double yc);
    double       xcoord(void) const;
    double       ycoord(void) const;
  private:
    double       x, y;    // coordinates
  };

  inline Point::Point(double xc, double yc)
   { x = xc; y = yc; }

  inline double   Point::xcoord(void) const
   { return x; }

  inline double   Point::ycoord(void) const
   { return y; }

#endif     // POINT

// ———— END: point.h ————
```

The coordinates are represented as a pair of doubles. The constructor `Point` initializes these private data members, whilst the accessor functions `xcoord` and `ycoord` provide controlled access. Since each function is trivially coded, they have been given inline.

A line segment is defined by a pair of points. The interface to the class `Line` is provided by the header file:

```
// ─────────── FILE: line.h ───────────

#ifndef LINE
  #define LINE

  #include "point.h"

  class Line {
  public:
    Line(Point pt1, Point pt2);
    Point          point1(void) const;
    Point          point2(void) const;
    double         length(void) const;
    double         slope(void) const;
    Point          intersection(const Line&) const;
  private:
    Point          p1, p2;
  };

  inline Line::Line(Point pt1, Point pt2)
          : p1(pt1), p2(pt2)
  {}

  inline Point    Line::point1(void) const
          { return p1; }

  inline Point    Line::point2(void) const
          { return p2; }

#endif    // LINE

// ─────────── END: line.h ───────────
```

and implemented by:

```
// ─────────── FILE: line.cpp ───────────

#include <math.h>
#include "line.h"

double    Line::length(void) const
{
  const double xdistance = p2.xcoord() - p1.xcoord();
  const double ydistance = p2.ycoord() - p1.ycoord();
  return sqrt(xdistance * xdistance + ydistance * ydistance);
}

double    Line::slope(void) const
{
  const double xdistance = p2.xcoord() - p1.xcoord();
  const double ydistance = p2.ycoord() - p1.ycoord();
  return ydistance / xdistance;
}

Point     Line::intersection(const Line& line) const
{
```

```
          // equation of first line: A1*x + B1*y + C1 = 0
          // equation of second line: A2*x + B2*y + C2 = 0
  const A1 = p1.ycoord() - p2.ycoord();
  const B1 = p2.xcoord() - p1.xcoord();
  const C1 = p1.xcoord() * p2.ycoord() - p2.xcoord() * p1.ycoord();

  const A2 = line.p1.ycoord() - line.p2.ycoord();
  const B2 = line.p2.xcoord() - line.p1.xcoord();
  const C2 = line.p1.xcoord() * line.p2.ycoord() -
               line.p2.xcoord() * line.p1.ycoord();

                      // solve linear equations to find intersection
  const double xi = (B1 * C2 - B2 * C1) / (A1 * B2 - A2 * B1);
  const double yi = (A1 * C2 - A2 * C1) / (A2 * B1 - A1 * B2);

  return Point(xi, yi);
}

// ---------- END: line.cpp ----------
```

The following program checks the behaviour of these two classes by creating a square with the vertices presented as points, and the diagonals of the square as two lines. The program then finds the intersection of these two diagonals and finds the slope for one of them.

```
// ---------- FILE: case01.cpp ----------

#include <iostream.h>
#include "line.h"

int main()
{
  Point origin(0, 0);              // four corners of a square
  Point fourzero(4, 0);
  Point fourfour(4, 4);
  Point zerofour(0, 4);

  Line    line1(origin, fourfour);// first diagonal
  Line    line2(zerofour, fourzero);    // second diagonal

                                   // length = 4 * sqrt(2) = 5.66
  cout << "Length of line1: " << line1.length() << "\n";
                                   // slope = 1
  cout << "Slope of line1: " << line1.slope() << "\n";

                                   // intersection at (2, 2)
  Point intersect = line1.intersection(line2);

  cout << "Intersection of line1 and line2: ";
  cout << "(" << intersect.xcoord() << ", " << intersect.ycoord() <<
")\n";

  return (0);
}

// ---------- END: case01.cpp ----------
```

CASE STUDY 9.2
Patient statistics

A doctor keeps statistics on the number of visits made by each patient in addition to the usual medical records. A doctor is responsible for a number of patients, and for each patient the doctor records their name, date of birth, and the number of visits made by that patient in one calendar year. The date of birth will be used by the doctor subsequently to analyze the distribution of visits according to age groups. In the first study, a doctor wishes to know what is the average number of visits across all patients, and have a printout of those patients with more than five visits above the average.

From the problem outline we highlight two candidate classes, namely, `Patient` and `Doctor`. Both classes have name properties, the name of the doctor and the name of the patient. In addition, the patient has a date of birth and a number of visits recorded. As in Figure 9.1 we may present class diagrams for the two relevant classes. More significantly, this problem identifies that there is a natural relationship between the classes. A doctor will be responsible for a number of patients, and a patient will be cared for by one doctor (strictly, in modern medical practices a more complex relationship will exist between doctors and patients). This we show in our class diagram (Figure 9.5) with the *relation* `registeredWith` between a patient and one doctor. The relation also shows that a number (`N`) of patients are under the care of one doctor.

All relations between classes are potentially binary with traversal in either direction. For example, we may cross the relation `registeredWith` from `Patient` to `Doctor` to obtain the name of the patient's doctor. Equally, we may determine if a patient is registered with a doctor by traversing the relation from `Doctor` to `Patient`. If in a particular application we only ever wish to traverse a relation in one direction, then some optimizations are possible in the chosen representation. For example, relation `registeredWith` is only ever traversed between `Doctor` and `Patient` in that direction to get the statistics for every patient. Hence we can represent this relationship with an array of type `Patient` in the `Doctor` class. Each new patient is entered into this array when they are registered with the doctor. The statistics are then determined and the printout produced by processing each `Patient` in the array.

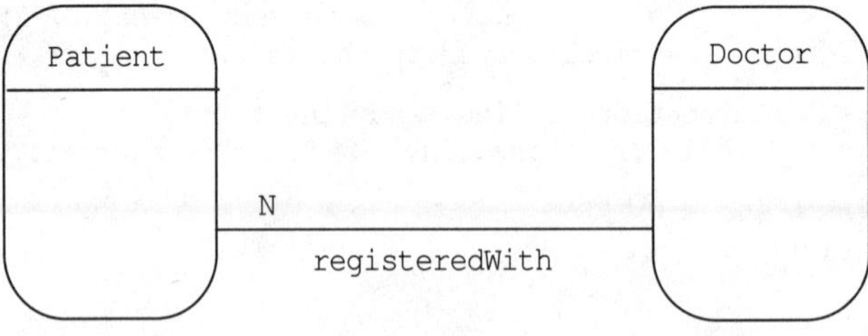

Figure 9.5

Class Patient is relatively straightforward. The name for the patient is held as a `String` data member, the date of birth as a `Date` data member, and the number of visits as a simple `int`. The `String` and `Date` data types are taken from our class library described in Chapter 12.

```
// ———— FILE: patient.h ————

#ifndef PATIENT
  #define PATIENT

  #include "cstring.h"
  #include "cdate.h"

  class Patient {
  public:
    Patient(const String& aName, const Date& aDOB, int aVisits);
    Patient(void);

    String        name(void) const;
    int           visits(void) const;

  private:
    String        theName;        // representation
    Date          theDOB;
    int           theVisits;
  };

  inline Patient::Patient(const String& aName, const Date& aDOB, int
aVisits)
   : theName(aName),
     theDOB(aDOB),
     theVisits(aVisits)
  {}

  inline Patient::Patient(void)          // default name and DOB
   : theVisits(0)
  {}

  inline String         Patient::name(void) const
   { return theName; }

  inline int            Patient::visits(void) const
   { return theVisits; }

#endif    // PATIENT

// ———— END: patient.h ————
```

The class `Doctor` has the added complication of handling the relationship with class `Patient`. As noted above this is represented by an array `thePatientsList` with member `thePatientsRegistered` acting as a high water mark for the number of array entries used. Obviously, a fixed size array restricts the number of patients we may associate with a doctor but in Chapter 12 we shall remove this limitation. As each new patient is registered with our doctor using operation `registerPatient`, we add this patient to the array using the high water mark.

```
// ——————— FILE: doctor.h ———————

#ifndef DOCTOR
  #define DOCTOR

  #include "patient.h"
  #include "cstring.h"

  const int PATIENTS = 100;               // maximum allowable

  class Doctor {
  public:
    Doctor(const String& aName);
    String name(void) const;
    void  registerPatient(const Patient& aPatient);

    double mean(void) const;                      // visit statistics

    void  printUpper(double limit) const;         // results

  private:
    String theName;                       // representation
    Patient      thePatientsList[PATIENTS];
    int          thePatientsRegistered;
  };

  inline Doctor::Doctor(const String& aName)
   : theName(aName)
  {
    thePatientsRegistered = 0;
  }

  inline String           Doctor::name(void) const
   { return theName; }

  inline void             Doctor::registerPatient(const Patient&
                                                           aPatient)
   { thePatientsList[thePatientsRegistered++] = aPatient; }

#endif    // DOCTOR

// ——————— END: doctor.h ———————

// ——————— FILE: doctor.cpp ———————

#include "doctor.h"

double    Doctor::mean(void) const
{
  long totalVisits = 0L;

  for(int k = 0; k < thePatientsRegistered; k++)
    totalVisits += thePatientsList[k].visits();

  return double(totalVisits)/thePatientsRegistered;
}

void      Doctor::printUpper(double limit) const
{
  cout << "Upper limit\n";
```

```
    for(int k = 0; k < thePatientsRegistered; k++)
      if(thePatientsList[k].visits() > limit)
        cout << "\t" << thePatientsList[k].name()
               << ", " << thePatientsList[k].visits() << "\n";
  }
  // ————— END: doctor.cpp —————
```

Finally the program reads a series of patient names, dates of birth and number of visits until the sentinel patient with unique name `ZZZ` is encountered. For each patient, a `Patient` object is established and the details entered into the array by registering that patient with the doctor. After all patients have been entered the average for the number of visits is determined. Those patients with five or more visits above this amount are then displayed.

```
// ————— FILE: case02.cpp —————
#include <iostream.h>
#include <iomanip.h>
#include "patient.h"
#include "doctor.h"

int main()
{
  Doctor   doctor("Wellbeing");
  String   patientName;

  cin >> patientName;
  while(patientName != "ZZZ"){
    int          day, month, year;       // patient details;
    char   separator;
    int          patientVisits;

    cin >> day >> separator >> month >> separator >> year;
    cin >> patientVisits;

    Date  patientDOB(day, month, year);
    Patient      patient(patientName, patientDOB, patientVisits);

    doctor.registerPatient(patient);

    cin >> patientName;
  }
  cout << "Patient statistics for Doctor ";
  cout << doctor.name() << "\n";

  double   average = doctor.mean();
  cout << "     Average number of visits: "
       << setw(5) << setprecision(2) << average << "\n";

  doctor.printUpper(average + 5);

  return (0);
}
// ————— END: case02.cpp —————
```

9.9 Static class members

It is common in programming to have variables persist throughout a program's lifetime. For example, a counter that is repeatedly updated during the program execution. Where this variable is required across the whole program it is declared as global. If the scope of the variable is to be restricted to file scope then static storage is employed.

Similarly, it may be useful for all the objects of some class to have access to the same (shared) variable. A *static data member* operates as a global variable shared by all instances of the class. While there may be many instances of a class there is only one instance of a static class member for that class. Whilst a program global variable can provide the same functionality, information hiding cannot be imposed except at file level. Additionally, a static class member has class scope and will not conflict with identifiers of the same name appearing elsewhere in the program.

Consider the class `Date` shown earlier. Suppose we wish to maintain a count of the number of occurrences of class `Date` which have been created. A static data member, `occurs`, in class `Date` is incremented by every constructor call:

```
class Date{
public:
  Date(int aDay, int aMonth, int aYear) { occurs++; .... }
  static int     getOccurs(void) const { return occurs; }
  // .....
private:
  static int   occurs;
  // .....
};
```

Only one copy of the data member `occurs` is present. Each `Date` object is able to access this member. We are assured that each `Date` class object accesses the same value by virtue of declaring `occurs` as `static`. Further, we need only update this member at one place in the program (the constructor) to maintain the correct count, reducing the likelihood of error.

A static data member of a class is initialized in the usual way. However, to indicate that this is the static data member of class `Date` and not a global variable the class scope syntax is obligatory. For example, we might initialize `occurs` with:

```
int Date::occurs = 0;
```

With ordinary global variables only one initialization appears in a program (see Chapter 7). This is also true for initialization of static data members. The above initialization should not appear in the class header file since multiple inclusion of this file into separate program units would introduce repeated definitions. The correct placement is in the program unit containing the code for the member functions.

Static data members are also subject to the private and public access rules. The static data member `occurs` needs to be protected from inadvertent modification by placing it in the private section. Static members obey the normal class member access rules excepting that they may be initialized.

The member function `getOccurs` is introduced to access the static class member `occurs`. Normally, we should have to call the functions of a class with some class object, for example, `hogmanay.getOccurs()`. Which particular object is used is, of course, irrelevant – only one instance of the data member `occurs` is being accessed and not any of the data members of the class object. A class object is necessary to be consistent with the calling syntax for class member functions. The resulting code is somewhat confusing since the class object plays no meaningful part.

Member functions may also be declared `static`. A *static member function* may, if required, be accessed through a class object or through a pointer to a class object (see next section). Alternatively, it may be called using the member class syntax. This is shown in the call to `getOccurs`, e.g.:

```
int count = Date::getOccurs();
```

Static class member functions can also be called directly even if no class object has been declared.

PROGRAM 9.9

```
// ────────── FILE: p09.cpp ──────────

#include <iostream.h>
#include "date09.h"

void      dateReport(void);        // prototype

int main()
{
  Date    hogmanay(31, 12, 1989);          // first variable
  Date    xmas(25, 12, 1989);      // second variable

  dateReport();                    // two Date variables thus far

  Date    birthday(27, 9, 1989); // third variable

  dateReport();                    // three date variables now

  return (0);
}

void dateReport(void)
{
  cout << "Report on date usage\n";
  cout << Date::getOccurs() << " dates created\n";
}

// ────────── END: p09.cpp ──────────

// ────────── FILE: date09.h ──────────
```

```
class Date {
public:
  Date(int aDay, int aMonth, int aYear);
  static int  getOccurs(void)
   { return occurs; }
private:
  int            theDay, theMonth, theYear;
  static int     occurs;
};

// ────────── END: date09.h ──────────

// ────────── FILE: date09.cpp ──────────

#include "date09.h"

Date::Date(int aDay, int aMonth, int aYear)
{
  theDay  = aDay;
  theMonth= aMonth;
  theYear = aYear;
  occurs++;
}

int       Date::occurs = 0;       // initialize

// ────────── END: date09.cpp ──────────
```

9.10 Pointers and class objects

We have shown how a pointer can be defined to point to a fundamental data type such as an `int` or a `char`. Pointers may also be defined to point to class objects. Using the `Date` class we define a variable as:

```
Date today(9, 1, 1990);
```

A variable defined as a pointer to a `Date` object is presented in the usual way:

```
Date*      ptr;
```

The variable `ptr` can then be used in the expected fashion. We can, for example, set it to point to the variable `today` with the assignment:

```
ptr = &today;
```

Having performed this assignment, we can indirectly access any public member of the class object pointed to by `ptr`. If `p` is a pointer to some class object, then the notation:

```
p->member-name                  // data member
p->member-name(arguments)       // function member
```

refers to the particular member name. Strictly, the symbol `->` is another C++

operator known as the *class pointer operator* and has precedence and associativity as shown in Appendix E. Using the pointer variable ptr we may reference the member function day for the class object today with the expression:

```
ptr->day()
```

To test if today belongs to 1990, the statement:

```
if(ptr->year() == 1990) .....
```

can be used.

While not really a sensible way to do things, we could write a program to establish an object of class Date and then to print it. The Date object is manipulated through pointers to illustrate the usage.

PROGRAM 9.10

```
// ---------- FILE: p10.cpp ----------

#include <iostream.h>
#include "date04.h"

int main()
{
  Date     today(4, 10, 1991);
  Date*    ptr = &today;

  cout << "Today\'s date: " << ptr->day()
     << "/" << ptr->month()
     << "/" << ptr->year() << "\n";

  return (0);
}

// ---------- END: p10.cpp ----------
```

The notation:

```
ptr->day()
```

refers to the member function day of the Date object to which the pointer variable ptr points. Since ptr points to a Date class object, then dereferencing with the expression *ptr gives the Date object itself and the expression:

```
(*ptr).day()
```

achieves the same as that above. However, since the former is both shorter and aethestically more pleasing it is preferred to the latter. Note that the first pair of parentheses in (*ptr).day() are necessary because of the precedences of the class member operator '.' and the indirection operator '*'.

9.11 The implicit pointer this

Every class instance possesses its own copy of the data members for that class. For example:

```
Date        today;
```

has its `theDay`, `theMonth` and `theYear` members. Equally,

```
Date        birthday;
```

has its own copy. Both `today` and `birthday` call the same copy of any member function. One question follows from this arrangement. If there is only one copy of a member function, then how does the function know to which class object it is being called, and as a consequence the object's data members? For example, when we call:

```
today.set(30, 12, 1992);
```

and:

```
birthday.set(31, 12, 1992);
```

how do we manage to assign `30` to the `theDay` data member for `today` and assign `31` to the `theDay` data member for `birthday`?

Every class member function has one hidden parameter additionally inserted by the compiler as the first argument. The parameter is given the name `this` and is a pointer to its class type. In a `Date` member function, `this` is of type `Date*`. For example, given the class definition:

```
class Date {
public:
  void      set(int aDay, int aMonth, int aYear);
  // .....
private:
  int       theDay;
  int       theMonth;
  int       theYear;
};
```

the compiler treats the member function `set` as if it had been defined as:

```
void Date::set(Date* this, int aDay, int aMonth, int aYear)
{
     this->theDay   = aDay;
     this->theMonth = aMonth;
     this->theYear  = aYear;
}
```

The call:

```
today.set(31, 12, 1990)
```

is translated by the compiler into:

```
set(&today, 31, 12, 1990);
```

It is perfectly valid for the programmer to explicitly reference `this` in a member function, but as we have shown throughout the chapter it is completely unnecessary. For example, a programmer supplied definition for the member function `set` might be:

```
void Date::set(int aDay, int aMonth, int aYear)
{
     this->theDay   = aDay;
     this->theMonth = aMonth;
     this->theYear  = aYear;
}
```

with an explicit use of the otherwise implicit `this` parameter.

A static member function does not have a `this` pointer since it does not associate with any class object. Any explicit reference to the pointer `this` in a static member function results in a compile time error. Accessing a non-static class data member in a static member function is an implicit reference to the pointer `this` and also produces a compile-time error. For example:

```
class Date {
public:
   Date(int aDay, int aMonth, int aYear);
  static void  initOccurs(void)
     { this->occurs = 0; }          // syntax error

  static int   getOccurs(void)
     { return theYear; }            // syntax error

private:
  int            theDay, theMonth, theYear;
  static int     occurs;
};
```

9.12 Class templates

The function template specified how a family of functions is constructed. In the same way, a *class template* specifies how a family of classes can be constructed. A class template, like a function template, is parameterized with one or more type names. For example, a class `Stack` similar to that introduced in Program 9.5 appears as:

```
// ———————— FILE: stack.h ————————

#ifndef STACK
  #define STACK

  enum Bool { FALSE, TRUE };

  template <class TYPE>
```

```
  class Stack {
  public:
    Stack(void);
    void  push(TYPE item);
    void  pop(void);
    TYPE  top(void) const;
    Bool  isEmpty(void) const;
    int   depth(void) const;
    void  reverse(void);
  private:
    TYPE          stack[100];    // array of ...
    int           stackTop;      // stack top
  };

  #include "stack.t"             // function bodies
#endif    // STACK
// ———————— END: stack.h ————————

// ———————— FILE: stack.t ————————

template <class TYPE>
inline Stack<TYPE>::Stack(void)
          { stackTop = -1; }

template <class TYPE>
inline void       Stack<TYPE>::push(TYPE item)
          { stack[++stackTop] = item; }

template <class TYPE>
inline void       Stack<TYPE>::pop(void)
          { stackTop--; }

template <class TYPE>
inline TYPE       Stack<TYPE>::top(void) const
          { return stack[stackTop]; }

template <class TYPE>
inline Bool       Stack<TYPE>::isEmpty(void) const
          { return (stackTop < 0) ? TRUE : FALSE; }

template <class TYPE>
inline int Stack<TYPE>::depth(void) const
          { return 1 + stackTop; }

template <class TYPE>
void      Stack<TYPE>::reverse(void)
{
  if(stackTop > 0){
    const int middle = (1 + stackTop) / 2;
    int ktop = stackTop;
    for(int k = 0; k < middle; k++, ktop--){
      const TYPE temp = stack[k];
      stack[k] = stack[ktop];
```

```
            stack[ktop] = temp;
        }
    }
}
// ———————— END: stack.t ————————
```

The prefix `template <class TYPE>` introduces a template class with `TYPE` representing some arbitrary type name. This type name `TYPE` has the class declaration as its scope in a manner similar to template functions. Hence within the class declaration the data member `stack`, for instance, is understood to represent an array of some type to be later defined.

Note how the member functions are specified as function templates. The additional notation includes the prefix `template <class TYPE>` again indicating a function template is being introduced. The class name to which (for example) member function `reverse` belongs is the name of the class template (here `Stack`) followed by the template parameter `TYPE`. Hence we have:

```
template <class TYPE>

void        Stack<TYPE>::reverse(void)
{
  // .....
}
```

This same naming device is then used to *instantiate* specific instances of the class. Replacing the parameter name `TYPE` with, say, `int`:

```
Stack<int>      myStack;            // stack of int's
```

defines an object `myStack` of some class `Stack<int>`. Equally, we may define:

```
Stack<Date>       holidays;
Stack<String>     names;
```

and codify some program with:

```
int main()
{
  Stack<Date>       holidays;
  Stack<String>     names;

  // .....

  holidays.reverse();
  String upperMost = names.top();
  // .....
}
```

Note that the template for the class and the templates for its member functions must be accessible to the compiler to permit it to instantiate the necessary versions. Hence the class declaration and the member function definitions must be available. Rather than have the function bodies clutter the appearance of the header file they are placed in a '`.t`' file (for template) and included into the header when it is included in some program file.

With the generic class `Stack` we repeat Program 9.5 in Program 9.11.

PROGRAM 9.11

```
// ———————— FILE: p11.cpp ————————
#include <iostream.h>
#include "stack.h"

int main()
{
  int            data;
  Stack<int>     stack;

  cout << "Start entering the data:\n";
  cin >> data;
  while(data >= 0){
    stack.push(data);
    cin >> data;
  }

  cout << "\nReversed data values:\n";
  while( ! stack.isEmpty()){
    data = stack.top();
    cout << data << "\n";
    stack.pop();
  }
  return (0);
}

// ———————— END: p11.cpp ————————
```

A template argument can include constant expressions in addition to type names. For example, an integer argument can be used to set the compile time size for our `Stack`:

```
// ———————— FILE: stack.h ————————

#ifndef STACK
  #define STACK

  template <class TYPE, int SIZE>
  class Stack {
  public:
    // .....
  private:
    TYPE           stack[SIZE];    // array of .....
    int            stackTop;       // stack top
  };
```

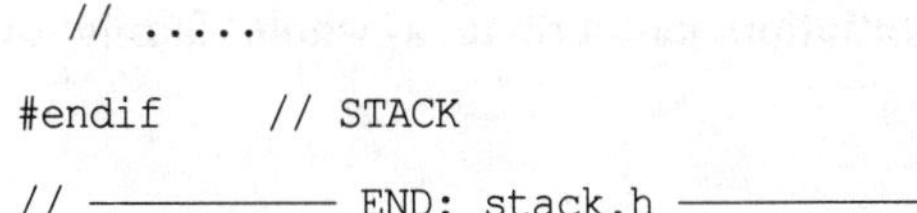

```
// ....

#endif    // STACK

// ———————— END: stack.h ————————
```

An instantiation for a `Stack` of `100` integers would then appear as follows:

```
Stack<int, 100>    myStack;
```

9.13 Summary

1. The C++ programming language supports the aggregate type known as a *class*. Components of a class can be both data items and functions.

2. The C++ keywords `public:` and `private:` indicates the accessibility of the class members. *Information hiding* aims to make inaccessible those details which do not concern other parts of the programming system.

3. A *constructor* member function is called to initialize the data members of a newly created class object. At the end of a class variable's life, a *destructor* is called to perform any necessary clean up before the space used by the variable is deallocated.

4. The scope rules of C++ are extended by incorporating class member declarations into the scheme.

5. A member function which does not modify the data members of a class object may be optionally designated as `const`. Any class variable of the appropriate type may use these functions. These are the only functions which a `const` class object may use since they do not change any data members.

6. A static data member in a class operates as a global variable for that class. Only one instance of a static class member exists. It acts as a single object shared by all objects of that class. C++ also supports static member functions in classes.

7. C++ has the special keyword `this` which allows access to the current class object. The keyword `this` is a pointer, referring to self.

8. An array of classes or a class with array members are all valid constructions in C++.

9. A family of classes is introduced with template classes. The class is parameterized with some arbitrary type which the compiler instantiates with

some user-specified type. Instantiation can create a whole family of like classes with different types.

9.14 Exercises

1. A distance in the imperial system is measured in yards, feet and inches (3 feet per yard, 12 inches per foot). Prepare the program unit to implement the class:

```
class Imperial {
public:
  Imperial(int aYard, int aFoot = 0, int anInch = 0);

  void       add(const Imperial&);
  void       mul(int factor);

  int        yards(void) const;
  int        feet(void) const;
  int        inches(void) const;

private:
  int        theYards, theFeet, theInches;
};
```

   Prepare a program to test the behaviour of the member functions. In particular, show that adding the zero distance and multiplying by unity leave an `Imperial` value unchanged, that is:

```
Imperial  distance(.....);
Imperial  zero(0);

distance.add(zero);            // no change
distance.mul(1);                // no change
```

2. The military time is represented by the three values `HH:MM:SS` (where `0` <= `HH` <= `23`, `0` <= `MM`, `SS` <= `59`). Complete the program unit for the class:

```
class MilitaryTime {
public:
  MilitaryTime(int anHour, int aMinute = 0, int aSecond = 0);
  MilitaryTime(long aSeconds);

  void       add(const MilitaryTime&);
  void       sub(const MilitaryTime&);
  long       difference(const MilitaryTime&) const;

  long       totalSeconds(void) const;
  int        hours(void) const;
  int        minutes(void) const;
  int        seconds(void) const;

private:
  int        theHours, theMinutes, theSeconds;
 };
```

The constructor with the single long argument initializes the time to the number of seconds past midnight. The member function `totalSeconds` converts the `MilitaryTime` to the number of seconds since midnight. The functions `add` and `sub` ignore any day wrap around.

Test this class in a program.

3. A rational number is a fractional value expressed as the quotient of two positive integers. Examples of rational numbers include 1/2, 3/4 and 8/5. The elements of a rational number are the *numerator* and *denominator*. The rational number 3/4 has numerator 3 and denominator 4.

   Generally, a rational number is expressed in its simplest form. The rational number 8/6 reduces to 4/3 in its simplest form. The reduced form is achieved by determining the highest common factor (hcf):

```
unsigned hcf(unsigned num, unsigned den)
{
  if(den > num){
    const unsigned temp = num;
    num = den;
    den = temp;
  }
  while(num % den != 0){
    const unsigned temp = den;
    den = num % den;
    num = temp;
  }
  return den;
}
```

Prepare the program unit for the class declaration:

```
class Rational {
public:
  Rational(unsigned aNumerator, unsigned aDenominator = 1);

  void          add(const Rational&);
  void          mul(const Rational&);

  unsigned      numerator(void) const;
  unsigned      denominator(void) const;

private:
  unsigned      theNumerator, theDenominator;
  unsigned      hcf(unsigned, unsigned);
};
```

The arithmetic of Rationals is:

$$\frac{a}{b} + \frac{c}{d} \equiv \frac{c * d + b * c}{b * d}$$

$$\frac{a}{b} * \frac{c}{d} \equiv \frac{a * c}{b * d}$$

Use this class to develop a program to compute the partial sums of the harmonic series. The program will evaluate $H(n)$ for various values of n, where:

$$H(n) \equiv 1 + \frac{1}{2} + \frac{1}{3} + \ldots.. + \frac{1}{n}$$

4. Use the `Point` and `Line` class of Case Study 9.1 to develop a new class `Triangle` declared as:

```
enum Bool { FALSE, TRUE };

class Triangle {
public:
 Triangle(Point, Point, Point);
 double              perimeter(void) const;
 double              area(void) const;
 Bool                isRight(void) const;         // boolean
 Bool                isIsosceles(void) const;     // boolean
private:
 Point               p1, p2, p3;                  // vertices
};
```

A right triangle is one with a right-angled vertex. An isosceles triangle is one with two sides of equal length. If the lengths of the sides of a triangle are `a`, `b` and `c`, then the perimeter, `p`, is:

```
p = a + b + c
```

and the semi-perimeter, `s`, is:

```
s = (a + b + c)/2
```

The area of a triangle is then given by:

```
area = sqrt(s(s-a)(s-b)(s-c))
```

5. Use the template class `Stack` of Section 9.12 to determine if a stream of positive integers (with negative terminator) is palindromic. The data stream `1, 2, 2, 1` and `1, 2, 3, 2, 1` are palindromic. The data sequence `1, 2, 3, 4` is not palindromic. Solve the problem:

   (a) Using the member function `reverse`.
   (b) Without using the member function `reverse`.

6. Use the template class `Stack` data type of Section 9.12 to implement a `Queue`. A queue is distinguished by inserting all new items on to the rear of the queue and removing and accessing items from the front of the queue. The class declaration is:

```
enum Bool { FALSE, TRUE };

template <class TYPE>
```

```
class Queue {
public:
  Queue(void);

  void          add(const TYPE& item);          // to rear
  void          remove(void);          // front item
  TYPE          atFront(void);
  Bool          isEmpty(void);          // boolean
private:
 Stack<TYPE>     queue;              // representation
};
```

The implementation is based on a design in which the stack top represents either the front or the rear of the queue.

Using a `Stack<int>` object and a `Queue<int>` object determine if an integer data stream is palindromic.

7. Extend Case Study 9.2 to find the average number of visits made by patients over a given age value.

   How would we produce a report of the total visits made by patients in a particular age category?

8. Prepare a class diagram showing the relation 'has capital' between a `Country` and a `City`. Develop classes for the latter both with name properties. Use these classes to develop a program to find how many countries have more than one capital (e.g. administrative and historical capitals).

9. Prepare a class diagram relating a `File` to its `Directory`. The latter has the property name, while the former has properties name and size.

   Use these classes to develop a program to find the space occupied by all the files in a named directory.

   How should we modify the class diagram to permit subdirectories?

10. An organization employs a number of employees. Each employee is directly responsible to a single employee manager. The class diagram for the relations is shown in Figure 9.6:

    1. Prepare suitable classes for this problem.
    2. Design some sample input data for this program.
    3. How should we deal with the most senior staff member who has no immediate superior?
    4. Develop the program to read the input and produce a list of employees under the direct supervision of a named manager.
    5. Develop a version of the program to find the manager for a named employee.
    6. Develop a version which identifies the most senior employee in the organization.

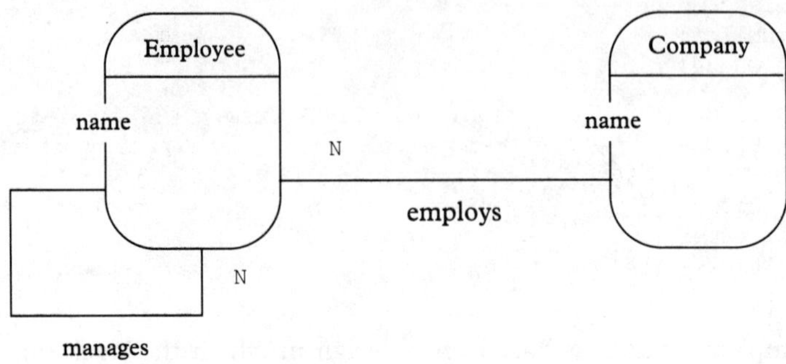

Figure 9.6

11. Why would it not be sensible for the copy constructor for some class `X` to have the signature `X::X(X)`?

12. Provide an efficient implementation for the template class `Queue`:

```
enum Bool { FALSE, TRUE };

const int QUEUEMAX = 100;

template <class TYPE, int SIZE>
class Queue {
public:
  Queue(void);

  void       add(const TYPE& item);          // to rear
  void       remove(void);                   // from rear

  TYPE       atFront(void) const;
  Bool       isEmpty(void) const;            // boolean

private:
  TYPE       theQueue[SIZE];                 // representation
  int        theFront;                       // indices
  int        theRear;
  int        theLength;                      // number of items
};
```

Then repeat Exercise 6 above.

10

Operator Overloading

A user defined abstract data type can include the definition of operators applicable to objects of that class. Consider class `Date`:

```
class Date {
public:
  // .....
  long int   difference(const Date&);
  // .....
};
```

in which the member function `difference` determines the number of days between two dates. Its use might appear as in:

```
Date holiday(25, 12, 1993);
Date today(30, 8, 1993);
long daystowork = holiday.difference(today);
```

Using this conventional message passing notation, we have been careful to name and define the member function so that it is logical to use. However, its usage is not as natural as that of the basic data types where we might have expected to express the above initialized definition as:

```
long int daystowork = holiday - today;
```

The operator symbol '`-`' represents the basic operations on `ints`, `floats`, etc. Here, we have envisaged extending its usage to be applicable to class `Date` objects. The result is a more natural means of expressing the desired effect. Defining operators to apply to class objects permits the same notation to be used with user defined classes.

10.1 Operator functions

A user defined abstract data type can include the definition of operators applicable to objects of that class. The operator symbols `+`, `-`, `*`, etc., represent the basic operations on `ints`, presented in a conventional manner. Defining operators to apply to class objects permits this same notation to be used with user defined classes.

Language defined operators can be overloaded to operate with operands of a class type. This is represented by a member operator function that has at least one class type object as an operand. This restriction ensures that the programmer cannot override the behaviour of the operators for the standard types. An operator function is introduced in the usual way except that the function name has the form `operator@`, where `@` is the operator symbol being overloaded. The operator symbol `@` may be any of the C++ operators shown in Table 10.1.

Table 10.1

<table>
<tr><td>+</td><td>-</td><td>*</td><td>/</td><td>%</td><td>^</td><td>&</td><td>|</td></tr>
<tr><td>~</td><td>!</td><td>,</td><td>=</td><td><</td><td>></td><td><=</td><td>>=</td></tr>
<tr><td>++</td><td>--</td><td><<</td><td>>></td><td>==</td><td>!=</td><td>&&</td><td>||</td></tr>
<tr><td>+=</td><td>-=</td><td>*=</td><td>/=</td><td>%=</td><td>^=</td><td>&=</td><td>|=</td></tr>
<tr><td><<=</td><td>>>=</td><td>[]</td><td>()</td><td>-></td><td>->*</td><td>new</td><td>delete</td></tr>
</table>

These standard operators all have a predefined precedence and associativity (see Appendix E). The precedences and associativities cannot be altered when used with user defined class types. As a consequence, irrespective of the types involved, the expression:

```
a + b * c
```

will always perform `operator*` before `operator+`. As usual, parentheses can be employed to override the predefined order.

Equally, every standard operator has a fixed *arity*. The arity of an operator defines the number of required operands. Again, this cannot be changed. Thus, a user defined `operator!` can only apply to a single operand. A user defined version for `operator<` can only be expressed in terms of operands.

To support the difference of two dates, the member operator would be declared as:

```
class Date {
public:
  long int operator- (const Date&);
  // .....
};
```

Given two `Date` objects `holiday` and `today`, then the expression:

```
daystowork = holiday - today;
```

would invoke:

```
holiday.operator-(today)
```

with the first operand of a member operator function as the implicit class object that invokes it. In effect, the expression `holiday - today` is translated into the latter by the compiler.

The C++ language places a number of restrictions on the use of operator overloading:

- The operators for the standard types cannot be redefined. We can only overload the operators for user defined classes.
- Only the predefined operator symbols may be used. New operator symbols cannot be introduced. The permissible set of operators are those in Table 10.1.
- The arity (the number of arguments) of the operator cannot be changed. The unary operator `!` cannot be defined as a binary operator. The binary operator `%` cannot become a unary operator.
- The operator `sizeof`, the member access operator `.`, the scope resolution operator `::`, the pointer to member access operator `.*`, and the conditional operator `?:` cannot be overloaded.
- The operators =, ->, ->*, ( ) and [ ] can only be overloaded as member functions. These operators can never be overloaded as non-member functions, including non-member friend functions (see Section 10.3).
- An overloaded operator cannot have default arguments.

Program 10.1 illustrates with a class `Time` containing a number of operators. All the operators have been overloaded to work with different operand (argument) types. For example, `operator+` can add together two clock times, or a clock time and a `long` number of seconds. This last version effectively advances the time by that number of seconds.

PROGRAM 10.1

```
// ———————— FILE: p01.cpp ————————

//
//  Create clock times adding them together and to
//      a long integer value.
//

#include <iostream.h>
#include "time01.h"

int main()
{
  Time    oneam(3600L);                  // Time(long)
  Time    twoam(2, 0, 0);                // Time(int, int, int)

  Time threeam = oneam + twoam;                 // Time + Time
  Time fouram = threeam + 3600L;         // Time + long

  cout << "Three am: ";   threeam.print();
```

```
  cout << "Four am:  ";   fouram.print();
  return (0);
}
// ——————— END: p01.cpp ———————

// ———————- FILE: time01.h ———————

//
//  A military style clock time in which the hours range
//       from 0 through 23 inclusive. The class provides
//       support for the overloaded addition operator
//       between two clock times and between a clock time
//       and a long integer representing a number of seconds.
//

#ifndef TIME
  #define TIME

  class Time {
  public:
    Time(int anHour, int aMinute, int aSecond);
    Time(long secondsPastMidnight);

    long          hms2secs(void) const;
    Time          operator+ (const Time&) const;
    Time          operator+ (long) const;
    void          print(void) const;
  private:
    int           theHours;       // representation
    int           theMinutes;
    int           theSeconds;
  };

#endif   // TIME

// ———————- END: time01.h ———————

// ———————- FILE: time01.cpp ———————

#include <iostream.h>
#include "time01.h"

Time::Time(int anHour, int aMinute, int aSecond)
{
  theHours   = anHour % 24;    // no day wraparound
  theMinutes = aMinute;
  theSeconds = aSecond;
}

Time::Time(long secondsPastMidnight)
{
  const int minutes = secondsPastMidnight / 60;

  theSeconds = secondsPastMidnight % 60;
  theMinutes = minutes % 60;
```

```
  theHours    = (minutes / 60) % 24;
}

long Time::hms2secs(void) const
{
  return (theHours * 60L + theMinutes) * 60L + theSeconds;
}

Time Time::operator+ (const Time& time) const
{
  const long second_operand_in_secs = time.hms2secs();
  const long first_operand_in_secs  = hms2secs();
  return Time(first_operand_in_secs + second_operand_in_secs);
}

Time Time::operator+ (long secondsPastMidnight) const
{
  const long first_operand_in_secs = hms2secs();
  return Time(first_operand_in_secs + secondsPastMidnight);
}

void Time::print(void) const
{
  cout << theHours << ":" << theMinutes << ":"
       << theSeconds << "\n";
}

// ---------- END: time01.cpp ----------
```

Here it is important to return a copy of the result of an operation when we overload an operator. This is because operators are generally used in expressions. For example, given the `Time` objects `t1`, `t2` and `t3`, the expression `t1 + t2 + t3` relies on the result of the operation `t1 + t2` being available to the second occurrence of `operator+` with operand `t3`. Hence the signature for `operator+` is:

```
Time Time::operator+ ( /* ..... */ );
```

Actually the issue is rather more complicated as we would have to give consideration to handling large class objects where returning a new result could involve expensive copying (see Section 9.3). For the present we shall simply return a class object. In later chapters we shall have to be more considered about this when the classes represent large objects.

Note the declaration of the two addition operators:

```
class Time {
public:
  // .....
  Time      operator+ (const Time&) const;
  Time      operator+ (long) const;
  // .....
};
```

A binary operator (such as `+`) may be declared as a non-static member function taking one argument (as above). Alternatively, a binary operator may be declared as a non-member function taking two arguments. For example, the first illustration above might also appear as:

```
                // external, non-member function
Time            operator+ (const Time&, const Time&);
```

This non-member version of the `operator+` function has no access to the private representation of a `Time` object and must rely on the public member functions to express its implementation.

Similarly, a unary operator may be declared as a non-static member function with no argument or as a non-member function taking one argument:

```
class Time {
public:
  // .....
  Time      operator! (void);
};
```

or

```
Time      operator! (const Time&);      // external function
```

10.2 X& X::operator=(const X&)

In Section 9.3 we noted that a definition of the form:

```
Time t1 = t2;
```

was implemented by the copy constructor `Time (const Time&)` and if not defined in the class `Time`, then the compiler provides a default version which implements memberwise initialization. Equally, the assignment of one class object with another is implemented as the memberwise assignment of the data members. The procedure is the same as that for initialization, discussed in Section 9.3.

By default, the compiler implicitly produces the assignment operator:

```
X& X::operator= (const X&)
```

for every class `X`. For example, class `Time` has implicitly:

```
class Time {
public:
  // ....
  Time& operator= (const Time& time)
  {
    theHours   = time.theHours;
    theMinutes = time.theMinutes;
    theSeconds = time.theSeconds;
    return *this;
  }
  // .....
};
```

A class may override this default, by providing an explicit version of the memberwise assignment operator. For the classes we are presently able to define, default memberwise assignment is appropriate and there is no need to provide a new version of this operator. However, for some classes (see Chapter 12) this simple-minded assignment must be overridden with a class specific version. For completeness, therefore, we note that a version of the assignment operator may be defined for the class.

We know that the keyword `this` refers to the address of the object for which a member–function is called. Since the dereferencing operator `*` delivers the value at the given address, then the special return statement used in `operator=` is interpreted as returning (a reference to) the class object on the left side of the assignment (suitably assigned with the value from the right side). Returning the reference to the value permits us to use the operator in multiple assignments, as in:

```
Time t1(3600L);
Time t2, t3;          // assume a default constructor

t3 = t2 = t1;
```

The assignment operator associates right to left and the statement is interpreted in the usual way as `t3 = (t2 = t1)`. Our user defined implementation for the operator performs a memberwise copy from `t1` to `t2` then makes available a reference to `t2`. This value, in turn, is employed as the right side for the assignment to `t3`.

10.3 Friend functions

Consider adding the long integer `2L` to a `Time` variable `time`. Assuming the declared member function `operator+` from Program 10.1, `time + 2L` is interpreted as `time.operator+(2L)`. However, we cannot express this as `2L + time` since there is no class `long` for which to define `operator+`. Since the compiler does not know the semantics of a user defined `operator+` it cannot assume the commutativity of `+` and interpret `2L + time` as `time + 2L`.

The problem is resolved using *friend functions*. A friend function is a non-member of a class which is given access to the non-public members of the class. To support the above illustration, we must implement two `Time` operator functions:

```
class Time {
  friend Time  operator+ (const Time&, long);
  friend Time  operator+ (long, const Time&);
public:
  // .....
};
```

Since friends are not members of the class, they are unaffected by the public or private sections. By convention, we will collect all friend function declarations immediately following the opening brace symbol of the class body, and before the first labelled section, as shown.

When the friend functions are defined they simply appear as normal function definitions. They are, however, effectively within scope of the class definition and are permitted access to the non-public members.

```
inline Time operator+ (const Time& time1, const Time& time2)
{
  const long time1_2secs = time1.hms2secs();
  const long time2_2secs = time2.hms2secs();
  return Time(time1_2secs + time2_2secs);
}

inline Time operator- (const Time& time1, const Time& time2)
{
  const long time1_2secs = time1.hms2secs();
  const long time2_2secs = time2.hms2secs();
  return Time(time1_2secs - time2_2secs);
}
```

The binary `operator+` shown in Section 10.1 was defined as a member function with one argument. The two operands to this operator call are the function argument (the second operand) and the implicit object `this` (the first operand). As demonstrated above, a binary operator can also be defined as a (friend) function taking two arguments. Hence for any binary operator `@`, `x @ y` can be interpreted as either `x.operator@(y)` or `operator@(x, y)`, respectively the member and non-member (friend) versions. A unary operator is defined by either a member function with no arguments, or a non-member (friend) function with one argument.

PROGRAM 10.2

```
// ———————— FILE: p02.cpp ————————
//
//  Create some clock times and combine them arithmetically
//

#include <iostream.h>
#include "time02.h"

int main()
{
  Time    oneam(1, 0, 0);
  Time    twoam(7200);

  Time oneoclock         = twoam - 3600;        // Time - long
  Time onepastmidnight   = twoam - oneam;       // Time - Time

  oneoclock.print();
  onepastmidnight.print();
```

```
  return (0);
}

// ———————— END: p02.cpp ————————

// ———————— FILE: time02.h ————————

//  Military clock style with the arithmetic operators
//       addition and subtraction overloaded with various
//       combinations of clock times and long integers.
//

#ifndef TIME
  #define TIME

  class Time {
    friend Time operator+ (const Time&, const Time&);
    friend Time operator+ (const Time&, long);
    friend Time operator+ (long, const Time&);

    friend Time operator- (const Time&, const Time&);
    friend Time operator- (const Time&, long);
    friend Time operator- (long, const Time&);

  public:
    Time(int, int, int);
    Time(long);

    long hms2secs(void) const;
    void print(void) const;

  private:
    int          theHours;
    int          theMinutes;
    int          theSeconds;
  };

  inline Time::Time(int anHour, int aMinute, int aSecond)
  {
    theHours   = anHour % 24;
    theMinutes = aMinute;
    theSeconds = aSecond;
  }

  inline Time::Time(long secondsPastMidnight)
  {
    const long minutes = secondsPastMidnight / 60;

    theSeconds = secondsPastMidnight % 60;
    theMinutes = minutes % 60;
    theHours   = (minutes / 60) % 24;
  }

  inline long Time::hms2secs(void) const
  { return (theHours * 60L + theMinutes) * 60L + theSeconds; }

  inline Time operator+ (const Time& time, long seconds)
  {
```

```
    const long time2secs = time.hms2secs();
    return Time(time2secs + seconds);
  }

  inline Time operator+ (const Time& time1, const Time& time2)
  {
    const long time1_2secs = time1.hms2secs();
    const long time2_2secs = time2.hms2secs();
    return Time(time1_2secs + time2_2secs);
  }

  inline Time operator- (const Time& time, long seconds)
  {
    const long time2secs = time.hms2secs();
    return Time(time2secs - seconds);
  }

  inline Time operator- (const Time& time1, const Time& time2)
  {
    const long time1_2secs = time1.hms2secs();
    const long time2_2secs = time2.hms2secs();
    return Time(time1_2secs - time2_2secs);
  }

#endif   // TIME

// ———————— END: time02.h ————————
```

10.4 Constructors as conversion operators

Through the introduction of friend functions, class `Time` can now introduce operator functions for each combination of `Time` and `long`. For example:

```
class Time {
  friend Time  operator+ (const Time&, const Time&);
  friend Time  operator+ (const Time&, long);
  friend Time  operator+ (long, const Time&);

  friend Time  operator- (const Time&, const Time&);
  friend Time  operator- (const Time&, long);
  friend Time  operator- (long, const Time&);

  // .....
};
```

An alternative approach to using several overloaded operator functions is to declare a constructor which when given a `long` creates a `Time`. For example:

```
class Time {
public:
  Time(long);
  // .....
};
```

A constructor with a single argument may be called explicitly in the usual way, or may be called implicitly. Where an initializing value is the type of the constructor's single argument, the constructor is called implicitly. Hence, in:

```
Time oneam      = Time(3600L);
Time oneoclock = 3600L;
```

both `oneam` and `oneoclock` are initialized by calling `Time(3600L)`, the first explicitly and the second implicitly.

A constructor with a single argument acts as a *conversion operator* between the argument type and the class type. When a value of the class type is required in some expression, and a value of the argument type is given, then the constructor is used to provide the conversion. Class `Time` can now be declared as:

```
class Time {
  friend Time  operator+ (const Time&, const Time&);
  friend Time  operator- (const Time&, const Time&);
public:
  Time(long);          // constructor/type conversion
  // .....
};
```

with the operators now able to support combinations of `Time` and `long` values. For a `Time` object called `time`, the expression `time + 2L` means:

```
operator+(time, Time(2L))
```

Equally, the expression `2L + time` means:

```
operator+(Time(2L), time)
```

where the conversion is applied before invoking the operator.

By the same token, an expression evaluating to a standard type is converted by the constructor conversion operation where required. Given:

```
void fff(Time);
int  k;

fff(k);            // implicit Time(long(k))
```

The effect is achieved by the compiler introducing a temporary `Time` object which is passed to function `fff`. The temporary object is destroyed immediately following the function call.

Finally, we note that a constructor conversion can be used to convert from one user defined class to another. For example, in:

```
class X {
  // .....
};

class Y {
public:
```

```
    Y(const X&);        // constructor conversion
    // .....
};
```

the single argument to the constructor for class `Y` is another user defined class type `X`.

PROGRAM 10.3

```
// ———————— FILE: p03.cpp ————————

#include <iostream.h>
#include "time03.h"

int main()
{
  Time   oneam(1, 0, 0);
  Time twoam(7200);

  Time oneoclock = twoam - 3600;       // Time - long
  Time onepastmidnight = twoam - oneam;      // Time - Time

  oneoclock.print();
  onepastmidnight.print();

  return (0);
}

// ———————— FILE: p03.cpp ————————

// ———————— FILE: time03.h ————————

//
//  Military clock with overloaded versions of the
//        arithmetical operators addition and subtraction.
//        One version of each is given with a constructor
//        acting also as a conversion operator.
//

#ifndef TIME
  #define TIME

  class Time {
    friend Time operator+ (const Time&, const Time&);
    friend Time operator- (const Time&, const Time&);

  public:
    Time(int, int, int);  // constructor
    Time(long);             // constructor and conversion operator

    long hms2secs(void) const;
    void print(void) const;

  private:
    int          theHours;
```

```
    int           theMinutes;
    int           theSeconds;
  };

  inline Time::Time(int anHour, int aMinute, int aSecond)
  {
    theHours   = anHour % 24;
    theMinutes = aMinute;
    theSeconds = aSecond;
  }

  inline Time::Time(long secondsPastMidnight)
  {
    const long minutes = secondsPastMidnight / 60;

    theSeconds = secondsPastMidnight % 60;
    theMinutes = minutes % 60;
    theHours   = (minutes / 60) % 24;
  }

  inline long Time::hms2secs(void) const
  { return (theHours * 60L + theMinutes) * 60L + theSeconds;}

  inline Time operator+ (const Time& time1, const Time& time2)
  {
    const long time1_2secs = time1.hms2secs();
    const long time2_2secs = time2.hms2secs();
    return Time(time1_2secs + time2_2secs);
  }

  inline Time operator- (const Time& time1, const Time& time2)
  {
    const long time1_2secs = time1.hms2secs();
    const long time2_2secs = time2.hms2secs();
    return Time(time1_2secs - time2_2secs);
  }

#endif   // TIME

// ---------- END: time03.h ----------

// ---------- FILE: time03.cpp ----------

#include <iostream.h>
#include "time03.h"

void Time::print(void) const
{
  cout << theHours << ":" << theMinutes << ":"
       << theSeconds << "\n";
}

// ---------- END: time03.cpp ----------
```

10.5 Conversion operators

Using a constructor as a conversion operator is asymmetric in the following sense:

- We can convert a basic type to the class type using the constructor, but we cannot convert the other way.
- We can convert an existing class type to the newly defined class type using the constructor, but we cannot achieve the opposite effect without modification to the definition of the original class.

A class X may also introduce member functions which provide a conversion from the class type to some other fundamental type or to some other user defined type. Such a function is known as a conversion operator and has the form X::operator T (void), where X is the class and T represents the converted type. T is the resulting type name.

For class Time, we can define a conversion to type long. Effectively, this conversion operator can be used in place of the member function hms2secs. An extract of the class definition is:

```
class Time {
public:
  operator long(void) const;  // conversion: Time -> long
  // .....
};
```

Note how neither argument types nor return types are specified.

A Time object may now be used in place of a long object, for example, as initializer expressions, in function actual argument expressions and function return values. For example, the expression in the declaration pair:

```
Time      now(1, 0, 0);
double    time = now + 0.5;
```

is resolved by invoking the conversion operator on the variable now, yielding the long integer value 3600L; this, in turn, is promoted to the double value 3600.0 and added to the double literal constant 0.5.

Program 10.4 illustrates the use of class Time supporting this conversion operator.

PROGRAM 10.4

```
// ———————— FILE: p04.cpp ————————

#include <iostream.h>
#include "time04.h"

int main()
{
```

```
  Time twoam(2, 0, 0);

  if(twoam > 3600)                    // conversion operator
    cout << "Two am is later than one am\n";
  else
    cout << "Two am is not later than one am\n";

  return (0);
}

// ——————— END: p04.cpp ———————

// ——————— FILE: time04.h ———————

//
// Military clock with overloaded arithmetic operators
//      and a conversion to a long operator.
//

#ifndef TIME
  #define TIME

  class Time {
    friend Time operator+ (const Time&, const Time&);
    friend Time operator- (const Time&, const Time&);

  public:
    Time(int, int, int);
    Time(long);

    operator    long(void) const;     // conversion operator
    void print(void) const;

  private:
    int         theHours;
    int         theMinutes;
    int         theSeconds;
  };

  inline Time::Time(int anHour, int aMinute, int aSecond)
  {
    theHours   = anHour % 24;
    theMinutes = aMinute;
    theSeconds = aSecond;
  }

  inline Time::Time(long secondsPastMidnight)
  {
    const long minutes = secondsPastMidnight / 60;

    theSeconds = secondsPastMidnight % 60;
    theMinutes = minutes % 60;
    theHours   = (minutes / 60) % 24;
  }

  inline Time::operator long(void) const
  { return (theHours * 60L + theMinutes) * 60L + theSeconds; }
```

```
  inline Time operator+ (const Time& time1, const Time& time2)
  {
    const long time1_2secs = time1;
    const long time2_2secs = time2;
    return Time(time1_2secs + time2_2secs);
  }

  inline Time operator- (const Time& time1, const Time& time2)
  {
    const long time1_2secs = time1;
    const long time2_2secs = time2;
    return Time(time1_2secs - time2_2secs);
  }

#endif   // TIME

// ——————— END: time04.h ———————

// ——————— FILE: time04.cpp ———————

#include <iostream.h>
#include "time04.h"

void Time::print(void) const
{
  cout << theHours << ":" << theMinutes << ":"
       << theSeconds << "\n";
}

// ——————— END: time04.cpp ———————
```

10.6 Overloading the input/output operators

Input and output of the basic types is provided by the extraction (>>) and insertion (<<) operators respectively. The class `ostream` (in `<iostream.h>`) is defined with the `operator<<` to handle output of the standard types:

```
class ostream {
public:
  ostream& operator<< (int);
  ostream& operator<< (double);
  // .....
};
```

Note that when, for example, we write:

```
int x = 27;
cout << x;
```

the output statement is considered to be:

```
cout.operator<< (x);
```

in which the member operator function `operator<<` is applied to the `ostream` object `cout`. Since this is an object of the class `ostream` we can present the `operator<<` as a member function.

All `operator<<` functions return a reference to the `ostream` it was called for, so that another operator can be applied to it:

```
cout << "x = " << x;
```

A class designer may overload the insertion operator to define output for that class:

```
#include <iostream.h>

class Time {
  friend ostream& operator<< (ostream&, const Time&);
  // .....
};
```

The insertion operator is a binary operator with the first argument an `ostream` reference and its second argument the class type reference. The value returned by the operator is the `ostream` reference. Since the first argument is an `ostream` reference and not the class type `Time`, the operator must appear as a friend function. Here is the definition:

```
ostream& operator<< (ostream& os, const Time& time)
{
  os << time.theHours << ":" << time.theMinutes << ":"
     << time.theSeconds;
  return os;
}
```

Input of the standard types is provided by the extraction operator >> defined for the input stream `istream`:

```
class istream {
  istream& operator>> (int&);
  istream& operator>> (double&);
  // .....
};
```

Again, a class designer may overload `operator>>` to provide an input operator for that class:

```
#include <iostream.h>

class Time {
  friend istream& operator>> (istream&, Time&);
  // .....
};
```

and:

```
istream& operator>> (istream& is, Time& time)
{
```

```
  int h, m, s;          // hours, etc.
  char ch;              // colon field delimiter
                        // format is HH:MM:SS
  is >> h >> ch >> m >> ch >> s;
  time = Time(h, m, s);
  return is;
}
```

Program 10.5 inputs a series of values of class `Time` and prints each value and the corresponding number of elapsed seconds from midnight. The sentinel value midnight is used as the data terminator.

PROGRAM 10.5

```
// ———————— FILE: p05.cpp ————————

#include <iostream.h>
#include "time05.h"
//
//  Input a series of military clock times in the form
//        HH:MM:SS and convert each to the number of seconds
//        past midnight. The input and output is achieved
//        with overloading of the input/output operators.
//

int main()
{
  const Time    midnight(0, 0, 0);
  Time          time(0, 0, 0);

  cout << "Enter first time: ";
  cin >> time;
  while( ! (time == midnight)){
    const long seconds = time;
    cout << time << " is " << seconds << " after midnight\n\n";
    cout << "Enter next time: ";
    cin >> time;
  }
  return (0);
}

// ———————— END: p05.cpp ————————

// ———————— FILE: time05.h ————————

//
//  A class to represent a military clock time with
//        the input/output operators overloaded.
//

#ifndef TIME
  #define TIME
```

```
  #include <iostream.h>

  class Time {
    friend istream& operator>> (istream&, Time&);
    friend ostream& operator<< (ostream&, const Time&);
    friend int operator== (const Time&, const Time&);

  public:
    Time(int, int, int);
    operator     long(void) const;

  private:
    int          theHours;
    int          theMinutes;
    int          theSeconds;
  };

#endif    // TIME

// ————— END: time05.h —————
```

10.7 Friend classes

As we have shown, functions that have been declared friend in a class declaration are not members of that class but have permission to access the private members of objects of the class. A class can also be declared friend of another class. In this case, all member functions of the friend class are friends.

```
class F;                     // forward reference

class G {
  friend class F;
public:
  // ..... remainder of class G
private:
  int     g;
};

class F {                    // definition proper
public:
  void     f(G&);
  // .....
};
```

The non-public members of the class `G` may now be accessed within any member functions of class `F`. The private member `g` of class `G` may be accessed in `F::f()`. Since only member functions have `this`, the member access operator must be used by friend functions. For example:

```
void F::f(G& gr) { ..... gr.g ..... }
```

Consider the class `Nat` representing the natural numbers 0, 1, 2, ...:

```
class Nat {
public:
  // .....
  unsigned     nat(void) const { return theNat; }
  // .....
private:
  unsigned     theNat;
};
```

and a variant of the class `Time` we have used throughout this chapter:

```
class Time {
public:
  Time(long);
  // .....
  int      hours(void) const { return theHours; }
  int      minutes(void) const { return theMinutes; }
  int      seconds(void) const { return theSeconds; }
private:
  int      theHours, theMinutes, theSeconds;
};
```

As expected, each class conceals its representation, and provides a suite of operations to manipulate objects of its type. Now consider defining a function to add a `Nat` to a `Time`. One possible solution is to define a non-member function like this:

```
Time add(const Time& time, const Nat& natural)
{
  const long totalseconds =
    (60L * time.hours() + time.minutes()) * 60L +
      time.seconds();
  return Time(totalseconds + natural.nat());
}
```

Every time `add` is called, calls to the accessor functions to obtain copies of the constituent parts of a `Time` and a `Nat` are required. This overhead can, of course, be removed by making all these accessor functions inline. However, in some circumstances, we find that these accessor functions may, in addition to performing their primary task, execute some other procedure necessary for normal usage but not required in this instance. For example, some accessor functions may perform checks which, in the context of this application, is not required.

We could dispense with the overhead of this extra code if we make `add` a member of class `Time` where the accessor functions for `Time` carried the extra code. Equally, if the accessor functions for `Nat` had the extras, then we could make `add` a member of class `Nat`. In either case we could then bypass the unnecessary program logic and access the data members directly. If the accessor functions for both classes did checks our problem then is that function `add` cannot be a member of both classes.

The language construct we require is a friend. Operation `add` can be a friend to both classes or, as shown below, `add` can be a member of class `Time` (say), which has a class friend `Nat`:

```
class Nat;          // forward reference

class Time {
  friend class Nat;
public:
     Time(const long);
  // .....
  Time    add(const Time&, const Nat&);
  // .....
private:
  int     theHours, theMinutes, theSeconds;
};

class Nat {
public:
  // .....
private:
  unsigned     theNat;
};

Time Time::add(const Time& time, const Nat& natural)
{
  const long totalseconds = (60L * theHours + theMinutes) * 60L +
           theSeconds;
  return Time(totalseconds + natural.theNat);
}
```

When making friends of two classes in this way we must provide convincing arguments to justify this breach of information hiding. Chapter 13 will provide an example in which the two classes are intimately bound and for which friendship is an appropriate mechanism for the members to interact.

CASE STUDY 10.1
Rational numbers

Consider developing a program to compute the partial sums of the harmonic series *H(n)*. The program evaluates *H(n)* for various values of *n*, where:

$$H(n) = 1 + \frac{1}{2} + \frac{1}{3} + ... + \frac{1}{n}$$

The output from the program is the table for the values of *n* and the partial sum, the latter expressed as a rational number. For example, for *n* = 4, the program output is:

```
2 : 3/2
3 : 11/6
4 : 25/12
```

To implement this program, we first define a class to represent *rational numbers*. A rational number is a fractional value expressed as the quotient of two positive integers. Examples of rational numbers include 1/2, 3/4 and 7/8. The constituents of a rational number are its *numerator* and *denominator*. The value 3/4 has numerator 3 and denominator 4. An appropriate class is:

```
class Rational {
public:
  // .....
private:
  unsigned      theNumerator, theDenominator;
};
```

The class constructor has two arguments representing the two elements of a rational number. If omitted, the denominator defaults to the value 1, so that the rational 3/1 may be established with `Rational(3)`:

```
class Rational {
public:
   Rational(unsigned aNumerator, unsigned aDenominator = 1);
  // .....
};
```

We want the rational value always expressed in its simplest form. Thus if the arguments to the constructor are 8 and 6 (i.e. the rational value 8/6), we should wish the function to establish the reduced rational number 4/3. To do so we must determine the highest common factor of the two arguments, and divide this value into both. This is implemented with the hidden function `hcf`:

```
class Rational {
public:
   Rational(unsigned aNumerator, unsigned aDenominator = 1);
  // .....
private:
  // .....
  unsigned      hcf(unsigned, unsigned);
};
```

In addition, the constructor will trap the error condition where the denominator has value zero.

The arithmetic operations addition and multiplication are to be supplied for this version of class `Rational`. A conversion operator delivers the decimal value corresponding to the rational number. The rational number 3/4 has decimal value 0.75. The relational operators <, <=, etc. are used to compare two `Rational` values.

```
enum Bool { FALSE, TRUE };

class Rational {
public:
  // .....
  Rational      operator+ (const Rational&);
  // .....
  Bool          operator< (const Rational&);
  // .....
```

```
                operator double() const;
    // .....
};
```

Given such a class with its specification supplied in the header file `rational.h`, we may program the harmonic series as follows:

```
// ———————— FILE: case01.cpp ————————

//
//  Program to compute the harmonic series:
//
//       H(n) = 1 + 1/2 + 1/3 + ..... + 1/n
//
//       for some given value for n. The arithmetic is
//       achieved with the class Rational representing the
//       value x/y for some positive integers x, y.
//

#include <iostream.h>
#include "rational.h"

int main()
{
  int n;

  cout << "Enter limit n: ";
  cin >> n;

  Rational sum(1);
  for(unsigned int k = 2; k <= n; k++){
    Rational term(1, k);
    sum += term;
    cout << k << " : " << sum << "\n";
  }
  return (0);
}

// ———————— END: case01.cpp ————————
```

The solution is a natural expression of the problem. In addition to the operators for class `Rational` identified above, the output insertion operator `<<` has been overloaded, and the compound assignment operator `+=` must be supplied with the appropriate semantics. The specification and implementation for the class is as follows:

```
// ———————— FILE: rational.h ————————

//
//  A class Rational to represent the rational values
//       x/y where x and y are positive integers. Support
//       is provided for a range of arithmetic operators
//       relational operators.
//

#ifndef RATIONAL
```

```
#define RATIONAL

#include <iostream.h>

enum Bool { FALSE, TRUE };

inline Bool   not(Bool b)
{ return (b == FALSE) ? TRUE : FALSE; }

inline Bool   or(Bool b1, Bool b2)
{ return (b1 == TRUE) ? TRUE : b2; }

class Rational {
  friend ostream&    operator<< (ostream&, const Rational&);

public:
     Rational(unsigned int aNumerator, unsigned int aDenominator
                                                            = 1);
  operator double() const;

  Rational    operator+ (const Rational&);
  Rational    operator* (const Rational&);
  Rational&   operator+= (const Rational&);
  Rational&   operator*= (const Rational&);

  Bool operator<  (const Rational&) const;
  Bool operator>  (const Rational& rat) const;
  Bool operator<= (const Rational& rat) const;
  Bool operator>= (const Rational& rat) const;
  Bool operator== (const Rational& rat) const;
  Bool operator!= (const Rational& rat) const;

private:
  unsigned int  theNumerator;
  unsigned int  theDenominator;
  unsigned int  hcf(unsigned int, unsigned int);
};

inline ostream&   operator<< (ostream& os, const Rational& rat)
{
  os << rat.theNumerator << "/" << rat.theDenominator;
  return os;
}

inline Rational::operator double() const
{ return (double)theNumerator / theDenominator; }

inline Bool   Rational::operator<  (const Rational& rat) const
{
  return (theNumerator * rat.theDenominator
       < rat.theNumerator * theDenominator) ? TRUE : FALSE;
}

inline Bool   Rational::operator>  (const Rational& rat) const
{ return rat < *this; }

inline Bool   Rational::operator<= (const Rational& rat) const
{ return not(*this > rat); }

inline Bool   Rational::operator>= (const Rational& rat) const
```

```
  { return not(*this < rat); }

  inline Bool    Rational::operator== (const Rational& rat) const
  { return not(or(*this < rat, rat < *this)); }

  inline Bool    Rational::operator!= (const Rational& rat) const
  { return not(*this == rat); }

#endif    // RATIONAL

// ————— END: rational.h —————

// ————— FILE: rational.cpp —————

#include <stdlib.h>
#include "rational.h"

Rational::Rational(unsigned int aNumerator, unsigned int
                                                  aDenominator)
{
  if(aDenominator == 0){
    cout << "Rational(....) with zero denominator\n";
    exit(EXIT_FAILURE);
  }
  const unsigned int gcd = hcf(aNumerator, aDenominator); //
                                        greatest common divisor
  theNumerator = aNumerator / gcd;
  theDenominator = aDenominator / gcd;
}

Rational Rational::operator+  (const Rational& rat)
{
  const unsigned int num = theNumerator * rat.theDenominator
        + rat.theNumerator * theDenominator;
  const unsigned int den = theDenominator * rat.theDenominator;
  return Rational(num, den);
}

Rational Rational::operator*  (const Rational& rat)
{
  const unsigned int num = theNumerator * rat.theNumerator;
  const unsigned int den = theDenominator * rat.theDenominator;
  return Rational(num, den);
}
Rational& Rational::operator+= (const Rational& rat)
{
  theNumerator = theNumerator * rat.theDenominator
             + rat.theNumerator * theDenominator;
  theDenominator = theDenominator * rat.theDenominator;
  const unsigned int gcd = hcf(theNumerator, theDenominator);
  theNumerator /= gcd;
  theDenominator /= gcd;
  return *this;
}

Rational&        Rational::operator*= (const Rational& rat)
```

```
{
  theNumerator = theNumerator * rat.theNumerator;
  theDenominator = theDenominator * rat.theDenominator;
  const unsigned int gcd = hcf(theNumerator, theDenominator);
  theNumerator /= gcd;
  theDenominator /= gcd;
  return *this;
}

unsigned int    Rational::hcf(unsigned int a, unsigned int b)
{
  if(a < b){
    const unsigned int temp = a;
    a = b;
    b = temp;
  }

  while(a % b != 0){
    const unsigned int temp = b;
    b = a % b;
    a = temp;
  }
  return b;
}

// ———————— END: rational.cpp ————————
```

10.8 Commentary

The advantage of using friends is that they permit two or more classes, or a class and one or more functions to be more tightly coupled. For example, we permitted class `Time` to have more privileges with class `Nat` than one would give users of class `Nat`. Equally, friend functions provide syntactic advantages over member functions. Firstly, a friend function `f` can be called like `f(object)`, whereas a member function is called by `object.f()`. Secondly, as we showed in class `Time`, a friend function proves a convenient way of handling binary infix operators, particularly when the first operand is not the class type.

Since the friends of a class are absorbed into the class one may view friends as a way to violate information hiding. One should not view friends this way or try to use them for this purpose. Friends are used to provide safe access to a class in a way that the class itself is unable to achieve.

10.9 Summary

1. A user-defined abstract data type can include the definition of operators applicable to objects of that class. Only the predefined operator symbols may be used. The arity and associativity of the operators cannot be changed.

2. The meaning of the operators for the standard types cannot be redefined.

3. The assignment operator may be overloaded. By default, the compiler implicitly produces a memberwise copy version for this operator.

4. A friend function is a non-member of a class which is given access to the non-public members of the class.

5. An operator named with a type name operates as conversion operator from the class type to the given type.

10.10 Exercises

1. Prepare and test the class `Boolean`:

```
enum Bool { FALSE, TRUE };

class Boolean {
public:
  Boolean(Bool b = FALSE) { bool = b; }
  Boolean      operator&& (const Boolean&);
  Boolean      operator|| (const Boolean&);
  Boolean      operator! (void);
private:
  Bool          bool;
};
```

2. Prepare and test a class which supports modulo arithmetic:

```
class Modulo {
public:
  Modulo(unsigned n = 0) { mod = n % modulo; }
  static void          setModulo(unsigned m) { modulo = m; }
  Modulo               operator+ (const Modulo&);
  Modulo               operator- (const Modulo&);
  Modulo               operator* (const Modulo&);
  Modulo               operator/ (const Modulo&);
private:
  unsigned             mod;
  static unsigned      modulo;
};
```

3. Repeat Exercise 3 of Chapter 9 using operator functions as appropriate.

4. Add suitable operator functions to the class `Date` developed in the previous chapter.

5. Prepare a class `Imperial` containing appropriate operators for the imperial measure yards, feet and inches (one yard is 3 feet, one foot is 12 inches).

6. Prepare a class `Metric` for a metric measure. The class should provide conversion operators between itself and `Imperial` measures.

11

Inheritance

Inheritance is a mechanism which simplifies the definition of a new class which is similar to an existing class. Inheritance is an important mechanism in support of code sharing and software re-use. Rather than creating a completely new class, the programmer inherits the properties and characteristics of an existing class. In addition, for the new class we can specialize and extend those general features into specifics appropriate to the new class.

If we identify the use of inheritance in object oriented programming (OOP) with the idea that a *base class* expresses a general concept of which all *derived classes* are specializations, then there is no distinction amongst groups of related classes. An object of the derived class may use the services of a member function of the base class as if it were defined for that class. Equally, an application program can apply a service operation to an instance of one of the base classes without regard for the specific derived class type. During program execution, the *dynamic binding* mechanism of C++ determines the particular class of the object, and invokes that class's implementation of the operation. The result is a form of *polymorphism*.

In this chapter we shall introduce the C++ features that provide direct support for OOP. In particular, we will focus on the inheritance and dynamic binding mechanisms through, respectively, derived classes and *virtual functions*. The themes of encapsulation, inheritance and dynamic binding as the cornerstone in program design will then influence the organization of programs throughout the remainder of this book.

11.1 Class derivation

We shall illustrate class inheritance through a simple complete example. Assume we are developing a program that operates with four-sided geometrical figures (quadrilaterals). A quadrilateral will be subject to the following operations: calculate its area, find the length of its perimeter, scale the figure by some multiplying factor, and translate the figure by some amount through the X–Y co-ordinate system. The class describing a quadrilateral is then:

```
// ———————— FILE: quad.h ————————
//
```

```
//  Representation for a general four sided figure.
//

#ifndef QUADRILATERAL
  #define QUADRILATERAL

  #include "point.h"
  #include <math.h>

  class Quadrilateral {
  public:
    Quadrilateral(Point pp1, Point pp2, Point pp3, Point pp4);
    void          scale(double factor);
    void          translate(double horizontal, double vertical);
    double        perimeter(void) const;
    double        area(void) const;

  private:
    Point p1, p2, p3, p4;

  private:
    double      triangleArea(Point q1, Point q2, Point q3) const;
  };

  // .....

  inline double Quadrilateral::perimeter(void) const
  {
    double perim =  p1.distance(p2);
           perim += p2.distance(p3);
           perim += p3.distance(p4);
           perim += p4.distance(p1);
    return perim;
  }

  // .....
#endif    // QUADRILATERAL

// ———————— END: quad.h ————————
```

The supporting class `Point` describes positions in a two dimensional Cartesian coordinate system and is modelled on the class type defined in Case Study 9.1. The four data members `p1`, `p2`, `p3` and `p4` of type `Point` represent the coordinates of the vertices of the figure.

```
// ———————— FILE: point.h ————————

//
//  Representation for a point in a two-dimensional
//         cartesian coordinate space.
//

#ifndef POINT
  #define POINT

  #include <math.h>

  class Point {
```

```
  public:
    Point(double xx, double yy);
    void        scale(double factor);
    void        translate(double horizontal, double vertical);
    double      distance(const Point& p) const;

  private:
    double      x, y;
  };

  inline Pcint::Point(double xx, double yy)
          { x = xx; y = yy; }

  inline void    Point::scale(double factor)
          { x *= factor; y *= factor; }

  inline void    Point::translate(double horizontal, double
  vertical)
          { x += horizontal; y += vertical; }

  inline double Point::distance(const Point& p) const
  {
    double xdistance = x - p.x;
    double ydistance = y - p.y;
    double xdistance2 = xdistance * xdistance;
    double ydistance2 = ydistance * ydistance;
    return sqrt(xdistance2 + ydistance2);
  }

#endif    // POINT

// ——————— FILE: point.h ———————
```

Suppose now we require a class representing rectangles. A rectangle is also a four-sided figure, distinguished by having adjacent edges forming right angles. A rectangle is, then, a special version of a quadrilateral. Class inheritance allows the members of one class to be used as if they are members of another class. The class `Rectangle` can be introduced, inheriting all the members of class `Quadrilateral`. All the operations that can be performed on a `Quadrilateral` can also be performed on an object of class `Rectangle`. A rectangle has properties that distinguish it from a general quadrilateral. We can, if necessary, extend the attributes and services of class `Quadrilateral` which are inherited by class `Rectangle` by providing additional data and function members. We can also replace some or all of the member operations inherited from `Quadrilateral` with specialized versions appropriate to rectangles.

Inheritance is probably the most distinguishing characteristic of an OOP language such as C++. The derivation of class `Rectangle` from the class `Quadrilateral` permits the former to inherit the members of the latter (see Figure 11.1).

This commonality is distinguished by defining class `Rectangle` as a *derived class* of `Quadrilateral`. All the services of the *base* class `Quadrilateral` are applicable to the derived class `Rectangle`. Thus we may write:

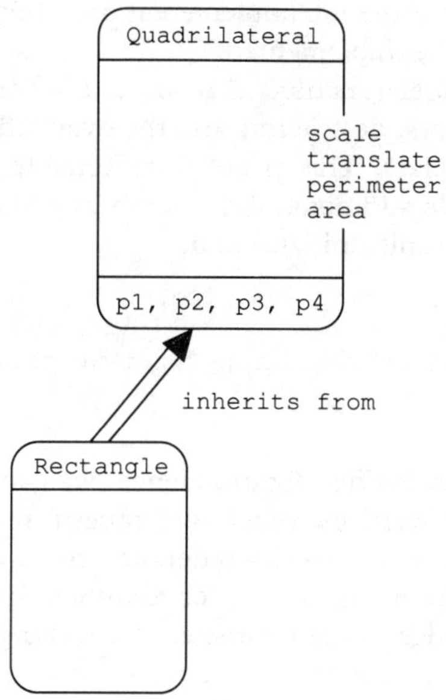

Figure 11.1

```
Rectangle       box(.....);                 // constructor
double length = box.perimeter();            // ok
```

To denote class derivation, the class header is extended to include a *derivation list* of classes from which to inherit members. The classes named in the list are the base classes. The class header for `Rectangle` would then appear as:

```
class Rectangle : public Quadrilateral {.....};
```

Note how the derivation list is set off from the class tag name by a colon symbol. The keyword `public` denotes that `Rectangle` is a publicly derived class of class `Quadrilateral`. This means that a public member of the base class is also a public member of the derived class. Derivations can be established as either public derivations or private derivations (see later), and dictate the visibility of inherited members.

Because of the derivation list, there is no need to repeat the inherited services of the base class. They are automatically exported to the derived class. The partial definition for `Rectangle` is then:

```
class Rectangle : public Quadrilateral {
  // ..... add nothing!
};
```

More commonly, a derived class incorporates some additional features not present in the base class. Alternatively, some functions of the base class are redefined in the derived class with a different implementation. Only the differences between the two classes needs to be implemented.

There are some member functions that are not automatically inherited by the derived class. Constructors, destructors and the overloaded assignment `operator=` only apply to the base class. This is not unreasonable since, as we have said, a derived class may include additional data members which will require appropriate treatment under, for example, initialization:

```
class Rectangle : public Quadrilateral {
public:
  Rectangle(Point pp1, Point pp2, Point pp3, Point pp4);
  // .....
};
```

A rectangle is still a four-sided figure. Hence, we can still represent it with the coordinates of its four vertices which we inherit from class `Quadrilateral`. However, it is appropriate to consider redefining some of the service functions of the base class. For function `perimeter`, for example, there is no need to compute the lengths of the four edges – the perimeter of a rectangle is simply twice the sum of the length of two adjacent edges.

The name, return type and signature for the redefined function appearing in the derived class must match exactly the definition in the base class. Here is the definition for `perimeter` in class `Rectangle`:

```
inline double Rectangle::perimeter(void) const
{
  double length = p1.distance(p2);
  double breadth = p2.distance(p3);
  return 2 * (length + breadth);
}
```

for which the class `Rectangle` appears as:

```
class Rectangle : public Quadrilateral {
public:
  // .....
  double        perimeter(void) const;    // specifies redefinition
  // .....
};
```

The problem with the implementation of `Rectangle::perimeter` is that the data members of class `Quadrilateral` are private and therefore not accessible to `Rectangle`. The principle of information hiding would be violated if we were to make the data members public. To resolve this conflict, an additional access level is supported, called *protected* class members. Protected class members under normal circumstances behave as private members, inaccessible to clients using the class. However, under inheritance a protected class member operates as a public member to the derived class. Member functions in the derived class may refer to protected data members in the base class as if they were public. A client using an instance of the derived class still finds these data members protected, and hence inaccessible. The proposed solution is corrected by changing the private data members of `Quadrilateral` to be protected members:

```
class Quadrilateral {
public:
  // ..... as above
protected:
  Point         p1, p2, p3, p4;
};
```

If we choose not to re-implement `perimeter` in class `Rectangle` we would still obtain the desired value when the function is called for an object of class `Rectangle`. Only a less efficient implementation is used.

The non-private member functions of a base class not redefined in the derived class are inherited by the derived class. The exception to this rule is that constructors and destructors and memberwise assignment operators are not inherited. The derived class constructor initializes the base class members through a member initialization list. The class `Rectangle` constructor initializes the base class members through the base class constructor, then, say, checks the integrity of the supplied figure ensuring that it is a proper rectangle. The check ensures that the diagonals are approximately equal by testing that their difference does not exceed some small value `epsilon`.

```
Rectangle::Rectangle(Point pp1, Point pp2, Point pp3, Point pp4)
  : Quadrilateral(pp1, pp2, pp3, pp4)
{
  if(fabs(p1.distance(p3) - p2.distance(p4)) > epsilon){
      cout << "Not a rectangle\n";
      exit(EXIT_FAILURE);
  }
  // .....
}
```

All these issues are consolidated into Program 11.1. Class `Quadrilateral` is defined as above, with member functions `area` and `perimeter`. The derived class `Rectangle` provides a specialized redefinition for the function `perimeter` but not function `area`. In addition, class `Rectangle` has been specialized to include the property of a diagonal. Class `Rectangle` is then made to operate as the public base class for `Square` which further redefines operation `perimeter`.

PROGRAM 11.1

```
// ——————— FILE: p01.cpp ———————

//
//  Program demonstrating derived classes and the
//        the determination of the member function
//        bodies from the function calls.
//
```

```
#include <iostream.h>
#include "quad.h"
#include "rect.h"
#include "square.h"

int main()
{
  Point origin(0, 0),   onezero(1, 0),oneone(1, 1);
  Point zeroone(0, 1), twozero(2, 0),twoone(2, 1);

  Quadrilateral quad(origin, twozero, oneone, zeroone);

  cout << "Quadrilateral, with perimeter: " << quad.perimeter()
       << ", area: " << quad.area() << "\n";

  Rectangle rect(origin, twozero, twoone, zeroone);

  cout << "Rectangle, with perimeter: " << rect.perimeter()
       << ", area: " << rect.area()
       << ", diagonal: " << rect.diagonal() << "\n";

  Square square(origin, onezero, oneone, zeroone);

  cout << "Square, with perimeter: " << square.perimeter()
       << ", area: " << square.area()
       << ", diagonal: " << square.diagonal() << "\n";

  return (0);
}

// ———————— END: p01.cpp ————————

// ———————— FILE: quad.h ————————

//
//  Representation for a general four sided figure.
//

#ifndef QUADRILATERAL
  #define QUADRILATERAL

  #include "point.h"
  #include <math.h>

  class Quadrilateral {
  public:
    Quadrilateral(Point pp1, Point pp2, Point pp3, Point pp4);
    void         scale(double factor);
    void         translate(double horizontal, double vertical);
    double       perimeter(void) const;
    double       area(void) const;

  protected:
    Point p1, p2, p3, p4;

  private:
    double       triangleArea(Point q1, Point q2, Point q3) const;
  };
```

```
inline Quadrilateral::Quadrilateral(Point pp1, Point pp2,
  Point pp3, Point pp4)
: p1(pp1), p2(pp2), p3(pp3), p4(pp4)
{}

inline void Quadrilateral::scale(double factor)
{
  p1.scale(factor);
  p2.scale(factor);
  p3.scale(factor);
  p4.scale(factor);
}

inline void Quadrilateral::translate(double horizontal, double
                                                       vertical)
{
  p1.translate(horizontal, vertical);
  p2.translate(horizontal, vertical);
  p3.translate(horizontal, vertical);
  p4.translate(horizontal, vertical);
}

inline double Quadrilateral::perimeter(void) const
{
  double perim =  p1.distance(p2);
         perim += p2.distance(p3);
         perim += p3.distance(p4);
         perim += p4.distance(p1);
  return perim;
}

inline double Quadrilateral::area(void) const
{
  const double triangle123 = triangleArea(p1, p2, p3);
  const double triangle134 = triangleArea(p1, p3, p4);
  return triangle123 + triangle134;
}

inline double Quadrilateral::triangleArea(Point q1, Point q2,
                                          Point q3) const
{
  const double side12 = q1.distance(q2);
  const double side23 = q2.distance(q3);
  const double side31 = q3.distance(q1);
  const double semiPerimeter = (side12 + side23 + side31) / 2;
  return sqrt(semiPerimeter * (semiPerimeter - side12) *
       (semiPerimeter - side23) * (semiPerimeter - side31));
}

#endif   // QUADRILATERAL

// ────────── END: quad.h ──────────

// ────────── FILE: rect.h ──────────
```

```
//
//  Representation for a rectangle
//

#ifndef RECTANGLE
  #define RECTANGLE

  #include "quad.h"

  class Rectangle : public Quadrilateral {
  public:
    Rectangle(Point pp1, Point pp2, Point pp3, Point pp4);
    double      perimeter(void) const;
    double      diagonal(void) const;

  private:
    double      theDiagonal;
  };

  inline double Rectangle::perimeter(void) const
  {
    double length = p1.distance(p2);
    double breadth = p2.distance(p3);
    return 2 * (length + breadth);
  }

  inline double Rectangle::diagonal(void) const
        { return theDiagonal; }

#endif   // RECTANGLE

// ────────── END: rect.h ──────────

// ────────── FILE: rect.cpp ──────────

#include <iostream.h>
#include <stdlib.h>
#include <math.h>
#include "rect.h"

static const double epsilon = 1.0e-4;

Rectangle::Rectangle(Point pp1, Point pp2, Point pp3, Point pp4)
  : Quadrilateral(pp1, pp2, pp3, pp4)
{
  if(fabs(p1.distance(p3) - p2.distance(p4)) > epsilon){
      cout << "Not a rectangle\n";
      exit(EXIT_FAILURE);
  }
  theDiagonal = p1.distance(p3);
}

// ────────── END: rect.cpp ──────────

// ────────── FILE: square.h ──────────

//
//  Representation for a square
```

```
//

#ifndef SQUARE
  #define SQUARE

  #include "rect.h"

  class Square : public Rectangle {
  public:
    Square(Point pp1, Point pp2, Point pp3, Point pp4);
    double       perimeter(void) const;
  };

  inline double Square::perimeter(void) const
  {
    double length = p1.distance(p2);
    return 4 * length;
  }

#endif   // SQUARE

// ——————— END: square.h ———————

// ——————— FILE: square.cpp ———————

#include <iostream.h>
#include <stdlib.h>
#include "square.h"

static const double epsilon = 1.0e-4;

Square::Square(Point pp1, Point pp2, Point pp3, Point pp4)
  : Rectangle(pp1, pp2, pp3, pp4)
{
  if(fabs(p1.distance(p2) - p2.distance(p3)) > epsilon){
    cout << "Not a square\n";
    exit(EXIT_FAILURE);
  }
}

// ——————— END: square.cpp ———————
```

As an object oriented system develops, new classes are constructed from existing classes. The new class is said to be a derived class (or *subclass*) of the original class. The old class is the base class (or *superclass*) of the new class. Thus, in Program 11.1, `Square` is the subclass of `Rectangle`, and `Quadrilateral` is the superclass of `Rectangle`.

A consequence of this development is that a *class hierarchy* is formed. The nodes represent the classes and the arcs represent the subclass/superclass relationships. Figure 11.2 shows the class hierarchy for Program 11.1.

It is appropriate to consider how objects of the base and derived classes find the code for some function applied to it. Consider, for example, the code:

```
Quadrilateral  quad(.....);          // constructor
double perim = quad.perimeter();     // member function
```

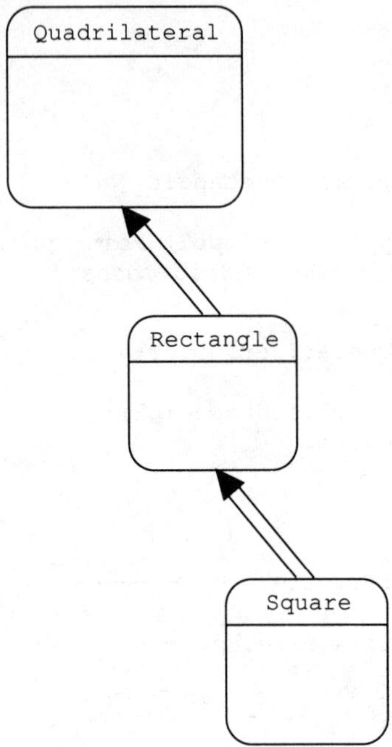

Figure 11.2

Here the `Quadrilateral` object `quad` executes the code for the member function `perimeter` defined in class `Quadrilateral`. This we show in Figure 11.3 with objects represented as rectangular figures and function execution as arrowed lines.

Equally, when we execute the fragment:

```
Rectangle      rect(.....);            // constructor
double perim = rect.perimeter();       // member function
```

the code for the member function `Rectangle::perimeter` is executed since class `Rectangle` redefines this function (see Figure 11.4). However, when we execute the fragment:

```
Rectangle        rect(.....);          // constructor
double area = rect.area();             // member function
```

the compiler will have first looked in the class `Rectangle` for the definition for function `area`. If it is not defined there then it looks for it in the immediate superclass, and so on up the class hierarchy. Here, since function `area` is defined in the base class `Quadrilateral` then the effect is as shown in Figure 11.5. Had no such function existed then, of course, a compile time error would have occurred.

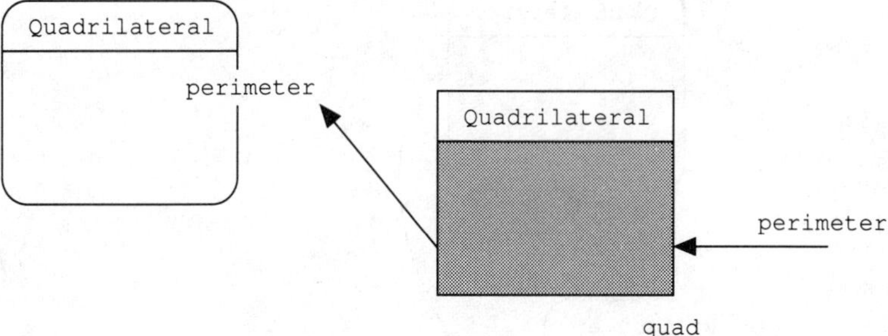

Figure 11.3

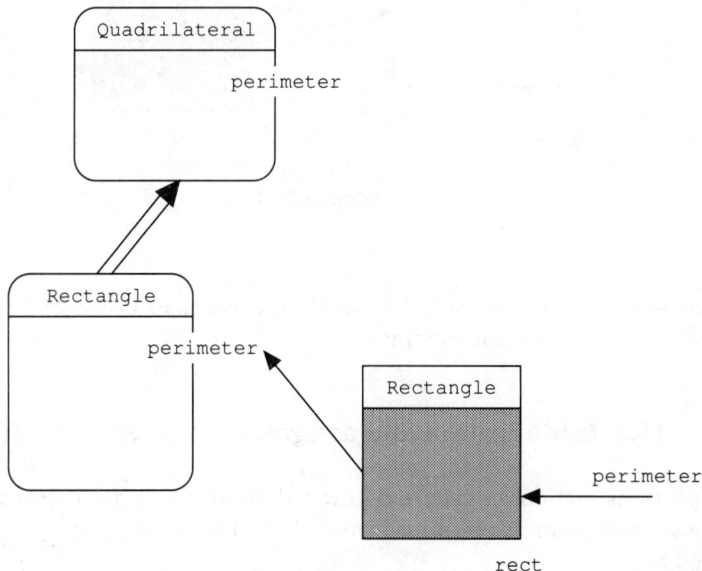

Figure 11.4

For an object to respond to a member function call it must look up and execute the body of the function. In a conventional programming language this association of the function name to the function body is performed by the compiler and the process is known as *binding*. In OOP languages when the binding is done at compile time we refer to it as *static binding*. This is the model for Figures 11.3, 11.4 and 11.5. In the code associated with Figure 11.5 the compiler statically binds the call to member function `area` to the code defined in class `Quadrilateral`. When the binding is performed at execution time we refer to it as *dynamic binding* (see later in the chapter). This distinction between function call

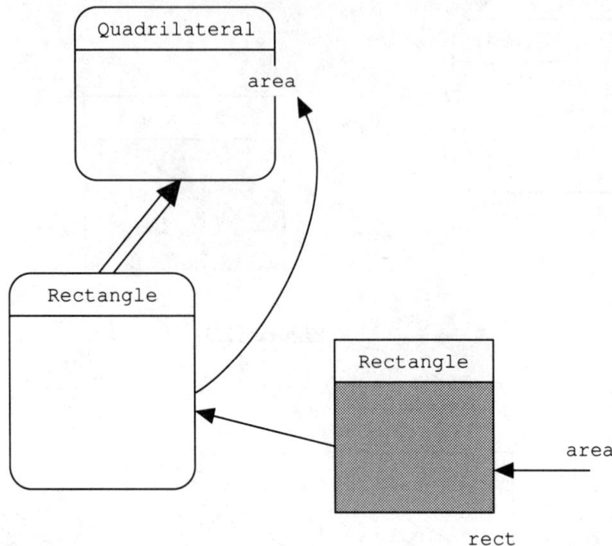

Figure 11.5

and function execution is central to OOP and we shall investigate the difference between static and dynamic binding.

11.2 Initialization and assignment under derivation

In the previous section we reported how a derived class constructor initializes the base class with a member initialization list. The class `Rectangle` constructor appeared as:

```
Rectangle::Rectangle(Point pp1, Point pp2, Point pp3, Point pp4)
  : Quadrilateral(pp1, pp2, pp3, pp4)
{
  // .....
}
```

The language defines a fixed order of constructor (and destructor) invocations. At its simplest, the base class constructors are invoked before the constructor of the derived class. In this example, the constructor for `Quadrilateral` is invoked before the constructor for `Rectangle`.

The member initialization list properly initializes all the data members of the base class inherited by the derived class. This is correctly achieved by calling the base class constructor since an object of class `Rectangle` has effectively a `Quadrilateral` subobject contained within it. The derived class may then not explicitly initialize a base class member since the effect has already been achieved. For example, the following is illegal:

```
Rectangle::Rectangle(Point pp1, Point pp2, Point pp3, Point pp4)
  : Quadrilateral(pp1, pp2, pp3, pp4), p1(pp1)
{
  // .....
}
```

The member initialization list passes arguments to the base class constructor. If the base class that does not define a constructor, or defines one that does not require an argument, then it need not appear in the member initialization list and the default constructor is called. For example:

```
class Quadrilateral {
public:
     Quadrilateral(void);      // default constructor
  // .....
};

class Rectangle : public Quadrilateral {
public:
     Rectangle(double r) { /* no initialization list */ }
  // .....
};
```

The full procedure for base class initialization is given by the following rules. To illustrate, consider a modified version of class `Square` containing the data member `middle` representing the co-ordinates of the centre of the figure:

```
class Square : public Rectangle {
public:
  // .....
private:
  Point   middle;
};
```

and the declaration:

```
Square    box(.....);
```

The constructors for `box` are invoked in the following order:

1. Each base class constructor is recursively applied in order of base class declarations:

```
Quadrilateral        // the base for Rectangle
Rectangle            // the base for Square
```

2 Each class member object is initialized with its constructor and called in the order of member object declarations:

```
Point                // to initialize middle
```

3. Finally, the derived class constructor is called:

```
    Square                    // to initialize box
```

The destructors for `box` are called in the reverse order of the invocations of the constructors.

Consider now initializing one class object with another. By default, memberwise initialization is performed. This same behaviour applies to derived class objects. For example, in:

```
Rectangle shape(.....);        // constructor
Rectangle box = shape;         // initialization
```

memberwise initialization is applied to the base class, then to each derived class member (if any).

11.3 Private base classes

The syntax:

```
class D : private B { ..... };
```

and

```
class D : B { ..... };
```

declares class `D` to be derived from class `B`. Further, `B` is a *private base class* of `D`. Note, how in the second example, when no explicit indication is provided, the base class is private by default. To avoid error, one is actively encouraged to present private base classes explicitly as shown by the first example.

A private base class is used where the internal representation for some derived data type is provided by the data type defined by the base class. The derived class `D` does not share the same operations that are appropriate to objects of the base class `B`. There is, therefore, no superclass/subclass relationship between classes `B` and `D`. The base class simply provides an implementation for the derived class.

For example, the abstract data type `Queue` is a storage device in which the first item which was inserted is always released first. It is customary to refer to the item to be released as the *front* of the queue. A new item is added to the *rear* of the queue. The usual queue operators are `add` (add an item to the queue rear), `remove` (release an item from the front of the queue), `front` (deliver a copy of the item at the front of the queue), `length` (count how many items are in the queue), and `isEmpty` (determine if the queue is empty).

The problem we are faced with is choosing an efficient representation for the `Queue` data type. However, we can exploit an existing data type and C++'s facility for software re-use to quickly produce an (inefficient) prototype.

A stack's behaviour is quite different from a queue. However, we propose to use a stack as a concrete representation for a queue. The problem with this implementation is that a stack operates from one end (the stack top), whilst a queue adds and removes items from, respectively, the queue rear and the queue front. If we choose to map the stack top on to the rear of the queue then the normally inaccessible stack bottom must correspond to the queue front, and we have the problem that we need to access the item at the queue front (see Figure 11.6).

Our implementation for a generic class `Stack` was defined in Section 9.12. It includes the (unusual) stack operation `reverse`. The availability of this operation makes it possible to consider using a `Stack` to realize a `Queue`. For example, the front of the queue is positioned at the bottom of the stack, and the rear of the queue is the stack top. The `Queue` operation `front` can be implemented by reversing the underlying `Stack` representation, obtain a copy of the stack top, then re-reversing the `Stack` to reinstate its original configuration.

```
// ———————— FILE: queue.h ————————

//
// Provide an inexpensive implementation for a queue
//      data type by utilising a stack as its implementation
//      through private inheritance.
//

#ifndef QUEUE
  #define QUEUE

  #include "stack.h"

  template <class TYPE>
  class Queue : private Stack<TYPE> {
  public:
    Queue(void);
    void add(const TYPE& item);
    void remove(void);
```

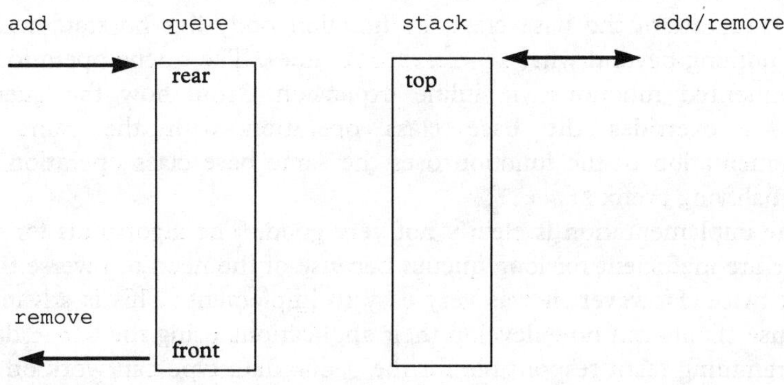

Figure 11.6

```
    TYPE        front(void);
    Bool  isEmpty(void) const;
    int         length(void) const;
  };

  template <class TYPE>
  inline Queue<TYPE>::Queue(void)
   {}
  template <class TYPE>
  inline void   Queue<TYPE>::add(const TYPE& item)
   { push(item); }
  template <class TYPE>
  inline void   Queue<TYPE>::remove(void)
   { reverse(); pop(); reverse(); }

  template <class TYPE>
  inline TYPE   Queue<TYPE>::front(void)
  {
    reverse();
    const TYPE frontItem = top();
    reverse();
    return frontItem;
  }

  template <class TYPE>
  inline Bool   Queue<TYPE>::isEmpty(void) const
   { return Stack<TYPE>::isEmpty(); }

  template <class TYPE>
  inline int    Queue<TYPE>::length(void) const
          { return depth(); }

#endif   // QUEUE

// ---------- END: queue.h ----------
```

The constructor `Queue::Queue` implicitly calls the default constructor `Stack::Stack` of the base class; its function body has no statements because it does nothing beyond what `Stack::Stack` does. The queue operations simply call the inherited functions via inline expansion. Note how the queue operation `isEmpty` overrides the base class operation with the same name. The implementation of the function uses the same base class operation and requires the qualifying prefix `Stack::`.

The implementation is clearly not very good. The algorithms for `remove` and `front` are inefficient for long queues because of the need to reverse the underlying stack twice. However, it was very easy to implement. This is advantage enough, because clients can now develop their applications using the `Queue` data type. The programming team responsible for the `Queue` data type can work on developing a better implementation (see Exercise 2 at the end of this chapter).

The problem we solve with data type `Queue<int>` is to input a series of positive integers and determine if the sequence is palindromic, i.e. reads the same both forwards and backwards. The data sets 1, 2, 2, 1 and 1, 2, 3, 2, 1 are palindromic. The data set 1, 2, 3, 4 is not palindromic. The input data uses a negative sentinel.

The solution is shown in Program 11.2. Here both a `Stack<int>` and a `Queue<int>` object are used in the following way: each single data item is both pushed on to the stack and added to the queue. Thus the queue will contain a copy of the data values in the order they appeared, whilst the stack has them reversed. When all the data is entered, items are repeatedly taken from both the stack (top) and the queue (front) and compared. If they differ the input data is not palindromic and the program terminates with a suitable message. Otherwise, the process repeats until the queue (or stack) is exhausted. Note that since both the queue and the stack are of equal length they will both be emptied simultaneously and it is sufficient to test just one.

PROGRAM 11.2

```
// ———————— FILE: p02.cpp ————————

//
// Determine if a series of positive integers is
//      palindromic, reading the same both forwards
//      and backwards.
//

#include <iostream.h>
#include <stdlib.h>
#include "stack.h"
#include "queue.h"

int main()
{
  Queue<int>     queue; // instantiate two containers
  Stack<int>     stack;
  int            data;

  cout << "Enter first data item: ";
  cin >> data;
  while(data >= 0){
    queue.add(data);
    stack.push(data);
    cout << "Enter next data item: ";
    cin >> data;
  }

  Bool isPalindromic = TRUE;
  while(queue.isEmpty() == FALSE){
    data = queue.front();
    if(data != stack.top()){
      isPalindromic = FALSE;
      break;
    }
```

```
    queue.remove();
    stack.pop();
  }
  if(isPalindromic)
    cout << "Data stream is palindromic\n";
  else
    cout << "Data stream is NOT palindromic\n";
  return (0);
}
// ———————— END: p02.cpp ————————
```

Note how similarities emerge if, alternatively, we had used a class member of type `Stack` to implement class `Queue` instead of derivation:

```
template <class TYPE>
class Queue<TYPE> {
  // .....
private:
  Stack<TYPE>      stack;
};
```

In both cases there is exactly one `Stack` subobject contained in a `Queue`. Equally, several distinctions must be emphasized. First, the latter form is necessary if, say, two or more `Stack` objects were to be contained by class `Queue`. Second, the inherited version permits functions of class `Queue` access to the protected members of the base class.

11.4 Scope rules and access control under derivation

The fundamental scope rules of C++ were defined in Chapters 5 and 7, and extended in Chapter 9 to accommodate classes. We further develop these rules to account for class derivation. The definition:

```
class Rectangle : public Quadrilateral {
public:
  Rectangle(Point pp1, Point pp2, Point pp3, Point pp4);
   double  diagonal(void);
protected:
  double theDiagonal;
};
```

declares `Rectangle` to be a new class derived from class `Quadrilateral`. `Rectangle` inherits all the members of class `Quadrilateral`, and adds its own: a value for the length of the diagonal, a function for accessing that value, and a constructor.

Class derivation results in a series of nested class scopes. In Chapter 5 we illustrated the effect on scoping when blocks are nested one within another. In a similar way, the scope of a derived class nests within the scope of its base class. If, say, we were to refer to data member `p1` in member function `Rectangle::diagonal`, then the compiler would first look for `p1` in class `Rectangle`, and failing that, check the base class `Quadrilateral`.

The syntax:

```
class Rectangle : public Quadrilateral
```

declares that the public members of the base class `Quadrilateral` are also public members of the derived class. A derived class has no special permissions to access private members of its base class. The privacy of class members is maintained under class derivation. Hence, a member function of class `Rectangle` may not refer to private members of its base class `Quadrilateral`. To do so would make the notion of privacy meaningless.

The declaration for a member function of a base class is invisible within the definition of the redefined version in the derived class. For example, were we not to optimize the implementation of `Rectangle::perimeter`, then a simple implementation would be to invoke the corresponding base class function. The scope resolution operator `::` is necessary here, since the re-use of such names makes the base class member invisible.

```
double Rectangle::perimeter(void)
{
  return Quadrilateral::perimeter();  // note qualification
}
```

Recognize that this example illustrates scope rules. The solution is quite unnecessary because we do not need to redefine `Rectangle::perimeter` this way since we get it for free through inheritance.

A non-terminating series of recursive calls (see Chapter 14) of `Rectangle::perimeter` would occur if we failed to observe this qualification.

```
double Rectangle::perimeter(void)
{
  return perimeter();             // trouble!!
}
```

We illustrate the visibility of members with a pictorial representation as shown in Figure 11.7. For some client program those accessible members of class `X` are drawn only from the public division of the class.

The public members of a base class `B` are also public members of a publicly derived class `D`. Hence public member functions of the base class can be applied to an object of the derived class. The scope rules under derivation also permit the definition of a derived class member function to be dependent upon a public member of the base class. This arrangement is shown in Figure 11.8. Observe how the protected members of a public base class are also protected members of the derived class.

A major distinction between private and public base classes is identified. When using a private base class the protected and public members of the base class are

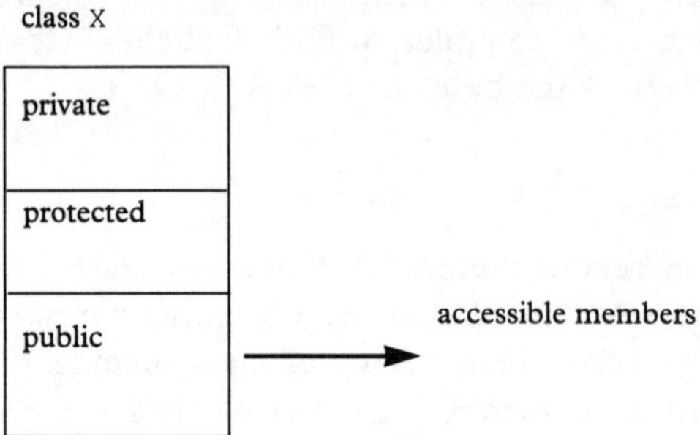

Figure 11.7

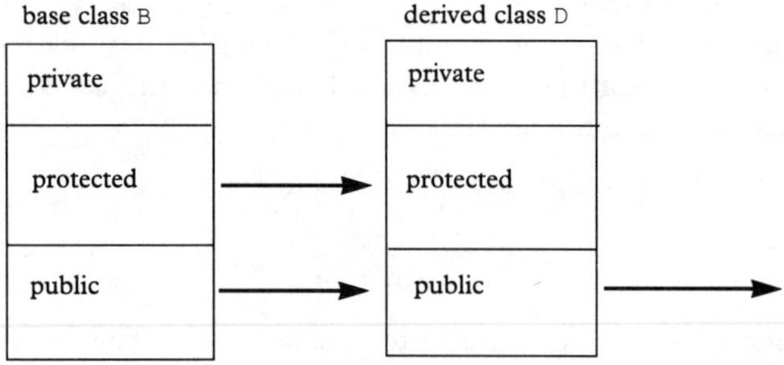

Figure 11.8

viewed as private members of the derived class (see Figure 11.9). In the last program the public operations of class `Stack` cannot be applied to an object of class `Queue`. This restriction protects the integrity of the `Queue` object, otherwise we would find ourselves permitted to `push` an item on to a queue – a meaningless operation on queue objects.

An *access declaration* may appear in the public section of a privately derived class. This is used to change the visibility of members from a private base class. A public member of the private base class can selectively be made public in the derived class through the notation:

```
class-name::member-name
```

For example, since class `Stack` provides the service `isEmpty`, we may simply inherit it for the same purpose with `Queue` objects (an empty queue is represented by an empty stack):

```
template <class TYPE>
class Queue : private Stack<TYPE> {
public:
```

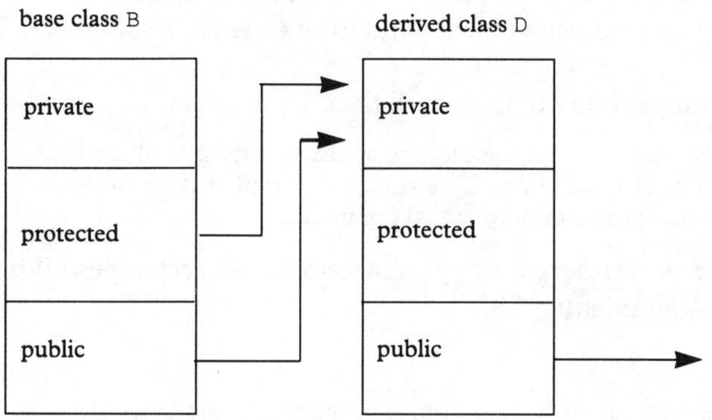

Figure 11.9

```
        // .....
        Stack<TYPE>::isEmpty;        // modify the access
        // .....
    };
```

11.5 Polymorphism and dynamic binding

Inheritance, as described in the introduction, is a mechanism in which one class is formed as a development of an existing class. This proves to be a particularly important concept which supports re-usability of existing code. Inheritance also gives rise to the notions of *polymorphism* and *dynamic binding*. These new concepts provide support by which software systems may be adapted to accommodate change in specification.

Polymorphism is defined as 'having several forms'. In an object oriented programming language this means that some object refers to instances of various classes during run time. In C++ static or compile time type checking is employed and, by definition, is incompatible with the notion of full polymorphism. This contention is resolved by the inheritance mechanism constraining the extent of the permitted polymorphism.

The class definition for `Rectangle` declares the explicit inheritance from `Quadrilateral` and reveals that a rectangle 'IS-A' quadrilateral with, perhaps, additional data and function members, and redefined functions. The class `Rectangle` has all the members of class `Quadrilateral` (and more), and hence the following assignment is correct:

```
    Quadrilateral         q;
    Rectangle             r;

    q  =  r;              // ok, rectangle IS-A quadrilateral
```

The conversion of a derived class object into an object of the base class is valid because every derived class object contains a base class subobject. This is shown in Figure 11.10.

The type compatibility of C++ is defined by the rule:

> The assignment `a = b`, where `a` is of class `A` and `b` is of class `B`, is only valid if `B` is a publicly derived class of `A`. This ruling also applies if a is a function formal argument and `b` is the corresponding actual argument.

The principle is illustrated by quadrilaterals and rectangles. Whereas `q = r` is allowed, the assignment:

```
r = q;
```

is illegal. The latter is only available if an explicit cast is used:

```
r = (Rectangle) q;
```

or

```
r = Rectangle(q);
```

The conversion of a derived class object into an object of its base class is valid because every derived class object contains all the members of the base class object. By a similar argument the opposite conversion is not safe, and is the reason why an explicit cast is required. The situation is similar to the cast:

```
(int)1.234
```

where the representation change is understood to result in information loss.

Equally, since `Quadrilateral` is a public base class of `Rectangle`, then there is a predefined conversion from `Rectangle*` to `Quadrilateral*`, and from `Rectangle&` to `Quadrilateral&`. Hence:

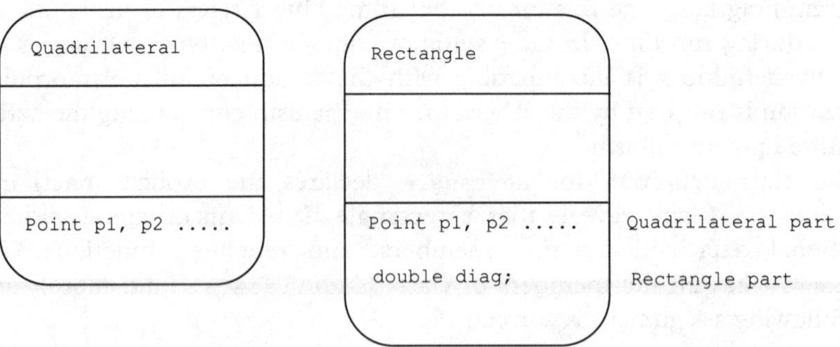

Figure 11.10

```
Square              s(.....);
Rectangle&          r = s;          // ok, s IS-A kind of Rectangle
Quadrilateral*      q = &r;         // ok, r IS-A kind of Quadrilateral
Quadrilateral*      p = &s;         // ok, s IS-A kind of Quadrilateral
```

Since the type system of C++ is consistent with inheritance, the following are also legal:

```
q->perimeter();         // ok, perimeter is defined for Quadrilateral

q->area(), q->translate(.....), q->scale(.....)
                        // ok, with legal arguments

r.diagonal();           // ok, diagonal is defined for Rectangle

r.translate(.....)
                        // ok, both defined for Quadrilateral
                        // and are inherited features for
                        // Rectangle

r.perimeter()
                        // ok, the redefined version for the
                        // first function is used, not the
                        // original in Quadrilateral
```

The above examples are all statically bound at compile time following the discussion in Section 11.1 (Figures 11.3, 11.4 and 11.5). We also noted there that C++ gives support to *dynamic binding* where the function's code is bound to the function call at run time. Consider Program 11.3(a).

PROGRAM 11.3(a)

```
// ---------- FILE: p03a.cpp ----------

#include <iostream.h>

//
//  Base class and two derived classes both providing
//       redefined versions of a member function
//

class Quadrilateral {
public:
  void   whoami(void) const
         { cout << "I am a Quadrilateral\n"; }
};

class Rectangle : public Quadrilateral {
public:
  void   whoami(void) const
         { cout << "I am a Rectangle\n"; }
};
```

```
class Square : public Rectangle {
public:
  void   whoami(void) const
    { cout << "I am a Square\n"; }
};


int main()
{
  Quadrilateral q;      // create some objects .....
  Rectangle     r;
  Square        s;

                        // put their addresses in an array .....
  Quadrilateral* figures[] = { &q, &r, &s };

  figures[0]->whoami(); // and call function
  figures[1]->whoami();
  figures[2]->whoami();

  return (0);
}

// ———————— END: p03a.cpp ————————
```

The program defines three classes related by inheritance. The base class `Quadrilateral` introduces the member function `whoami` and the two derived classes redefine it. Instances of each of the three class types are defined and their addresses are stored in an array. Note that the array type is `Quadrilateral*` and exploits the predefined conversions discussed above.

The program prints the message '`I am a Quadrilateral`' three times even though the calls to the function `whoami` are made with three distinct actual types. This behaviour is correct because static binding determines that the elements of the array `figures` are of type `Quadrilateral*`.

If we would like the proper `whoami` function to be determined by the actual object type, and not by the type of the elements of the array, then we must declare the function `Quadrilateral::whoami` to be `virtual`. In this case the modified program's output is:

```
I am a Quadrilateral
I am a Rectangle
I am a Square
```

The program producing this result is shown as Program 11.3(b).

PROGRAM 11.3(b)

```
// ———————— FILE: p03b.cpp ————————

#include <iostream.h>

//
```

```
//  Base class and two derived classes both providing
//       redefined versions of a virtual member function
//

class Quadrilateral {
public:
  virtual void  whoami(void) const
        { cout << "I am a Quadrilateral\n"; }
};

class Rectangle : public Quadrilateral {
public:
  void   whoami(void) const
        { cout << "I am a Rectangle\n"; }
};

class Square : public Rectangle {
public:
  void   whoami(void) const
        { cout << "I am a Square\n"; }
};

int main()
{
  Quadrilateral q;      // create some objects .....
  Rectangle     r;
  Square        s;

                        // put their addresses in an array .....
  Quadrilateral* figures[] = { &q, &r, &s };

  figures[0]->whoami(); // and call function
  figures[1]->whoami();
  figures[2]->whoami();

  return (0);
}

// ———— END: p03b.cpp ————
```

If, additionally, we were to remove the redefined version of function `whoami` from class `Rectangle`, then the latter inherits the definition of this function from its base class. Implicitly, `Square::whoami` is still a virtual function and redefines the base class version. This program's (Program 11.3(c)) output would be:

```
I am a Quadrilateral
I am a Quadrilateral
I am a Square
```

PROGRAM 11.3(c)

```
// ———— FILE: p03c.cpp ————

#include <iostream.h>
```

```
//
//  Base class and two derived classes one providing
//        redefined versions of a virtual member function
//

class Quadrilateral {
public:
  virtual void  whoami(void) const
        { cout << "I am a Quadrilateral\n"; }
};

class Rectangle : public Quadrilateral {
public:
};

class Square : public Rectangle {
public:
  void    whoami(void) const
        { cout << "I am a Square\n"; }
};


int main()
{
  Quadrilateral q;      // create some objects .....
  Rectangle     r;
  Square        s;

                        // put their addresses in an array .....
  Quadrilateral* figures[] = { &q, &r, &s };

  figures[0]->whoami();         // and call function
  figures[1]->whoami();
  figures[2]->whoami();

  return (0);
}

// ———————— END: p03c.cpp ————————
```

Consider now the geometrical figures quadrilateral, rectangle and square, and a non-member function called `dimensions` which computes both the perimeter and area of a four-sided figure. The relationships between inherited class types give rise to a polymorphic style of programming. The definition of function `dimensions` allows it to be called with any class type for which `Quadrilateral` is a public base class no matter how far removed.

The purpose of function `dimensions` is to take an actual argument of any of these three related class types and invoke the appropriate service functions. An implementation without any object oriented features would have the following logic:

```
const int QUADRILATERAL        = 0;
const int RECTANGLE            = 1;
const int SQUARE               = 2;
```

```
void dimensions(const Quadrilateral& figure, double& a, double& p)
{
  if(figure.isA() == QUADRILATERAL){
    a = figure.area();
    p = figure.perimeter();
  } else if(figure.isA() == RECTANGLE){
    a = ((Rectangle&)figure).area();
    p = ((Rectangle&)figure).perimeter();
  } else {
    a = ((Square&)figure).area();
    p = ((Square&)figure).perimeter();
  }
}
```

where the hypothetical function `isA` determines the run time type of the actual argument delivered to the function. The conditional statement contains clauses to handle each possible variant. The problem with this style of programming is that to change or to add a new strain to the kind of figures means we must modify the conditional statement. Commonly, there is more than one such statement throughout a program and we must identify and change them all. This is obviously a tiresome, maintenance activity.

In the solution above, resolution of the type of the variant is achieved with the programmer-defined conditional statement. In OOP the variant is resolved by the compiler. This we refer to as *dynamic binding*, and is demonstrated in the following coding:

```
void dimensions(Quadrilateral& figure, double& a, double& p)
{
  a = figure.area();
  p = figure.perimeter();
}
```

With each activation of function `dimensions`, the correct `perimeter` and `area` member functions are called.

Note how the function definition is greatly simplified. This will undoubtedly improve the quality and reliability of the code. The code is also implicitly extendible without the need for change. A further derivation can be added to the class hierarchy for figures without having to modify `dimensions` or any other similar functions.

Function `dimensions` can be called with a first actual argument of any class type that has `Quadrilateral` as its base class. The derived type can be any number of class derivations from the base class. Any unrelated actual argument will, of course, produce a compiler error:

```
Quadrilateral   q(.....);            // create some objects
Rectangle       r(.....);
Square          s(.....);
Point           p(.....);
double          surface, length;     // results of function call
```

```
dimensions(r, surface, length);
        // ok, r IS-A kind of Quadrilateral

dimensions(s, surface, length);
        // ok, s IS-A kind of Quadrilateral

dimensions(q, surface, length);
        // ok, perfect argument match

dimensions(p, surface, length);
        // error, p is not a Quadrilateral
```

Operations defined on all variants of `Quadrilateral` need not be implemented identically. This is the case for service function `perimeter`, having different versions for quadrilaterals and rectangles and squares. The fundamental question we must answer in function `dimensions` is what happens to its polymorphic first argument when the routines `area` and `perimeter` are applied?

In the code fragment:

```
Quadrilateral  quad(.....);
double         x = quad.perimeter();
```

no ambiguity exists, and it is clear that `Quadrilateral::perimeter` is called. Equally, in:

```
Rectangle      rect(.....);
double         y = rect.perimeter();
```

the function `Rectangle::perimeter` is invoked. However, for the polymorphic object `q`, declared as a `Quadrilateral` and dynamically bound to a rectangle, as in:

```
Quadrilateral& q = rect;       // ok, rect IS-A quadrilateral
double         z = q.perimeter();
```

Then dynamic binding determines that `Rectangle::perimeter` is applied when `z` is initialized. The `perimeter` operation automatically adapts to the object to which it is applied. In this case `q` is a (reference to a) `Rectangle`.

Thus when function `dimensions` is called with first actual argument `r` (a rectangle), routines `Rectangle::perimeter` and `Quadrilateral::area` are applied (class `Rectangle` redefines function `perimeter` but not `area`).

The rule for using virtual functions is that it must be called through a public base class reference or pointer. Argument `figure` in function `dimensions` is a reference to a base class (`Quadrilateral`) object. The actual routine (for `area` and `perimeter`) called is bound dynamically at run time, determined by the class type of the actual object addressed by the pointer or reference. A second version for this function using a `Quadrilateral*` argument is:

```
void dimensions(Quadrilateral* figure, double& a, double& p)
{
  a = figure->area();
  p = figure->perimeter();
}
```

The point to be emphasized is that we cannot define this function with simply an argument of type `Quadrilateral` and gain the same benefits of dynamic binding. Any actual first argument of type `Quadrilateral`, `Rectangle` or `Square` will simply be assigned to the formal argument `figure` which will then call statically the member functions `Quadrilateral::perimeter` and `Quadrilateral::area`:

```
void dimensions(Quadrilateral figure, double& a, double& p)
{
  // no dynamic binding behaviour
}
```

These issues are demonstrated in Program 11.4 which includes the function `dimensions` and for which the class `Quadrilateral` has been modified to mark the member functions `perimeter` and `area` as virtual:

```
// ———————— FILE: quadvirt.h ————————

//
//  Representation for a general four sided figure. The
//       perimeter and area functions have been tagged as
//       virtual so that they may engage in dynamic binding.
//

#ifndef QUADRILATERAL
  #define QUADRILATERAL

  #include "point.h"
  #include <math.h>

  class Quadrilateral {
  public:
    Quadrilateral(Point pp1, Point pp2, Point pp3, Point pp4);
    void           scale(double factor);
    void           translate(double horizontal, double vertical);
    virtual double perimeter(void) const;
    virtual double area(void) const;

  protected:
    Point       p1, p2, p3, p4;

  private:
    double      triangleArea(Point q1, Point q2, Point q3) const;
  };

  // .....

#endif   // QUADRILATERAL

// ———————— END: quadvirt.h ————————
```

PROGRAM 11.4

```
// ———————— FILE: p04.cpp ————————

#include <iostream.h>
```

```
#include "quadvirt.h"
#include "rectvirt.h"
#include "squarevirt.h"

void dimensions(const Quadrilateral&, double&, double&);
                                                    // prototype

int main()
{
  Point origin(0, 0),   onezero(1, 0),   oneone(1, 1);
  Point zeroone(0, 1), twozero(2, 0),   twoone(2, 1);
  double area, perimeter;

  Quadrilateral quad(origin, twozero, oneone, zeroone);

  dimensions(quad, area, perimeter);
  cout << "Quadrilateral, with perimeter: " << perimeter
       << ", area: " << area << "\n";

  Rectangle rect(origin, twozero, twoone, zeroone);

  dimensions(rect, area, perimeter);
  cout << "Rectangle, with perimeter: " << perimeter
       << ", area: " << area << "\n";

  Square square(origin, onezero, oneone, zeroone);

  dimensions(square, area, perimeter);
  cout << "Square, with perimeter: " << perimeter
       << ", area: " << area << "\n";

  return (0);
}

void dimensions(const Quadrilateral& figure, double& a, double& p)
{
  a = figure.area();
  p = figure.perimeter();
}

// ———————— END: p04.cpp ————————
```

In the first call to function `dimensions` with first argument `quad`, dynamic binding determines that `Quadrilateral::area` and `Quadrilateral::perimeter` are applied. Equally, the second call to `dimensions` with first actual argument `rect` determines that `Quadrilateral::area` and `Rectangle::perimeter` are invoked. The program's output is then:

```
Quadrilateral, with perimeter: 5.414214, area: 1.5
Rectangle, with perimeter: 6, area: 2
Square, with perimeter: 4, area: 1
```

As we have illustrated above a pointer or reference to an object can, through dynamic binding of virtual functions, lead to executing the function of the derived type and not that defined in the base class. Hence the run-time type of the object is used to determine the function to call. If the function is non-virtual the call will resolve statically to the member function associated with the class of the original pointer or reference.

At compile time, however, we have only the static type of the pointer or reference. Type safety is ensured by static type checking the call which means referring to the (static) type of the pointer or reference. If the type of the pointer or reference supports the member function call then so too will the pointer or reference since it refers to an object from a class derived from the pointer or reference class.

To permit a derived class to redefine a polymorphic member function of the base class, the latter must provide an explicit indicator to this effect. A member function of the base class labelled with the keyword `virtual` is known as a *virtual member function*. A virtual member function belongs to a class that is expected to be the subject of derivation, in which the function may be redefined.

As noted, the keyword `virtual` is attached to those function declarations where the implementation of a function is type dependent, and where the associated class expects to be an object of derivation. Hence in class `Quadrilateral` function `perimeter` is so labelled, so that any specialized form of four sided figure could provide its own way of computing these values:

```
class Quadrilateral {
public:
  // ..... as before
  virtual double perimeter(void) const;       // dynamic binding
  double         area(void) const;
private:
  // ..... as before
};
```

In this context the `virtual` keyword can only occur within the class body. It does not appear in the function definition when the latter is given separate from the class body. Further, the keyword `virtual` is not applicable to data members.

Notice that `Rectangle::perimeter` is virtual without having explicitly declared it to be so. However, we could have included the keyword `virtual` to emphasize this characteristic. The rule for determining when a function is virtual is simple: a function is virtual if it is declared virtual (such as `Quadrilateral::perimeter`), or if there is a base class function with the same signature that is virtual (`Rectangle::perimeter`).

A function declared in a derived class with the same name and signature as a virtual function in the base class is a polymorphic redefinition for that function. The keyword `virtual` in the base class indicates that it is likely that the function will be redefined in a derived class. If the derived class provides no redefinition, then it inherits the virtual function from the base class in the usual manner.

If in the derived class the redeclaration is not an exact match for the function, then it is not interpreted as a virtual for the derived class. If `Rectangle`, for example, declared `perimeter` as:

```
class Rectangle : public Quadrilateral {
public:
  // .....
  int      perimeter(void);          // different return type
};
```

then this function is not virtual for class `Rectangle`.

Class `Square` which is subsequently derived from `Rectangle` can still provide a virtual instance of `perimeter`, providing, once again, it is an exact match of the virtual declaration in `Quadrilateral`:

```
class Square : public Rectangle {
public:
  // .....
  double       perimeter(void);       // virtual version
};
```

11.6 Abstract base classes

The graphic illustration shown earlier consisted of the class `Quadrilateral` at the root of the class hierarchy. `Quadrilateral` defines the data and function members that are common to all four-sided figures. Derivations from `Quadrilateral` define what is unique to a specific class of such figures. Subsequent derivations refine this further.

The class `Quadrilateral` is designed as one from which others may be derived. Each derivation effectively extends it. The C++ rules specify that virtual functions must be defined in the class in which they are first declared. Our class `Quadrilateral` looked like:

```
// ———————— FILE: quadvirt.h ————————
//
// Representation for a general four sided figure. The
//         perimeter and area functions have been tagged as
//         virtual so that they may engage in dynamic binding.
//

#ifndef QUADRILATERAL
  #define QUADRILATERAL

  #include "point.h"
  #include <math.h>

  class Quadrilateral {
  public:
    Quadrilateral(Point pp1, Point pp2, Point pp3, Point pp4);
    void           scale(double factor);
    void           translate(double horizontal, double vertical);
    virtual double perimeter(void) const;
    virtual double area(void) const;
```

```
  protected:
    Point       p1, p2, p3, p4;

  private:
    double      triangleArea(Point q1, Point q2, Point q3) const;
  };

  // .....

  #endif    // QUADRILATERAL

  // ────────── END: quadvirt.h ──────────
```

Classes derived from `Quadrilateral` either inherited unchanged the member functions defined there or redefined them as a specialization. In a class hierarchy a polymorphic operation introduced in a base class is usually redefined in the derived classes. Sometimes it is useful to include in the base class an operation for which there is no meaningful definition. The expectation is that such an operation only has meaning in a derived class redefinition. The operation is incorporated into the hierarchy by its presence in the base class but its behaviour is deferred.

The solution to this kind of problem is to indicate that a virtual function does not have a definition. This gives rise to what is known as a *pure virtual function.* This we indicate with the initializer `'= 0'`:

```
class Quadrilateral {
public:
  // .....
  virtual double area(void) const =0;     // pure virtual function
  // .....
};
```

A class with one or more pure virtual functions is called an *abstract base class.* An abstract base class can only be used as the base class for another class. An abstract class makes it incumbent on the programmer to provide implementations for the pure virtual function in the derived classes. A class derived from an abstract base class must either define the pure virtual functions of its base, or once again declare them as pure virtual functions expecting further derivation. The derived class may also introduce additional pure virtual functions.

An abstract class is never used to declare class objects. One may not declare a variable whose type is given by an abstract base class. For class `Quadrilateral` defined above, objects of this class may not be created. But we can declare polymorphic objects of this type, for example, the first argument to non-member function `dimensions` introduced earlier.

Much of the power of C++ comes from arranging its classes into hierarchies. Each class has an immediate superclass (its base class) and possibly one or more subclasses (its derived classes). Classes higher in the hierarchy represent more general characteristics, while classes lower in the hierarchy represent more specific characteristics. For example, fish and tree are more abstract than salmon and pine respectively, and `Quadrilateral` is more abstract than `Rectangle`.

Inheritance provides the capability in C++ to allow one to re-use software by specializing already existing general solutions. In the class hierarchy we develop a generic problem solution using abstract classes, and then develop more application specific solutions which specialize the general solution by adding a small amount of code and data in subclasses. To see this, we will define a new class hierarchy for three- and four-sided figures (see Figure 11.11).

All the classes in the hierarchy are subclasses of the abstract base class `Figure` (shown with a dotted border). Class `Figure` provides the operation protocols inherited by its subclasses. Each closed figure supports determination of the length of its perimeter and its area. Class `Figure` assumes its subclasses implement the specialized versions for these operations.

```
class Figure {
public:
  virtual double  perimeter(void) const = 0;
  virtual double    area(void) const = 0;
  // ....
};
```

Based on the availability of these operations in derived classes, class `Figure` can provide a generic implementation for an operation on one or more figures. For example, `operator<` implements a comparison operation using the area of the closed figures as the measure. This generic operation is then inherited by all `Figure` classes.

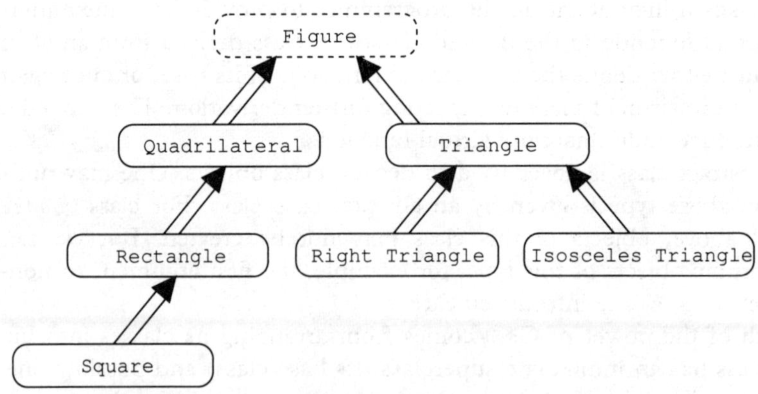

Figure 11.11

```
class Figure {
public:
      virtual double       perimeter(void) const =0;
      virtual double       area(void) const = 0;
      int operator< (const Figure& fig1, const Figure& fig2)
            { return fig1.area() < fig2.area(); }
      // .....
};
```

Hence given the definitions:

```
Rectangle         rect(.....);            // constructors
RightTriangle     hypo(.....);
```

we may issue the code:

```
if(rect < hypo) .....
```

and dynamic binding will correctly determine that the area of the `Rectangle` object `rect` is compared against the area of the `RightTriangle` object `hypo`.

The idea is to move the definition of operations as high as possible in the class hierarchy, so that it may be shared (without the need to repeat its definition) by the greatest possible number of descendant classes.

Abstract base classes also mean that we can set up containers such as arrays to hold objects of various types. For example:

```
Figure*   shapes[] = { &rect, &hypo };
```

The array will contain instances of each of the different types. Such assignments are possible since a pointer of class `Figure` may contain instances of pointers to subclasses of that class. We may correctly ask each object in the array for its `area` for each instance will belong to a subclass for which the operation has been defined.

CASE STUDY 11.1
Number classes

This case study draws together the object oriented concepts we have developed in this and the previous two chapters. In particular, exploitation of inheritance, polymorphism and dynamic binding exemplify how to develop code through re-use.

Consider the numerical classes `Natural` and `Rational` which appeared in the previous chapter. They both define objects that can be compared, measured and ordered. Further, they both respond to arithmetical operators and numerical functions.

Much of C++'s power comes from arranging its classes in a hierarchy. Each class has an immediate superclass and possibly one or more subclasses. Classes higher in the hierarchy represent more general characterstics, while classes lower down represent more specific properties.

In the previous two chapters we saw how C++ organizes its functions by class. Here we shall demonstrate how we can develop generic problem solutions using abstract classes, and then develop more application specific solutions which specialize the general solution by adding a small amount of code in the subclasses.

Inheritance is the capability whereby we can re-use software by specializing existing general solutions. Here, we shall incorporate the classes `Natural` and `Rational` into a class hierarchy `Number` (see Figure 11.12).

In this example, class `Number` is an abstract base class. That is, one that is not designed to be used to create objects, but designed to be inherited. It specifies an interface at a general level, and provides a *form* or *protocol* upon which other derived classes can be created. All numbers must support the relational operators `operator<` and `operator>`, and the numerical function `min` (minimum). `isEven` (is the number an even number), `isOdd` are operations peculiar to `Natural` numbers, whilst `reciprocal` (find the inverse of the number) is appropriate for `Rational` numbers.

The partial class definition for `Number` is:

```
class Number {    // abstract base class
  friend Number& min(const Number&, const Number&);
public:
  // .....
  Bool           operator< (const Number&) const;
  // .....
};
```

If `operator<` was made a pure virtual function, then our derived classes would be required to redefine it. Similarly for `operator>` and the other numerical functions. However, we can exploit polymorphism to facilitate re-use of existing code. Polymorphism permits different objects to respond to the same operation with their own unique behaviour. For example, introduce into class `Number` the pure virtual function `less` which determines if one `Number` is less than another. Classes `Natural` and `Rational` will provide their own specialized versions for this function. Based on particular implementations for this function, class `Number` can provide generic implementations for `operator<` and `operator>` which are inherited by all classes derived from `Number`:

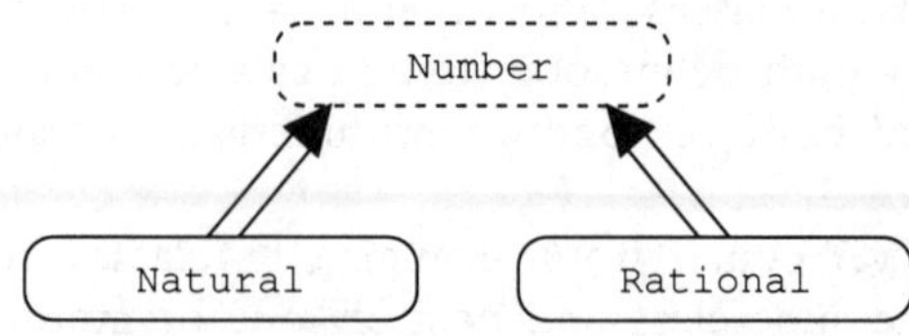

Figure 11.12

```
class Number {   // abstract base class
  friend Number&          min(const Number&, const Number&);
public:
  Bool            operator< (const Number& num2) const
          { return this->less(num2); }
  Bool            operator> (const Number& num2) const
          { return num2.less(*this); }
private:
  virtual Bool  less(const Number&) const = 0;

  // .....
};

class Natural : public Number {
  // .....
private:
  Bool   less(const Number&) const;        // redefined
  // .....
};

class Rational : public Number {
  // .....
private:
  Bool   less(const Number&) const;        // redefined
  // .....
};
```

Note how, for example, in the definition for `operator>` the actual version of function `less` which is invoked is dependent upon the actual type of `Number` given for the argument `num2`. Note also how we have placed the supporting function `less` in the private sections of the classes. Client programs can then only compare numbers using `operator<` and `operator>`.

Now in some application we are permitted to apply `operator<` and `operator>` to pairs of `Natural` or `Rational` values. For example, in:

```
int main()
{
  Natural        one(1), two(2);
  Rational       half(1, 2), quarter(1, 4);

  if(one < two) .....
  if(quarter > half) .....
  // .....
}
```

the second if statement invokes the operator function `operator>` from the base class `Number`. This occurs because the derived class `Rational` does not redefine this operator. In the definition for the `operator>` function in class `Number`, the polymorphic argument `num2` is of type (reference to) `Number`. The corresponding actual argument is the variable `half` of type `Rational`. Dynamic binding causes the function `Rational::less` to be called to deliver the required result. This function will, of course compare two `Rational` values as required.

One problem exists, however. The operator function `operator>` employs a polymorphic argument, with run time determination of which subordinate function `less` is to be called. Since both the classes `Natural` and `Rational` are publicly derived from the base class `Number`, then the following construct is syntactically valid:

```
if(two > half) .....
```

By the reasoning given above, dynamic binding will call the function `Rational::less` which expects an argument of type (reference to) `Number`. Strictly, the function will expect this to be an object of the derived type `Rational` to permit the comparison to be performed meaningfully. The problem is that the actual argument to `Rational::less` is of type `Natural` which the code will try to interpret as the structure for a `Rational`.

One solution is to introduce a private integer data member into each derived class which is uniquely encoded for each class. The function `Rational::less` could then interrogate this value for its actual argument to check that it is a `Rational`. Since all objects of the same class are encoded with the same value, we could make this discriminating value a static member.

The need to discriminate among types reintroduces the kind of problem we are endeavouring to overcome in this chapter. Another solution is not to compare the values of each static member from each class, but compare their addresses. There is a single instance of these static members for each class. Every class has its single copy, located at different addresses. We could compare addresses, rather than compare values which require careful organization.

Rather than simply use a static object of type `int` in every class definition, we shall use a static object of a user defined type. This *class descriptor* object can be used to contain information about an object's class, such as its name, its base class, etc. For the present, we will not associate any such attributes with this class descriptor object. Every class derived from `Number` has a private static member `classdescriptor` of type `Class`. For this problem `Class` is simply defined as:

```
class Class {};        // empty!
```

Every derived class also implements the function `classDescriptor`, returning the address of the private static data member:

```
class Number {
public:
  virtual Class*    classDescriptor(void) const =0;
  // .....
};

class Natural : public Number {
public:
  // .....
  Class* classDescriptor(void) const
     { return &classdescriptor; }
```

```
private:
  unsigned      nat;
  static Class  classdescriptor;
};
```

The call to the functions `less` redefined in every derived class, determines if the argument object is of a comparable class. For example, in class `Natural` the function ensures that the argument is a `Natural` object. The coding is:

```
class Natural : public Number {
  // .....
private:
  unsigned      nat;
  static Class  classdescriptor;

  Bool   less(const Number& num2) const
  {
    if(&classdescriptor != num2.classDescriptor()){
      cout << "Natural::less - bad argument type\n";
      exit(EXIT_FAILURE);
    }
    return Bool(nat < ((Natural&)num2).nat);
  }
};
```

Other case studies have addressed problems larger and richer than the small illustrative examples. This case study has been used as a draw-string, pulling together the object oriented concepts we have developed. These architectures will be carried forward into case studies later in the text. The program we develop simply tests the classes by calling a range of services. The program's output is:

```
one less than two
quarter NOT greater than half
Min of 1 and 2 is 1
Min of 1/2 and 1/4 is 1/4
2 is even
reciprocal of quarter is 4/1
Rational::less - bad argument type
```

```
// ————— FILE: case01.cpp —————

#include <iostream.h>
#include "number.h"
#include "natural.h"
#include "rational.h"

int main()
{
  Natural         one(1), two(2);
  Rational        half(1, 2), quarter(1, 4);

  if(one < two)
    cout << "one less than two\n";
  else
```

```
        cout << "one NOT less than two\n";

      if(quarter > half)
        cout << "quarter greater than half\n";
      else
        cout << "quarter NOT greater than half\n";

      cout << "Min of " << one << " and " << two << " is "
           << (Natural&)min(one, two) << "\n";

      cout << "Min of " << half << " and " << quarter << " is "
           << (Rational&)min(half, quarter) << "\n";

      if(one.isEven()) cout << one << " is even\n";

      if(two.isEven()) cout << two << " is even\n";

      quarter.reciprocal();
      cout << "reciprocal of quarter is " << quarter << "\n";

      if(two > half)          // ERROR
        cout << "two less than half\n";
      else
        cout << "two NOT less than half\n";

      return (0);
    }
    // ────────── END: case01.cpp ──────────

    // ────────── FILE: class.h ──────────

    #ifndef CLASS
      #define CLASS

      class Class {};

    #endif    // CLASS

    // ────────── END: class.h ──────────

    // ────────── FILE: number.h ──────────

    #ifndef NUMBER
      #define NUMBER

      #include "class.h"

      enum Bool { FALSE, TRUE };

      class Number {          // abstract base class
        friend const Number& min(const Number& num1, const Number&
                                                              num2);

      public:
        Bool          operator< (const Number& num2) const;
        Bool          operator> (const Number& num2) const;

        virtual Class* classDescriptor(void) const = 0;
```

```
  private:
    virtual Bool less(const Number&) const = 0;
  };

  inline const Number& min(const Number& num1, const Number&
                                                            num2)
         { if(num1.less(num2)) return num1; else return num2; }

  inline Bool    Number::operator< (const Number& num2) const
         { return this->less(num2); }

  inline Bool    Number::operator> (const Number& num2) const
         { return num2.less(*this); }

#endif    // NUMBER

// ────────── END: number.h ──────────

// ────────── FILE: natural.h ──────────

#ifndef NATURAL
  #define NATURAL

  #include <iostream.h>
  #include <stdlib.h>
  #include "number.h"

  class Natural : public Number {
    friend ostream& operator<< (ostream& os, const Natural&
                                                       natural);

  public:
    Natural(const unsigned n = 0);

    Bool          isEven(void) const;
    Bool          isOdd(void) const;

    Class*               classDescriptor(void) const;

  private:
    unsigned             nat;
    static Class classdescriptor;

    Bool          less(const Number& num2) const;

  };

  inline ostream& operator<< (ostream& os, const Natural& natural)
         { os << natural.nat; return os; }

  inline Natural::Natural(const unsigned n)
         { nat = n; }

  inline Bool      Natural::isEven(void) const
         { return Bool(nat % 2 == 0); }

  inline Bool      Natural::isOdd(void) const
         { return Bool(nat % 2 != 0); }

  inline Class*    Natural::classDescriptor(void) const
```

```
        { return &classdescriptor; }

  inline Bool   Natural::less(const Number& num2) const
    {
      if(&classdescriptor != num2.classDescriptor()){
         cout << "Natural::less - bad argument type\n";
         exit(EXIT_FAILURE);
      }
      return Bool(nat < ((Natural&)num2).nat);
    }

#endif   // NATURAL

// ———————— END: natural.h ————————

// ———————— FILE: natural.cpp ————————

#include "natural.h"

Class    Natural::classdescriptor;   // create static instance

// ———————— END: natural.cpp ————————

// ———————— FILE: rational.h ————————

#ifndef RATIONAL
  #define RATIONAL

  #include <iostream.h>
  #include <stdlib.h>
  #include "number.h"

  class Rational : public Number {
    friend ostream& operator<< (ostream& os, const Rational& rat);

  public:
    Rational(unsigned n, unsigned d = 1);

    void         reciprocal(void);

    Class*                classDescriptor(void) const;

  private:
    unsigned              numer, denom;
    static Class classdescriptor;

    Bool         less(const Number& num2) const;

  };

  inline ostream& operator<< (ostream& os, const Rational& rat)
    { os << rat.numer << "/" << rat.denom; return os; }

  inline Rational::Rational(unsigned n, unsigned d)
    { numer = n; denom = d; }

  inline void   Rational::reciprocal(void)
    { const unsigned temp = numer; numer = denom; denom = temp; }

  inline Class* Rational::classDescriptor(void) const
```

```
    { return &classdescriptor; }

  inline Bool   Rational::less(const Number& num2) const
  {
    if(&classdescriptor != num2.classDescriptor()){
      cout << "Rational::less - bad argument type\n";
      exit(EXIT_FAILURE);
    }
    return Bool(numer * ((Rational&)num2).denom <
                denom * ((Rational&)num2).numer);
  }

#endif   // RATIONAL

// ---------- END: rational.h ----------

// ---------- FILE: rational.cpp ----------

#include "rational.h"

Class    Rational::classdescriptor;   // static instance

// ---------- END: rational.cpp ----------
```

CASE STUDY 11.2
Patient statistics (revisited)

In Case Study 9.2 a system modelling doctors and patients was established. A `Patient` has a name and a date of birth as well as a count of the number of visits made by the patient to see the doctor. A `Doctor` has a name and a list of registered patients. We can now view a `Patient` and a `Doctor` as a specialization of class `Person` in which the general properties are a name and a date of birth. The `Patient` is specialized to keep count of the number of visits and the `Doctor` is specialized to maintain the record of the patients (see Figure 11.13).

```
// ---------- FILE: person.h ----------

//
//  A Person class with name and date of birth for
//       its attributes
//

#ifndef PERSON
  #define PERSON

  #include "cstring.h"
  #include "cdate.h"

  class Person {
  public:
    Person(const String& aName, const Date& aDOB);
    String      name(void) const;
```

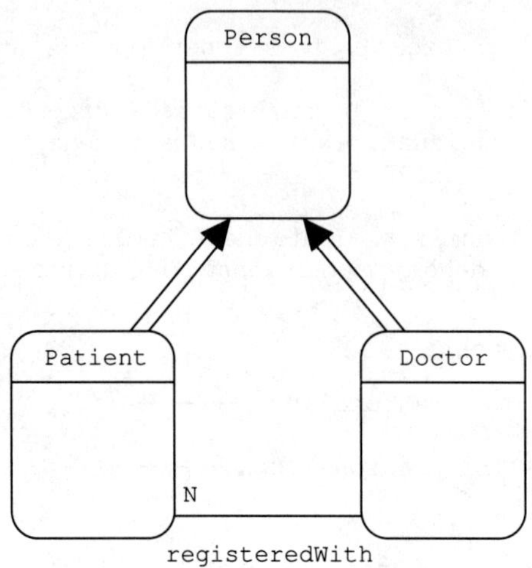

Figure 11.13

```
  protected:
    String      theName;
    Date  theDOB;
  };

  inline Person::Person(const String& aName, const Date& aDOB)
          : theName(aName),
            theDOB(aDOB)
  {}

  inline String Person::name(void) const
          { return theName; }
#endif   // PERSON

// ———————— END: person.h ————————

// ———————— FILE: patient.h ————————

#ifndef PATIENT
  #define PATIENT

  #include "person.h"

  class Patient : public Person {
  public:
    Patient(const String& aName, const Date& aDOB, int aVisits);
    Patient(void);

    int          visits(void) const;

  private:
    int          theVisits;
  };
```

```
    inline Patient::Patient(const String& aName, const Date& aDOB,
                                                        int aVisits)
            : Person(aName, aDOB),
              theVisits(aVisits)
    {}

    inline Patient::Patient(void)           // default name and DOB
    : Person(String(""), Date()),
            theVisits(0)
    {}

    inline int            Patient::visits(void) const
            { return theVisits; }

#endif    // PATIENT

// ---------- END: patient.h ----------

// ---------- FILE: doctor.h ----------

#ifndef DOCTOR
    #define DOCTOR

    #include "person.h"
    #include "patient.h"

    const int PATIENTS = 100;               // maximum allowable

    class Doctor : public Person {
    public:
      Doctor(const String& aName, const Date& aDOB);
      void registerPatient(const Patient& aPatient);

      double       mean(void) const;           // statistics
      void printUpper(double limit) const;     // results

    private:
      Patient      thePatientsList[PATIENTS];
      int          thePatientsRegistered;
    };

    inline Doctor::Doctor(const String& aName, const Date& aDOB)
              : Person(aName, aDOB),
            thePatientsRegistered(0)
    {}

    inline void    Doctor::registerPatient(const Patient& aPatient)
            { thePatientsList[thePatientsRegistered++] = aPatient; }

#endif    // DOCTOR

// ---------- END: doctor.h ----------
```

11.7 Assessment

In the first case study the classes `Natural` and `Rational` were immediately derived from the abstract base class `Number`. Typically, abstract classes cover a spectrum between fully abstract classes like `Number` and an *implementation class* like `Rational`. Intermediate abstract classes describe partially implemented abstract data types.

For example, the class hierarchy diagram in Figure 11.14 illustrates a container class library (see next chapter). The most abstract class `Collection` describes the most general services of a collection class. For example, we would expect operations to add and remove items from a collection, and ask the questions 'is the collection empty?'; 'is some item in the collection?'.

An `Indexed` collection is a more specialized version of the general collection. An indexable collection is one in which we can ask for the first item in the collection, the last in the collection, or the Nth in the collection. Removal of an item from an `Indexed` collection will be done by specifying with an index which particular item is to be deleted. When we remove a member, all subsequent items are repositioned so that there are no holes in the collection. Adding an item is also performed relative to some index position. We might, for example, add after the first position, putting the new item in the second position.

A `Sorted` collection is yet a more specialized version of an `Indexed` collection. Once again, we are able to request the first item, the last item and the Nth item from a sorted collection. These services are the same as those from an `Indexed` collection and are simply inherited. The difference is that when we ask for the first item we actually get the smallest (assuming the items are in increasing sort order). Removal of an item from an indexed position in the `Sorted` collection is inherited from the `Indexed` collection. Removing still retains the sort order of the items. Adding an item to a `Sorted` collection must not be done at some arbitrary index position. This would destroy the sort order of the items. The `add` operation is a redefinition of the `Indexed` operation.

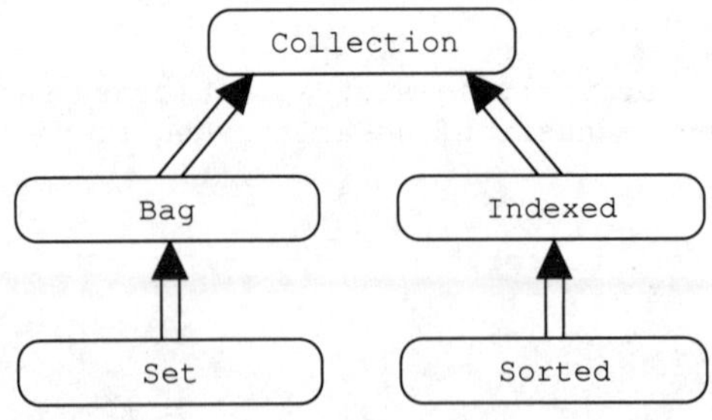

Figure 11.14

We have considered that a class describes one implementation of an abstract data type. The material of this chapter presents a more expanded view. A class describes an implementation, or in the case of abstract classes a group of related implementations, of an abstract data type.

11.8 Summary

1. Object oriented programming (OOP) is a technique which supports an explicit expression of commonality between related abstract data types. This commonality is presented as a hierarchy of class types.

2. Inheritance is a mechanism which simplifies the definition of a new class which is similar to an existing class. Rather than create a completely new class, the programmer inherits the properties of an existing class, specializing and extending the features of the old class.

3. Inheritance gives rise to the notion of polymorphism. Polymorphism is defined as having several forms, and in C++ means that some object refers to instances of various classes at run-time. In OOP the actual type is resolved by run-time execution of compiler generated code referred to as dynamic binding.

4. The scope rules of C++ are extended so that the scope of a derived class nests within the scope of its base class.

5. A class designed as one from which others will be derived is called an abstract base class. Abstract base classes are distinguished by having pure virtual function members. An abstract base class is used to describe a group of related implementations of an abstract data type.

11.9 Exercises

1. From Program 11.1 provide redefinitions for `Rectangle::area` and `Square::area`.

2. Re-implement the queue by stack by using the stack top as the queue front (see Figure 11.6).

3. From Section 11.3 provide an efficient implementation for the class `Queue` using an array representation whose size is compile time specified.

4. Optimize Program 11.2 so that not all the items in the stack and queue are compared.

5. Prepare the program unit for the class `Triangle` representing a three-sided figure:

```
class Triangle {
public:
  Triangle(Point pp1, Point pp2, Point pp3);
  virtual void    scale(double factor);
  virtual void    translate(double horiz, double vert);
  virtual double  perimeter(void) const;
  virtual double  area(void) const;
protected:
  Point   p1, p2, p3;
};
```

If the lengths of the sides of a triangle are `a`, `b` and `c`, then the perimeter, `p`, is:

```
p = a + b + c
```

and the semi-perimeter, `s`, is:

```
s = (a + b + c)/2
```

The area of a triangle is then given by:

```
sqrt(s(s-a)(s-b)(s-c))
```

Test this class in a program.

6. Derive the class `RightTriangle` and the class `IsoscelesTriangle` as specialized versions of class `Triangle`. The resulting class hierarchy is shown in Figure 11.15. In particular, class `RightTriangle` redefines service function `area` and additionally supports the member function `hypotenuse` which determines the length of the longest side:

```
class RightTriangle : public Triangle {
public:
  RightTriangle(Point pp1, Point pp2, Point pp3);
  double  area(void) const;
  double  hypotenuse(void) const;
};
```

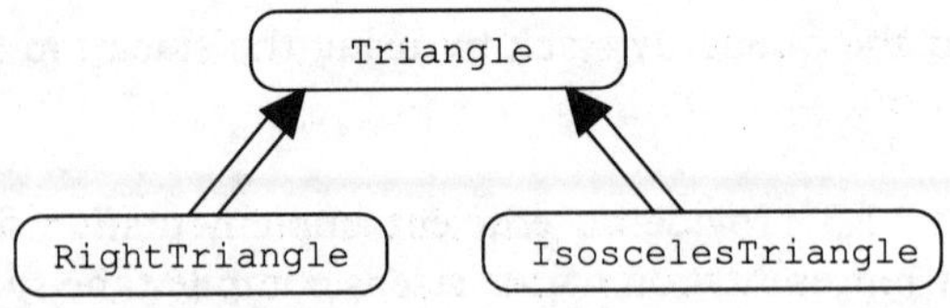

Figure 11.15

Class `IsoscelesTriangle` supports the member function `height` which finds the height of the triangle from the vertex between the two sides of equal length:

```
class IsoscelesTriangle : public Triangle {
public:
  IsoscelesTriangle(Point pp1, Point pp2, Point pp3);
  double  height(void) const;
};
```

If the length of the two equal sides is `a` and the length of the third side is `b`, then the height of the triangle is:

```
sqrt(a*a - b*b/4)
```

All constructors are to check the integrity of their arguments.

7. From Section 11.6 further develop the abstract base class `Figure` (see Figure 11.11). The class `Quadrilateral` of Section 11.1 and class `Triangle` of Exercise 2 are to be the immediate subclasses of class `Figure`.

```
class Figure {              // abstract class
  friend int operator< (const Figure& fig1, const Figure& fig2)
     { return fig1.area() < fig2.area(); }
  friend int operator> (const Figure& fig1, const Figure& fig2)
     { return fig1.area() > fig2.area(); }
  virtual double    perimeter(void) const =0;
  virtual double    area(void) const =0;
  virtual Class*    classDescriptor(void) const =0;
  Bool                isSimilar(const Figure& fig) const
     { return this->similar(fig); }          // bool
private:
  virtual Bool      similar(const Figure&) const =0;
};
```

Two figures are `similar` if they have the same number of sides, and the corresponding sides are proportional to each other.

Redesign non-member function `dimensions` with the polymorphic first argument of type `Figure&`.

8. Predict the output from the following program:

```
#include <iostream.h>

class Ten {
public:
  int     identify(void) const { return 10; }
};

class Twenty : public Ten {
public:
  int     identify(void) const { return 20; }
};

class Thirty : public Ten {
```

```
public:
  int    identify(void) const { return 30; }
};

int main()
{
  Ten     ten;
  Twenty  twenty;
  Thirty  thirty;

  cout << ten.identify() << "\n";
  cout << twenty.identify() << "\n";
  cout << thirty.identify() << "\n";
  return (0);
}
```

Identify a likely misinterpretation in the program and make the necessary changes.

9. **Show how inheritance can be used to package and supply a set of figurative (symbolic) constants to other classes.**

10. **If a rectangle is parallel to the X–Y axes, then the coordinates of two diagonally opposite vertices may be given to construct a rectangle. Show the definition for this constructor:**

```
class Rectangle : public Quadrilateral {
public:
     Rectangle(Point, Point);     // lower left, upper right
  // .....
};
```

11. Rework Exercise 10 from Chapter 9 so that class Employee is derived from class Person. The revised class diagram is given in Figure 11.16.

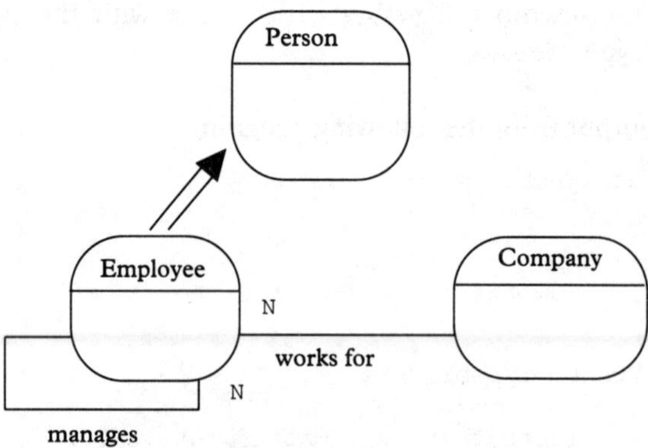

Figure 11.16

12

Storage Management

A *variable-sized* data structure is one in which the number of components may change dynamically during program execution. The major types of variable sized data structures include *lists*, *stacks*, *sorted collections*, *queues* and *trees*.

Variable sized data objects are used when the amount of data in a problem is not known in advance. Use of fixed sized arrays require that large amounts of storage are reserved in advance for the maximum size of data that might be encountered. Variable sized data structures, however, allow storage to be allocated incrementally during program execution.

There are two fundamentally different approaches to implementing these dynamic data structures. In some languages they are provided directly. In others, a pointer data type is provided, with facilities for the dynamic allocation of storage explicitly by the programmer. This is the approach taken in C++. Several language features are then necessary to make this possible:

1. An elementary data type *pointer*. A pointer data object contains the location of another data object, or it may contain the special null pointer, `NULL`. Pointers are ordinary objects that may be simple variables or components of arrays or classes. Pointers were the subject of Chapters 5 and 8.
2. A *creation operation* for data objects of fixed size, such as elementary types or class objects or arrays. The creation operation both allocates a block of storage for the data object and returns a pointer to its location. The creation operator differs in two ways from the ordinary creation of variables caused by declarations:
   - The data objects created have no names, their values are accessed through pointers; and
   - Data objects may be created in this way at any point during program execution, and persist until an explicit deletion operator is applied.
3. A *selection operation* for a pointer value that allows the data object to which it points to be accessed.
4. A *deletion operator* to recover blocks of storage not otherwise deleted automatically when variables leave scope.

12.1 Implementation

Function variables are allocated on a structure referred to as the program's *run time stack*. When a function is called, storage for that function's automatic variables is allocated at the top of the stack. The storage remains on the stack until the function terminates at which point the space is deallocated.

In addition, every program may utilize a region of otherwise unallocated memory. This pool of memory is referred to as the *heap*. The heap is manipulated at run time using the operators `new` and `delete`. Dynamic data structures are created on the heap.

The unary creation operator `new` allocates storage for a fixed sized data object and delivers a pointer to that object. The programmer defines the type of storage required and the heap manager returns a pointer to an item of that type.

The syntax for the `new` operator is:

```
new type-name [number-of-elements]
```

where the `[number-of-elements]` part is optional. If this part is omitted, then storage for a simple object of type `type-name` is allocated. Here are some simple examples:

```
int* ptr = new int;
Date* dp = new Date(31, 12, 1991);
```

The second illustration dynamically allocates space for a `Date` object to which `dp` then points. This dynamic object is properly initialized by calling the `Date` constructor. If the default constructor is defined, then:

```
Date* dp = new Date;
```

also produces a properly initialized dynamic `Date` object.

The following program demonstrates one use of the operator `new`. The program inputs two integer data values and outputs them in reverse order. Instead of declaring two integer variables to represent the data items, pointers are employed. Space for two integers is created dynamically and pointers assigned to the space. The program then operates in terms of the pointers rather than in terms of integer variables. The example is intended to illustrate dynamic storage. It is not recommended as the solution to this problem. The conventional solution is given in Program 5.3.

PROGRAM 12.1

```
// ———————— FILE: p01.cpp ————————

//
//  This program reads two integer values from the
//      standard input, and outputs them in reverse order.
```

```
//       The locations for the two integers are created
//       dynamically using the operator new.
//

#include <iostream.h>

int main()
{
  int* first = new int;          // pointers to the data values
  int* second = new int;

  cout << "Enter the data: ";
  cin >> *first >> *second;
  cout << "Reversed data: " << *second << " " << *first << "\n";

  return (0);
}

// ———————— END: p01.cpp ————————
```

Since memory is frequently a critical resource, available in limited quantities, it is desirable that the storage allocated by a call to operator `new` is returned to the system for later re-use when it is no longer required. The operator `delete` allows the programmer to deallocate a region of memory previously allocated by `new`. The specification for this operation is:

```
delete pointer
```

The argument to `delete` is a pointer to a region of memory previously returned by `new`. Once a region of memory has been freed, it should no longer be referenced by the program. The storage manager recycles the memory for use with subsequent calls to `new`.

Program 12.2 repeats the previous example, but additionally explicitly frees the region of memory dynamically established by `new`. Once again, the example is merely for illustrative purposes. Practical uses of `delete` will be shown later.

PROGRAM 12.2

```
// ———————— FILE: p02.cpp ————————

//
//  This program reads two integer values from the
//       standard input, and outputs them in reverse order.
//       The locations for the two integers are created
//       dynamically using the operator new.
//

#include <iostream.h>

int main()
{
  int* first = new int;      // pointers to the data values
  int* second = new int;
```

```
    cout << "Enter the data: ";
    cin >> *first >> *second;
    cout << "Reversed data: " << *second << " " << *first;

    delete first;              // free memory
    delete second;

    return (0);
}

// ———————— END: p02.cpp ————————
```

If the optional `[number-of-elements]` is present in an application of `new`, then a dynamic array object is allocated. Like statically allocated arrays, if the array elements are class types then the default constructor must be defined, and is used to initialize each array element. For example:

```
const int DATESIZE = 12;
Date* datep = new Date[DATESIZE];

for(int k = 0; k < DATESIZE; k++)
  datep[k] = Date(1, 1, 1990);
```

Note how in the `for` statement the variable `datep` is treated as an array which we can index. Alternatively, we might have initialized this array using a pointer:

```
for(Date* dp = datep; dp < &datep[DATESIZE]; dp++)
  *dp = Date(1, 1, 1990);
```

When deallocating an array of class objects we have to specify that it is an array:

```
delete [ ] datep;
```

The array notation is required to invoke the correct number of destructor calls. Without this additional notation only the first object in the array will be destroyed properly as described earlier.

A destructor is not invoked automatically for a pointer to a class object when it exits scope. Rather, the `delete` operator must be given explicitly, causing the destructor for the class object to be applied. In the example:

```
int main()
{
  Date  hogmanay(31, 12, 1990);
  Date* hp = &hogmanay;
  Date* dp = new Date(1, 1, 1991);
  // .....
  delete dp;

  return (0);
}
```

we would not want the destructor applied to `hp` since it is simply the address of a `Date` object which is otherwise properly initialized and deinitialized on the stack. However, we require the destructor to be applied to the object to which `dp` points, and this we get only by an explicit application of the `delete` operator.

Illustrating these ideas, data to a program consists of a single integer followed by a series of floating point values, the number of which is given by the leading integer. The floating point values are read and printed in reverse order by the program. The values are stored in an array during input. The array is dynamically created; the size is determined by the initial data item.

PROGRAM 12.3

```
// ———————— FILE: p03.cpp ————————

//
// Read a series of floats from the standard input and
//      write them to the standard output in reverse order.
//      The values are preceded by an integer count of the
//      number of data items. This value is used to
//      dynamically create an array to store the data.
//

#include <iostream.h>

int main()
{
  int   n;

  cout << "Enter the number of data items: ";
  cin >> n;

  float *const base = new float[n];    // allocate the array space

  float* ptr = base;                   // read the data values
  cout << "Enter the data values: ";
  for(int k = 0; k < n; k++)
    cin >> *ptr++;

  cout << "Reversed values:\n";        // print results
  for (ptr = base + n, k = 0; k < n; k++)
    cout << *(–ptr) << "\n";

  delete [] base;              // free memory

  return (0);
}

// ———————— END: p03.cpp ————————
```

Note the use of `*const` for the identifier `base`. This is done to ensure that, once initialized, we do not break the reference to the allocated array space.

If it is impossible for some reason to perform the required allocation, `new` returns the null pointer `NULL`, as defined in the standard header `<stdio.h>`. The programmer is then responsible for checking this situation and taking the appropriate action:

```
Date* datep = new Date[DATESIZE];
if(datep == NULL){
    // error handling action
    // .....
}
```

Alternatively, we can employ the `set_new_handler` function to specify the programmer-defined actions if `new` fails due to insufficient heap storage. The actions are described by a function whose name is given to the library function `set_new_handler`. This programmer-defined error handler must have no arguments and no return value. For example:

```
#include <new.h>                // set_new_handler()

void      noheapspace(void);  // prototype
set_new_handler(noheapspace);
```

The simplest function to give `set_new_handler` reports the error then terminates via the library function `exit`. Program 12.4 repeats the last program. This time, an error handler is incorporated. When we run the program and request a very large array size the program terminates giving the appropriate message.

PROGRAM 12.4

```
// ———————— FILE: p04.cpp ————————

#include <iostream.h>
#include <new.h>                // set_new_handler
#include <stdlib.h>             // exit()

void      noheapspace(void);

int main()
{
  long    n;                    // allow big sizes

  set_new_handler(noheapspace);       // set up error handler

  cin >> n;
  float *const base = new float[n];    // fail if n is large

  for(float* ptr = base; ptr < &base[n]; ptr++)
    cin >> *ptr;

  for(ptr = &base[n-1]; ptr >= base; ptr--)
    cout << *ptr << "\n";

  delete [] base;
  return (0);
}

void      noheapspace(void)
```

```
{
  cout << "No heap space\n";
  exit(1);
}
// ———— END: p04.cpp ————
```

CASE STUDY 12.1
Dynamic vectors

An array in C++ is of fixed constant length, has bounds starting at zero, and is not subject to any array bound checking at run time. Using the techniques presented in this chapter we can construct arrays or *vectors* of our own design which remove these constraints and weaknesses.

The idea is to have a structure allocated dynamically using the free storage allocator `new`. This space is encapsulated into a fixed sized structure that controls access to the actual storage. The C++ class mechanism is used to provide this encapsulation:

```
// ———— FILE: intvec.h ————
//
// A vector of integers which behaves like an
//       in-built C++ array. In addition, the vector
//       size is specified at run time and supports
//       run time checking of subscripts.
//

#ifndef INTVEC
  #define INTVEC

  class IntVec {
  public:
    IntVec(int aSize);
    // .....
  protected:
    int*        theVector;
    int         theSize;
  };

  // .....

#endif   // INTVEC

// ———— END: intvec.h ————
```

Here, we shall initially consider a one-dimensional vector of integers. In the next case study we will consider how to generalize the vector so that it is capable of storing values of differing types.

In this example the vector is realized by two data members: `theSize` which holds the number of elements represented by the array, and `theVector` which addresses the memory in which the elements are contained. This space is allocated dynamically using the operator `new`. This space is requested by the constructor:

```
IntVec::IntVec(int aSize)
{
  if(aSize <= 0){
    cout << "Bad Vector size\n";
    exit(1);
  }

  theVector = new int[theSize = aSize];
}
```

One can now declare `IntVec` objects as elegantly as the in-built array types:

```
IntVec    v1(100);                  // implicit form
IntVec    v2 = IntVec(200);         // explicit form
IntVec    v3(2 * nelements + 4);    // variable size
```

The subscript operator accepts an index value and delivers the appropriate element. This provides statements of the form:

```
int first = v1[0];
```

in which the subscripted variable appears in an expression on the right side of the assignment. Such a usage delivers the value of that particular element. In order for `v1[.....]` to appear as the target of an assignment:

```
v1[99] = last;
```

the overloaded subscript operator returns a reference type (an alias for the required object). Hence:

```
inline int&      IntVec::operator[] (int index)
  { return theVector[index]; }
```

When a vector goes out of scope all its space must be reclaimed for re-use. The `IntVec` destructor deletes the space allocated by the constructor:

```
inline IntVec::~IntVec(void)
  { delete [] theVector; }
```

A second constructor handles initialization of one `IntVec` object with another. It is called for definitions of the form:

```
IntVec v4 = v1;
```

The implementation is similar to the first constructor, except that the elements are copied from the source `IntVec` argument:

```
IntVec::IntVec(const IntVec& iv)
{
  theVector = new int[theSize = iv.theSize];
  for(int k = 0; k < theSize; k++)
```

```
        theVector[k] = iv.theVector[k];
    }
```

Without this explicit programmer-defined intialization constructor, memberwise initialization would copy each data member from one class object to another. For example, given the program outline:

```
IntVec    v1(5);

int main()
{
    IntVec v2 = v1;              // initialization constructor
    // .....
}
```

then the definition for `v2` is initialized in the following way:

```
v2.theSize = v1.theSize;
v2.theVector = v1.theVector;
```

Default memberwise initialization is inappropriate for this example. Figure 12.1 illustrates the resulting storage allocation for `v1` and `v2`. The principal problem is that the `theVector` members of both `v1` and `v2` address the same memory since only one `IntVec` is constructed. Further, upon completion of function `main` two destructors will have been called, once to deallocate the dynamic storage space associated with `v2` and once with `v1`. Since both refer to the same dynamic space, the program is in error when the destructor tries to remove the same space twice. In general, default memberwise initialization is inappropriate for classes that contain pointer members.

As has been shown, initialization of one class object with another requires more control than is provided by the simple default memberwise initialization. This additional control for `IntVec` is provided by an explicit instance of the

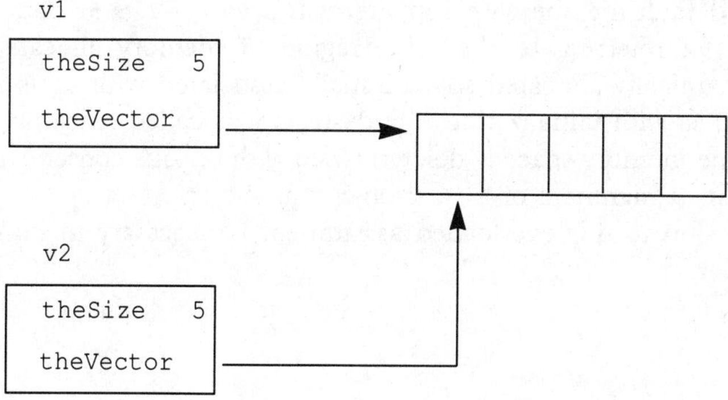

Figure 12.1

`IntVec(const IntVec&)` constructor. When explicitly defined within a class, it is invoked for every initialization of one class object with another. The code for this constructor ensures that each `theVector` member will address a distinct area of memory.

The assignment of one `IntVec` object to another is handled by the overloaded assignment operator:

```
IntVec&   IntVec::operator= (const IntVec& iv)
{

  delete [] theVector;

  theVector = new int[theSize = iv.theSize];
  for(int k = 0; k < theSize; k++)
    theVector[k] = iv.theVector[k];

  return *this;
}
```

Note how this assignment sizes the target array to be the same size as the source array and removes the original space occupied by the `IntVec` on the left side of the assignment.

The solution defines proper assignment of `IntVec` objects. Without an explicit version for this overloaded operator, default memberwise copying is performed. This can cause trouble similar to default memberwise initialization. Consider:

```
int main()
{
  IntVec  v1(10);
  IntVec  v2(20);

  v1 = v2;                    // assignment
  // .....
}
```

The constructor is called twice and allocates two integer arrays. The assignment `v1 = v2`, using default memberwise copying, will have `theVector` data members of both `v1` and `v2` referring to the same region of memory allocated for `v2`. Further, the dynamically allocated space initially associated with `v1` is no longer accessible. Then, as with initialization, the destructor is called twice on exit from `main` and the same memory space is deleted twice with serious consequences. The solution is to define assignment of `IntVec` objects as shown.

One small revision to this overloaded assignment is necessary to make it safe, however. Consider:

```
int main()
{
  IntVec  v1(30);

  v1 = v1;                    // assignment
  // .....
}
```

The new assignment operator fails to properly handle assignment of one class object with itself. Following the execution of the user-defined assignment operator:

```
delete [] theVector;
```

removes the dynamic space associated with the target `v1`. The data member `theVector` no longer refers to a region of memory associated with the program. Then:

```
theVector = new int[theSize = iv.theSize];
```

allocates new space for the target with the same size as the source. Then the `for` loop:

```
for(int k = 0; k < theSize; k++)
  theVector[k] = iv.theVector[k];
```

copies the array members from the source to the target. The problem here is that both the source and target are the same object and because of the `delete` operation neither now refers to the original data values.

We correct this problem by checking if both the source and target object have the same address, i.e. are the same class object:

```
if(this == &iv) return *this;
```

Here, however, the compiler would elicit an error message. The problem is the compiler identifies that permitting the programmer to take the address of `iv` one may then use the pointer to change something that is supposed to be constant. In this case a cast is necessary to alert the compiler:

```
IntVec&   IntVec::operator= (const IntVec& iv)
{
  if(this == &((IntVec&)iv)) return *this;

  // ..... as before
}
```

The function `reSize` expands an `IntVec` object. The increment is given as a positive integer argument. First, a new larger array is created; then the values of the original array are copied into the new space; and finally, the original space is removed:

```
void      IntVec::reSize(int incr)
{
  if(incr <= 0){
    cout << "Negative increment\n";
    exit(1);
  }

  int newtheSize = theSize + incr;
  int* newtheVector = new int[newtheSize];

  for(int k = 0; k < theSize; k++)
    newtheVector[k] = theVector[k];
```

```
    delete [] theVector;
    theVector = newtheVector;
    theSize = newtheSize;
  }
```

We now illustrate an application for the `IntVec` class by solving the following problem. A program reads a series of integer values and determines if they are palindromic. The sequence is palindromic if it reads the same both forward and backward. The number of integer values to process is given as user input in response to the initial prompt. The values are stored in the `IntVec` object `sequence`. After reading the values, the `sequence` is scanned simultaneously from both ends.

```
// ———————— FILE: case01.cpp ————————

//
//  Determine if a series of integers is palindromic
//        using the class IntVec to record the data values.
//

#include <iostream.h>
#include "intvec.h"

enum Bool { FALSE, TRUE };

int main()
{
  int      size;

  cout << "Enter number of data values: ";
  cin >> size;

  IntVec sequence(size);

  cout << "Enter the data values:\n";
  for(int k = 0; k < size; k++)
    cin >> sequence[k];

  Bool ispalindromic = TRUE;
  int j = size-1;

  for(k = 0; k < (size+1)/2; k++)
    if(sequence[k] != sequence[j--]){
      ispalindromic = FALSE;
      break;
    }

  if(ispalindromic)
    cout << "Sequence is palindromic\n";
  else
    cout << "Sequence is NOT palindromic\n";

  return (0);
}

// ———————— END: case01.cpp ————————
```

```
//  ────────── FILE: intvec.h ──────────

//
//  A vector of integers which behaves like an
//       in-built C++ array. In addition, the vector
//       size is specified at run time and supports
//       run time checking of subscripts.
//

#ifndef INTVEC
  #define INTVEC
  class IntVec {
  public:
    IntVec(int aSize);
    IntVec(const IntVec& iv);
    ~IntVec(void);
    IntVec&       operator= (const IntVec& iv);

    virtual int&  operator[] (int index);
    virtual void  reSize(int incr);
  protected:
    int*          theVector;
    int           theSize;
  };

  inline IntVec::~IntVec(void)
                { delete [] theVector; }

  inline int&     IntVec::operator[] (int index)
  { return theVector[index]; }

#endif   // INTVEC

//  ────────── END: intvec.h ──────────
```

Notice how the class body uses protected access privilege for the data members and declares some member functions as virtual. By exploiting inheritance we can define a new version of class `IntVec` for which the user can specify the index bounds:

```
//       File:  intvector.h

#ifndef INTVECTOR
  #define INTVECTOR

  #include "intvec.h"

  class IntVector : public IntVec {
  public:
     IntVector(int lowb, int upb);
     IntVector(const IntVector& iv);
     ~IntVector(void) { delete [] vector; }
    IntVector&   operator= (const IntVector& iv);

    int&         operator[] (int index);
    int          lowerbound(void) const
```

```
          { return lowerb; }
    int          upperbound(void) const
          { return upperb; }

  private:
    int          lowerb;
    int          upperb;
  };

#endif    // INTVECTOR
```

In an application program we may declare arrays in which the subscript range is specified in the constructor call, appropriate to the application:

```
IntVector year(1990, 1999);

for(int k = 1990; k < 2000; k++)
     cin >> year[k];
```

Class `IntVector` modifies class `IntVec` by providing a constructor that requires the user to specify the two index bounds, rather than the size for which the lower bound was implicitly zero. Further, the access function performs any necessary checks to ensure there are no subscript violations.

The constructor can be written like this:

```
IntVector::IntVector(int lowb, int upb)
   : IntVec(upb-lowb+1)
{
   lowerb = lowb;
   upperb = upb;
}
```

If the bounds are meaningless:

```
IntVector      v(10, 5);
```

then the initialization of the base class constructor is invoked with a negative argument, reports an error and terminates the program.

The access function `operator[]` for `IntVector` is readily programmed in terms of the `operator[]` for `IntVec`:

```
int&      IntVector::operator[] (int index)
{
   if(index < lowerb || index > upperb){
     cout << "Subscript violation [" << index << "]\n";
     exit(1);
   }

   return IntVec::operator[] (index-lowerb);
}
```

The scope resolution operator `::` is used to avoid an infinite recursion by calling `IntVector::operator[]` from itself. If efficiency is a consideration, then we may express the return statement by:

```
return vector[index - lowerb];
```

since the derived class `IntVector` has direct access to the protected members of the base class `IntVec`.

12.2 Containers

A *container* is a group of related objects. Containers are central to computer programming. Many programming activities involve recording objects in containers; looking up the details of an object in a container; and removing an object from a container. In this section we shall investigate the construction of a *container class library* consisting of several different data structures which serve as containers. These containers make it possible to build the complex data structures which are necessary for solving many programming problems.

Examples of container classes include implementations for *ordered collections* (e.g., a list of suppliers ordered chronologically), *sorted collections* (e.g., an alphabetical list of student names) and *sets* (e.g., an equipment inventory). The container classes are useful because they provide similar protocols for:

- Adding and removing elements.
- Searching a collection for a particular object.
- Accessing and changing elements.
- Iterating over the elements of a collection.

Figure 12.2 shows the container class hierarchy. The scheme is modelled on the class hierarchy used in the Smalltalk programming language [Gol83; see also Gor90].

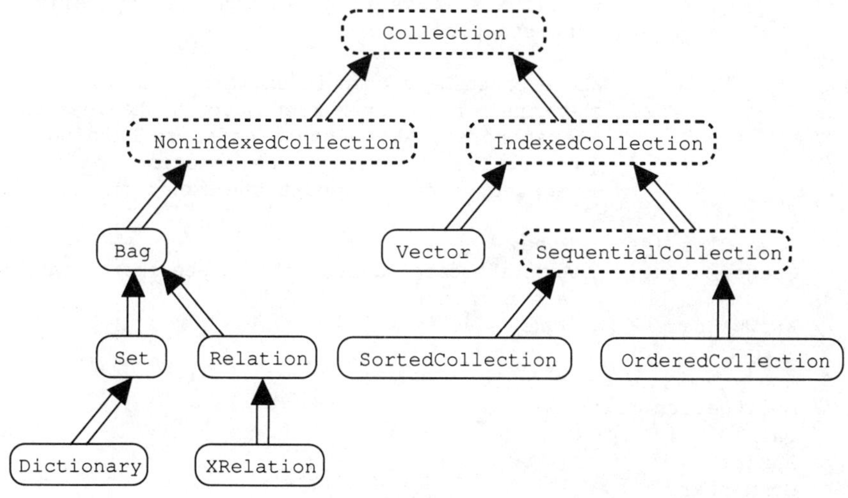

Figure 12.2

The container classes are generic, making them useful for a range of applications. The genericity is achieved using the template class mechanism introduced in Chapter 9. Further, inheritance is used in the class library to impose common behaviour and to permit code re-use.

Each specialized container class, for example `Bag`, uses an array (but see later) to record the elements in its collection. In effect, an array of `TYPE` items is maintained by every container, where `TYPE` is the name for the generic member types. Since `int` and `Date` are type names then we may have `Bag<int>`, `Bag<Date>` or `OrderedCollection<Date>`. Further, since `Bag<Date>` is a type, then `Bag< Bag<Date> >` can be readily constructed (a `Bag` whose members are `Bag<Date>` items). These capabilities enable us to build structures which accurately model real world entities.

Class `Collection` is an abstract class that serves as the base class for all container classes. This class declares virtual member functions that apply to all containers and includes operations to determine the current capacity of the container or to request that the container increase its size, etc. These operations will all have to be defined in the derived concrete classes.

```
// ====================================================================
// File Name     : COL.H
// File Type     : C++ header file for class COLLECTION
// Author        : Ken Barclay
// Date Created  : 2 Apr 1993
//
// ------------------------------------
// Description   : A Collection is an abstract class at the root
//                 of the container class library. All working
//                 containers are ultimately derived from this class.
//                 Associated with this class is an iterator which
//                 will iterate over the elements of any derived
//                 concrete class.
//
//                 Where containers compare existing and new members
//                 then the member types must support the less than
//                 operator (<). Where containers use hashing to
//                  provide fast access to the members then the
//                  member type must support the function hash.
//
// Base Class(es) : None
// Usage          : Abstract base class; no concrete instantiations
//                   are permitted
// Known Bugs     : None
//
// ------------------------------------
// Modification History
// Date           :
// Author         :
// Commentary     :
//
```

```
// ——————————————————————————————————————
// Version         : 2.0
//
================================================================

#ifndef COLLECTION
  #define COLLECTION

  #include "..\ticlass\classlib.h"

  template <class TYPE>
  ABSTRACT class Collection {
  public:
    virtual UInt     capacity(void) const =0;
                     // current storage capacity of the container

    virtual void         reSize(UInt increment) =0;
                     // increase the size of the container

    // .....

  };

  #include "..\ticlass\col.t"         // function bodies

#endif  // COLLECTION

// ================= End of header file COL.H ====================
```

Recollect that the template member functions of these classes must be accessible to the compiler so that it may instantiate them to the specific form. Rather than have them populate and clutter the associated header file we achieve the same by moving them into a file with suffix `'t'` (for template) and include it from the header file.

The header file `classlib.h` is used to collect common definitions used throughout the class library. For example, the macro `ABSTRACT` has been defined as null so that class definitions may be so prefixed and commented (see `Collection` above). The type `Bool` introduces the enumerated values `TRUE` and `FALSE`. The type names `UInt` and `ULong` are aliases for their obvious counterparts. The named constant `DEFAULTSIZE` is used throughout many containers to specify their initial default size.

```
//
================================================================
// File Name         : CLASSLIB.H
// File Type         : C++ header file for common definitions
// Author            : K. Barclay
// Date Created      : 24 Jan 1993
//
// ——————————————————————————————————————-
// Description       : A collection of enumerated types, typedefs
//                     for the primitive language types, used
//                     throughout the template class library.
//
```

```
// Base Class(es)   : None
// Usage            :
// Known Bugs       : None
//
// ------------------------------------
// Modification History
// Date             :
// Author           :
// Commentary       :
//
// ------------------------------------
// Version          : 1.21
//
==================================================================

#ifndef CLASSLIB
  #define CLASSLIB

  #include "..\ticlass\checks.h"

  #define ABSTRACT
    // Sets up the keyword ABSTRACT for use in the hierarchy as a
    // descriptive term to alert the user to the abstract classes
    // as against the concrete ones. It is defined with no value
    // for this purpose.

  #define EQ(A, B)       (((A) < (B) || (B) < (A)) ? FALSE : TRUE)
    // This defines the relation equals (==) under the pseudonym EQ
    // and this is used later in the hierarchy to allow the
    // comparison of containers (or their objects) either with
    // other containers or with a numerical value.

  #define NE(A, B)       (((A) < (B) || (B) < (A)) ? TRUE : FALSE)
    // This defines the relation not equal to (!=) under the
    // pseudonym NE & this is used later in the hierarchy to
    // allow the comparison of containers (or their objects)
    // either with other containers,or with a numerical value.

  enum Bool { FALSE, TRUE };
    // Setting up the Boolean type for use in the class library.

  enum { UNMANAGED, MANAGED};
    // setting up the storage management for the containers

  enum ClassType {
    // setting up the various class types for the hierarchy

    BAGTYPE,
    DICTIONARYTYPE,
    LISTTYPE,
    ORDEREDCOLLECTIONTYPE,
    ORDEREDLISTTYPE,
    RELATIONTYPE,
    SETTYPE,
    SORTEDCOLLECTIONTYPE,
    SORTEDLISTTYPE,
```

```
    VECTORTYPE,
    XRELATIONTYPE
  };

  typedef unsigned int        UInt;
    // Defining a shorthand for the type unsigned int for use in
    // the container class hierarchy

  typedef unsigned long       ULong;
    // Defining a shorthand for the type unsigned long for use in
    // the container class hierarchy

  const UInt     DEFAULTSIZE    = 32;
  const UInt     DEFAULTLEVEL    = 32;
    // sets the default size for the UInt type in the container
    // classes, this is used in places to set the size of the
    // containers

#endif   // CLASSLIB

// ================ End of header file CLASSLIB.H ================
```

As shown in Figure 12.2 the container class divides into two distinct groups – those which are indexable such as a `Vector`, and those which are not (such as a `Set`). An `IndexedCollection` represents collections with elements ordered externally by integer indices. Class `IndexedCollection` is an abstract class providing the common protocol for all the indexable collection subclasses. Indexable collections can be accessed using integer subscripts (through function `at` and `operator[]`):

```
// ============================================================
// File Name     : XCOL.H
// File Type     : C++ header file for class INDEXEDCOLLECTION
// Author        : Ken Barclay
// Date Created  : 1 Apr 1993
//
// ------------------------------------
// Description   : Class IndexedCollection is an abstract class
//                 providing the common protocol for all indexable
//                 be collection subclasses. Indexable collections
//                 can be accessed using integer indices.
// Base class(es): Collection (COL: abstract)
//                 |
//                   IndexedCollection (XCOL: abstract)
//
// Usage         : This is an abstract class; there can be no
//                 concrete instances of this class.
// Known Bugs    : None
//
// ------------------------------------
// Modification History
// Date          :
// Author        :
```

```
// Commentary    :
//
// ------------------------------------------
// Version       : 1.00
//
================================================================

#ifndef INDEXEDCOLLECTION
  #define INDEXEDCOLLECTION

  #include "..\ticlass\col.h"

  template <class TYPE>
  ABSTRACT class IndexedCollection : public Collection<TYPE> {
  public:

    virtual const TYPE&       operator[] (UInt index) const =0;
        // indexing operator

    virtual const TYPE&       at(UInt index) const =0;
        // indexing operator

    // .....
  };

#endif   // INDEXEDCOLLECTION

// ================ End of header file XCOL.H ===================
```

In this class hierarchy we classify a `Vector` and a `SequentialCollection` as particular forms of `IndexedCollection`. In a `Vector` we may position items at any arbitrary index value. In a `SequentialCollection` all the items are in adjacent storage locations, with the first at index position zero.

Class `SequentialCollection` is given below:

```
// ==============================================================
// File Name     : SEQCOL.H
// File Type     : C++ header file for class SEQUENTIALCOLLECTION
// Author        : Ken Barclay
// Date Created  : 1 Apr 1993
//
// ------------------------------------------
// Description   : SequentialCollection is a specialized
//                 IndexedCollection in which all the elements are
//                 held sequentially from the base index position
//                 (zero), without any absent members. All additions
//                 and deletions are achieved through various
//                 add.....and remove..... operations. No direct
//                 (indexed) access update operation is available
//                 to destroy the integrity of the container.
// Base class(es): Collection (COL: abstract)
//                      |
//                   IndexedCollection (XCOL: abstract)
//                             |
//                          SequentialCollection (SEQCOL: abstract)
```

```
//
// Usage          : This is an abstract class; there can be no
//                  concrete instances of this class.
// Known Bugs     : None
//
// ________________________________________
// Modification History
// Date           :
// Author         :
// Commentary     :
//
// ________________________________________
// Version        : 1.01
//
==================================================================

#ifndef SEQUENTIALCOLLECTION
  #define SEQUENTIALCOLLECTION

  #include "..\ticlass\xcol.h"
  #include "..\ticlass\vvector.h"

  template <class TYPE>
  ABSTRACT class SequentialCollection : public
    IndexedCollection<TYPE> {
  public:
    // .....

    virtual void              add(const TYPE& object) =0;
    // include given item into the container; the exact semantics
    // for this operation is dependent upon the descendent
    // concrete class

    Bool                      isMember(const TYPE& object) const;
    // is given object present in the container?

    void                      removeFirst(void);
    // remove the first item from the container; if the
    // collection is empty no action is performed

    // .....

  protected:
    VVector     theCollection;        // representation
    UInt        theCardinality;       // current position
    // .....
  };

  #include "..\ticlass\seqcol.t"          // function bodies

#endif  // SEQUENTIALCOLLECTION

// ================ End of header file SEQCOL.H =================
```

The class `SequentialCollection` **is represented by a variable length array type called** `VVector` **(see later) which can grow automatically to accommodate more**

elements if the original size is not large enough; and a counter which maintains a record of the number of items in the collection. Placing, removing and accessing items in the `SequentialCollection` is simply achieved by manipulating the items in the `VVector` and updating the counter. Since addition and removal of elements other than at the end cause the other members to be moved, applications using large `SequentialCollections` (as a base class for some concrete class such as `SortedCollection`) might result in the unnecessary overhead of member shuffling. In this case a more appropriate container class should be developed and used (see next chapter).

As an example of the coding, consider the operation `removeFirst`. The implementation is relatively straightforward. All members, except the first, are moved into the next lower index position within the `VVector`.

```
template <class TYPE>
void            SequentialCollection<TYPE>::removeFirst(void)
{
  if(theCardinality == 0)
    return;

  // .....

  for(register int k = 1; k < theCardinality; k++)
    theCollection[k-1] = theCollection[k];
  theCardinality--;
}
```

The code for the member function `isMember` is equally obvious:

```
template <class TYPE>
Bool      SequentialCollection<TYPE>::isMember(const TYPE& object)
                                                              const
{
  for(int k = 0; k < theCardinality; k++)
    if(EQ(*((TYPE*)theCollection[k]), object))
      return TRUE;

  return FALSE;
}
```

The function argument `object` is compared against all the items currently held by the container. If any item matches the argument value the search is stopped and the value `TRUE` is returned; otherwise `FALSE` is returned.

Note the if statement in the search loop:

```
if(EQ(*((TYPE*)theCollection[k]), object)) .....
```

where the argument value and the current container item at index position `k` are compared for equality. If in some concrete class such as `SortedCollection` derived from this `SequentialCollection` class:

```
SortedCollection<int>  numbers;
```

then the inherited function `isMember` will perform an equality test on two `int`s in the above statement. Hence the instantiated type (such as `int` here) we expect to provide support for the equality test. In the instantiated definition:

```
SortedCollection<Date>        holidays;
```

then the user defined class `Date` would need to overload `operator==`. As we shall see later the instantiated types must also support the comparison `operator<`. Since equality can be defined in terms of `operator<` we require that only the latter be defined while the equality is given by the `EQ` macro (see `classlib.h` above).

`OrderedCollections` are ordered by the sequence in which the objects are added to and removed from them. `OrderedCollections` are dynamic container objects that can be expanded at both ends and in the middle. Operations are provided to `add` (`addAt`, `addFirst`, `addLast`), `remove` (`removeAt`, `removeFirst`, `removeLast`) and access (`first`, `last`) members. The `add` operation inherited from class `SequentialCollection` is given the semantics of `addLast`. Member function `remove`, also inherited from class `SequentialCollection`, removes the first object in the `OrderedCollection` which is equal to the given function argument.

```
// ===============================================================
// File Name     : ORDCOL.H
// File Type     : C++ header file for class ORDEREDCOLLECTION
// Author : Ken Barclay
// Date Created : 1 Apr 1993
//
// ------------------------------------
// Description   : An OrderedCollection behaves as a
//                 SequentialCollection with additional add
//                 operators. In all cases these add operations
//                 increase the size of the container if presently
//                 full. The container size is automatically
//                 doubled.
//
// Base class(es): Collection (COL: abstract)
//                      |
//                   IndexedCollection (XCOL: abstract)
//                             |
//                         SequentialCollection (SEQCOL: abstract)
//                                    |
//                      OrderedCollection (ORDCOL: concrete)
// Usage         :
//       OrderedCollection<String>   names;
//       .....
//       names.add(*new String("Ken"));
//       names.addLast(*new String("Irene"));
//       names.addFirst(*new String("Ria"));
//       .....
//       const String& name = names.first();
//
// Known Bugs    : None
//
```

```
// ─────────────────────────────────────────────-
// Modification History
// Date          :
// Author        :
// Commentary    :
//
// ─────────────────────────────────────────────
// Version       : 1.00
// ==================================================================

#ifndef ORDEREDCOLLECTION
  #define ORDEREDCOLLECTION

  #include "..\ticlass\seqcol.h"

  template <class TYPE>
  class OrderedCollection : public SequentialCollection<TYPE> {
  public:
    OrderedCollection(UInt = DEFAULTSIZE, UInt = UNMANAGED);
         // constructor with default settings

    // .....

    void                addAt(UInt, const TYPE& object);
         // add the given item into the container at the given
         // index position; if the index position would destroy
         // the adjacency of the elements the operation fails;
         // elements in the container from the index position
         // are moved to the right to accommodate the new item

    void                addFirst(const TYPE& object);
         // insert the new element at index position zero,
         // moving all existing items one position rightward

    void                addLast(const TYPE& object);
         // incorporate the new element immediately following
         // the present final item

    void                add(const TYPE& object);
         // include given item into the container; the exact
         // semantics for this operation is that for addLast

    // .....

  };

  #include "..\ticlass\ordcol.t"             // function bodies

#endif   // ORDEREDCOLLECTION

// =============== End of header file ORDCOL.H =================
```

`OrderedCollection` is a concrete class of the library from which we can create real containers. Strictly, all containers in the library hold not objects themselves but pointers to objects. The expectation is that the application program will create an object on the heap and the container will record that address in its internal storage structure. For example, we might set up an `OrderedCollection` of `Date` values with:

```
int main()
  {
    OrderedCollection<Date>  holidays;   // establish a container

  // create some data values
    Date* xmas           = new Date(25, 12, 1993);
    Date* hogmanay       = new Date(31, 12, 1993);

    holidays.addLast(*xmas);                // store in container
    holidays.addLast(*hogmanay);
    // .....
  }
```

in which the member function `addLast` appears as:

```
template <class TYPE>
void          OrderedCollection<TYPE>::addLast(const TYPE& object)
{
  if(theCardinality == theCollection.capacity())
    theCollection.reSize(theCardinality);
          // double the size of the collection if full.

  theCollection[theCardinality++] = &((TYPE&)object);
}
```

Observe how the function argument is an alias for the actual object to be entered in the container and how the function simply takes the address of that actual object as the value to be recorded.

Note the form of the constructor for class `OrderedCollection`:

```
OrderedCollection(UInt = DEFAULTSIZE, UInt = UNMANAGED);
```

The first argument specifies the initial size of the container. The second argument dictates the storage management strategy to be employed by the container class for the members it contains. If an application requires that the objects maintained by the container be deleted when the container goes out of scope then the second constructor argument should be specified as `MANAGED`:

```
const int NUMBEROFHOLIDAYS = 40;
OrderedCollection<Date>     holidays(NUMBEROFHOLIDAYS, MANAGED);
```

If the application maintains control of the objects (perhaps in some other container) then the default value `UNMANAGED` is used:

```
OrderedCollection<Date>     holidays(NUMBEROFHOLIDAYS);
```

The derived class `SortedCollection` maintains a sort order list of its members. Like an `IndexedCollection` we can access the items at some given subscript position. Like a `SequentialCollection` we can request the first item or remove the last item. Many of the operations for `SortedCollection` are inherited directly without further programming from the latter.

```
// ===============================================================
// File Name    : SORCOL.H
// File Type    : C++ header file for class SORTEDCOLLECTION
// Author       : Ken Barclay
// Date Created : 1 Apr 1993
//
// ------------------------------------
// Description  : A SortedCollection contains elements sorted
//                according to the sort order of the elements.
//                When elements are added or removed from a
//                SortedCollection, the collection remains in
//                order. To ensure proper ordering of the
//                elements in the sorted container, the generic
//                type must support the operator<  (see COL.H).
//
// Base class(es): Collection (COL: abstract)
//                      |
//                  IndexedCollection (XCOL: abstract)
//                          |
//                     SequentialCollection (SEQCOL: abstract)
//                                  |
//                             SortedCollection (SORCOL: concrete)
// Usage         :
//       SortedCollection<String>    names;
//       .....
//       names.add(*new String("Ken"));
//       names.add(*new String("Irene"));
//       names.add(*new String("Dawn"));
//       .....
//       const String& name = names.last();
//
// Known Bugs    : None
//
// ------------------------------------
// Modification History
// Date          :
// Author        :
// Commentary    :
//
// ------------------------------------
// Version       : 1.00
// ===============================================================

#ifndef SORTEDCOLLECTION
  #define SORTEDCOLLECTION

  #include "..\ticlass\seqcol.h"

  template <class TYPE>
  class SortedCollection : public SequentialCollection<TYPE> {
  public:
    SortedCollection(UInt size = DEFAULTSIZE, UInt manage=
                                                     UNMANAGED);
```

```
  // constructor with default settings

    // .....

    virtual void              add(const TYPE& object);
           // include given item into the container; the item
           // is located in the container, retaining the sort
           // order among the elements and permitting duplicates

    // .....

  };

  #include "..\ticlass\sorcol.t"      // function bodies

#endif    // SORTEDCOLLECTION

// ================ End of header file SORCOL.H ==================
```

Since the items are maintained in sort order, the operation `add` must be programmed to give the necessary semantics. As before the types of the items held by the container must provide the comparison `operator<`.

```
template <class TYPE>
void            SortedCollection<TYPE>::add(const TYPE& object)
{
  if(theCardinality == theCollection.capacity())
    theCollection.reSize(theCardinality);
  // double the size of the collection if full.

  for(int k = 0; k < theCardinality; k++)
    if(object < *((TYPE*)theCollection[k])){
      for(int j = theCardinality-1; j >= k; j-)
        theCollection[j+1] = theCollection[j];
  // find the correct position for the object and shuffle the other
  // objects to leave a space

      theCollection[k] = &((TYPE&)object);
      theCardinality++;
      return;
    }
  // if object is larger than all objects in the collection then:
   theCollection[theCardinality++] = &((TYPE&)object);
}
```

Program 12.5 is a short illustration to read a series of names and produce an ordered list. The solution is readily achieved by recording the names in a `SortedCollection`.

PROGRAM 12.5

```
// ———————— FILE: p05.cpp ————————

//
```

```
//  Read a series of names and list them in alphabetical
//        order using a SortedCollection.
//

#include <iostream.h>
#include "cstring.h"
#include "sorcol.h"

int main()
{
  SortedCollection<String>     names(DEFAULTSIZE, MANAGED);

  String                 name;

  cout << "Start entering names:\n";
  cin >> name;
  while(name != "ZZZ"){
    names.add(*new String(name));
    cin >> name;
  }

  cout << "Sorted names list:\n";
  int cardinality = names.cardinality();
  for(int k = 0; k < cardinality; k++)
    cout << "\t" << names[k] << "\n";

  return (0);
}

// ———————— END: p05.cpp ————————
```

CASE STUDY 12.2
Patient statistics (yet again)

In this exercise we repeat Case Study 11.2 which revisited Case Study 9.2. The problem was described by Figures 9.5 and 11.13 and concerned statistics of patient visits to their doctor. In both solutions the patients registered with a doctor were represented in a fixed sized array. In this new solution we will use the container classes of the previous section. Specifically we shall use a `SortedCollection` so that when we produce the required list of patients they will appear in name order. To achieve this the class `Patient` must provide a definition for `operator<`.

In this version we hold pointers to the patient objects created dynamically on the heap. In the application program we create a `Patient` object and register it with the `Doctor` object. This involves placing the pointer to that object in the `SortedCollection<Patient>` data member maintained by class `Doctor`. The `Doctor` class constructor initializes this data member for some given initial size and to have responsibility for the memory management of these objects. When the `Doctor` object goes out of scope at the end of function `main`, then so too does the collection data member and the `Patient` objects maintained by it.

```
// ——————— FILE: case02.cpp ———————

#include <iostream.h>
#include <iomanip.h>
#include "patient.h"
#include "doctor.h"

int main()
{
  Doctor doctor("Wellbeing", Date(1, 1, 1950));

  String patientName;

  cin >> patientName;
  while(patientName != "ZZZ"){
    int         day, month, year;    // patient details;
    char separator;
    int         patientVisits;

    cin >> day >> separator >> month >> separator >> year;
    cin >> patientVisits;

    Date patientDOB(day, month, year);
    Patient*    patient = new Patient(patientName, patientDOB,
                                              patientVisits);

    doctor.registerPatient(*patient);

    cin >> patientName;
  }

  cout << "Patient statistics for Doctor ";
  cout << doctor.name() << "\n";

  double average = doctor.mean();
  cout << "    Average number of visits: "
       << setw(5) << setprecision(2) << average << "\n";

  doctor.printUpper(average + 5);

  return (0);
}
// ——————— END: case02.cpp ———————

// ——————— FILE: patient.h ———————

#ifndef PATIENT
  #define PATIENT

  #include "person.h"

  class Patient : public Person {
    friend Bool operator< (const Patient&, const Patient&);
  public:
    Patient(const String& aName, const Date& aDOB, int aVisits);
    Patient(void);

    int         visits(void) const;
```

```
  private:
    int          theVisits;
  };

  inline Bool    operator< (const Patient& pat1, const Patient&
                                                          pat2)
        { return pat1.theName < pat2.theName; }

  inline Patient::Patient(const String& aName, const Date& aDOB,
                                                   int aVisits)
   : Person(aName, aDOB),
     theVisits(aVisits)
   {}

  inline Patient::Patient(void)       // default name and DOB
        : Person(String(""), Date()),
      theVisits(0)
   {}

  inline int          Patient::visits(void) const
        { return theVisits; }

#endif   // PATIENT

// ———————— END: patient.h ————————

// ———————— FILE: doctor.h ————————

#ifndef DOCTOR
  #define DOCTOR

  #include "person.h"
  #include "patient.h"
  #include "sorcol.h"

  class Doctor : public Person {
  public:
    Doctor(const String& aName, const Date& aDOB);
    void registerPatient(const Patient& aPatient);

    double      mean(void) const;            // statistics
    void printUpper(double limit) const;     // results

  private:
    SortedCollection<Patient> thePatientsList;
  };

  inline Doctor::Doctor(const String& aName, const Date& aDOB)
        : Person(aName, aDOB),
      thePatientsList(DEFAULTSIZE, MANAGED)
   {}

  inline void   Doctor::registerPatient(const Patient& aPatient)
        { thePatientsList.add(aPatient); }

#endif   // DOCTOR

// ———————— END: doctor.h ————————
```

```
// ———————— FILE: doctor.cpp ————————

#include "doctor.h"

double    Doctor::mean(void) const
{
  long totalVisits = 0L;
  const int thePatientsRegistered = thePatientsList.cardinality();

  for(int k = 0; k < thePatientsRegistered; k++)
    totalVisits += thePatientsList[k].visits();

  return double(totalVisits)/thePatientsRegistered;
}

void      Doctor::printUpper(double limit) const
{
  const int thePatientsRegistered = thePatientsList.cardinality();

  for(int k = 0; k < thePatientsRegistered; k++)
    if(thePatientsList[k].visits() > limit)
      cout << "\t" << thePatientsList[k].name()
     << ", " << thePatientsList[k].visits() << "\n";
}

// ———————— END: doctor.cpp ————————
```

12.3 Sets, bags and iterators

A `Bag` (sometimes called a multi-set) is a container in which the items are unordered. The class has no notion of first or last object, or of one object coming before or coming after another object. Because the items are without order, we cannot access them with an integer index. For this reason `Bag`s have been derived from the non-indexed container class `NonIndexedCollection`.

A `Set` is also a container of items without order. The distinction is that whilst a `Bag` permits duplicate items to be present, a `Set` does not. Since a `Set` is a specialized kind of `Bag`, little redefinition is necessary. The `Set` gets most of its functionality programmed from `Bag` and `NonIndexedCollection`.

These classes introduce two new issues. The first is the need to find a suitable representation which gives fast access to the members. The second problem is how we can, say, visit all the items in a `Set` if there is no notion of ordering and indexing.

It would be a simple enough task to use an `OrderedCollection` for the representation for a `NonIndexedCollection` (and hence `Bag` and `Set`). Items added to a `Bag` could simply be implemented with `addLast` on the underlying `OrderedCollection` representation. Equally, operations to remove a member and determine if an item is a member of a `Bag`, etc. are implemented with the corresponding operation for `OrderedCollection`.

However, whilst the operation to add an object to a `Bag` is implemented effectively with the operation `OrderedCollection::addLast`, operations such as isMember (is some item in the Bag) and occurrencesOf (how many occurrences of some given item are in the Bag) have poor performance because of the need to linearly scan the OrderedCollection. As the number of items in the Bag grows, so too does the number of searches required by these two operations.

An alternative strategy is to use a VVector in the implementation and randomly distribute the objects in the Bag throughout the VVector. This method is known as *hashing*. The distribution is achieved by every item possessing a *hash function* which delivers some random value. This arbitrary value is restricted (by modulo arithmetic) to the size of the VVector, and the resulting value is used as the index into the VVector in which to place the new item. Each instantiated version of these containers then requires that there is a hash function on the item type available (similar to the requirement that a version of operator< be available). Since these containers permit both fundamental types and user-defined class types as members then the hash operation must be provided in the usual functional style and not as a member of a class (though it may be a friend to a class).

To implement the operation isMember the same strategy is employed as that to introduce an item into the container (see Figure 12.3). The incoming argument applies its hash function and the result is reduced to the size of the VVector. This index value is used to access the VVector and if the item at that location matches the argument, the function isMember returns TRUE. The outcome is effectively direct access to the item in the container.

It is possible, however, for two or more items to produce the same index value from the randomizing algorithm. For example, consider adding two items K and B to a Bag in which the hashing process delivers the index value 8. Item K will find the VVector unoccupied at location 8 and it is written to that position. Strictly, location 8 is initially occupied with the NULL pointer which we interpret as empty. The VVector is initialized this way when the Bag constructor is called. When item B is added to the same Bag it too delivers the index position 8. When two or more items index the same VVector position we describe this as a *collision*. A number of

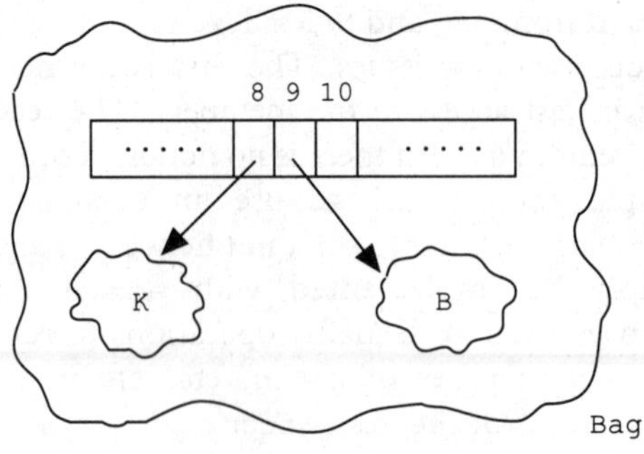

Figure 12.3

strategies exist for dealing with this problem. The simplest, called *open hash*, moves the index to the next highest position and tries again to find an unoccupied `VVector` location. If that too is occupied the index is incremented again, and so on. The index value is incremented modulo the size of the `VVector` so that it wraps around to index position zero in its search for a vacant position in the `VVector`.

As the number of items in the `Bag` increases and the underlying `VVector` fills up, then the number of collisions occurring increases. As a result, more and more linear searching caused by the open hash algorithm occurs, and there is a consequential performance penalty. If f represents how full the `Vector` is, then an estimate for the average number of searches is given by the formula:

$$\frac{2-f}{2(1-f)}$$

Table 12.1 illustrates the number of searches required for various values of f. The tabulated values show how the number of searches quickly rise beyond $f = 0.75$.

Table 12.1

f	searches
0	1
0.25	1.17
0.5	1.5
0.75	2.5
0.8	3
0.85	3.83
0.9	5.5
0.95	10.5

In the implementation for `Bag::add` if the value for f reaches 0.75, then the size of the underlying `VVector` is doubled and the items are redistributed throughout the new `VVector`. This is implemented with the operation `NonIndexedCollection::reSize`. Doubling the size of the `VVector`, halves the value for f and reduces the search length accordingly. This improvement is achieved at a cost – the overhead of doubling the `Vector` and redistributing its content. If an accurate assessment of the expected size of the `Bag` is available it should be used in the constructor call to minimize this cost.

```
template <class TYPE>
void            Bag<TYPE>::add(const TYPE& object)
{
  UInt maxsize = theCollection.capacity();

  if(theCardinality >= 3 * maxsize / 4){// if container rapidly
    this->reSize(maxsize);             // .. filling then double
    maxsize += maxsize;                // .. its size at 75% full
```

```
    }

    UInt position = hash(object) % maxsize;    // find free slot
    while(theCollection[position] != NULL)
      position = (1 + position) % maxsize;

    theCollection[position] = &((TYPE&)object);
                                         // set parameter into
                                         // the collection
    theCardinality++;
  }
```

Using this representation strategy the final outcome for class `Bag` is given below. Most of the `Bag` operations are inherited from class `NonIndexedCollection` which represents a general non-indexed collection of simple values. This abstract class is implemented as an open hash `VVector`. Note how the `VVector` is protected so that it is available to its descendant class `Bag`.

```
// =============================================================
// File name     : NXCOL.H
// File type     : C++ header file for class NONINDEXEDCOLLECTION
// Author        : Ken Barclay
// Date Created  : 2 Apr 1993
//
// ------------------------------------
// Description   : A NonIndexedCollection represents an abstract
//                 base class for containers for which there is
//                 no notion of ordering among the elements.
//                 Typical of such collections are Sets, Bags,
//                 Relations, and Dictionaries.
//
//                 All non-indexed containers use a hash method
//                 to provide fast access to its members. The
//                 member type must then be supported by an
//                 external function hash, e.g.:
//
//                 ULong hash(const String&);
//                 Set<String>       names;
//
// Base Classes  :  Collection(COL: abstract)
//                           |
//                     NonIndexedCollection(NXCOL: abstract)
//
// Usage         : See the containers mentioned in the description.
// Known Bugs    : None
//
// ------------------------------------
// Modification History
// Date          :
// Author        :
// Commentary    :
//
// ------------------------------------
```

```
// Version      :  1.00
// =================================================================

#ifndef NONINDEXEDCOLLECTION
  #define NONINDEXEDCOLLECTION

  #include "..\ticlass\col.h"
  #include "..\ticlass\vvector.h"

  template <class TYPE>
  ABSTRACT class NonIndexedCollection : public Collection<TYPE> {
  public:

    // .....

    Bool         isMember(const TYPE&) const;
                 // is the given argument held by the container

    virtual void add(const TYPE&) =0;
                 // incorporate the given item into the container

    // .....

  protected:
    VVector             theCollection;       // representation
    UInt                theCardinality;
    // .....

  };

  #include "..\ticlass\nxcol.t"              // function bodies

#endif   // NONINDEXEDCOLLECTION

// ============= End of header file NXCOL.H ======================

// =================================================================
// File name     : BAG.H
// File type     : C++ header file for class BAG
// Author        : Ken Barclay.
// Date Created  : 2 Apr 1993
//
// ------------------------------------
// Description   : A Bag is a collection of unordered elements in
//                 which duplicates are permitted. It cannot be
//                 accessed through external keys but it can be
//                 visited via the iterator and there is a hashing
//                 algorithm for fast access to the unordered
//                 objects.
//
// Base Classes :  Collection (COL: abstract)
//                   |
//                  NonIndexedCollection (NXCOL: abstract)
//                              |
//                             Bag (BAG: concrete)
//
// Usage         : A Bag of integers in which is stored two 9s
```

```
//                  and one 1
//
//                          Bag<int>   numbers(4, MANAGED);
//                          int*  number;
//
//                          number = new int(9);
//                          numbers.add(*number);
//                          number = new int(9);
//                          numbers0.add(*number);
//                          number = new int(1);
//                          numbers.add(*number);
// Known Bugs               :
// ------------------------------------------
// Modification History
// Date            :
// Author          :
// Commentary      :
//
// ------------------------------------------
// Version         : 1.20
// ===============================================================

#ifndef BAG
  #define BAG

  #include "..\ticlass\nxcol.h"

  template <class TYPE>
  class Bag : public NonIndexedCollection<TYPE> {
  public:
    Bag(UInt = DEFAULTSIZE, UInt = UNMANAGED);      // constructor

    // .....

    void          add(const TYPE&);
                  // add given object to the container; object is
                  // permitted to duplicate one already present

    // .....

  };

 #include "..\ticlass\bag.t"// include function bodies from T file

#endif  // BAG

// ================ End of header file BAG.H =====================
```

Class Set is a direct descendant of class Bag. The majority of the operations for class Set are inherited without change from class Bag. Operation Set::add follows the same logic as Bag::add and additionally checks that no duplicates are incorporated into the Set. Hence like class SortedCollection, classes Bag and Set require comparison operations on the members.

```
// ===============================================================
// File name     : SET.H
```

```
// File type     : C++ header file for class SET
// Author        : Ken Barclay
// Date Created  : 2 Apr 1993
//
// ———————————————————————————————————
// Description    : A Set represents an unordered collection of
//                  unique objects with no external keys. Set is a
//                  direct descendant of class bag and inherits
//                  most of bags operations without change except
//                  'add' which additionaly checks that no
//                  duplications are made.
//
// Base Classes   :  Collection (COL: abstract)
//                        |
//                    NonIndexedCollection (NXCOL: abstract)
//                               |
//                             Bag (BAG: concrete)
//                                   |
//                                 Set (SET: concrete)
// Usage          :
//
//       Set<String>                     names(3, MANAGED);
//       String*                            name;
//       Set<String>                     dames(3, MANAGED);
//       String*                            dame;
//
//       name = new String("gerry");  names.add(*name);
//       name = new String("jill");   names.add(*name);
//       name = new String("dick");   names.add(*name);
//
//       dame = new String("jill");   dames.add(*dame);
//       dame = new String("joan");   dames.add(*dame);
//       dame = new String("jessie"); dames.add(*dame);
//
// Known Bugs           : None
// ————————————————————————————————————-
// Modification History
// Date           :
// Author         :
// Commentary     :
//
// ————————————————————————————————————-
// Version        : 1.30
// =================================================================

#ifndef SET
  #define SET

  #include "..\ticlass\bag.h"
  #include <iostream.h>

  template <class TYPE>
  class Set : public Bag<TYPE> {
    friend Set<TYPE>  operator+  (const Set<TYPE>&, const
```

```
      Set<TYPE>&);
    friend Set<TYPE>  operator*   (const Set<TYPE>&, const
      Set<TYPE>&);
    friend Set<TYPE>  operator-   (const Set<TYPE>&, const
      Set<TYPE>&);
         // set union(+), intersection(*), and difference(-)
  public:
    Set(UInt = DEFAULTSIZE, UInt = UNMANAGED);

    // .....

    void add(const TYPE&);
         // add the given item to the container, ensuring no
         // duplicates are introduced; if the container is 3/4 full
         // then double its size

    // .....

  };
  #include "..\ticlass\set.t"          // function bodies

#endif   // SET

// ================ End of header file SET.H =====================
```

These two new classes introduce one further issue – how to access the members of the collection. Classes derived from the abstract class `IndexedCollection` permit client programs to access the items in the containers with the operations `at` and `operator[]`. No equivalent facility exists for class `Bag` and class `Set` since there is no natural ordering of the items in `NonIndexedCollection` containers.

This section introduces our final abstraction mechanism, the *iteration abstraction*, or *iterator* for short. Iterators are a generalization of the iteration methods available in most programming languages. Iterators permit us to iterate over arbitrary container types in a natural and convenient way. For example:

```
OrderedCollection<Date>    diary(10);

// ..... add the items

                // FORALL elements of diary DO
int cardinality = diary.cardinality();
for(int k = 0; k < cardinality; k++){
  const Date& date  = diary.at(k);
  cout << "Year: " << date.year() << "\n";
}
```

uses the fact that an `OrderedCollection` is also an `IndexedCollection` for which the member functions `at` and `operator[]` are available.

By the same token, an obvious use for a `Set` is to perform some action for each of its elements:

```
Set<Date>        s(10);       // of element type Date

FORALL elements of s DO
```

```
  some action upon the element
ENDFOR
```

Such a loop might visit all the items in the `Set`, printing the members. Or, we might search for an element that satisfies some criterion, in which case the loop can stop as soon as the desired element is found.

To support iteration adequately, we need to access all elements in a collection. Whilst this need for iterators is identified when introducing the classes `Bag` and `Set`, it can be seen as a general requirement for all `Collection` classes. This way, the same iteration abstractions can be developed in programs that use the `Bag` or `Set` or `SortedCollection` classes. The same consistent interface is presented, giving a uniform way to iterate over such containers.

The abstract base class `Collection` is augmented with an associated iterator class `Iterator`. The constructor for this iterator is given any `Collection` container type (e.g. `Bag`) and scans the underlying representation to find the first non-empty position. Member function `Iterator::selection` makes available a copy of the container item at the non-empty position. Operation `Iterator::advance` moves through the representation to the next non-empty position, and `Iterator::isExhausted` determines when there are no further items to locate.

```
// ==============================================================
// File Name    : COL.H
// File Type    : C++ header file for class COLLECTION
// Author       : Ken Barclay
// Date Created : 2 Apr 1993
//
// .....

#ifndef COLLECTION
  #define COLLECTION

  #include "..\ticlass\classlib.h"

  template <class TYPE>
  ABSTRACT class Collection {
    friend class    Iterator<TYPE>;
  public:

    // .....

  private:
    virtual void                iteratorInitialize(void) =0;
    virtual Bool                iteratorIsExhausted(void) const =0;
    virtual const TYPE&         iteratorSelection(void) const =0;
    virtual void                iteratorAdvance(void) =0;
          // iterator functions to be provided
          // by the concrete classes

  };

  template <class TYPE>
  class Iterator {
```

```
  public:
    Iterator(const Collection<TYPE>& aCollection);
    Bool              isExhausted(void) const;
    const TYPE&       selection(void) const;
    void              advance(void);
  private:
    Collection<TYPE>*  theCollection;        // representation
  };

  #include "..\ticlass\col.t"          // function bodies

#endif  // COLLECTION

// =============== End of header file COL.H ======================
```

Strictly, the `Iterator` class has no knowledge of the underlying representation of each container. For example, the `Iterator` does not know that an `OrderedCollection` holds the items in adjacent cells of a `VVector` while a `Bag` scatters the elements randomly across a `VVector` or that some other storage scheme is used. However, the `Iterator` class is given indirect access to the items in any specific container through the four pure virtual functions `iteratorInitialize`, `iteratorIsExhausted`, etc. specified in the container base class `Collection`. The concrete classes (or their base classes which provide the representation) will know what storage management scheme is employed and how to support the iteration. For example, here is `NonIndexedCollection::iteratorInitialize` which finds the position of the first non-empty cell in the representation:

```
template <class TYPE>
void
NonIndexedCollection<TYPE>::iteratorInitialize(void)
{
  const UInt theCapacity = theCollection.capacity();

  theIteratorIndex = 0;
  while(theIteratorIndex < theCapacity){
    if(theCollection[theIteratorIndex] != NULL)
      break;
    theIteratorIndex++;
  }
}
```

For any concrete class these pure virtual functions will have been defined and the `Iterator` class can then operate on these as the interface to the container and its hidden representation:

```
template <class TYPE>
Iterator<TYPE>::Iterator(const Collection<TYPE>& aCollection)
{
  theCollection = &((Collection<TYPE>&)aCollection);
  theCollection->iteratorInitialize();
}
```

The code fragment for the diary given above may also be expressed as:

```
OrderedCollection<Date>   diary(10);      // of Date objects

// ..... add the items

Iterator<Date>  iter(diary);
while(iter.isExhausted() == FALSE){
  const Date& date = iter.selection();
  cout << "Year: " << date.year() << "\n";
  iter.advance();
}
```

Note how the `Iterator` constructor lends support to the polymorphic effect, prepared to accept any container to iterate across. If later we decide that a `Set` was the best representation for the diary, then we need only change the definition. The iterator code remains unchanged.

We must be careful not to add or remove objects from a container while iterating through its members. Operations to add and remove items will most likely change the order or position of the objects in the container and this will mislead the indexing mechanism maintained by the iterator. Program 12.6 illustrates the problem. The program builds an `OrderedCollection` of names then iterates through them simultaneously removing any name alphabetically before `"Name"`.

PROGRAM 12.6

```
// ———————— FILE: p06.cpp ————————

//
//  Adding and/or removing items from a container
//      while simultaneously iterating across the
//      container can produce unexpected results.
//

#include <iostream.h>
#include "cstring.h"
#include "ordcol.h"

int main()
{
  char* names[] = { "Alfred", "Bernard", "Norman", "Robert" };
  const int NAMESIZE = sizeof(names) / sizeof(names[0]);

  OrderedCollection<String>    nameList;

                               // fill container
  for(int k = 0; k < NAMESIZE; k++)
    nameList.addLast(*new String(names[k]));

                               // iterate through collection
                               // and remove any item
                               // alphabetically before "Name"
```

```
                                // CARE! intention not satisfied
    Iterator<String>       iter(nameList);
    while(iter.isExhausted() == FALSE){
      const String& name = iter.selection();
      if(name < "Name")
        nameList.remove(name);
      iter.advance();
    }

                                        // print result
    Iterator<String>      print(nameList);
    while(print.isExhausted() == FALSE){
      cout << "\t" << print.selection() << "\n";
      print.advance();
    }

    return (0);
  }
  // ———————— END: p06.cpp ————————
```

The output from the program shows that we have not succeeded in our intention:

```
Bernard
Norman
Robert
```

The problem is that the first iteration removes `'Alfred'` from the list and `'Bernard'` now becomes the first item, with `'Norman'` in position 2 and so on. The `Iterator` is unaware of this change and correctly finds the second object on the next iteration. Unknown to the `Iterator` it has skipped the name `'Bernard'` and fails to remove it.

Program 12.7 presents a small example using `Sets` to produce the solution. The program builds two `Sets` for the names of students studying mathematics and computing then produces a list of those students studying both subjects. The solution is readily obtained using the overloaded `operator*` which finds the intersection of the two sets, i.e. those items common to both sets.

PROGRAM 12.7

```
// ———————— FILE: p07.cpp ————————

//
//  Produce a list of those students studying both
//        mathematics and computing.
//

#include <iostream.h>
#include "cstring.h"
#include "set.h"

int main()
```

```
{
  char* mathematics[]  = { "Ken", "Lesley", "Bob" };
  char* computing[]    = { "Ken", "Lesley", "Brian" };
  const int MATH       = sizeof(mathematics) /
                         sizeof(mathematics[0]);
  const int COMP       = sizeof(computing) /
                         sizeof(computing[0]);

  Set<String>    mathSet;
  Set<String>    compSet;

  for(int k = 0; k < MATH; k++)
    mathSet.add(*new String(mathematics[k]));

  for(k = 0; k < COMP; k++)
    compSet.add(*new String(computing[k]));

  Set<String>    bothSet = mathSet * compSet;

  cout << "Students attending both mathematics and computing:\n";
  Iterator<String>      iter(bothSet);
  while(iter.isExhausted() == FALSE){
    cout << "\t" << iter.selection() << "\n";
    iter.advance();
  }

  return (0);
}
// ———————— END: p07.cpp ————————
```

12.4 Dictionaries and Relations

A `Dictionary` is a collection of key/value pairs of objects. The keys in a `Dictionary` are unique, acting as the lookup keys for the collection. Associated with each key is its value. Two or more keys may be associated with the same value.

An example of a `Dictionary` is the internal telephone directory of an organization in which the keys are the staff surname (which we shall assume are unique), and the values are the office extensions. Where two or more staff share the same extension, then two distinct keys (surnames) are associated with one value (extension number).

A `Dictionary` may be searched for the value corresponding to some given key using the member function `lookUp`. Dictionaries are hashed for efficient key lookup and hence operate as a specialized kind of `NonIndexedCollection`.

Internally a `Dictionary` stores the key/value pair as an `Association` which contains the lookup key and its corresponding value. The comparisons performed by operations such as `lookUp` and `isMember` involves comparing the key component of an `Association` which is provided by the class.

```
// ==============================================================
// File Name       : ASSOC.H
```

```
// File Type        : C++ header file for class ASSOCIATION
// Author           : Ken Barclay
// Date Created     : 18 Jun 1993
//
// ---------------------------------------------
// Description      : An Association is a key/value pair
// Base Class(es)   : None
// Usage            :
// Known Bugs       : (Borland) Member functions must NOT be
//                    inlined!
//
// ---------------------------------------------
// Modification History
// Date             :
// Author           :
// Commentary       :
//
// ---------------------------------------------
// Version          : 2.0
//
================================================================

#ifndef ASSOCIATION
  #define ASSOCIATION

  template <class KEYTYPE, class VALUETYPE>
  class Association {
    friend Bool operator< (const Association<KEYTYPE,
                VALUETYPE>&, const Association<KEYTYPE,
                VALUETYPE>&);
    friend ULong hash(const Association<KEYTYPE, VALUETYPE>&);

  public:
    Association(const KEYTYPE&, const VALUETYPE&);
    ~Association(void);
    const KEYTYPE&       key(void) const;
    const VALUETYPE&     value(void) const;
    void                 setValue(const VALUETYPE&);

  private:
    KEYTYPE*             theKey;                // representation
    VALUETYPE*           theValue;
  };

  #include "..\ticlass\assoc.t"                 // function bodies

#endif   // ASSOCIATION

// =============== End of header file ASSOC.H ==================
```

A `Dictionary` is like a `Set` containing an unordered collection of items without duplicates. Here, the items are `Associations` rather than simple objects and duplication is based on the key component of the association. A `Dictionary` is derived from class `Set`, specialized to handle the key/value look up. Class `Dictionary` appears as:

```
// ==============================================================
// File name     : DICTIONARY.H
// File type     : C++ header file for class DICTIONARY
// Author        : Ken Barclay
// Date Created  : 2 Apr 1993
//
// -------------------------------------
// Description   : A Dictionary is collection of key/value pairs
//                 of objects. The keys in a dictionary are
//                 unique, whereas values may be duplicated. A
//                 Dictionary may be searched by key using hashing
//                 for efficiency. The key and value types may be
//                 diferent.
//
// Base Classes :  Collection (COL: abstract)
//                      |
//                  NonIndexedCollection (NXCOL: abstract)
//                      |
//                     Bag (BAG: concrete)
//                          |
//                        Set (SET: concrete)
//                               |
//                              Dictionary (DICTIONARY: concrete)
//
// Usage : e.g. for a directory of names/numbers.
//
//       const int SIZE  = 5;
//       typedef Dictionary<String, int>    Directory;
//
//       int main()
//       {
//         Directory   directory(SIZE, MANAGED);
//         String*   name;
//         int*        number;
//
//         name = new String("terry"); number = new int(1);
//         directory.addKeyValue(*name, *number);
//         name = new String("bobby"); number = new int(2);
//         directory.addKeyValue(*name, *number);
//         name = new String("tobby"); number = new int(3);
//         directory.addKeyValue(*name, *number);
//         name = new String("bill");  number = new int(4);
//         directory.addKeyValue(*name, *number);
//         .....
//       }
//
// Known Bugs          : None
//
// -------------------------------------
// Modification History
// Date                :
// Author              :
```

```
// Commentary          :
//
// ---------------------------------------
// Version             : 1.40
//
=================================================================

#ifndef DICTIONARY
  #define DICTIONARY

  #include "..\ticlass\set.h"
  #include "..\ticlass\assoc.h"

  template <class KEYTYPE, class VALUETYPE>
  class Dictionary : public Set< Association<KEYTYPE, VALUETYPE>
                                                              > {

  public:
    Dictionary(UInt = DEFAULTSIZE, UInt = UNMANAGED);
    Dictionary(const Dictionary<KEYTYPE, VALUETYPE>&);
    ~Dictionary(void);
    Dictionary<KEYTYPE, VALUETYPE>&
         operator= (const Dictionary<KEYTYPE, VALUETYPE>&);

    void         addKeyValue(const KEYTYPE&, const VALUETYPE&);
         // add the key/value pair to the collection; if a key
         // in the container is the same as that given, then the
         // given value overwrites the original, unless the
         // DEBUG_ON option is used then abort the program via
         // PRECONDITIONS; if necessary,the collection will
         // double in size if it is 75% full

    void         removeKey(const KEYTYPE&);
                 // remove the key/value pair where the key
                 // matches that which is given; if no match is
                 // found then no operation is performed unless
                 // the DEBUG_ON option is used then abort the
                 // program via PRECONDITIONS.

    Bool         hasKey(const KEYTYPE& aKey) const;
                 // finds if such a key is present

    const VALUETYPE& lookUp(const KEYTYPE& aKey) const;
                 // find the value corresponding to the given key;
                 // fails if key not present

    // .....

  };

  #include "..\ticlass\dictionary.t"          // function bodies

#endif   // DICTIONARY

// ============== End of header file DICTIONARY.H ==============
```

Program 12.8 illustrates a simple application of class `Dictionary` in which we implement a small language dictionary. Words from the dictionary are paired with their meaning which the program displays in response to look up words.

PROGRAM 12.8

```
// ———— FILE: p08.cpp ————

//
// Construct a language dictionary then lookup a seies
//      of input words.
//

#include <iostream.h>
#include "cstring.h"
#include "dictionary.h"

char*   word[]   = { "object",
                   "abstract",
                   "binding",
                   "polymorphism",
                   "paradigm"
                   };

char*  meaning[] = { "tangible thing",
                   "having no reference to material objects",
                   "process by which a name is associated with a
                      type",
                   "having many forms",
                   "an illustrative model"
                   };

const int SIZE  = sizeof(word) / sizeof(word[0]);

int main()
{
  Dictionary<String, String>  dictionary(DEFAULTSIZE, MANAGED);

  for(int k = 0; k < SIZE; k++){
    String* wordp = new String(word[k]);
    String* meaningp = new String(meaning[k]);
    dictionary.addKeyValue(*wordp, *meaningp);
  }

  cout << "Enter look up words\n";
  String inputWord;

  cout << "First word: ";
  cin >> inputWord;
  while(inputWord != "ZZZ"){
    if(dictionary.hasKey(inputWord) == TRUE)
      cout << inputWord << ": " << dictionary.lookUp(inputWord)
        << "\n";
    else
      cout << inputWord << ": " << "UNKNOWN\n";

    cout << "Next word: ";
    cin >> inputWord;
  }
```

```
    return (0);
}

// ————— END: p08.cpp —————
```

Note how we have introduced member function `hasKey` which determines if the given key value matches any key of the key/value pairs in the `Dictionary`. This would appear to duplicate the role of `isMember` inherited by the `Dictionary` class. However, we must remember that a `Dictionary` is a specialized kind of `Set` with `Association` members and in Program 12.8, for example, if we were to use `isMember` we should have to supply an `Association` argument:

```
if(dictionary.isMember(Association(*inputWord, *inputWord)) ==
                                                        TRUE) .....
```

Here we require a second argument for the `Association` constructor which is otherwise ignored. Since the key and values types are `String`, we use the `inputWord` again. Had the types been different then some temporary value would be required.

A similar comment is made for member function `Dictionary::add`. Its argument is also an `Association` which must be created on the heap by the application program so that its address may be included into the container:

```
dictionary.add(*new Association(*wordp, *meaningp));
```

Finally note that when we iterate across a `Dictionary` then the items we select on each iteration is an `Association`. For example, the code fragment to tabulate the dictionary might appear as:

```
Iterator< Association<String, String> >      iter(dictionary);
while(iter.isExhausted() == FALSE){
  const Association<String, String>& assoc = iter.selection();
  const String& word = assoc.key();
  const String& meaning = assoc.value();
  cout << word << ": " << meaning << "\n";
  iter.advance();
}
```

A (binary) `Relation` between two sets `S` and `T` is defined to be the subset of the cartesian product `S x T`. The resulting relation `R` is a set of pairs (`s`, `t`) drawn from the sets `S` and `T`. For example, if the set `S` is `{Ken, Brian, Lindsay, George}`, and the set `T` is `{Irene, Iris, Margaret}`, then the relation `R` might contain:

```
{(Ken, Irene), (Lindsay, Iris), (George, Margaret)}
```

The inverse of a relation `R` is the relation formed from pairs (`t`, `s`), such that the pair (`s`, `t`) is a member of the relation `R`. Hence the inverse of the relation `R` above is the relation:

```
{(Irene, Ken), (Iris, Lindsay), (Margaret, George)}
```

Sometimes we wish to extract from a relation `R` only that part applying to some subset `A` of the set `S`. Given a set `A` containing `{Ken, George}` then the restriction `R` to `A` is:

```
{(Ken, Irene), (George, Margaret)}
```

Similarly, the co-restriction to some subset `B` of the set `T` is a subset of the relation `R` in which the second of the pairs in `R` are members of the set `B`. If `B` is `{Margaret, Iris}`, then the co-restriction of `R` to the set `B` is:

```
{(George, Margaret), (Lindsay, Iris)}
```

Another operation on the relation `R` is to determine which things in `T` are related to the members of the set `A`, a subset of the set `S`. This we call the image. Given `R` and `A` above, then the image of `R` on `A` is:

```
{ Irene, Margaret }
```

Finally, the `domain` (`range`) of a relation `R` are those elements forming a set from the first (second) of the pairs in `R`.

```
// ================================================================
// File name    : RELATION.H
// File type    : C++ header file for class RELATION
// Author       : Ken Barclay
// Date Created : 2 Apr 1993
//
// ------------------------------------
// Description  : A Relation is collection of pairs of objects.
//                If the first of the pair is drawn from the set S
//                and the second from the set T, then we describe
//                the relation R as: R = {(s,t) is member of S x T},
//                that is, R is a subset of the cartesian
//                product S x T.
//
// Base Classes  :  Collection (COL: abstract)
//                        |
//                     NonIndexedCollection (NXCOL: abstract)
//                            |
//                         Bag (BAG: concrete)
//                               |
//                            Relation (RELATION: concrete)
//
// Usage        : e.g. a  pair of related members
//                in a family tree:
//
//       Relation<String, String>    tree(32, MANAGED);
//       String                                parent, child;
//
//       cout << "Enter family tree:";
//       cin >> parent >> child;
//       while(parent != "ZZZ"){
//         tree.addKeyValue(*new String(parent), *new
                                               String(child));
```

```
//          cin >> parent >> child;
//        }
//        .....
//        Iterator< Association<String, String> >   iter(tree);
//        while(iter.isExhausted() == FALSE){
//          const Association<String, String>& assoc =
                                                  iter.selection();
//          cout << assoc.key() << ", " << assoc.value() << "\n";
//          iter.advance();
//        }
//
//  Known Bugs          : None
//
// ------------------------------------------------------------
// Modification History
// Date          :
// Author        :
// Commentary    :
//
// ------------------------------------------------------------
// Version       : 1.30
//
==================================================================

#ifndef RELATION
  #define RELATION

  #include "..\ticlass\bag.h"
  #include "..\ticlass\assoc.h"
  #include "..\ticlass\set.h"

  template <class KEYTYPE, class VALUETYPE>
  class Relation : public Bag< Association<KEYTYPE, VALUETYPE> > {
  public:
    Relation(UInt = DEFAULTSIZE, UInt = UNMANAGED);
    Relation(const Relation<KEYTYPE, VALUETYPE>&);
    ~Relation(void);
    Relation<KEYTYPE, VALUETYPE>&
         operator= (const Relation<KEYTYPE, VALUETYPE>&);

    void         addKeyValue(const KEYTYPE&, const VALUETYPE&);
   // add the key/value pair to the collection; if a key
   // in the container is the same as that given, then the
   // given value overwrites the original, unless the
   // DEBUG_ON optionis used then abort the program via
   // PRECONDITIONS; if necessary, the collection will double in
   // size if it is presently full

    void         removeKeyValue(const KEYTYPE&, const VALUETYPE&);
   // remove the key/value pair from the collection; if
   // no such pair exists then no operation is performed unless the
   // DEBUG_ON option is used then abort the program via
   // PRECONDITIONS.

    Set<KEYTYPE>        domain(void) const;
```

```
  // deliver a set of the domain values of the relation R;
  // if (s, t) is in R, then s is in the domain

    Set<VALUETYPE>      range(void) const;
  // deliver a set of the range values of the relation R;
  // if (s, t) is in R, then t is in the range

    Set<VALUETYPE>      image(const Set<KEYTYPE>&) const;
  // deliver a set of the range values which pair with
  // the domain values of the Set S given as the argument;
  // if s is in S and (s, t) is in the relation R then
  // t is in the result set

    Relation<KEYTYPE, VALUETYPE>restriction(const Set<KEYTYPE>&)
                                                          const;
  // deliver a relation drawn from the original restricted
  // by the members of the Set argument S; if s is in S
  // and (s,t) is in the relation R then (s, t) is in
  // the result relation

    Relation<KEYTYPE, VALUETYPE>      corestriction(const
      Set<VALUETYPE>&) const;
  // deliver a relation drawn from the original restricted
  // by the members of the Set argument T; if t is in T
  // and (s,t) is in the relation R then (s, t) is in
  // the result relation

    Relation<VALUETYPE, KEYTYPE>      inverse(void) const;
  // deliver a relation which is the inverse of the pairs
  // in the relation R; if (s, t) is in R then (t, s) is
  // in the result

    // .....

  };

  #include "..\ticlass\relation.t"

#endif    // RELATION

// ================= End of header file RELATION.H ===============
```

The class `Relation` has been parameterized on the types for the key and value. Hence we may have a `Relation` with different key and value types. Two examples include:

```
    Relation<String, int>        telephone;     // name and extension
    Relation<Doctor, Patient>    patients;
```

Of course, both the key and value types may be the same as in:

```
Relation<String, String>family;
  // name of parent and name of child
```

We define a `Relation` in which both the key and value types are the same as `XRelation`, derived from class `Relation` and extended to include additional operations.

```
// ==============================================================
// File name    : XRELATION.H
// File type    : C++ header file for class XRELATION
// Author       : Ken Barclay
// Date Created : 2 Apr 1993
//
// ------------------------------------
// Description  : A Relation is collection of pairs of objects. If
//                the first of the pair is drawn from the set S
//                and the second from the set T, then we describe
//                the relation R as: R = {(s, t) is member of S x
//                T}, that is, R is a subset of the cartesian
//                product S x T. Class XRELATION is an extension
//                of the class RELATION to include operations
//                such as transitiveClosure which requires the
//                sets S and T to be the same.
//
// Base Classes  : Collection (COL: abstract)
//                       |
//                   NonIndexedCollection (NXCOL: abstract)
//                                |
//                     Bag (BAG: concrete)
//                                |
//                            Relation (RELATION: concrete)
//                                        |
//                              XRelation (XRELATION: concrete)
//
// Usage         :
// Known Bugs    : None
//
// ------------------------------------
// Modification History
// Date          :
// Author        :
// Commentary    :
//
// ------------------------------------
// Version       : 1.10
//
// ==============================================================

#ifndef XRELATION
  #define XRELATION

  #include "..\ticlass\relation.h"

  template <class TYPE>
  class XRelation : public Relation<TYPE, TYPE> {
  public:
    XRelation(UInt = DEFAULTSIZE, UInt = UNMANAGED);
    XRelation(const XRelation<TYPE>& relation);
    XRelation(const Relation<TYPE, TYPE>& relation);
    ~XRelation(void);
    XRelation<TYPE>&    operator= (const XRelation<TYPE>&);
```

```
    void          identityRelation(const Set<TYPE>&);
          // fill the Relation with the pairs (s, s), where
          // s is an element of the Set argument

    XRelation<TYPE>     composition(const XRelation<TYPE>&);
          // if (r, s) are members of the first relation (object)
          // and (s, t) is a member of the second (argument), the
          // the composition consists of those elements (r, t)

    XRelation<TYPE>     kthComposition(UInt);
          // repeated application of the composition function

    XRelation<TYPE>     transitiveClosure(void);

    // .....
  };

  #include "..\ticlass\xrelation.t"

#endif    // XRELATION

// ================ End of header file XRELATION.H ==============
```

The function `composition` between two `XRelation` objects is the set of pairs `(s, u)` such that there exists an item `t` with the pair `(s, t)` a member of the first `XRelation` and the pair `(t, u)` a member of the second `XRelation`.

For example, if the `Relation Reg` consists of the pair `(s, r)` where student `s` is registered in region `r`, then the composition `Reg.composition(InvReg)` is the set of pairs `(s, t)` of students both registered in some region `r`. `InvReg` denotes the inverse of the relation `Reg`.

Member function `kthComposition` forms the kth composition of the `XRelation` with itself. If some `XRelation Rel` consists of the pair `(s, t)` where person `s` is parent-of person `t`, then `Rel.kthComposition(2)` produces the grandparent-of relation. Similarly, `Rel.kthComposition(3)` is the great-grandparent-of relation. By definition, `Rel.kthComposition(1)` delivers `Rel`, and `Rel.kthComposition(0)` is the identity relation.

The `transitiveClosure` is the set of all pairs directly or indirectly related by the original relation. The `transitiveClosure` of the relation parent-of are all the ancestors of the persons in the relation.

CASE STUDY 12.3
Class hierarchies

Referring to Figure 12.2, observe how each class has at most one base or ancestor class. The exception to this rule is the root class `Collection`. We might model this information in the class diagram given in Figure. 12.4. A `Class` has a `name` property and operates as a base class for any number of derived classes.

Previously we would have represented the `derived` relation by either having a pointer in a derived class instance to its base class instance, or a set of pointers

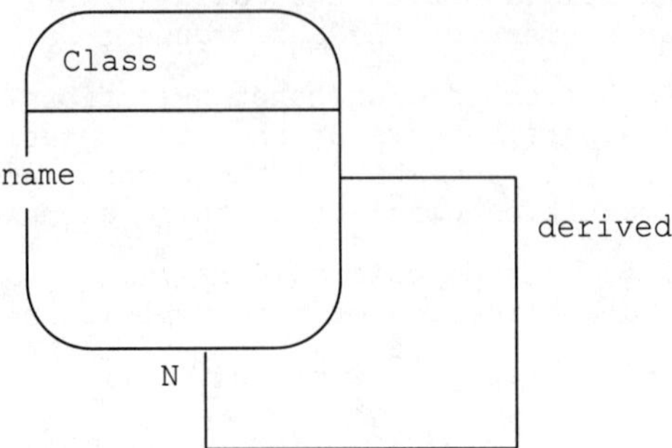

Figure 12.4

from base class instances to derived classes, or both if traversal in each direction is necessary (see Case Study 12.2).

Alternatively, if classes `B` and `D` are related through direct inheritance then the pair may be recorded in an inheritance `XRelation` called, say, `classHierarchy`. The `transitiveClosure` of this relation would produce the descendent classes for all classes. The `inverse` operation determines the ancestor classes and the `image` of this with a `Set` containing a single class name are the ancestors of that named class.

```
// ———————— FILE: case03 ————————

#include <iostream.h>
#include "cstring.h"
#include "xrelation.h"

                              // prototype
void      readHierarchy(XRelation<String>&);

int main()
{
  String        className;
  Set<String>                nameSet;
  XRelation<String>          classHierarchy;

  readHierarchy(classHierarchy);

  cout << "\n\nEnter class name for ancestors:";
  cin >> className;
  nameSet.add(*new String(className));

  XRelation<String> derivedClasses(classHierarchy.transitive
                                                      Closure());
  XRelation<String> ancestorClasses(derivedClasses.inverse());
  Set<String>   ancestorNames = ancestorClasses.image(nameSet);

  cout << "Ancestors of: " << className << "\n";
```

```
  Iterator<String>      iter(ancestorNames);
  while(iter.isExhausted() == FALSE){
    const String& name = iter.selection();
    cout << "\t" << name << "\n";
    iter.advance();
  }

  return (0);
}

void      readHierarchy(XRelation<String>& classHierarchy)
{
  String terminator("ZZZ");
  String className;

  cout << "Enter hierarchy:\n";
  cout << "Enter base class name:";
  cin >> className;
  while(className != terminator){
    String* baseClassName = new String(className);
    cout << "\tEnter derived class name:";
    cin >> className;
    while(className != *baseClassName){
      String* derivedClassName = new String(className);
      classHierarchy.addKeyValue(*baseClassName,
        *derivedClassName);
      cout << "\tEnter derived class name:";
      cin >> className;
    }
    cout << "Enter base class name:";
    cin >> className;
  }
}

// ———————— END: case03 ————————
```

12.5 Representation

We have already noted that the containers use a user–defined array class called `VVector`. Had we used the obvious class `Vector` defined by the library then instantiation of, say, the generic class `Bag` to `Bag<Date>` would instantiate the underlying generic `Vector` class as `Vector<Date>`. Equally, `SortedCollection<Time>` implies generation of `Vector<Time>`. Clearly this will result in the same vector code generated, one for `Date` and one for `Time` objects. To avoid replication of the code and having `Vector` of `Date` pointers and `Vector` of `Time` pointers we employ an array of untyped (void) pointers `VVector`. The containers are made type-safe by encapsulating `VVector` in the generic container classes. The outline for class `VVector` is:

```
// ================================================================
// File Name     : VVECTOR.H
// File Type     : C++ Header file for class VVECTOR
// Author        : K. Barclay
// Date Created  : 24 Jan 1993
//
// ------------------------------------
// Description   : A VVector is an indexed collection which has
//                 the semantics of a conventional C++ array. In
//                 addition, VVectors may be created at run-time
//                 of some computed size; further, it may be
//                 increased in size during program execution.
//                 Unlike ordinary arrays, VVectors may also be
//                 assigned. A VVector is a vector of untyped
//                 (void) pointers.
// Base Class(es): None
// Usage         :
// Known Bugs    : None
//
// ------------------------------------
// Modification History
// Date          :
// Author        :
// Commentary    :
//
// ------------------------------------
// Version       : 1.01
//
=================================================================

#ifndef VVECTOR
  #define VVECTOR

  #include "..\ticlass\classlib.h"

  class VVector {
  public:
    VVector(UInt = DEFAULTSIZE);
      // Standard Constructor setting the size of the VVector to
      // the default size of 32

    VVector(const VVector&);
      // Copy Constructor

    ~VVector(void);
      // Standard Destructor

    VVector&          operator= (const VVector&);
      // Overloading the assignment operator to allow the
      // assignment of the contents of one VVector to another

    void*&            operator[] (UInt);
      // indexing operator applicable to left or right side
      // of assignment
```

```
    void*        operator[] (UInt) const;
      // indexing operator applicable only to constant
      // objects and only appearing on the right side
      // of assignments (inherited from IndexedCollection)

    void*        at(UInt) const;
      // indexing operator (inherited from IndexedCollection

    UInt         capacity(void) const;
      // the current capity of the VVector (inherited from
      // Collection)

    void         reSize(UInt);
      // increase the size of the VVector (inherited from
      // Collection)

  private:
    void**       theVVector;    // representation
    UInt         theSize;       // holds the size of the the VVector
  };

  // .....

#endif    // VVECTOR

// ================ End of Header file VVECTOR.H ================
```

The interesting part here is the declaration for the data member `theVVector`. The interpretation of this declaration is that `theVVector` is a pointer to an array of elements which are untyped pointers (`void*`). An untyped pointer in C++ is used as a general pointer. Any pointer may be converted to `void*` without loss of information. Further, if the result is converted back to the original pointer type, then the original pointer value is restored.

12.6 Summary

1. Variable sized data objects are used when the amount of data is not known in advance. In C++, a pointer data type is provided and standard operators for the dynamic allocation and deallocation of storage.

2. The operator `new` returns a pointer to dynamically allocated memory of some given type. Storage allocated by `new` is returned to the system for subsequent recycling with the operator `delete`. It is the programmer's responsibility to ensure that `new` operation is successful, and that the memory that has been freed is not referenced.

3. An initial version of a class library has been developed. The class library serves to collect together a group of related objects. The collection classes define several different data structures which serve as containers for arbitrary objects. For example, a `Set` is an unordered collection of non-duplicated objects.

4. The collection classes are useful because they provide similar protocol for:

   - Iterating over the elements of a collection.
   - Searching a collection for a particular element.
   - Adding and removing elements.
   - Accessing and changing elements.

12.7 Exercises

1. The classical algorithm for enumerating prime numbers is the *Sieve of Eratosthenes*. Suppose that we wish to find all the prime numbers less than 12. We start by placing all the numbers from 2 to 12 inclusive on to the sieve:

   2 3 4 5 6 7 8 9 10 11 12

   We then repeat the following actions until the sieve is empty:

   (a) Select and remove the lowest number from the sieve, claiming that it is a prime.
   (b) Remove all multiples of that number from the sieve.

   After step (a), we have 2 as a prime. From step (b), the sieve now contains the odd numbers:

   3 5 7 9 11

   Repeating the process, we know that 3 is the next prime number and only 5, 7 and 11 remain on the sieve. The process continues until the sieve is empty. The identified primes not exceeding 12 are then 2, 3, 5, 7 and 11.

   There are many ways to program this problem. One possibility is to employ the `SortedCollection` abstraction. The sieve is represented by a `SortedCollection` and is initially established to contain 2, 3, ... , N for some data value N. Members are entered onto the sieve with the operation `SortedCollection::add` and deleted with `SortedCollection::remove`. Since the items in the sieve are ordered by the underlying representation, then the smallest sieve member is determined with the operation `SortedCollection::first`.

   Prepare a program which accepts a single integer and prints all prime numbers not exceeding this value.

2. Repeat Exercise 1 this time viewing a sieve as a class derived from `SortedCollection`:

```
class Sieve : private SortedCollection<int> {
public:
  Sieve(const int limit);
```

```
        Bool        isEmpty(void) const;
        int         smallest(void) const;
        void        removemultiples(const int small);
    };
```

3. Repeat Program 11 from Chapter 9 using class `OrderedCollection` to act as a stack with a 'last in first out' behaviour.

4. Repeat Case Study 12.2 using a `Relation` to represent the `registeredWith` relationship between a `Patient` and a `Doctor`.

5. Re-implement Exercises 8, 9 and 10 from Chapter 9 using appropriate container classes.

6. Let `M` represent the `Set` of male students and `F` the `Set` of female students. Let `G` be the `Set` of students studying geography and `H` be the `Set` of students studying history. Prepare a program to input these `Sets` of names and find:

   (a) Those male students studying geography.
   (b) Those female students not studying history.
   (c) Those male students studying both geography and history.
   (d) The student not enrolled for either subject.

7. Add the new member `sort` to the class `OrderedCollection`. Use any sorting method you are familiar with or take the Shell sort algorithm from Chapter 8.

   To class `OrderedCollection` also add the member function `reverse` which reorders the items in the container.

8. To class `SortedCollection` add the following two constructors:

```
SortedCollection(const OrderedCollection&);
  // with template arguments
SortedCollection(const Set&);
```

   In both cases the items in the container arguments are incorporated into the `SortedCollection`.

9. To class `Relation` add the following constructor:

```
Relation(const OrderedCollection&, const
  OrderedCollection&); // templates
```

   in which the keys are drawn from the first `OrderedCollection` and the values from the second `OrderedCollection`. The key/value pairs are taken from the same position in both containers.

10. In class `Relation` member functions `domain`, `range` and `image` return `Sets` for their values. This is a relatively expensive operation because of the need

to copy the `Set`. Suggest how we may modify this to reduce the cost.

Following the developments of classes `Dictionary` and `Relation`, develop a new class `KeySortedCollection` which represents a sorted collection of key/value pairs sorted according to the keys. Class `KeySortedCollection` is to be derived from class `SortedCollection`.

11. An invoice consists of a number of invoice item lines containing the item number, the item description, the quantity, the unit cost and the final cost. From the object model suggested by Figure 12.5, print an invoice as:

```
Name:         Joe
Order No:     123                                 Invoice
Invoice No:   456
                  Item         Item           Quantity   Unit       Cost
                  No           Description    Cost

                   6           Needles          20        0.20       4.00
                  10           Pins            100        0.01       1.00
                  .....
Total                                                                8.90
```

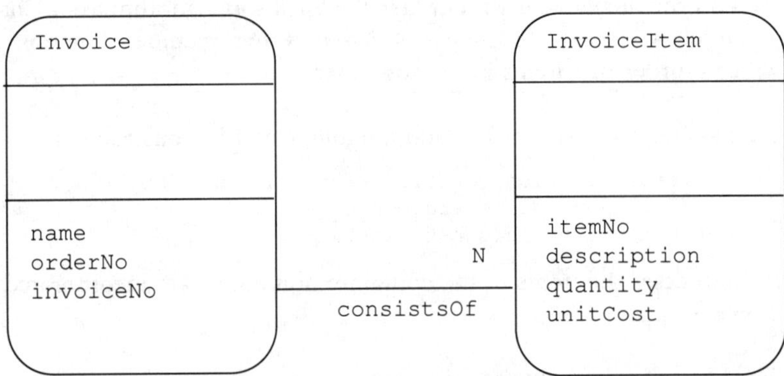

Figure 12.5

12. In a certain organization a person works on a number of projects, and a project involves one or more staff. Using the object model shown in Figure 12.6, in which the number of person hours attached to each project is recorded, find how many hours a person worked on a given project, and for

a given staff member find the number of distinct projects with which he/she was associated.

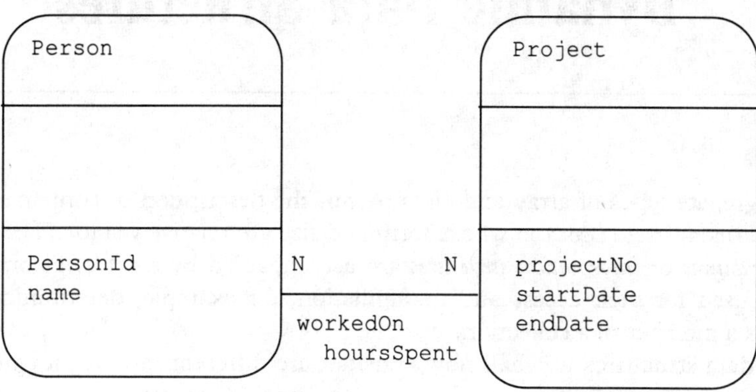

Figure 12.6

13

Dynamic Data Structures

The aggregate types of array and class permit the description of containers such as `Set` and `OrderedCollection` whose form and size are relatively static. These various *data structures* or *information structures* are accompanied by a set of algorithms that can be used for their access and manipulation, for example, determining if some object is a member of a collection.

The data structures we shall now consider are different in that they use storage or memory dynamically, whereby the amount of storage in use is directly proportional to the amount of information stored at a given stage in the computation.

The static data structures have a role to play in the creation of these dynamic data structures. The aggregates array and class form the basic unit of storage for these dynamic data structures. These basic units are commonly referred to as the *nodes* of the data structure. These nodes are linked together in some way to form the structure, with the *linkage information* contained within each node. A given data structure is characterized by the structure imposed on the data by these linkages. Generally, there are three forms: *linear*, *hierarchical* and *graph* structures.

The *linear linked list* is the simplest of these categories. Normally each node has associated with it a data field and a single *link* field. The link associates one node with the next node in the list. The result is a chain-like structure, logically appearing as shown in Figure 13.1.

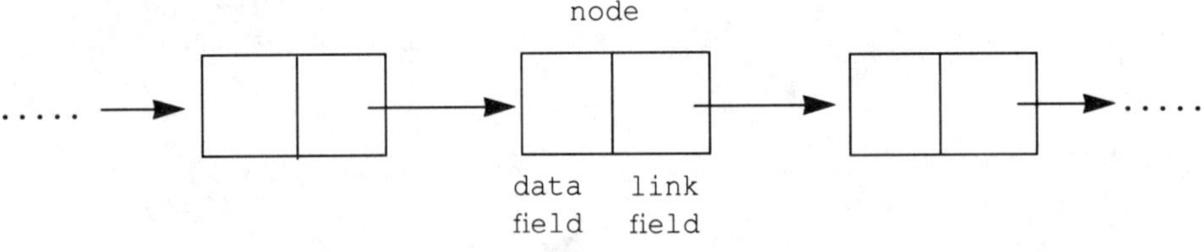

Figure 13.1

A common example structure from the hierarchical class is the *binary tree*. Each node in the structure can have one predecessor or ancestor and as many as two successors or descendants. Thus each node contains data and the links to its two descendants as shown by Figure 13.2.

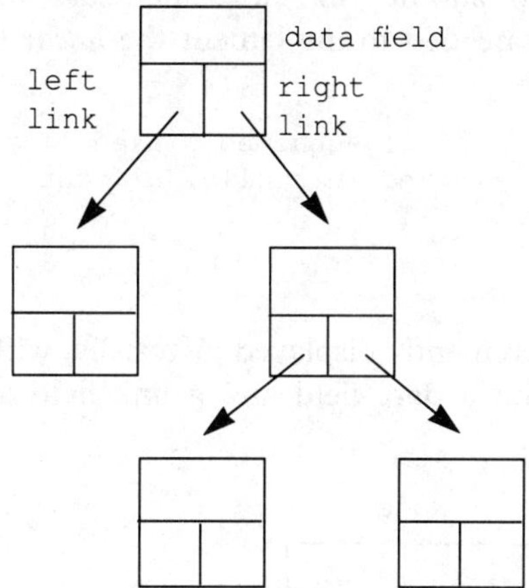

Figure 13.2

The *graph* is a generalization of the tree structure which allows loops. Each node of a graph links to one or more other nodes as shown by Figure 13.3. We shall not consider trees or graphs in this book.

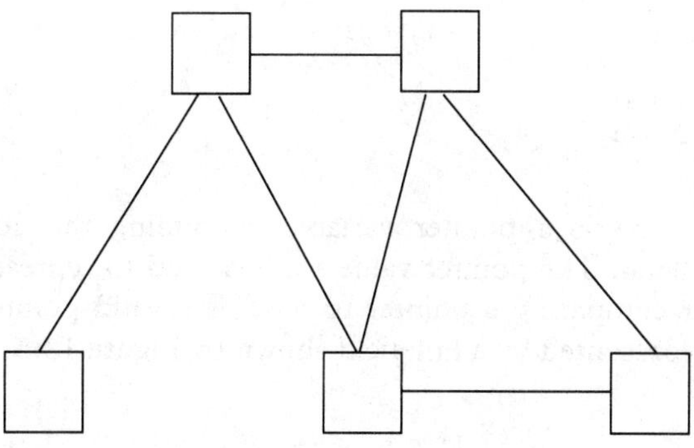

Figure 13.3

13.1 The linear linked list

A class in which a member is a pointer to other instances of the same such class is known as a *self referential structure.* A self referential structure permits one instance of the class to refer to another of the same class through a pointer. The declarations that will be needed to implement the *linear linked list* data structure are of the form:

```
class Node {      // singly-chained linked list
public:           // note: initially, all data members are public
  int    data;
  Node*  link;
};
```

These structures are conveniently displayed pictorially, with the `Nodes` represented by a partitioned box with a data field and a link field and the links shown by arrows (see Figure 13.4).

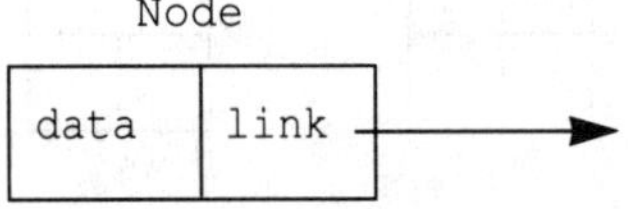

Figure 13.4

The member `data` is, in this example, a data item of type `int`. It can, of course, be any valid C++ type, including aggregate types array and class. Using a class data member, a node can be made to carry a large quantity of associated data. For example, information in a node may be represented by the declaration:

```
class Info {*/...../*};
```

and then the `Node` by:

```
class Node {          // aggregate data in list
public:
  Info    data;
  Node*   link;
};
```

The member `link` is a pointer variable containing the address of another instance of type `Node`. The pointer value `NULL` is used to represent the end of the list. Assigning or comparing a pointer to `NULL` is a valid pointer operation. The `NULL` pointer is represented by a link field shown by Figure 13.5.

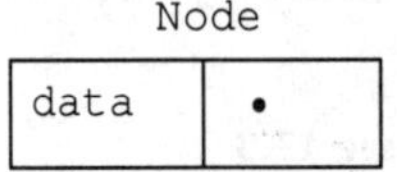

Figure 13.5

Let us now define some variables of type `Node` with integer data items:

```
Node        first, second, third;
```

and perform some assignments on these structures:

```
first.data        = 1;
second.data       = 2;
third.data        = 3;

first.link = second.link = third.link = NULL;
```

A chain-like structure can be established by having the `link` member of `first` address the node `second`, and for its link in turn to address the node `third`. The statements are:

```
first.link        = &second;
second.link       = &third;
```

These pointer assignments result in linking `first` to `second` and `second` to `third`. We now have a linear linked list (see Figure 13.6).

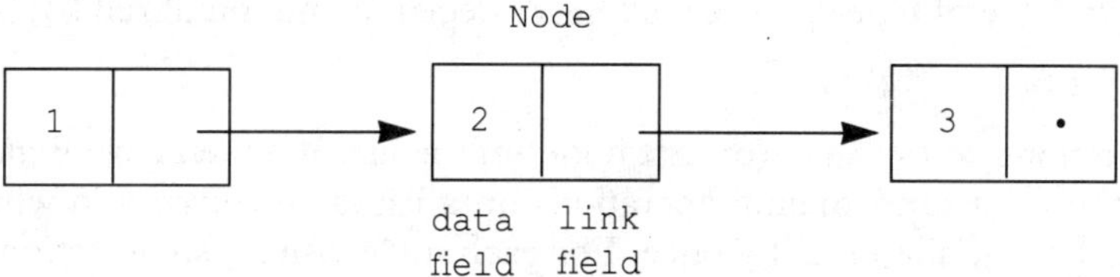

Figure 13.6

To reference the data items on this linked list there are a number of equivalent expressions. To retrieve the data item `'1'`, the expression is:

```
first.data
```

The expression:

```
first.link
```

is an object of type `Node*`. It does, of course, point to the `Node` object called `second`. From Section 9.10, a pointer to a class object permits a member of that object to be accessed by:

```
class-pointer->member-name
```

The expression to reference the data value `'2'` is:

```
second.data
```

or, indirectly:

```
first.link->data
```

The two operators, pointer to class member reference (->) and class member reference (.) are of equal precedence and associate left to right. Therefore, the `link` member of `first` will be determined, and then the member `data` of the `Node` class object addressed by this pointer.

Similarly, the member `link` of the object `second` can be referenced through:

```
first.link->link
```

and, in turn, the data item `'3'` by:

```
first.link->link->data
```

The essential feature here is that the `data` members of the objects `second`, `third` and any more which may be linked into this list are accessible not only by their name (e.g. `second.data`) but also through the pointers which refer to them (`first.link -> data`). Excepting `first`, the nodes in the linked list may be treated *anonymously*. Location `first` can also be processed this way if we have an additional variable of type `Node*` called `head`, declared and initialized by:

```
Node* head = &first;
```

to act as a pointer to the `head` (or first node) of the list. We then have Figure 13.7.

One of the most fundamental operations on a list is *list traversal* in which every node of the list is visited exactly once. For each node visited, some action, such as printing the data item associated with the node, is performed. Using the list

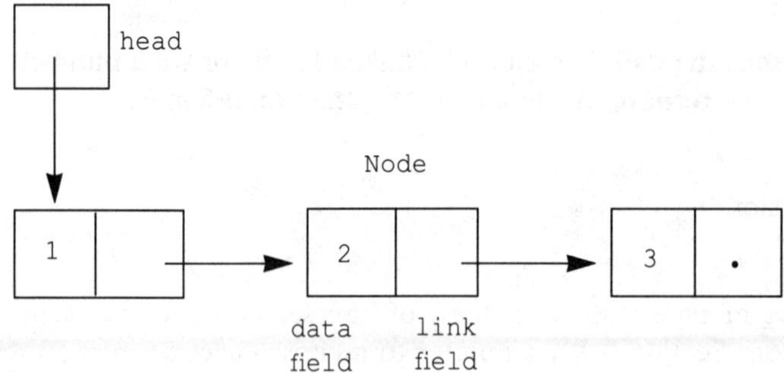

Figure 13.7

established above, Program 13.1 prints each integer in the list. List traversal is achieved by setting a pointer to the head of the list, then advancing through the list via the `link` pointer until the value `NULL` is determined, denoting the end of the list.

PROGRAM 13.1

```
// ———————— FILE: p01.cpp ————————

//
// Manually establish a linear linked list then
//      perform a list traversal. Initialize a pointer
//      to the first list node, then cycle through the
//      nodes via the link member until the end of list
//      is recognized.
//

#include <iostream.h>

class Node {        // singly chained linked list
public:
  int               data;
  Node*             link;
};

int main()
{
  Node    first, second, third;
                                   // build a list
  first.data   = 1;     first.link  = &second;
  second.data  = 2;     second.link = &third;
  third.data   = 3;     third.link  = NULL;
  Node* head   = &first;

  Node* ptr = head;                    // list traversal
  while(ptr != NULL){                  // more nodes?
    cout << ptr->data << "\n";       // access data
    ptr = ptr->link;                 // advance to next node
  }

  return (0);
}

// ———————— END: p01.cpp ————————
```

Anonymous locations can be created dynamically whilst the program is executing. These dynamic data structures can then expand and contract freely as required. The linked list offers the advantage that it can be made just as long as necessary – no more and no less. The array, by comparison, has its size fixed in advance and an arbitrary limit on the number of elements must be imposed (though, as we showed in Chapter 12, we can dynamically reallocate an array to a larger size).

We can dispense completely with the named nodes and operate solely with anonymous nodes if each node can be created dynamically. A new region of memory can be allocated using the storage management operator `new`. The operator allocates a region of memory and returns a pointer to it. To create space for one `Node` the code is:

```
Node* ptrnode = new Node;
```

Pictorially, we have Figure 13.8. The members of this dynamically created node can be assigned values with expressions of the form:

```
ptrnode->data = .....;
ptrnode->link = .....;
```

or by having a `Node` constructor to do the work.

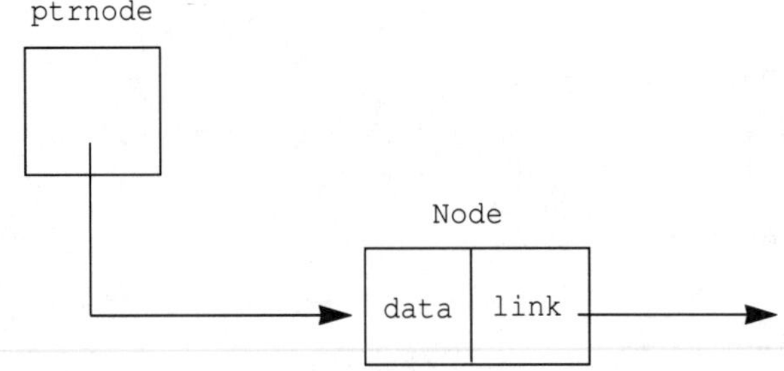

Figure 13.8

We combine this idea and list traversal in Program 13.2. Data to the program consists of a series of positive integers of unknown length and a negative terminator. The program reads the data and prints the values in reverse order. Each data value is entered onto a dynamically created linked list. Since the `head` object provides access to the front of the list, inserting a new node onto the list is most easily achieved at that point. The new node has its data field filled, and its link field is set to the value referenced by `head`, i.e. the first node. The `head` is then set to point to the new node, incorporating it into the front of the list.

PROGRAM 13.2

```
// ———————— FILE: p02.cpp ————————
//
//  Read a series of positive integers terminated
//       with a negative sentinel. Enter each data value
//       on to the front of a dynamically created linked
```

```
//      list. Print the values in reverse order by removing
//      from the front of the list.
//

#include <iostream.h>

class Node {      // singly chained linked list
public:
  Node(int, Node*);       // constructor

  int           data;   // representation
  Node*         link;
};

Node::Node(int aData, Node* aLink)
  : data(aData), link(aLink)
{}

int main()
{
  int           data;
  Node*         head = NULL;          // empty list

  cout << "Enter data:\n";
  cin >> data;
  while(data >= 0){
    Node* ptr = new Node(data, head); // new node on front of list
    head      = ptr;
    cin >> data;
  }

  cout << "\n\nReversed data:\n";
  Node* ptr = head;
  while(ptr != NULL){
    cout << ptr->data << "\n";
    ptr = ptr->link;
  }

  return (0);
}

// ———————— END: p02.cpp ————————
```

13.2 List processing

Classes SequentialList, SortedList and OrderedList are the list processing counterparts of, respectively, SequentialCollection, SortedCollection and OrderedCollection. SequentialList is an abstract class providing the representation structures, operation protocols and implementations for a number of functions. No instances of this class can, of course, be created. Its use is as a base class for the two concrete classes SortedList and OrderedList. Items placed in a SortedList are recorded according to their sort order. Items placed in an

OrderedList are placed according to their positioning. Figure 13.9 is an extract of the original class hierarchy given in Chapter 12 and shows the position of these new classes.

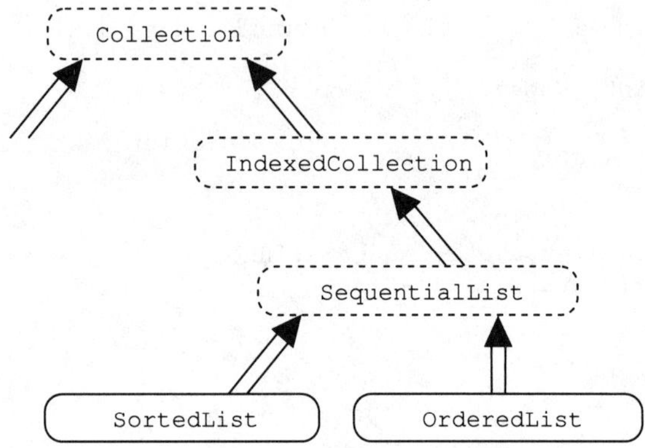

Figure 13.9

Class SortedList, for example, is listed below. In addition to the usual constructors some member functions inherited from ancestor classes have been defined, whilst others such as first, removeFirst, etc., are simply inherited unchanged from the immediate base class SequentialList.

```
// ==============================================================
// File Name       : SORLIST.H
// File Type       : C++ header file for class SORTEDLIST
// Author          : Ken Barclay
// Date Created    : 23 Jun 1993
//
// ---------------------------------------
// Description     : A SortedList contains elements sorted
//                   according to their sort order. When elements
//                   are added or removed from the list, the
//                   collection remains in order. A SortedList is
//                   permitted to contain duplicates.
//
// Base class(es)   : Collection (COL: abstract)
//                          |
//                     IndexedCollection (XCOL: abstract)
//                             |
//                            SequentialList (SEQLIST: abstract)
//                                   |
//                                 SortedList (SORLIST: concrete)
//
// Usage                    :
```

```
// Known Bugs      : None
//
// ----------------------------------------
// Modification History
// Date            :
// Author          :
// Commentary      :
//
// ----------------------------------------
// Version         : 1.01
//
=================================================================

#ifndef SORTEDLIST
  #define SORTEDLIST

  #include "..\ticlass\seqlist.h"

  template <class TYPE>
  class SortedList : public SequentialList<TYPE> {
  public:
    SortedList(UInt size = DEFAULTLEVEL, UInt manage= UNMANAGED);
          // constructor with default settings for size and
                                                 management scheme

    SortedList(const SortedList<TYPE>& aSorted);
          // copy constructor

    ~SortedList(void);
          // destructor

    SortedList<TYPE>&
                operator= (const SortedList<TYPE>& aSorted);

    void        add(const TYPE& object);
          // include given item into the container; duplicates
          // are permitted

    void        remove(const TYPE& object);
          // locate given item in the container and remove it; if
          // the item is absent no action is performed

    Bool        isMember(const TYPE& object) const;
          // is given object present in the container?

    UInt        occurrencesOf(const TYPE& object) const;
          // how many occurrences of given object in the
                                                        container?

    // .....

  };

  #include "..\ticlass\sorlist.t"          // function bodies

#endif // SORTEDLIST

// ================ End of header file SORLIST.H ================
```

Program 13.3 produces a *word concordance* for some input text. The concordance is an alphabetical list of all the distinct words in the text. This is readily achieved using the container class `SortedList`. In the program we demonstrate that the iterator is still valid for this class since it is ultimately derived from class `Collection`.

PROGRAM 13.3

```
// ———————— FILE: p03.cpp ————————

//
// Examine a piece of text and produce a list, in
//      alphabetical order, of all the distinct words
//      which appear in the text.
//

#include <iostream.h>
#include "cstring.h"
#include "sorlist.h"

int main()
{
  SortedList<String>    concordance;
  String         word;

  cout << "Start entering text:\n";
  cin >> word;
  while(word != "ZZZ"){
    concordance.add(*new String(word));
    cin >> word;
  }

  cout << "Word concordance:\n";
  Iterator<String>      iter(concordance);
  while(iter.isExhausted() == FALSE){
    const String& concordanceWord = iter.selection();
    cout << "\t" << concordanceWord << "\n";
    iter.advance();
  }

  return (0);
}

// ———————— END: p03.cpp ————————
```

13.3 List representation

As shown earlier in the chapter, a list of objects may be represented by a singly-chained structure with pointers which follow from the first item through to the last item. The list itself is represented by a pointer to the first item. For example, a list containing the data items L1, L2, ... is shown in Figure 13.10. Then to insert a new item before, say, the node labelled `Lj` (referred to as the *cursor*) the pointer field of the new node links to the cursor node and the predecessor node (`Li`) links to the new item as in Figure 13.11.

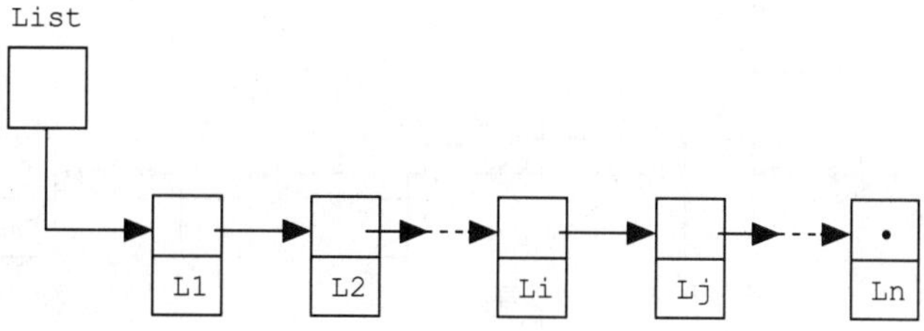

Figure 13.10

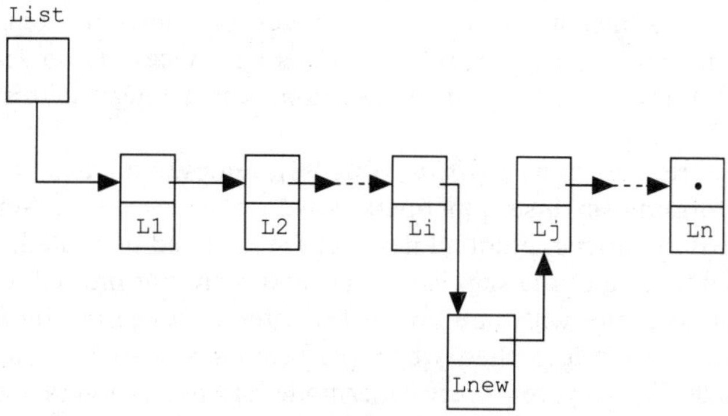

Figure 13.11

Two further variations to this implementation simplifies the processing. Incorporating the list length into the list cell avoids having to repeatedly count the number of list items each time operation `cardinality` is called. For every insertion the counter is incremented. For every deletion the counter is decremented (see Figure 13.12). Inserting a new item on to the front of the list requires special processing of the node and list pointers and is different from that required for an internal insertion point. By introducing a *sentinel node* and connecting the data nodes from this sentinel node we remove this difficulty. The head of the list is a pointer to this sentinel node and the successor of the sentinel is the first item in the list. Inserting and removing at the front of the list then only involves nodes and not the list cell.

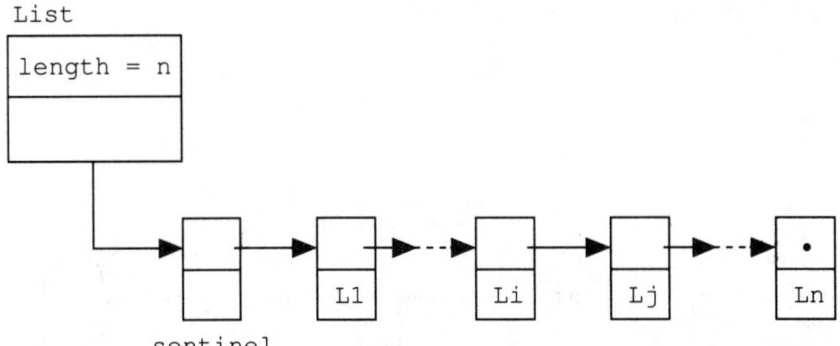

Figure 13.12

The poor performance of `SortedCollection` was alluded to earlier. The problem is having to reposition the members to effect inserting an item in its correct position. Whilst a `SortedList` removes the need for repositioning by simply updating pointers as shown above, it is still necessary to scan the list of items to identify the correct point of insertion. For a long list this could prove quite time consuming.

A data structure, known as a *skip list* [Pug 90], removes the need to scan the full list when performing an insertion operation on a `SortedList`. Similarly, when searching for list membership not all items in the list need be visited.

The essential feature of the skip list is that nodes are not limited to one pointer. Consider a list structure with one forward pointer as suggested by Figure 13.12. For a list with N members then when performing a search we might need to examine N nodes. If, however, every other node had two pointers, one to the next node and one to the node two ahead of it (see Figure 13.13) we have to examine at most N/2+1 nodes.

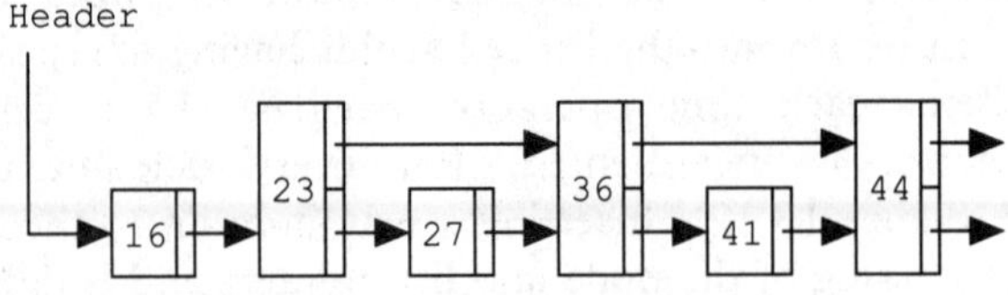

Figure 13.13

Giving every fourth node three pointers, one to the next node, one to the node two ahead, and one to the node four ahead (see Figure 13.14) only requires at most N/4+1 nodes to be examined during a search or insertion operation.

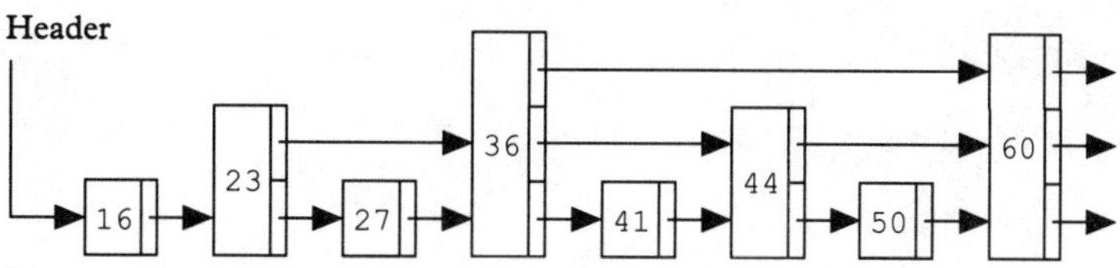

Figure 13.14

In general, a node with k forward pointers is known as a *level k* node. If the nodes are distributed as shown as Figure 13.14, then 50 per cent of the nodes are at level 1, 25 per cent are at level 2, 12.5 per cent are at level 3, etc. A node's ith pointer (i >= 1) points to the next node at level i or higher. The forward pointers of a level k node are numbered 1 to k.

Two special nodes, much like the sentinel node of the previous section, are employed by this structure. One node, labelled NIL, terminates the skip list. It effectively has a data value that exceeds all others in the list. The other node is referred to as the *header*. The first m pointers of the header refer to the other nodes of the list. The value m is the current maximum level of the list (data member `theLevel` in class `SequentialList`, see below). The remaining pointers in the header refer to NIL. The last figure is redrawn as Figure 13.15 and shows the arrangement for the header and NIL nodes.

The *header* node is established at some `maxLevel` number of pointers. This value is given to the `SortedList` constructor. Initially `theLevel` of the list is 1 and all the (`maxLevel`) header pointers refer to NIL.

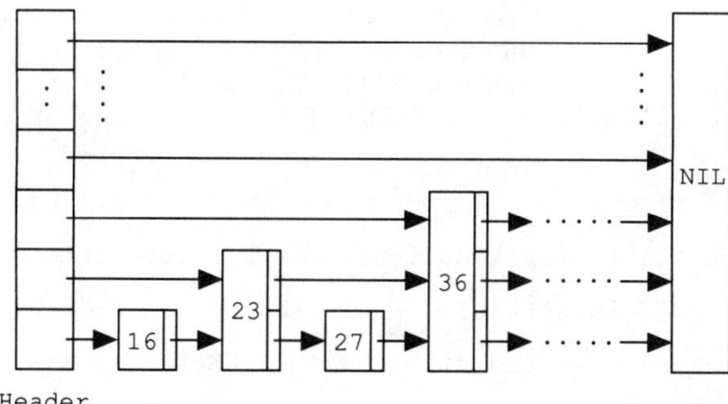

Figure 13.15

The classes used by this structure are given below. The `SortedList` representation consists of a pointer to the dynamically created header node (`theHeader`) and the current level of the list (`theLevel`). This representation structure is inherited from the immediate base class `SequentialList`.

```
// ================================================================
// File Name    : SEQLIST.H
// File Type    : C++ header file for class SEQUENTIALLIST
// Author       : Ken Barclay
// Date Created : 23 Jun 1993
//
// .....

#ifndef SEQUENTIALLIST
  #define SEQUENTIALLIST

  #include "..\ticlass\xcol.h"
  #include "..\ticlass\listnode.h"

  template <class TYPE>
  ABSTRACT class SequentialList : public IndexedCollection<TYPE> {
  public:
    SequentialList(UInt size = DEFAULTLEVEL, UInt manage=
                                                    UNMANAGED);
            // constructor with default settings for size and
               management scheme

    SequentialList(const SequentialList<TYPE>& aSequential);
            // copy constructor

    ~SequentialList(void);
            // destructor

    SequentialList<TYPE>&
         operator= (const SequentialList<TYPE>& aSequential);

    // .....

  protected:
    ListNode<TYPE>* theHeader;           // representation
    UInt            theLevel;            // present level
    UInt            theMaxLevel;         // upper limit
    UInt            theCardinality;      // current position
    UInt            theManagementScheme; // storage arrangements
    ListNode<TYPE>* theIteratorIndex;    // iterator control

    void         freeList(void);
  };

  #include "..\ticlass\seqlist.t"      // function bodies

#endif  // SEQUENTIALLIST

// =============== End of header file SEQLIST.H ================
```

The constructor for `SortedList` properly initializes its data members `theCardinality`, `theLevel` and `theMaxLevel`. Data member `theHeader` refers to a

dynamically allocated `ListNode` (see below) whose pointers refer to the C++ pointer `NULL` (the realization of the NIL node). The number of member pointers of the header is given by the constructor argument `maxLev`. For `maxLev` = 16, the skip list will be capable of containing up to 2^{16} elements.

```
// ==================================================================
// File Name      : LISTNODE.H
// File Type      : C++ header file for class LISTNODE
// Author         : Ken Barclay
// Date Created   : 23 Jun 1993
// ------------------------------------
// Description    : Nodes used in list processing structures.
// Base Class(es) : None
// Usage          :
// Known Bugs     : None
//
// ------------------------------------
// Modification History
// Date           :
// Author         :
// Commentary     :
//
// ------------------------------------
// Version        : 2.0
//
==================================================================

#ifndef LISTNODE
  #define LISTNODE

   #include "..\ticlass\classlib.h"

   template <class TYPE>
   class ListNode {
   public:
     ListNode(UInt aLevel, TYPE* anObject);
     ~ListNode(void);
     const TYPE&          object(void) const;
     ListNode<TYPE>*&     forward(UInt index);
     UInt                 level(void) const;

   private:
     TYPE*                theObject;      // object at node
     ListNode<TYPE>**     theForward;     // pointers to next node
     UInt                 theLevel;       // number of pointers to
                                             next node
   };

   #include "..\ticlass\listnode.t"

#endif   // LISTNODE

// ================== End of header file LISTNODE.H ==============
```

Member function `isMember` is implemented with the following algorithm:

```
nodep = header
FOR i FROM level-1 DOWNTO 0 DO
  nodeq = ith forward pointer of nodep
  WHILE object of nodeq < search object DO
    nodep = nodeq
    nodeq = ith forward pointer of nodep
  ENDWHILE
ENDFOR
nodep = 0th forward pointer of nodep
IF object of nodep = search object
THEN
  return TRUE
ELSE
  return FALSE
ENDIF
```

The procedure consists of advancing through the pointers ensuring that we do not overshoot the search item. If, at the current level of forward pointers, no further progress can be made, then the search continues at the next lower level. When no more progress can be made at the lowest level, then the search object, if it exists, is at the following node. The resulting code for the function is:

```
template <class TYPE>
Bool            SortedList<TYPE>::isMember(const TYPE& obj) const
{
  ListNode<TYPE>* nodep = theHeader;

  for(int i = theLevel-1; i >= 0; i–){
    ListNode<TYPE>* nodeq = nodep->forward(i);
    while(nodeq && nodeq->object() < obj){
      nodep = nodeq;
      nodeq = nodep->forward(i);
    }
  }
  nodep = nodep->forward(0);

  if(nodep == NULL)
    return FALSE;

  if(EQ(nodep->object(), obj))
    return TRUE;
  else
    return FALSE;
}
```

Inserting or deleting an item follows the search algorithm given above. To properly insert a new node an array of node pointers called `update` is maintained. This array of pointers is used to update the pointers of the nodes to the left of the newly inserted node. The code for the member function `add` is as follows:

```
template <class TYPE>
void            SortedList<TYPE>::add(const TYPE& obj)
{
  ListNode<TYPE>** update = new ListNode<TYPE>*[theMaxLevel];
  ListNode<TYPE>* nodep = theHeader;

  for(int i = theLevel-1; i >= 0; i--){
    ListNode<TYPE>* nodeq = nodep->forward(i);
    while(nodeq && nodeq->object() < obj){
      nodep = nodeq;
      nodeq = nodep->forward(i);
    }
    update[i] = nodep;
  }

  nodep = nodep->forward(0);
  if(nodep && nodep != theHeader && EQ(nodep->object(), obj))
    return;

  theCardinality++;
  const UInt newlevel = randomLevel(theMaxLevel);
  if(newlevel > theLevel){
    for(i = theLevel; i < newlevel; i++)
      update[i] = theHeader;
    theLevel = newlevel;
  }

  TYPE*  newObject = new TYPE(obj);

  nodep = new ListNode<TYPE>(newlevel, newObject);
  for(i = 0; i < newlevel; i++){
    ListNode<TYPE>* updatep = update[i];
    nodep->forward(i) = updatep->forward(i);
    updatep->forward(i) = nodep;
  }

  delete update;
}
```

The new node inserted into the list is at level `newlevel` which is an arbitrary value not exceeding `maxLevel`. This arbitrary value is produced from the function `randomLevel`, based on the library function `rand` (see Appendix F.3).

An `OrderedList` operates a specialized version of class `SequentialList`. The primary distinction is the way each `ListNode` is established through its constructor call with only one forward pointer, effectively implementing the linear linked list discussed earlier. Like the `SortedList` the full representation details are inherited from the base class `SequentialList`. Most of the functionality of the class such as the operations `first`, `last`, `removeFirst` and `removeLast` are defined in the base class and only a few functions are redefined.

13.4 Summary

1. Static data objects are used to build dynamic data structures. These static objects, or nodes, contain pointers to other such nodes and are known as self referential structures. The nature of the linkages reflects the underlying information structure.

2. A linear linked list is a dynamic data structure composed of one or more nodes chained together by single pointers.

3. A `OrderedList` has the same protocol as an `OrderedCollection`. Items are inserted and deleted from an `OrderedList` by updating the links.

4. A `SortedList` is implemented using skip lists. Here, nodes are not restricted to one or two links. Such structures give better performance for insertion, deletion and search operations.

13.5 Exercises

1. Develop the member functions:

```
void        reverse(void);
void        sort(void);
```

   for the class `OrderedList`.

2. Develop the class `KeySortedList` derived from class `SortedList` in the manner of Exercise 10 from Chapter 12.

3. Prepare a class `Student` outlined as follows:

```
class Student {
public:
  Student(const String& aName, UInt anAge);
  // .....
private:
  String    theName;
  UInt      theAge;
  // .....
};
```

   Program an application to maintain two `KeySortedLists` one based on the student name and one the student age.

4. **Develop classes `Stack` and `Queue` using an `OrderedList` representation.**

5. **Develop the member function `OrderedList::append` which incorporates the members of the `OrderedList` argument onto the `OrderedList` object.**

14

More on Functions

Chapters 5 and 7 gave a comprehensive coverage of functions, and program structure. In this section we consider three further aspects of functions: recursive functions, that is functions that call themselves either directly or indirectly; function pointers; and functions with a variable number of arguments.

14.1 Recursive functions

Any function may invoke any other function, as we have already seen. Programmers exploit this facility to build programs constructed hierarchically, in which some function invokes sub-functions F1, F2,..... to perform subsidiary tasks; these sub-functions in turn invoke further sub-functions G1, G2,..... to perform simpler tasks; and so on.

This is not the only way of exploiting the use of functions. In particular, a function may call or invoke itself. Such a function is said to be *recursive.* Many programming problems have solutions which are expressible directly or indirectly through recursion. The ability to map these solutions onto recursive functions lead to elegant and natural implementations.

Recursion is commonly used in applications in which the solution can be expressed in terms of successively applying the same solution to subsets of the problem. Common applications involve the searching and sorting of recursively defined data structures. A recursive solution is frequently an alternative to using iteration.

To illustrate, consider a function to evaluate the factorial of a number. The factorial of a positive integer `n`, written `n!`, is defined as the product of the successive integers `1` through `n` inclusive. The factorial of zero is treated as a special case and is defined equal to `1`. So:

```
n! = n * (n-1) * (n-2) * ..... * 3 * 2 * 1        for n >= 1
```

and

```
0! = 1
```

It follows that:

```
5! = 5 * 4 * 3 * 2 * 1 = 120
```

The iterative solution is:

```
long int factorial(int n)
{
  if(n == 0)
    return (1L);
  else {
    long int product = 1L;
    for(int k = n; k > 0; k—)
      product *= k;
    return (product);
  }
}
```

Customarily, the mathematical definition of factorial is given recursively. We observe that:

```
n! = n * (n-1) * (n-2) * ..... * 3 * 2 * 1
```

which we can group as:

```
n! = n * [(n-1) * (n-2) * ..... * 3 * 2 * 1]
```

The bracketed group is, of course, the definition for `(n-1)!` Thus the recursive definition is:

```
n! = n*(n-1)!
```

with the special case (the so called *base case*):

```
0! = 1
```

We can now develop a function to calculate the factorial of an integer `n` according to this recursive definition. Such a function is illustrated in Program 14.1.

PROGRAM 14.1

```
// ——————— FILE: p01.cpp ———————

//
//  Tables of factorials for 0, 1, 2, ..... , 10. The
//      factorials are determined by a recursive function.
//

#include <iostream.h>
#include <iomanip.h>

int main()
{
  long int factorial(int);
  for(int j = 0; j <= 10; j++)
```

```
    cout << setw(2) << j << "! is " << factorial(j) << "\n";
  return (0);
}

long int factorial(int n)
{
  if(n == 0)
    return (1L);
  else
    return (n * factorial(n-1));
}

// ———————— END: p01.cpp ————————
```

The program's output is:

```
 0! is 1
 1! is 1
 2! is 2
 3! is 6
 4! is 24
 5! is 120
 6! is 720
 7! is 5040
 8! is 40320
 9! is 362880
10! is 3628800
```

The function `factorial` is recursive since it includes a call to itself. Let us see what happens in the case where the function is called to calculate the factorial of `5`, for example. When the function is entered, the formal parameter `n` is set to `5`. The conditional if statement determines that this `n` is not zero, and returns with the value obtained by evaluating `n * factorial(n-1)` with `n = 5`, namely:

```
5 * factorial(4)
```

The expression specifies that the `factorial` function is to be called again, this time to obtain `factorial(4)`. The multiplication of `5` by this value is left pending while `factorial(4)` is computed.

We call the `factorial` function again. This time, the actual argument is `4`. Each time any C++ function is called it is allocated its own set of automatic variables and formal parameters with which to work. This applies equally to recursive or non-recursive functions. Therefore, the formal argument `n` that exists when the `factorial` function is called to calculate the factorial of `4` is distinct from that used in the first call to calculate the factorial of `5`.

With `n = 4` this time, the function executes the return with the expression:

```
4 * factorial (3)
```

Once again, the multiplication by `4` is left pending while the `factorial` function is called to calculate the factorial of `3`. The process continues in this manner until formal argument `n` has value `0`. The situation is then as described by Table 14.1.

Table 14.1

factorial(n)	return (n * factorial(n-1))
5	5 * factorial (4) = 5 * ?
4	4 * factorial (3) = 4 * ?
3	3 * factorial (2) = 3 * ?
2	2 * factorial (1) = 2 * ?
1	1 * factorial (0) = 1 * ?

When the formal argument `n` is reduced to zero, the conditional if statement causes an immediate return with `long` value `1`. The recursive descent can now start to unwind and all the pending multiplications can be evaluated in reverse order. Repeating the above table, but in reverse sequence, we obtain Table 14.2.

Table 14.2

factorial (n)	return (n * factorial (n-1))
1	1 * factorial (0) = 1 * 1 = 1
2	2 * factorial (1) = 2 * 1 = 2
3	3 * factorial (2) = 3 * 2 = 6
4	4 * factorial (3) = 4 * 6 = 24
5	5 * factorial (4) = 5 * 24 = 120

Lest it be argued that this last example is an artificial example, consider the *Euclidean algorithm* to determine the highest common factor HCF of two positive integers `n` and `m`. The procedure can be written:

```
IF m > n
THEN HCF(m, n)
ELSE IF m = 0
  THEN n
  ELSE HCF(m, remainder when n is divided by m)
  ENDIF
ENDIF
```

The recursive function can be written directly from the definition:

```
int hcf(int n, int m)
{
  if(m > n)
    return (hcf(m,n));
  else if(m == 0)
    return (n);
  else
    return (hcf(m, n % m));
}
```

On the other hand, the non-recursive form requires a certain amount of programmer skill. The implementation is also much less obvious:

```
int hcf(int n, int m)
{
  if(m > n)
  {
    int temp = m;
    m = n;
    n = temp;
  }

  while(n % m ! = 0){
    int temp = m;
    m = n % m;
    n = temp;
  }

  return (m);
}
```

It is also permissible to write a function which calls a second function which in turn calls the original function. This is known as *indirect recursion* and involves a circle of function calls. For example, function `A` calls function `B`, `B` calls `C`, and `C` calls `A` again.

Recursion is not always the most efficient solution to a problem. Many problems which can be solved recursively can also be solved using iteration, as shown above. The solution may be less elegant but can be more efficient in terms of program execution time and memory requirements. For each recursive function call a separate region of memory is established to hold the values of the arguments and local variables. Hence, recursive algorithms are expensive in terms of memory space utilization. Further, for each recursive call, processor time is used to pass function arguments, establish the new memory area for that call, and to return its result upon completion.

The most persuasive argument in support of recursive functions is that they reflect recursively defined data structures and algorithms which are defined recursively. Further, some recursive algorithms are very difficult to construct iteratively.

14.2 Pointers to functions

Functions in C++ have been introduced in our program code in two ways: function definitions and function prototype declarations. For example, `square` is a function definition:

```
int square(int x)
{
  return x * x;
}
```

whilst a prototype declaration for it might appear as in:

```
int square(int);
```

In C++ we may also define *pointers to functions* – variables which effectively hold the address of a function's executable code. To declare such a pointer we give the functions full signature. In the definition:

```
int  (*fp)(int);
```

the identifier `fp` is declared as a 'pointer to a function returning an `int` with an `int` argument'. We may then assign to `fp` any such function. The latter is delivered by the name of a suitably declared function. For example:

```
fp = square;
```

Variable `fp` is a pointer to the function object known in the program as `square`. The function call:

```
y = square(x);
```

can also be achieved indirectly with the indirection operator applied to an expression of type 'pointer to function returning `int` with an `int` argument'. An equivalent call is:

```
y = (*fp)(x);
```

The use of `fp` in this example must coincide fully with its definition. Since `fp` is a function pointer, then application of the indirection operator dereferences the pointer. Hence `*fp` is the function itself. In the same way that the syntax `abs(x)` is a function call then so too is `(*fp)(x)` since `*fp` is the function. Note that the parentheses are necessary for without them `*fp(x)` would be interpreted as a call to a function named `fp` whose return value is expected to be a pointer which is subsequently dereferenced.

Since this notation is unwieldy, a function call of the form introduced in Chapter 5 is permitted. The designated function may be a function name or an identifier which is a pointer to a function. Hence we might present the last statement more clearly as:

```
y = fp(x);
```

Program 14.2 illustrates the use of this construct. The pointer to function variable `func` is first assigned to the function object `square` which in turn is called indirectly to determine 5 squared. The process is then repeated using the function `cube`.

PROGRAM 14.2

```
// ———————— FILE: p02.cpp ————————

//
```

```
//  Determine the square and the cube of the value 5.
//      The squaring and cubing functions are called
//      through indirect function calls.
//
#include <iostream.h>

int       square(int);   // prototype declarations
int       cube(int);

int main()
{
  int y, x = 5;
  int (*func)(int);               // pointer to function

  func = square;                  // not a call to square !!
  y = func(x);                    // indirect call on square
  cout << "Square of " << x << " is " << y << "\n";

  func = cube;
  y = func(x);
  cout << "Cube of " << x << " is " << y << "\n";
  return (0);
}

int square(int x)
{
  return (x * x);
}

int cube(int x)
{
  return (x * x * x);
}

//  ———————— END: p02.cpp ————————
```

Whilst a default argument means that an actual argument may be omitted, the argument type is still part of the function declaration. Hence:

```
void f(int, int = 0);
void (*pf)(int, int) = f;       // ok
void (*qf)(int) = f;            // error
```

The syntax of the C++ language in handling function pointers makes the program text very difficult to read. The `typedef` statement can improve matters by introducing a suitable type name. For example, the definition:

```
typedef int         (*Pfi)(int, float);
```

introduces `Pfi` as a pointer to a function returning an `int` with an `int` and a `float` argument. The declaration for a variable of this type is then:

```
Pfi         func;
```

14.3 Functions as arguments

We have written programs in which one function invokes another. Indeed, without this facility, large programs would be very difficult to write. We sometimes encounter circumstances in which we wish to write a function that will invoke another function whose effect is not determined until program execution time. This is achieved by passing a pointer to a function as a formal *function argument*. The specification for this formal argument indicates a function pointer. For example, the definition:

```
void ppp( ....., int (*f)(int), .....)
{
  int x, y;
//  .....
  y = f(x);
//  .....
}
```

introduces a function `ppp` with a formal function argument `f` which returns an `int` and has an `int` argument. Within the body of `ppp`, `f` is used like any other pointer to a function returning an `int`. When the function `ppp` is called, the actual parameter corresponding to `f` must be the identifier of a function with the same argument specifications and the same result type. A legal call to `ppp` would be:

```
ppp( ....., square, .....);
```

with function `square` as defined in the previous section.

Consider the function `tabulate` which generates a succession of values for `x`, as determined by the arguments `lower`, `upper` and `increment`, and to evaluate and print `f(x)`. Function `tabulate` takes `f` as a function argument. The function definition is:

```
void tabulate(double (*f)(double),
          double lower, double upper, double increment)
{
  double x;

  for(x = lower; x <= upper + 0.5 * increment; x += increment)
    cout << x << "  " << f(x) << "\n";
}
```

The function call:

```
tabulate(f1, 0.0, 1.0, 0.1);
```

would cause the values of `x` and `f1(x)` to be tabulated for `x` in the range `0.0` to `1.0` at intervals of 0.1. Function `f1` should possess one `double` argument and return a value of type `double`. Program 14.3 employs function `tabulate` to display `x` and `x*x` for `x` = `0.0, 0.1, 0.2, ....., 2.0`.

PROGRAM 14.3

```
// ——————— FILE: p03.cpp ———————
//
// Demonstration of a pointer to function argument.
//     A series of values are tabulated for some
//     given function. The tabulation function
//     receives the function as one of its arguments.
//

#include <iostream.h>

                                // prototypes:
double square(double);
void   tabulate(double (*)(double), double, double, double);

int main()
{
  tabulate(square, 0.0, 2.0, 0.1);
  return (0);
}

void tabulate(double  (*f)(double),
  double lower, double upper, double increment)
{
  double x;

  for(x = lower; x <= upper + 0.5 * increment; x += increment)
    cout << x << " " << f(x) << "\n";
}
double square(double x)
{
  return (x * x);
}

// ——————— END: p03.cpp ———————
```

14.4 Functions with variable number of arguments

All the functions we have introduced have had a fixed number of arguments. Certain standard library functions can, however, be called with a variable number of arguments. The C++ language provides a set of routines to implement such *variadic functions*. The header `<stdarg.h>` provides facilities for stepping through the list of arguments when they are of unknown number and type.

The following example shows the definition and prototype for such a function.

```
int sum(int, ...);              // prototype

int sum(int number, ...)        // definition
```

```
{
  //.....
}
```

The ellipsis '...' appearing at the end of the argument list indicates that the function can take a variable number of arguments. To access the arguments within the function definition, a new type called `va_list`, and three functions (macros) that operate on objects of this type called `va_start`, `va_arg` and `va_end` are introduced from the header `<stdarg.h>`.

The type `va_list` is a typedef declared in `<stdarg.h>`. Its actual type is machine dependent but is commonly an array or a pointer. We declare a variable of this type in the usual way:

```
va_list   args;
```

Before any attempt is made to access a variable argument list, `va_start` must be called. It is effectively defined as:

```
void va_start(va_list ap, lastarg);
```

The macro initializes `ap` to point to the first unnamed argument. The initialization is performed by naming the last named argument appearing in the function's formal argument list. Hence, we might have, for function `sum`:

```
va_start(args, number);
```

Note that there must be at least one named argument in the function definition.

Following initialization, the actual arguments can be accessed sequentially by the `va_arg` macro. It is defined as:

```
type va_arg(va_list ap, type);
```

Note how the type returned by this 'function' is determined by its second argument. No real function could be defined this way. `va_arg` is therefore a macro. Each macro call delivers the next actual argument from the list of actual arguments as a value of the specified type. For example, to obtain the next argument as an `int`, we write:

```
int myint = va_arg(args, int);
```

Finally, when all the arguments have been processed, the function `va_end` should be called. It is effectively defined as:

```
void va_end(va_list ap);
```

The function effectively implements a clean-up process. It is obligatory that this function be called to ensure that the defined function performs a normal return.

We illustrate these issues with Program 14.4, which completes function `sum` to form the sum of the variable number of integer arguments if the first named argument gives the number of arguments following.

PROGRAM 14.4

```
// ———————— FILE: p04.cpp ————————
//
// Form the sum of a variable number of integer
//      values presented as arguments to a variadic
//      function.
//

#include <iostream.h>
#include <stdarg.h>

int main()
{
  int sum(int, ...);             // prototype

  cout << "Sum of 10, 20, 30 and 40 is "
       << sum(4, 10, 20, 30, 40) << "\n";
  return (0);
}

int sum(int number, ...)
{
  va_list args;          // list of arguments
  int           arg;             // individual argument
  int           k, total = 0;

  va_start(args, number);
  for(k = 0; k < number; k++){
    arg = va_arg(args, int);
    total += arg;
  }
  va_end(args);
  return total;
}
// ———————— END: p04.cpp ————————
```

Note that the macro `va_arg` can only operate correctly if the type argument can be converted to a pointer to such an object by simply appending a pointer operator symbol `'*'`. Simple types such as `int`, `char` and `Date` work without difficulty. If the argument is an array object say, `int[]`, then the correct argument type is `int*` and not `int[]`, since the latter is not a valid pointer type when we attach the pointer operator.

CASE STUDY 14.1
Quicksort

Of all the various sorting techniques, *quicksort* is perhaps the most widely used internal sort. An internal sort is one in which all the data to be sorted is held in primary memory.

Let us suppose that we want to sort an array of integers of size `n` into ascending order. The essential characteristic of the quicksort algorithm is that it partitions the original array by rearranging it into groups. The first group contains those elements less than some arbitrarily chosen value from the set, and the second group contains those elements greater than or equal to the value. The chosen value is known as the *pivot* element. Once the array has been rearranged with respect to the pivot, the same partitioning is then applied to each of the two subsets. When all subsets have been partitioned, the original array is sorted. Since the partitioning is applied in turn to the subsets, quicksort is best described recursively.

Suppose we wish to sort the elements `a[lo], a[lo+1], ..... , a[hi]` of the integer array `a` into ascending order. We denote this task by:

```
rquick(a, lo, hi)
```

If, by some means, we are able to identify the pivotal element `a[piv]` and perform the rearrangement, then the problem divides into:

```
IF lo < hi
THEN
  partition the elements a[lo], ....., a[hi] so that
  a[lo], a[lo+1], ....., a[piv-1] < a[piv] <= a[piv+1],
  ....., a[hi], where lo <= piv <= hi
  rquick (a, lo, piv-1)
  rquick (a, piv+1, hi)
ENDIF
```

Ideally, the pivot should be chosen so that at each step the array is partitioned into two sets with equal (or nearly equal) numbers of elements. This would then minimize the total amount of work performed by the quicksort algorithm. Since we do not know in advance what this value should be, we select for the pivot the first value that will provide a partition. Assuming that the array elements are randomly distributed, this is equivalent to choosing the pivot value randomly. We select as the pivot element the last in the set, `a[hi]`. The elements are rearranged entirely within the subset of `a` between `a[lo]` and `a[hi]`. An outline of the partitioning algorithm is:

```
low = lo
high = hi
pivot = a[hi]
REPEAT
  increase low until low >= high or a[low] > pivot
  decrease high until high <= low or a[high] < pivot
  IF low < high
  THEN
    exchange a[low] and a[high]
  ENDIF
UNTIL low >= high
exchange a[low] and a[hi]
```

Putting these elements together we arrive at a program to read a series of integer values, to sort them into ascending order using the quicksort algorithm, and then to print the sorted list. The data is preceded by an integer N representing the number of data items. The program is subdivided into three principal functions performing input, sorting and output respectively.

```
//———————— FILE: case01.cpp ————————-
//
//  Sort a sequence of values using the quicksort
//     algorithm. The set of data values is preceded
//     by the integer N representing the number of items.
//

#include <iostream.h>

const int MAXTABLE      = 1000;

template <class TYPE>
void     swap(TYPE& data1, TYPE& data2)
{
  TYPE temp = data1;
  data1 = data2;
  data2 = temp;
}

template <class TYPE>                    // prototype declarations
void    readInput(TYPE*, int*, int);

template <class TYPE>
void     writeOutput(TYPE*, int);

template <class TYPE>
void     quickSort(TYPE*, int);

template <class TYPE>
void     rQuick(TYPE*, int, int);

int main()
{
  int table[MAXTABLE];                   // data items
  int number;                            // number of values

  readInput(table, &number, (int)MAXTABLE);// read the data
  if(number <= MAXTABLE){                // check sizes
    quickSort(table, number);            // apply algorithm
    writeOutput(table, number);          // print results
  } else
    cout << "Too many data items\n";
  return (0);
}

template <class TYPE>
void readInput(TYPE* table, int* number, int limit)
{
```

```
  cout << "Enter the number of data values: ";
  cin >> *number;
  if(*number > limit)
    return;
  cout << "Enter the data values:\n";
  for(int k = 0; k < *number; k++)
    cin >> table[k];
}

template <class TYPE>
void writeOutput(TYPE* table, int number)
{
  cout << "Sorted values:\n";
  for(int k = 0; k < number; k++)
   cout << table[k] << "\n";
}

template <class TYPE>
void quickSort(TYPE* table, int number)
{
  rQuick(table, 0, number-1);          // recursive quicksort
}

template <class TYPE>
void rQuick(TYPE* table, int lo, int hi)
{
  int     low, high;
  TYPE    pivot;

  low = lo;
  high = hi;
  if(low < high){
    pivot = table[high];
    do {
      while(low < high && (table[low] <= pivot))
        low++;
      while(high > low && (pivot <= table[high]))
        high-;
      if(low < high)                   // out of order pair
        swap(table[low], table[high]);
    } while (low < high);
    swap(table[low], table[hi]);     // move pivot to low
    rQuick(table, lo, low-1);
    rQuick(table, low+1, hi);
  }
}

// ———————— END: case01.cpp ————————-
```

CASE STUDY 14.2
Higher order functions

We have shown how a function can be the argument to another function. Such functions are sometimes described as *higher order functions* [Har88]. They make it possible to define very general functions that are useful in a variety of applications. Because of their nature they can appear highly abstract – yet this quality embodies them with their general applicability. In some cases they may not prove as efficient as some alternate implementations and so they may find initial use in a program prototype.

Consider the Doctor/Patient model from Case Study 12.2. To produce the desired report we first had to determine the average number of visits made by each patient and involved totalling the visits of all the patients. If we had an `OrderedList<int>` of the visits made by each patient, then finding the total might be readily implemented with the function `sum`:

```
template <class ITEMTYPE, class SUMTYPE>
SUMTYPE
  sum(const OrderedList<ITEMTYPE>& list, const SUMTYPE& initial)
{
  SUMTYPE total = initial;
  Iterator<ITEMTYPE>    iter(list);

  while(iter.isExhausted() == FALSE){
    const ITEMTYPE& listItem = iter.selection();
    total += listItem;
    iter.advance();
  }

  return total;
}
```

Note how the `SUMTYPE` may differ from the `ITEMTYPE` if, for example, we need to form a total of `int`s producing a `long`.

Now an `OrderedList<int>` containing the visits by each patient might be produced in the usual way. However, at a more abstract level, what we are actually trying to achieve is a mapping between an `OrderedList<Patient>` and an `OrderedList<int>` where the latter maps out from each Patient the visits made by that instance. If we call this process `map`, then we convert one list into another in which we 'map out' some component of each item in the first list into the second list:

```
template <class ITEMTYPE, class RESULTTYPE>
OrderedList<RESULTTYPE>&
  map(OrderedList<ITEMTYPE>& list,
        RESULTTYPE (*function)(const ITEMTYPE&))
{
  OrderedList<RESULTTYPE>*     result = new
          OrderedList<RESULTTYPE>(MANAGED);
```

```
    Iterator<ITEMTYPE>          iter(list);

    while(iter.isExhausted() == FALSE){
      const ITEMTYPE&     listItem       = iter.selection();
      const RESULTTYPE    resultListItem= function(listItem);
      result->addLast(*new RESULTTYPE(resultListItem));
      iter.advance();
    }

    return *result;
  }
```

Here, argument `function` represents the mapping scheme. It is presented as a function pointer and applies itself to `ITEMTYPE` objects producing `RESULTTYPE` values. In the function body for `map`, the iteration loop fetches each item from the argument list, applies `function` to it, and puts the outcome into a `result` list.

Note how this `map` function returns not the `OrderedList` itself which would be an expensive copying process, but a reference to one created on the heap. Function `map` then expects the application to be responsible for its deletion.

Function `map` is an example of a higher order function. Its usefulness derives from its generality. Given a list of some type (`ITEMTYPE`), and a function for converting an `ITEMTYPE` into a `RESULTTYPE` we can produce a list of `RESULTTYPE` objects. For example, given the function `getVisits` which extracts the number of visits made by a Patient:

```
int       getVisits(const Patient& aPatient)
          { return aPatient.visits(); }
```

then we may find this list of visits by:

```
OrderedList<Patient>&   thePatients = thePatientsList;
OrderedList<int>& patientVisits = map(thePatients, getVisits);
```

and the average number of visits by:

```
long      totalVisits = sum(patientVisits, 0L);
double    meanVisits = double(totalVisits) /
          patientVisits.cardinality();

delete &patientVisits;
```

Producing a list of these patients with above average visits to the doctor now involves filtering out from the patient list those which exceed the criteria. The higher order function `filter` achieves this effect:

```
template <class ITEMTYPE, class CONDITIONTYPE>
OrderedList<ITEMTYPE>&
  filter(const OrderedList<ITEMTYPE>& list,
      Bool (*comparison)(const ITEMTYPE&, const CONDITIONTYPE&),
                const CONDITIONTYPE& condition)
{
```

```
  OrderedList<ITEMTYPE>*       result = new
    OrderedList<ITEMTYPE>(MANAGED);
  Iterator<ITEMTYPE>           iter(list);

  while(iter.isExhausted() == FALSE){
    const ITEMTYPE& listItem = iter.selection();
    if(comparison(listItem, condition) == TRUE)
      result->addLast(*new ITEMTYPE(listItem));
    iter.advance();
  }

  return *result;
}
```

Given a list of ITEMTYPE objects, function filter produces a new list with the same type of objects but only those which fit some comparison. The iteration loop fetches each item from the argument list and if it meets the criteria puts it into the result list.

The comparison function we require for the problem compares the visits for each Patient argument against the limit, and returns TRUE if the former exceeds the latter:

```
Bool      isUpper(const Patient& aPatient, const double& aLimit)
          { return Bool(aPatient.visits() > aLimit); }
```

Member function printUpper from class Doctor would then appear as:

```
void      Doctor::printUpper(double limit) const
{
  OrderedList<Patient>& thePatients = thePatientsList;
  OrderedList<Patient>& theUpperPatients = filter(thePatients,
                                                  isUpper, limit);

  cout << "Doctor: " << theName << "\n";

  Iterator<Patient>     iter(theUpperPatients);
  while(iter.isExhausted() == FALSE){
    const Patient& patient = iter.selection();
    cout << "\t" << patient.name() << ", " << patient.visits()
      << "\n";
    iter.advance();
  }

  delete &theUpperPatients;
}
```

14.5 Summary

1. Recursion is a powerful tool for solving particular categories of problems. Using recursion can result in an elegant and natural program solution.

2. A recursive function either calls itself directly or indirectly. Recursion usually consists of a general case and one or more base cases. It is vital in the program implementation that the recursive function terminate through its base conditions.

3. Recursive functions can be written in an equivalent iterative form. Due to system overheads, a recursive function may be less efficient than the iterative version.

4. The C++ language supports the type 'pointer to function returning .....' which can be used as the element type of an array, as a function argument, etc. Functions as arguments are useful for constructing general purpose functions whose effect is not determined until execution time.

5. Where it is impossible to list the type and number of all the arguments to a function, the ellipsis '...' can be specified in the function signature. Its presence informs the compiler that zero or more arguments may follow and that their types are unknown.

14.6 Exercises

1. Prepare a recursive function to form the sum of the first `n` positive integers using the recursive definition:

   ```
   sum(n)  = n + sum(n-1)
   ```

   What is the base case for this definition?

2. The following equations define the Fibonacci sequence of numbers:

   ```
   Fib(1)  = 1
   Fib(2)  = 1
   Fib(n)  = Fib(n-1) + Fib(n-2)          for n > 2
   ```

   Produce a recursive C++ function directly from these definitions.

3. Write a recursive function to calculate values of Ackermann's function, `Ack(m, n)`, defined for `m >= 0` and `n >= 0` by:

   ```
   Ack(0, n)  = n + 1
   Ack(m, 0)  = Ack(m-1, 1)
   Ack(m, n)  = Ack(m - 1, Ack(m, n - 1))
                for m > 0 and n > 0
   ```

   What is the value for `Ack(3, 2)`?

4. Write a function, `digit(n, k)`, that returns the value of the `kth` digit from the right of the number `n`. For example:

```
digit(234567, 2)  = 6
digit(1234, 7)    = 0
```

5. Write a function, `count(n, k)`, that returns a count of the number of occurrences of the digit `k` in the number `n`. For example:

```
count(4214, 4) = 2
count(73, 5)   = 0
```

6. Write a function, `reverse(n)`, that returns a number made up of the digits of the number `n` reversed. For example:

```
reverse(1234)  = 4321
reverse(222)   = 222
```

7. A game called the Tower of Hanoi consists of a platform carrying three posts and a number of discs of different size. The object of the game is to move a tower of discs, arranged as a pyramid, from the left hand rod to the right hand rod using the middle rod. The conditions of the game are that only one disc may be moved at a time, and that at no stage may a larger disc rest on a smaller disc.

   Develop a program to read an integer representing the number of discs in the initial pyramid and to trace the steps involved in moving the discs to the target rod.

8. Provide template functions to find the minimum and maximum values for its two arguments.

9. Present an implementation for `OrderedList<TYPE>::sort(void)` using the quicksort algorithm.

10. The function `forAll` ensures all the members of the `OrderedList` argument meet some condition:

```
template <class ITEMTYPE, class CONDITIONTYPE>
Bool  forAll(const OrderedList<ITEMTYPE>& list,
           Bool (*comparison)(const ITEMTYPE&, const
             CONDITIONTYPE&),
                   const CONDITIONTYPE& condition)
{
  Iterator<ITEMTYPE>       iter(list);

  while(iter.isExhausted() == FALSE){
    const ITEMTYPE& listItem     = iter.selection();
    if(comparison(listItem, condition) == FALSE)
      return FALSE;
    iter.advance();
  }
```

```
    return TRUE;
  }
```

Develop its counterpart `thereExists` which returns `TRUE` if any one member of the `OrderedList` satisfies the given condition.

In Case Study 14.2 use these functions to determine if all patients have made at least one visit, and if there are any patients with over 10 visits.

11. Develop the function length to count the number of items in an `OrderedList` using the `map` and `sum` functions presented in Case Study 14.2.

12. A very general and adaptable function is `reduce`:

```
template <class ITEMTYPE, class RESULTTYPE>
RESULTTYPE  reduce(OrderedList<ITEMTYPE>& list,
                 RESULTTYPE (*function)(const ITEMTYPE&,
                 const RESULTTYPE&),
                 const RESULTTYPE& identity)
{
  if(list.isEmpty() == TRUE)
    return identity;
  else {
    ITEMTYPE firstItem = list.first();
    list.removeFirst();
    return function(firstItem, reduce(list, function,
                                              identity));
  }
}
```

Describe its behaviour then develop a version of `sum` using this function.

13. Prepare a version of the overloaded `operator==` for two `OrderedLists`:

```
template <class TYPE>
Bool    operator== (const OrderedList<TYPE>&,
const   OrderedList<TYPE>&);
```

and a function to `reverse` a list:

```
template <class TYPE>
OrderedList<TYPE>&          reverse(const OrderedList<TYPE>&);
```

then use them both to develop `isPalindromic` which determines if two `String` lists are palindromic:

```
Bool   isPalindromic(const OrderedList<String>&,
const  OrderedList<String>&);
```

15

Stream Input/Output

The programs we have studied have all produced some output, and in the majority of cases accepted some input. This has been achieved by using the standard input and standard output *streams*. These simple programs are unrepresentative of the majority of computer programs. Many applications involve the storage of permanent data. To retain the data between program executions, they are held in computer *files* on some auxiliary storage medium such as magnetic disc. In this chapter we consider the standard streams and other file streams in some detail.

The C++ input/output library is composed of a series of classes formed into a class hierarchy. The essential elements of this hierarchy are given in Fig. 15.1. Input and output operations are provided by the `istream` (input stream) and `ostream` (output stream) classes. Both these classes are derived from the base class `ios` which provides the fundamental functionality associated with input/output, for example, error control and the representation of numbers.

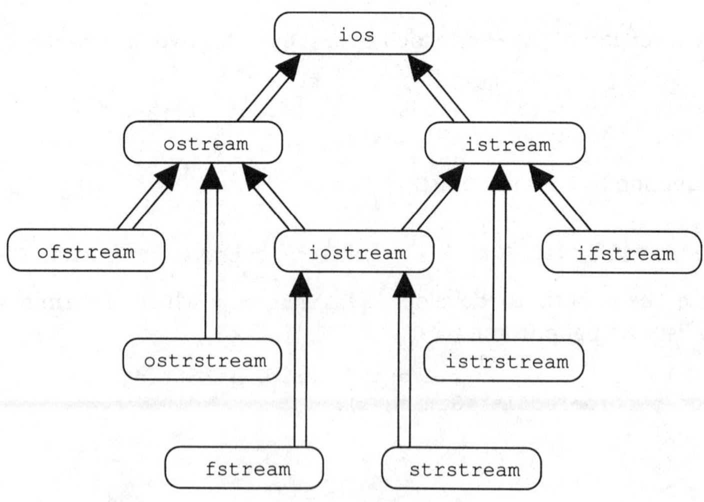

Figure 15.1

Class `ifstream` is derived from class `istream` and associates a file with the program for data input. Similarly, class `ofstream` is derived from class `ostream` to permit a program to produce output to a file. Using the inheritance mechanism these two classes inherit much of their functionality from their immediate base classes.

Class `iostream` is derived from both `istream` and `ostream`. This class is a mixture of its two base classes permitting both input and output on a stream. Figure 15.1 is not a simple class hierarchy diagram because of the use of *multiple inheritance*. Here class `iostream` inherits functionality from two base classes. We shall discuss this subject in a later chapter.

Class `fstream` is derived immediately from class `iostream` supporting both input and output on a file.

The `iostream` library effectively supports reading and writing a sequence of characters to and from a stream. By the same token, class `strstream` allows one to read/write a sequence of characters to/from a character array. Specifically, class `istrstream` reads characters from an array while class `ostrstream` writes characters to an array.

In Chapter 4 we outlined simple input/output through the extraction (>>) and insertion (<<) operators. For example:

```
cout << "Hello\n";
```

From Chapter 10 we have that the insertion operator is an operator defined in class `ostream` and overloaded for all the fundamental types:

```
class ostream {
public:
  ostream&      operator<< (char*);      // strings
  ostream&      operator<< (char);
  ostream&      operator<< (int);
  ostream&      operator<< (long);
  ostream&      operator<< (double);
  // .....
  ostream&      put(char);
  // .....
};
```

Hence we may have:

```
cout << "Hello";          // first operator<< version
cout << 123;              // third operator<< version
```

where we now recognize that `cout` is an instance of the class `ostream`.

Similarly, the extraction operator is overloaded in class `istream` for input of the standard types:

```
class istream {
public:
  istream&      operator>> (char*);  // string
  istream&      operator>> (char&);
```

```
    istream&        operator>> (int&);
    istream&        operator>> (long&);
    istream&        operator>> (double&);
    // .....
    istream&        get(char&);
    int             get(void);
    // .....
  };
```

Again, we may use:

```
char      name[NAMESIZE];
char      ch;
int       age;

cin >> name;              // first operator>> version
cin >> age;               // third operator>> version
cin.get(ch);              // first get version
```

with `cin` an instance of the class `istream`.

15.1 File access

Before a file can be read or written it must first be opened. This is performed by defining either an `ifstream` (input file) or an `ofstream` (output file) class object. The constructors for objects of these types take two arguments. The first is the name of the file to be opened, presented as a null-terminated string. The second argument denotes how the file is to be opened. For example:

```
#include <fstream.h>

ofstream  ofp("results", ios::out);     // output file
```

An `ofstream` file can either be opened in *output mode* (`ios::out`) or *append mode* (`ios::app`). The mode parameter is an enumerated constant defined in the class `ios`. If a file does not exist and is opened for output or appending, then it is automatically created. If it already exists and is opened for output, then its original content is irretrievably lost. If it already exists and is opened in append mode, then output values are appended to the file end. The input and output modes defined in class `ios` might appear as (the actual values are, of course, implementation dependent):

```
class ios {
public:
  enum open_mode {
    in  = 0x01,   // open for reading
    out = 0x02,   // open for writing
    app = 0x08,   // append mode: all additions at end of file
    // .....
  };
```

```
    // .....
};
```

Since class `ofstream` is derived from class `ostream`, all the `ostream` operations can be applied to an `ofstream` object:

```
ofp << "message";
ofp.put('\n');
ofp << "Sum is: " << sum << "\n";
```

Opening a file may cause an error indicator to be set. This may arise for a number of reasons. For example, opening a file (in append mode) which does not exist sets an error indicator. This we can test with:

```
if( ! ofp){
  cout << "Cannot open \'results\' file\n";
  return (1);
}
```

The following program reads a stream of characters from the standard input and copies them to the file named on the command line. Copying continues until a period symbol is read.

PROGRAM 15.1

```
// ——————— FILE: p01.cpp ———————

//
// Copy a series of characters from the input
//       stream to a file named in the command line.
//

#include <iostream.h>
#include <fstream.h>

const int PERIOD = '.';

int main(int argc, char* argv[])
{
  if(argc != 2){
    cout << "Usage: " << argv[0] << " filename\n";
    return (1);
  }

  ofstream      ofp(argv[1], ios::out);     // constructor call

  if( ! ofp){
    cout << argv[0] << ": canot open " << argv[1] << "\n";
    return (2);
  }

  char   ch;
  while(cin.get(ch), ch != PERIOD)
    ofp.put(ch);
```

```
  return (0);
}
// ———————— END: p01.cpp ————————
```

Observe how when we open a file with a constructor call, then the file is automatically closed by the corresponding destructor call when the `ofstream` object goes out of scope.

An input stream is associated with an `ifstream` class object. Again, the class `ifstream` is a derived class from `istream`. The `ifstream` constructor expects the file name and mode as arguments:

```
ifstream  ifp("data", ios::in);
```

The following program copies a file on to the standard output. The file name is given as the command line argument. Copying continues until a period is read from the input stream. The `typedef` used in this program is explained in the next section.

PROGRAM 15.2

```
// ———————— FILE: p02.cpp ————————

//
//  Copy a series of characters from a file
//        named in the command line to the standard
//        output
//

#include <iostream.h>
#include <fstream.h>

typedef int      Character;

const int PERIOD = '.';

int main(int argc, char* argv[])
{
  if(argc != 2){
    cout << "Usage: " << argv[0] << " filename\n";
    return (1);
  }

  ifstream      ifp(argv[1], ios::in);       // constructor call

  if( ! ifp){
    cout << argv[0] << ": canot open " << argv[1] << "\n";
    return (2);
  }

  Character     ch;
  while((ch = ifp.get()) != PERIOD)
    cout.put(ch);
```

```
    return (0);
}
// ———————— END: p02.cpp ————————
```

15.2 The functions get and put

Function `put` writes a single character to an `ostream` or any derived class such as an `ofstream`. The prototype declaration for `put` in class `ostream` is:

```
ostream&  put(char ch);
```

Examples of its use include:

```
cout.put('\n');              // send newline to standard output
ofp.put(ch);                 // send ch to file
```

Note that the function returns a reference to the `ostream` class object that invokes it. Hence application of function `put` may be cascaded as in:

```
cout.put('K').put('e').put('n');
```

Function `get` reads a single character from an input stream. One prototype declaration for `get` in class `istream` is:

```
istream&  get(char& ch);
```

Examples include:

```
cin.get(initial);
cin.get(letter1).get(letter2);         // cascaded
ifp.get(ch);                           // some ifstream object
```

The operation may be used in the condition of a while loop. End of file processing is determined by the following type of logic:

```
char ch;
while(cin.get(ch)) .....             // stop at file end
```

The function `get` is overloaded in class `istream` with a second variant:

```
int     get(void);
```

which again reads a single character from the input stream returning with its value. The set of return values also includes the symbolic constant `EOF` denoting the file end. Thus we might have:

```
int  c;
while((c = ifp.get()) != EOF) .....
```

Care is required to ensure that the variable `c` used to represent the data character returned by `get` is of type `int`. This is necessary to ensure that the loop operates correctly. To illustrate the difficulties, assume we are operating on a machine with sixteen bit integers, and the `EOF` value is `-1`. The representation for `EOF` is:

```
-1 (decimal) = 1111111111111111 (binary)
```

If `get` returns `EOF` and this is assigned to the variable `c` which is erroneously declared as a character variable of 8 bits, then `c` is assigned the low order 8 bits returned by `get` (`EOF`), namely:

```
c = 11111111 (binary)
```

The inequality test (`!=`) will then fail to recognize the `EOF` value, since:

```
11111111 != 1111111111111111
```

evaluates to logical `TRUE`. The loop would thus cycle indefinitely.

To explicitly indicate that a variable is to operate as a character variable, but is represented as an integer to correctly handle detection of `EOF`, we recommend the type name `Character` be introduced. The name implies the variable type but conceals its representation as an `int`:

```
typedef int        Character;

Character c;

while((c = ifp.get()) != EOF) .....
```

We now write a program called `copy` to copy the content of one file to a second file. The two file names are supplied as command line arguments with the source file named first.

PROGRAM 15.3

```
// ———————— FILE: p03.cpp ————————
//
//  Copy the content of a source file to a destination
//      file. The two file names are given as command line
//      arguments.
//

#include <iostream.h>
#include <fstream.h>

typedef int      Character;

int main(int argc, char* argv[])
{
  if(argc != 3){
    cout << "Usage: " << argv[0] << " file file\n";
    return (1);
  }

  ifstream        ifp(argv[1], ios::in);
  if( ! ifp){
    cout << argv[0] << ": cannot open " << argv[1] << "\n";
    return (2);
```

```
    }
    ofstream        ofp(argv[2], ios::out);
    if( ! ofp){
      cout << argv[0] << ": cannot open " << argv[2] << "\n";
      return (3);
    }

    Character       ch;
    while((ch = ifp.get()) != EOF)
      ofp.put(ch);
    return (0);
}
// ———— END: p03.cpp ————
```

It is not necessary to open a file when an `ifstream` or an `ofstream` object is defined. At some later point in the program a file can be associated with the class object with the member function `open`. For example:

```
ofstream  ofp;              // stream class object
// .....
ofp.open("data", ios::out);
if( ! ofp) .....
```

The file connected to the stream class object is explicitly closed using the member function `close`:

```
ofp.close();
```

Program 15.4 copies the content of a number of files to the standard output. The files to be copied are named in the program command line.

PROGRAM 15.4

```
// ———— FILE: p04.cpp ————

//
//  Copy the content of a number of files to the
//        standard output. The files are named in the
//        program command line.
//

#include <iostream.h>
#include <fstream.h>

typedef int       Character;

int main(int argc, char* argv[])
{
    if(argc < 2){
      cout << "Usage: " << argv[0] << " file file .....\n";
      return (1);
    }
```

```
    ifstream       ifp;
    for(int k = 1; k < argc; k++){
      ifp.open(argv[k], ios::in);
      if( ! ifp)
        cout << argv[0] << ": cannot open " << argv[k] << "\n";
      else {
        Character ch;
        while((ch = ifp.get()) != EOF)
          cout.put(ch);
        ifp.close();
      }
    }

    return (0);
}

//  ──────────  END: p04.cpp  ──────────
```

15.3 Manipulators

Each `iostream` library class object maintains various *format state flags* which determine, among other things, how a value is to be presented when displayed and read. The states are determined by values contained in class `ios` and can be set and unset through member operations of that class.

Class `ios`, for example, has members that specify the base of an integer when it is read or written; the precision of floating point numbers when read or written; the width of a field into which a value is written; the padding character if a value requires fewer positions than its field width; etc. These values can be manipulated with the appropriate operations:

```
class ios {
public:
     int          width(int);                // set field width
     int          width(void) const;         // get field width
     char         fill(char);                // set padding character
     char         fill(void) const;          // get padding character
     int          precision(int);            // set precision
     int          precision(void) const;     // get precision
     // .....
};
```

Member function `width` specifies the field width for the next string or numeric output operation:

```
int age = 21;
cout.width(5);
cout << '[' << age << ']';
```

producing the output:

```
[   21]
```

with the three blank (space) characters filling the field width to five as required. This padding character can be changed with the function `fill`:

```
cout.width(5);
cout.fill('*');
cout << '[' << age << ']';
```

producing:

```
[***21]
```

If the field width setting is not large enough, then the minimum number of positions is used to display the value. This ensures that the full value is displayed. It will, of course, disrupt the planned layout:

```
cout.width(2);
cout << '[' << "Ken" << ']';
```

produces:

```
[Ken]
```

rather than:

```
[Ke]
```

A convenient way to change some of these formatting states is through the application of operators called *manipulators*. Manipulators have a stream reference as argument and return a reference to the same stream. As a consequence, we can include these manipulators with the extraction and insertion operators. They produce no input or output of values but have the effect of altering the stream state.

The parameterized manipulator `setw` sets the field width for the next immediate value. For example:

```
cout << setw(2) << monthNumber << setw(4) << yearNumber;
```

Other parameterized manipulators are `setbase`, `setfill`, `setprecision`, `setiosflags` and `resetiosflags`. Their effect is summarized in Table 15.1 and detailed in Appendix F.4. To use these manipulators the header file `<iomanip.h>` must be included.

Some further examples of using the manipulators include:

```
cout << flush;                      // flush output to terminal
cout << x << endl;                  // display x and newline

int i = 10;
cout << dec << i << oct << i << hex << i << endl;
                                    // displays 10, 12, and A

int i = 1234;
cout << setfill('*') << setw(6) << i << endl;
                                    // displays **1234
```

Table 15.1

Manipulator	*Action*
`dec`	apply decimal conversion
`oct`	apply octal conversion
`hex`	apply hexadecimal conversion
`ws`	discard whitespace on input
`endl`	insert newline into output and flush
`ends`	insert terminal null in string
`flush`	flush output stream
`setbase(int)`	set conversion base to argument value n (0, 8, 10 or 16); 0 is the default value and denotes decimal
`resetiosflags(long)`	clear the format states as determined by argument
`setiosflags(long)`	set the format state as specified by the argument
`setfill(int)`	set the fill character to the argument value
`setprecision(int)`	set the floating point precision to the argument value
`setw(int)`	set the field width to the argument value

```
char buffer[BUFFERSIZE];
cin >> setw(BUFFERSIZE-1) >> buffer;
                                        // avoids overflow
```

This code ensures that the character array `buffer` is not overfilled with too many characters. Any characters in excess of the size (strictly, `BUFFERSIZE-1`) of the array are left in the input stream.

```
float x = 27.0;
cout << x << endl;                 // displays 27.000000
                                   // default precision is 6

cout << setprecision(4) << endl;
                                   // displays 27.0000
```

15.4 String stream processing

The class `istrstream` (`ostrstream`) is directly derived from class `istream` (`ostream`), and consequently all the `istream` (`ostream`) functions are available for the derived class. The functions of class `istream` parse the sequence of characters received from the input device, placing the formed value into memory locations. For example, the statements:

```
int  day;
char month[MONTHSIZE];
cin >> day >> month;
```

read and convert a stream of input characters from the `istream` object `cin` into an integer value and a string value.

The functions of class `istrstream` operate as for class `istream` above. The difference is the input is read from a program character array and not from the input device. Given:

```
char*     buffer = "123 is an integer";
```

the statements:

```
istrstream      iss(buffer, strlen(buffer));
iss >> day >> month;
```

assigns the decimal value `123` to the variable `day` and the string `'is'` to the character array variable `month`.

The class `istrstream` thus permits input operations from a program string variable. The constructors for this class:

```
class istrstream : public istream {
public:
     istrstream(const char*);
     istrstream(const char*, int n);
     // .....
};
```

either specify a string or the first n characters of one.

The operations from class `ostrstream` complement those of class `istrstream`. For example, a numerical value may be converted into a null-terminated character string with:

```
int  number = 123;
char numeric[NUMERICSIZE];

ostrstream      oss(numeric, NUMERICSIZE);
oss << number;
cout << "[" << numeric << "]";        // outputs [123]
```

15.5 The functions getline, read and write

Recall from Chapter 4 that the extraction operator >> uses whitespace characters as input separators. Hence:

```
char buffer[BUFFERSIZE];
// .....
while(cin >> buffer) .....
```

will repeatedly read character strings separated with whitespace symbols.

To read an entire line from an input stream including possible whitespace characters we use the function `getline` from class `istream` with prototype:

```
istream&  getline(char* buf, int limit, char delim = '\n');
```

The input characters are stored in the character array `buf`. At most, `limit-1` characters will be read, and a terminating `NULL` character is appended onto the end of `buf`. If the character `delim` is encountered in the input stream, or the file end is detected, then fewer than `limit-1` characters are transferred. The terminating character defaults to the newline symbol. Whatever character is used for this terminator, it is not stored in `buf`.

We have used the `#include` facility of the preprocessor to assemble most of the programs in this book. In the following example we demonstrate how we might actually implement this useful facility. The general outline of our version of `include` is:

```
WHILE get one line of the source file; not the end of file DO
  IF the line starts with #include
  THEN
    include this new file
  ELSE
    output the line to the destination file
  ENDIF
ENDWHILE
```

If the included file contains further `#includes`, this naturally leads to a recursive solution. Nested `#includes` are useful and readily implemented in C++ with a recursive implementation of the appropriate function.

The program is invoked with the command line:

```
include source-file-name destination-file-name
```

As described by the PDL, the lines of text are copied from the source file to the destination file. If at any time a line from the source file consisting of:

```
#include file-name
```

is met, then the include operation applies to this new source file, continuing to send the output to the same destination file as the first. When the new source file is exhausted, the copying continues with the original file or the program terminates if it is the first file.

PROGRAM 15.5

```
// ———————— FILE: p05.cpp ————————

//
// Copy the content of a source file to a
```

```
//      destination file. The two file names are given
//      as command line arguments. A line of text of the
//      form:
//
//              #include filename
//
//      appearing in the source file is replaced with
//      the content of the named file. Nested include
//      statements are supported to the depth permitted
//      by the maximum number of open files allowed by
//      the host operatimg system.
//

#include <iostream.h>
#include <fstream.h>
#include <strstream.h>
#include <string.h>

const int LINESIZE = 256;
const char* INCLUDE = "#include";

void    file_include(istream&, ostream&);

int main(int argc, char *argv[])
{
  ifstream      ifp;
  ofstream      ofp;

  if(argc != 3)
    cout << "Usage: " << argv[0] << " file1 file2\n";
  else {
    ifp.open(argv[1], ios::in);
    if( ! ifp){
      cout << argv[0] << ": cannot open " << argv[1] << "\n";
      return (1);
    }

    ofp.open(argv[2], ios::out);
    if( ! ofp){
      cout << argv[0] << ": cannot open " << argv[2] << "\n";
      ifp.close();
      return (2);
    }
    file_include(ifp, ofp);
    ifp.close();
    ofp.close();
  }
  return (0);
}

//
//  Perform a line by line copy of the source file
//      to the destination file. Expand all #include
//      lines. Permit nested #include's.
//
```

```
void file_include(istream& ifp, ostream& ofp)
{
  char line[LINESIZE], word1[LINESIZE], word2[LINESIZE];

  while(ifp.getline(line, LINESIZE)){          // eof input?
    istrstream  ins(line, strlen(line));
    ins >> word1 >> word2;
    if(strcmp(word1, INCLUDE) != 0)            // #include line?
       ofp << line << "\n";                    // no, copy
    else {
      ifstream  fp;
      fp.open(word2, ios::in);
      if( ! fp)
         cout << "Cannot open: " << word2 << "\n";
      else {
         file_include(fp, ofp);                // nested include
         fp.close();
      }
    }
  }
}

// ———————— END: p05.cpp ————————
```

The member function `write` of class `ostream` sends a specified number of bytes to some output stream. The function prototype is:

```
ostream&  write(const char* buf, int len);
```

The first `len` bytes of the array `buf` are written to the stream. The machine representation of the information is stored without first converting to a readable form. For example:

```
char buffer[BUFFERSIZE];
cin >> buffer;
ofp.write(buffer, strlen(buffer));
```

The counterpart of function `write` is member function `read` of class `istream`. The function signature is similar to that of `write`, but this time `len` is the number of bytes to be read, and `buf` is the target address of the input:

```
Date     input;                  // user-defined class
ifp.read((char*)&input, sizeof(Date));
```

Note the need for the explicit cast and the use of the compile time function `sizeof` to determine the number of bytes in some storage structure. Whilst a user-defined type such as `Date` consists of both data members and member functions, only the data for such objects is read/written from/to the file.

15.6 cin, cout and cerr

When a C++ program executes, three streams are automatically opened by the system and class objects provided for them. The streams are the *standard input*, the *standard output* and the *standard error*. The respective class objects are called `cin`, `cout` and `cerr`. These class objects are predefined in the standard input/output header `<iostream.h>`.

Normally, these class objects associate with the user's terminal. The class object `cerr` has not been used before. It is intended that any error messages produced by a program be written to this 'standard error' stream. In an interactive environment, this stream is associated with the user's terminal. `cerr` exists so that error messages can be logged to a device or file other than where the normal output is written. This is particularly desirable when the program's output is *redirected* to a file or sent down a *pipe* by the operating system. In the programs of this chapter, error messages should therefore have been delivered by statements of the form:

```
ofstream  ofp(argv[1], ios::out);
if( ! ofp){
  cerr << argv[0] << ": cannot open " << argv[1] << "\n";
  return (1);
}
```

using `cerr` instead of `cout`.

15.7 Direct access

A number of different file structures are possible and supported by functions in the standard library. The simplest file organization is the *serial file* and is the type of file we have processed so far. A serial file is constructed by writing new records to the end of the file. When the file is subsequently read, the components are input in the same order as they were originally written to the file.

A different file structure, one which permits direct access to a specified component of the file, is also supported by the standard I/O library. A *direct access file* can be interpreted as a number of data blocks or *record areas*. Each record area is of some fixed size measured as a number of bytes. To read (or write) a record, we must first position the reading (writing) head at the first byte of the record area. The required number of bytes is then transferred to (from) memory.

.....	record area	record area	record area	.....

Figure 15.2

The function `seekg` (`seekp`) allows direct access within an input (output) file. The prototype for the function `seekg` is:

```
istream&  seekg(long offset, seek_dir direction = ios::beg);
```

The second argument, if present, must have the enumerated value `ios::beg`, `ios::cur` or `ios::end`. If it is `ios::beg` then the position in the file is set equal to the value of the first argument considered as a byte count. The first byte of the file is numbered `0`. The `direction` value `ios::beg` is used when we wish to locate the read/write head at some *absolute* position in the file. In particular, the call:

```
ifp.seekg(0L, ios::beg);
```

will rewind the file to the beginning.

If the second argument is `ios::cur` then the position in the file is set equal to the current position plus the signed `offset`. A positive offset will advance the position away from the beginning of the file, while a negative offset moves toward the beginning of the file. The direction value `ios::cur` is used for *relative* positioning within the file.

If the second argument is `ios::end` then the position is set to the end of the file plus the signed `offset`. This functionality is often used to extend a file. To seek to the end of the file before, say, writing, the call is:

```
ofp.seekp(0L, ios::end);
```

Once the required location in the file has been obtained with a call to `seekg` (`seekp`), subsequent reading (and writing) will begin at that position. The input (or output) is performed by the appropriate stream operation.

The following two programs illustrate a simple use for these functions. The first program reads a series of dates given by the user and writes them serially to a file. The second program then treats this file as an array of date values and fetches the required date value given an index position.

One additional function associated with direct access files is `tellg` (`tellp` on an output file). The function heading is:

```
long tellg(void)
```

The function `tellg` takes a stream class object that is currently open and returns the byte position in the stream. Thus:

```
ifp.seekg(0L, ios::end);
long size = ifp.tellg();
```

will determine the number of bytes currently in the file identified by the stream object `ifp`.

PROGRAM 15.6a

```
// ———————— FILE: p06a.cpp ————————

//
//  Input a series of dates from the user and write
//       them to a file.
//

#include <iostream.h>
#include <fstream.h>
#include "cdate.h"

int main(int argc, char* argv[])
{
  if(argc != 2){
    cerr << "Usage: " << argv[0] << " filename\n";
    return (1);
  }

  ofstream       resultsFile(argv[1], ios::out);
  if( ! resultsFile){
    cerr << argv[0] << ": cannot open " << argv[1] << "\n";
    return (2);
  }

  Date           terminator(1,1,2000);

  int            day, month, year;
  char           separator;

  cout << "Enter first date: ";
  cin >> day >> separator >> month >> separator >> year;
  Date           input(day, month, year);

  while(input != terminator){
    resultsFile.write((char*)&input, sizeof(Date));

    cout << "Enter next date: ";
    cin >> day >> separator >> month >> separator >> year;
    input = Date(day, month, year);
  }

  return (0);
}

// ———————— END: p06a.cpp ————————
```

PROGRAM 15.6b

```
// ———————— FILE: p06a.cpp ————————

//
// Read a series of date values from a file in response
```

```
//        to the index values given by the user.
//

#include <iostream.h>
#include <fstream.h>
#include "cdate.h"

int main(int argc, char* argv[])
{
  if(argc != 2){
    cerr << "Usage: " << argv[0] << " filename\n";
    return (1);
  }

  ifstream       dataFile(argv[1], ios::in);
  if( ! dataFile){
    cerr << argv[0] << ": cannot open " << argv[1] << "\n";
    return (2);
  }

  dataFile.seekg(0L, ios::end);
  long           fileSize = dataFile.tellg();
  int            numberOfRecords = fileSize / sizeof(Date);

  int            index;
  cout << "Enter first index: ";
  cin >> index;

  while(index >= 0){
    if(index >= numberOfRecords)
      cout << "Bad index!\n";
    else {
      dataFile.seekg(index * sizeof(Date), ios::beg);
      Date       input;
      dataFile.read((char*)&input, sizeof(Date));

      cout << "Date at index: "<< index << ": ";
      cout << input.day() << "/" << input.month() << "/" <<
        input.year() << "\n";
    }
    cout << "Enter next index: ";
    cin >> index;
  }

  return (0);
}
// ────────── END: p06a.cpp ──────────
```

15.8 Commentary

C++ programs may use library functions from other languages, notably, C. A C++ program might, for example, choose to use I/O routines from the standard C library [Ker88, Bar90], rather than the services offered by `<iostream.h>`. However, we should recognize the benefits which accrue from using the latter.

First, the C++ I/O facilities are *type safe* – the object being transferred is known statically by the compiler, rather than dynamically at run time as in the C input/output library. This makes the implementation more efficient too since the correct low-level library routine to perform the transfer is selected by the compiler.

Second, the C++ I/O mechanism is extensible to new user-defined types. This makes I/O of user classes look and operate like basic language types (see Chapter 10).

15.9 Summary

1. A file is a collection of records of some base type. File access methods determine how the records of a file are processed, and include serial and direct access organization. A serial file is constructed by writing new records to the end of the file. When the file is subsequently read, the elements are input in the same order as they were originally written. A direct access file can be written or read to/from any position within the file.

2. Before a file can be read or written it must first be opened. This operation is performed by a library function which returns a stream class object that is then used in subsequent I/O operations. When processing a file is complete it must be closed in an orderly manner. Both effects can be achieved by normal object creation and destruction.

3. Serial processing of a file is provided by the library functions `get`, `put`, etc. Direct access within a file is provided by functions such as `seekg`.

4. Three files automatically provided in all C++ programs are known by the stream objects `cin`, `cout` and `cerr`.

15.10 Exercises

1. Implement your own version of the library function `getline`.

2. Use the file handling functions of the standard library to double space a text file. The names of the files are given as command line arguments, with the source file named first and the target file named second.

3. Write a program to copy one file to another, removing any blank lines in the source file. The file names are given as command line arguments.

4. Write a program to number the lines in a text file. The input file name should be passed as a command line argument. The program should write to `cout`.

5. Write a program to display the content of a text file on to the standard output, 20 lines at a time. The input file is given as a command line argument. Each 20 lines are displayed following receipt of a return character entered from the standard input.

6. Given two files of integers sorted into ascending order, write a program to merge the files into a third file of sorted integers. All three file names are given as command line arguments.

7. Write a program called `find` that searches for patterns. If the command:

   ```
   find pattern filename
   ```

   is given, then the string pattern is searched in the named file. All lines containing the pattern are printed.

   Modify this program to support the command line option `-n` which, if present, requests that the line number should be printed as well.

8. Write a program which operates as a file printer. The program `print` is invoked with one or more file names as arguments. It prints the files with top and bottom margins on each page, and, at the top of each page the file name and the page number.

9. Rework Case Study 12.2 with the details of the doctor and the patients recorded on a file.

16

Structures, Unions and Bit Fields

In Chapter 9 we introduced the class – an aggregate of values of possibly different types. C++ also supports a second aggregate type known as a *structure.* A structure is a class declared with the keyword `struct`. The distinction is that a structure has all its members public by default. Hence:

```
class Demo { public: ..... };
```

and

```
struct Demo { ..... };
```

are equivalent. Members of a structure can, of course, be made private using an explicit access specifier:

```
struct Date {
  Date(int aDay, int aMonth, int aYear);     // public by default
  // .....
private:
  int       theDay, theMonth, theYear;
};
```

If a structure participates in a derivation, then the base of a derived structure is public by default. That is:

```
struct Derived : Base { ..... };
```

is equivalent to:

```
class Derived : public Base { ..... };
```

Otherwise, structures and classes are identical. Generally, structures are used when information hiding is considered inappropriate. Historically, record structures are inherited from the C programming language and only supports data members. In C++ it is probably appropriate to reserve their use as that for C, and only consider classes as the means of implementing abstract data types.

16.1 Unions

The `union` data type in C++ is similar to *variant records* in other programming languages. The union data type is like the class and structure data type in that it can contain members of different types and sizes. Unlike classes and structures, however, a union can hold at most one of its components at a time. Effectively, the members are overlaid in the storage allocated for the union. The compiler allocates sufficient storage to accommodate the largest of the specified members. By default, the members of a union are public.

A union is a variable which can legitimately hold any one of several types. We demonstrate this in the following illustration. The notation used to declare and access members of a union is identical to that used with classes and structures, with the keyword `union` replacing `class` or `struct`. Consider:

```
union Number {          // members are overlaid:
  int     integer;
  float   decimal;
};

Number    data;
```

The variable `data` will be large enough to hold the larger of the two types (`int` or `float`), regardless of which machine it is compiled on. Providing the program usage is consistent, either of the types may be assigned to `data` and used in expressions. If something is stored as one type and extracted as another, then the results are machine dependent. This is illustrated in Program 16.1.

PROGRAM 16.1

```
// ———————— FILE: p01.cpp ————————

//
//  A program to illustrate how a system overlays an int
//      and a float. The program also shows how in C++ it is
//      the programmer's responsibility to maintain
//      consistency.
//

#include <iostream.h>
#include <iomanip.h>

union Number {            // members are overlaid:
  int     integer;
  float   decimal;
};

int main ()
{
  Number      data;

  data.integer = 20000;
  cout << "int: " << setw(6) << data.integer
       << ", float: " << setw(10) << setprecision(4) <<
         data.decimal
       << "\n";
```

```
  data.decimal = 123.0;
  cout << "int: " << setw(6) << data.integer
       << ", float: " << setw(10) << setprecision(4) <<
data.decimal
       << "\n";

  return (0);
}
// ———— END: p01.cpp ————
```

The program demonstrates how a system overlays an `int` and a `float`. The program output, which is dependent upon the computer system on which it is run, might be:

```
int: 20000, float: 1.7968e-13
int:     0, float:        123
```

Members of unions are accessed just as for classes and structures. Syntactically, we use:

```
union-variable.member-name
```

or:

```
union-pointer -> member-name
```

when using, respectively, a union object and a union pointer.

There is no provision in C++ to enquire which component of a union was last assigned. The programmer can, however, enclose a union in a class or structure that includes a tag component to indicate which member of a union is active. For example, we might add to the union `Number`:

```
enum Tag { INT, FLOAT };

union Number {
  int           integer;
  float         decimal;
};

struct Pair {
  Tag           tagged;
  Number        value;
};

Pair            data;
```

To assign to the union, we write either:

```
data.tagged            = INT;
data.value.integer     = 123;
```

or:

```
data.tagged            = FLOAT;
data.value.decimal     = 123.0;
```

We can then write portable functions that can discriminate among the possible values of the union. For example, we repeat the last program, including the above definitions and a function to print a `Pair` value, whatever it may contain.

PROGRAM 16.2

```
// ———————— FILE: p02.cpp ————————
//
//  Associate a tag value with a union to permit
//       descrimination among possible values of the union.
//
#include <iostream.h>

enum Tag { INT, FLOAT };

union Number {  // number pair template:
  int            integer;
  float          decimal;
};

struct Pair {  // tagged number pairs:
  Tag              tagged;
  Number           value;
};

void print(Pair);

int main ()
{
  Pair         data;

  data.tagged        = INT;
  data.value.integer = 20000;
  print(data);

  data.tagged        = FLOAT;
  data.value.decimal = 123.0;
  print(data);

  return (0);
}

void print(Pair d)
{
  switch (d.tagged){
    case INT:
      cout << "Integer: " << d.value.integer << "\n";
      break;

    case FLOAT:
      cout << "Decimal: " << d.value.decimal << "\n";
      break;
```

```
    }
}

// ———————— END: p02.cpp ————————
```

The output from this program is:

```
Integer: 20000
Decimal: 123
```

The `print` function correctly discriminates between the fields `integer` and `decimal` according to the value assigned to the tag.

C++ unions may be initialized using either an expression delivering a value of the same type or by a brace enclosed initializer. When using the latter, however, only the first member can be set in this way. Thus in the union `Number` of Program 16.1, only the field member `integer` may be initialized. For example:

```
Number num1 = { 27 };          // ok
Number num2 = num1;            // ok
```

are legal initializers for a union. In contrast, the following are all invalid ways to initialize a union:

```
Number num3 = { 27, 3.1416 }; // only initialize first member
Number num4 = { 3.1416 };     // cannot initialize second member
Number num5 = 27;             // must be brace enclosed
```

Like classes and structures, unions may have member functions. Overloaded constructor functions can be defined to initialize any of the union's members:

```
union Number {
  Number(int i) { integer = i; }
  Number(float d) { decimal = d; }

  int             integer;
  float           decimal;
};
```

A union is used to conserve storage space. As such, it is not expected to participate in a class hierarchy. A union is restricted so that it may not be used as a base class, may not be derived from a base class, and may not have virtual functions.

None of the data members of a union can be static. This is necessary since all union members have the same address. A static member would exist separate from the union yet somehow have the same address – an impossible situation. By the same argument, if a member of a union is a class object then that class may not have a constructor, a destructor, or a user-defined assignment operator.

A union declaration in which the tag name is omitted and no variables are defined is known as an *anonymous union*. For example:

```
int main()
{
  union {             // anonymous
```

```
    int       integer;
    float     decimal;
  };

  integer = 27;      // no member access syntax required
  // .....
  decimal = 3.1416;
  // .....
}
```

The names of the union's members must be different from other names in the scope in which the union is introduced. This is necessary since the members are considered part of the enclosing scope. As such, they are referenced directly without recourse to the usual member access syntax. Frequently, anonymous unions are members of classes or structures:

```
class Pair {
public:
  enum Tag { INT, FLOAT };
  Pair(int i) : tagged(INT), integer(i) {}
  Pair(float f) : tagged(FLOAT), decimal(f) {}
private:
  Tag     tagged;
  union {           // anonymous
    int   integer;
    float decimal;
  };
};
```

16.2 Bit fields

Systems programming activities are often required to manipulate data not only at the byte level, but also at the bit level. *Bit fields* are typically used in machine dependent programs which require data structures to correspond to some fixed hardware representation.

The C++ compiler allows integral values to be packed into spaces smaller than that ordinarily allowed. These components are called *bit fields* and are specified by following the member declarator with a colon symbol and a constant integer expression specifying the width of the field in bits:

```
struct Packed {
  unsigned int        a : 2;
  unsigned int        b : 4, c : 7;
} bits = { 1, 7, 33 };
```

The intent is that member a is allocated the first two bits of the structure, member b the next four bits, and finally member c the next seven bits. The two-bit field a is capable of representing the four values 0 to 3 inclusive; b is capable of storing the values 0, 1, 2, ... , 15; and the seven-bit field c may represent the values 0 to 127 inclusive.

The compiler assigns in either a left-to-right or a right-to-left order of the bits in a machine word needed to store the fields. The internal representation of bit fields, therefore, is machine dependent. A machine word usually equates with the data type int, and the memory allocation for ints differs among machines. Further, while the majority of machines store fields left-to-right, some store right-to-left. Assuming a 16-bit int and a left-to-right storage format, the memory representation for variable bits as declared and initialized above is shown in Figure 16.1.

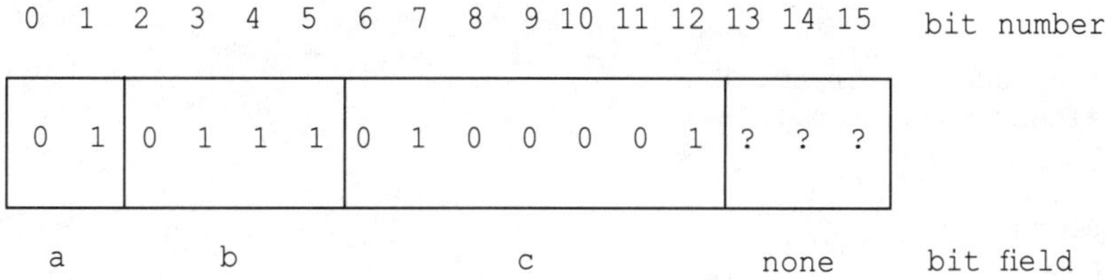

Figure 16.1

A field may overlap an int boundary. If the bit field width would cause this to happen, the field may be aligned at the next int boundary. Thus the declaration:

```
struct Filled {
  unsigned int        a : 4;
  unsigned int        b : 10;
  unsigned int        c : 10;
};
```

might require two 16-bit words with the fields a and b in the first word and field c in the second word.

Without qualification, bit fields must be considered as highly machine dependent. For example, an implementation may choose to use a long in place of an int when a bit field is defined with more bits than a single precision int.

Field members are restricted to integral type. Arrays of fields are not allowed. Fields cannot be addressed directly by pointers, and the address operator cannot be applied to a bit field member.

The use of bit fields is likely to be non-portable and therefore should only be used in appropriate situations. In the following program the day number of a date has (maximum) range 1 to 31 inclusive, month number is 1 to 12 inclusive, and the year is 0 to 99 if we discount the century. If memory is at a premium, we may choose to pack the day, month and year into respectively 5-bits (0 to 31 inclusive),

4-bits (0 to 15 inclusive) and 7-bits (0 to 127 inclusive) fields. The resulting program is as follows.

PROGRAM 16.3

```
// ——————— FILE: p03.cpp ———————
//
//  Program illustrating bit fields. The program
//      determines a person's age measured in years
//      given that person's date of birth and today's
//      date. The dates are packed into bit fields
//      of a 16-bit integer.
//

#include <iostream.h>
#include "cstring.h"


class Date {
public:
  Date(unsigned int aDay, unsigned int aMonth, unsigned int
                                                        aYear);
  unsigned int  day(void) const;
  unsigned int  month(void) const;
  unsigned int  year(void) const;

private:
                        // packed date template:
  unsigned int    theDay : 5;
  unsigned int    theMonth : 4;
  unsigned int    theYear : 7;
};

inline Date::Date(unsigned int aDay, unsigned int aMonth,
unsigned int aYear)
   : theDay(aDay),
     theMonth(aMonth),
     theYear(aYear)
{}

inline unsigned int     Date::day(void) const
  { return theDay; }

inline unsigned int     Date::month(void) const
  { return theMonth; }

inline unsigned int     Date::year(void) const
  { return theYear; }

Date    askfordate(const String&);    // prototype

int main ()
```

```
{
  int           age;

  Date dateofbirth = askfordate("Date of birth?: ");
  Date today = askfordate("Today\'s date?: ");

  if(today.month() > dateofbirth.month() ||
      (today.month() == dateofbirth.month() &&
        today.day() > dateofbirth.day()))
    age = today.year() - dateofbirth.year();
  else
    age = today.year() - dateofbirth.year() - 1;

  cout << "Age: " << age << " years\n";

  return (0);
}

Date askfordate(const String& prompt)
{
  unsigned int  day, month, year;
  char          separator;

  cout << prompt;
  cin >> day >> separator >> month >> separator >> year;

  return Date(day, month, year);
}

// ———————— END: p03.cpp ————————
```

16.3 Summary

1. A structure is an example of an aggregate type consisting of a collection of subcomponents treated as a single entity. In all respects a `struct` operates like a class with the differences highlighted in the text. `structs` are perhaps best used as intended in C, namely, record structures.

2. `Unions` have the same syntactic form as structured objects. `Union` members share the same storage overlaid upon each other.

3. Bit fields are members of a structure packed into a machine word. The internal representation of bit fields is highly machine dependent.

16.4 Exercises

1. Define an array of structures that could be used for a telephone directory. Include the name, area code and phone number for a maximum of 40 records.

2. Write a program that uses bit fields to display the bit representation of the simple data types int and float. The program is to operate upon a series of data values of both types.

3. An input stream consists of a mixture of alphabetic character strings, integers (strings of decimal digits), and punctuation symbols (such as `, ; [ }` etc.). A program is required to display only the integers in the input.

   The problem can be tackled by using a lexical analyzer to separate the input into a sequence of tokens. The analyzer and associated declarations are provided by the header file:

```
//   File:      lex.h

#ifndef LEXICAL
  #define LEXICAL

  enum TokenTag { INTSY, STRSY, PUNCSY, EOFSY };
                // integer, string, punctuation, end-of-file

  class Lexical {
  public:
    Lexical(const String& filename);
    TokenTag   lexical(void);
    String     symbol(void) const { return string; }
    int        integerCode(void) const { return integer; }
    // .....
  private:
    int        integer;         // integer or punctuation value
    String     string;
    // .....
  };

#endif    // LEXICAL
```

17

Operations on Bits

A particular feature of system programming is the processing of individual bit patterns within a computer word. These facilities are supported in C++ by the provision of a number of *bitwise operators*.

17.1 Bitwise operators and expressions

In addition to the bit fields associated with structured values, C++ also supports six operators to manipulate bit values of integral types. The six bitwise operators are shown in Table 17.1. Like all C++ operators, the bitwise operators have rules of precedence and associativity which determine how expressions involving these and other operators are evaluated. Further, all these bitwise operators, except the *unary complement*, operate in conjunction with the assignment operator. The full table of operators is given in Appendix E.

Table 17.1

Category	*Bitwise operator*	*Symbol*
Bitwise operators:	(unary) bitwise complement	~
	bitwise and	&
	bitwise or	|
	bitwise exclusive or	^
Shift operators:	left shift	<<
	right shift	>>

All the bitwise operators apply to integral types only. Thus these operators may not be applied to type `float` and `double`. We will restrict our discussion to a machine with a 16-bit, 2's complement representation for a standard sized `int`. Other architectures are processed similarly.

The *bitwise complement* operator ~, also known as the 'one's complement operator', computes the bitwise negation of its single operand. The usual unary conversions apply to the operand. Every bit in the binary representation of the result is the inverse or complement of the operand. If the integer variable `t` has decimal value 12, the binary representation for this value is:

```
0000000000001100
```

then `~t` has the binary representation:

```
1111111111110011
```

This 2's complement value equates to decimal –13.

The bitwise operators *and* (`&`), *or* (`|`) and *exclusive or* (`^`) are binary operators. Each operand is treated in terms of its binary representation. Each bit of the result is computed by applying the operator *and*, *or* or *exclusive or* to the corresponding bits of both operands. The semantics of these three operators is given by Table 17.2.

Table 17.2

x	y	x & y	x | y	x ^ y
0	0	0	0	0
0	1	0	1	1
1	0	0	1	1
1	1	1	1	0

In the context of the following definitions:

```
int p = 123, q = -17;
```

Table 17.3 shows a series of expressions, the binary representation of the result of evaluating the expression, and the corresponding decimal value.

Table 17.3

Expression	*Binary representation*	*Decimal value*
p	0000 0000 0111 1011	123
q	1111 1111 1110 1111	-17
p & q	0000 0000 0110 1011	107
p | q	1111 1111 1111 1111	-1
p ^ q	1111 1111 1001 0100	-108

A *mask* is used to extract the desired bit pattern from an expression. For example, the `int` constant 3 has the binary representation:

```
0000 0000 0000 0011
```

and can be used in conjunction with the bitwise *and* operator to determine the low order 2 bits of an int expression value. For example, the expression:

```
y = x & 3;
```

assigns to y the rightmost (least significant) 2 bits of the integer variable x. If x has the value 17 (binary: 0000000000010001), then y has the value 1 (binary: 0000000000000001). To find the value of a particular group of bits in an expression, a mask with 1s in those bit positions and 0s elsewhere is used. Thus, the hexadecimal constant 0x30 is a mask for bits 5 and 6 from the right.

To clear the low-order byte of a 16-bit integer, the mask 0xFF00 can be used. To allow the code to work properly, independent of the size of an integer, the bitwise complement can be used to construct the necessary mask:

```
high_byte = word & (~ 0xFF)
```

Finally, there are the two *shift operators*. Both are binary operators with two integral operands. The right operand is converted to an int. The type of the expression result is that of its left operand. The left shift operator << shifts the binary representation of its left operand the number of places to the left as specified by the right operand. The low order bits are zero filled. The right shift operator >> shifts the binary representation of its left operand the number of places to the right as specified by its right operand. The bits shifted in from the left are machine dependent. If the left operand is unsigned, then 0s are shifted in from the left. If the left operand is a signed operand, then whether 0s or 1s are shifted in is at the discretion of the implementor. On some implementations, 0s are always shifted in; on others the leftmost sign bit is regenerated as the shifted in bit. Right shifting a signed value is unlikely to be portable and should be avoided. Table 17.4 shows a number of expressions, the binary representation after evaluating the result, and the corresponding decimal value. The integer variable p is assumed to have the decimal value 123.

Table 17.4

Expression	*Binary representation*	*Decimal value*
p	0000 0000 0111 1011	123
p << 4	0000 0111 1011 0000	1968
p >> 2	0000 0000 0001 1110	30
(p >> 2) & 0xF	0000 0000 0000 1110	14

Bitwise expressions can be used for data compression, making useful savings in program storage requirements. For example, on a machine with 32-bit unsigned ints, four bytes may be packed into one int. The function pack uses the bitwise operators to perform byte by byte packing:

```
unsigned int pack(char a, char b, char c, char d)
{
  unsigned int packed;

  packed = a;
  packed = (packed << 8) | b;
  packed = (packed << 8) | c;
  packed = (packed << 8) | d;

  return (packed);
}
```

The four bytes in a packed unsigned integer can be recovered with the function `unpack`:

```
const int MASK  = 0xFF;

void unpack(unsigned p, char *a, char *b, char *c, char *d)
{
  *a = p & MASK;
  *b = (p >> 8) & MASK;
  *c = (p >> 16) & MASK;
  *d = (p >> 24) & MASK;
}
```

Program 16.3 used bit fields to pack the elements of a date. We repeat the same problem in Program 17.1 below, this time using the bitwise operators to perform the packing and unpacking.

PROGRAM 17.1

```
// ———————— FILE: p01.cpp ————————
//
//  The program determines a person's age measured
//      in years given that person's date of birth and
//      today's date. The dates are packed into 16 bits
//      and stored left to right as day (5 bits), month
//      (4 bits) and year (7 bits).
//

#include <iostream.h>
#include "cstring.h"

typedef unsigned int            Date;    // packed representation

inline Date      makeDate(int d, int m, int y)
  { return (((d << 4) | m) << 7) | y; }

inline int       day(Date d) { return d >> 11; }
inline int       month(Date d)  { return (d >> 7) & 0xF; }
inline int       year(Date d)  { return d & 0x7F; }

Date askfordate(const String&);                    // prototype
```

```
int main()
{
  int          age;

  Date dateofbirth = askfordate("Date of birth?: ");
  Date today = askfordate("Today\'s date?: ");

  if(month(today) > month(dateofbirth) ||
      (month(today) == month(dateofbirth) &&
   day(today) > day(dateofbirth)))
    age = year(today) - year(dateofbirth);
  else
    age = year(today) - year(dateofbirth) - 1;

  cout << "Age: " << age << "\n";

  return (0);
}

Date askfordate(const String& prompt)
{
  unsigned int day, month, year;
  char           separator;

  cout << prompt;
  cin >> day >> separator >> month >> separator >> year;

  return makeDate(day, month, year);
}

// ———————— END: p01.cpp ————————
```

CASE STUDY 17.1
Bit vectors

A college offers ten courses in Mathematics, Physics, Chemistry, Biology, English, French, German, Italian, Accounting and Economics. Each student's enrolment is recorded in a text file, one record per line. The student's surname appears in columns 1–20 inclusive. Each course taken by a student is shown by the presence of the letter `X` in columns 21–30, representing respectively the ten courses. Design and write a program which reads the enrolment file and prints a class list for every course.

The problem is most naturally expressed in terms of the set concept. Each student record consists of the student's name and the set of courses on which that student is enrolled. As each student record is input, each occurrence of the letter `X` in columns 21–30 causes the corresponding course to be included in the set of courses that the student attends. Producing a class list for a given subject is expressed by determining whether the course is a member of the set of courses attended by a student.

The problem naturally divides into two parts. The first phase builds the register of student records. Each record matches the student's name against the set of courses for which that student is enrolled. The second phase then produces the class lists for each subject.

The internal data structure for the problem is a `KeySortedCollection`, pairing the student name and course enrolments. We might consider using a `Set` of course names to realize the enrolments, however, this would prove expensive in terms of storage requirements. An alternative would be to use 10 single-bit flags. If a given bit flag has value `1`, then that corresponding subject is studied by the student.

A bit vector is a linear array of bits. Each element in that array may take the value `0` or `1`. However, since the smallest unit manipulated in C++ is an 8-bit byte, then a bit vector implementation will have to manipulate a sequence of bytes as if they were a vector of bits.

File `bitvector.h` offers three variants, `BitVector16`, `BitVector32` and `BitVector`. Class `BitVector16` (`BitVector32`) uses one (two) 16-bit words of storage supporting a maximum of 16 (32) bits. Class `BitVector` is a general bit vector of user-defined size.

To permit mixing these bit vectors and to give them the same protocol, they are derived from the common base `BitVec`. The common protocol includes `operator[]` and function `bit` which deliver the value of the bit as given by the index argument. Functions `set` and `reset` set or unset the specified bit respectively. Function `capacity` delivers the number of bits in the `BitVec` object. For example, the capacity of a `BitVector16` object is 16 bits. The header file for these classes is then:

```
// ==================================================================
// File Name    : BITVECTOR.H
// File Type    : C++ header file for the bit vector classes
// Author       : Ken Barclay
// Date Created : 2 Apr 1993
//
// -----------------------------------
// Description  : A range of bitvectors including
//                BitVector16, .....
// .....

#ifndef BITVECTOR
  #define BITVECTOR

  #include <iostream.h>

  #ifndef CLASSLIB
    #include "..\ticlass\classlib.h"
  #endif

  ABSTRACT class BitVec {
  public:
    virtual UInt  operator[] (UInt) const = 0;
         // get bit for given index value

    virtual void shiftRight(UInt index) = 0;
         // shfit right by given number of bits
```

```
    virtual void shiftLeft(UInt index) = 0;
         // shfit left by given number of bits

    virtual void rotateRight(UInt index) = 0;
         // rotate right a given number of places

    virtual void rotateLeft(UInt index) = 0;
         // rotate right a given number of places

    virtual UInt  bit(UInt) const = 0;
         // get bit for given index value

    virtual void  set(UInt) = 0;
         // set bit to one for given index value

    virtual void  reset(UInt) = 0;
         // set bit to zero for given index value

    virtual UInt  capacity(void) const = 0;
         // how many bits are recorded

    virtual ULong hashValue(void) const =0;
         // return decimal representation

  };

  // .....

// ==================================================================
// Start of class BitVector16.  Derived from ABSTRACT base class
   BitVec
// It is used to create objects representing 16-bit bit vectors.
   Note:
//
//    UInt  operator[] (UInt) const; UInt  bit(UInt) const;
//    void  set(UInt);               void  reset(UInt);
//    UInt  capacity(void);          ULong hashValue(void) const;
//
// are redefinitions of virtual functions in the ABSTRACT base
   class
// BitVec
//
==================================================================

  class BitVector16 : public BitVec  {
    friend UInt        operator* (const BitVector16&, const
      BitVector16&);
    friend BitVector16 operator+ (const BitVector16&, const
      BitVector16&);

  public:
    BitVector16(UInt = 0);
         // standard constructor

    BitVector16(const BitVec& bit);
         // copy constructor
    ~BitVector16(void);
  // destructor
```

```
    BitVector16&        operator= (UInt bit);
    BitVector16&        operator= (const BitVec& bit);
          // overloaded assignment operators

    UInt          operator[] (UInt index) const;
    UInt          bit(UInt index) const;
          // indexing operators

    void          shiftRight(UInt index);
          // shfit right by given number of bits

    void          shiftLeft(UInt index);
          // shfit left by given number of bits

   void           rotateRight(UInt index);
          // rotate right a given number of places

   void           rotateLeft(UInt index);
          // rotate left a given number of places

   void           set(UInt index);
          // set bit at given index position

   void           reset(UInt index);
          // reset bit at given index position

   UInt           capacity(void) const;
          // how many bits are recorded

   ULong hashValue(void) const;
          // return decimal representation

  private:
    UInt          bits;         // representation

    void          replicate(const BitVec& bit);
                  // replicate function called by copy constructor
                  // and overloaded assignment operator
                  // BitVector16::operator= (const BitVec& bit)

 };

  // .....

#endif   // BITVECTOR

// ================= End of header file BITVECTOR.H ==============
```

From these new services and those of our existing class library, the problem solution is straightforward and appears as follows:

```
// ———————— FILE: case01.cpp ————————

#include <iostream.h>
#include <fstream.h>
#include <string.h>
#include "cstring.h"
#include "bitvector.h"
#include "ksorcol.h"

const UInt LINESIZE = 64;
```

```
const UInt MATHEMATICS = 0;
const UInt ECONOMICS = 9;

String courseName[] = {
  "MATHEMATICS", "PHYSICS", "CHEMISTRY", "BIOLOGY", "ENGLISH",
  "FRENCH",  "GERMAN", "ITALIAN",  "ACCOUNTING", "ECONOMICS"
};

int main(int argc, char* argv[])
{
  if(argc != 2){
    cerr << "Usage: " << argv[0] << "filename\n";
    return (1);
  }

  ifstream              ifp(argv[1], ios::in);
  if( ! ifp){
    cerr << argv[0] << ": cannot open " << argv[1] << "\n";
    return (2);
  }

  KeySortedCollection<String, BitVector16>  studentRegister(4);
  char                                      textLine[LINESIZE];

  while(ifp.getline(textLine, LINESIZE)){
    String      textString(textLine);

    String*     studentName = new String(textString(0,20));

    BitVector16* courses = new BitVector16(0);
    for(int column = 20; column < 30; column++)
      if(textString[column] == 'X')
        courses->set(column-20);

    studentRegister.addKeyValue(*studentName, *courses);
  }

                                     // print the registers
  const int registerLength = studentRegister.cardinality();
  for(int subject = MATHEMATICS; subject <= ECONOMICS;
                                                      subject++){
    cout << "\n\n\n" << courseName[subject] << "\n";

    for(int enrollee = 0; enrollee < registerLength; enrollee++){
      const Association<String, BitVector16>& assoc =
                                  studentRegister.at(enrollee);
      const String& student = assoc.key();
      const BitVector16& classes = assoc.value();
      if(classes.bit(subject))
         cout << "\t" << student << "\n";
    }
  }

  return (0);
}

// ———————— END: case01.cpp ————————
```

17.2 Summary

1. Bitwise expressions allow storage compaction and operations on the machine dependent bit representation of integral data values. Bitwise operations are highly machine dependent and make programs difficult to port. Where appropriate, consideration should be given to portability aspects when using bitwise operators. In particular, code should be conditionally compiled for a number of architectures.

2. Packing is the name given to placing bit patterns into integral data values. Unpacking is used to access these bit patterns. Masks are used to perform these operations.

17.3 Exercises

1. Develop a C++ function called `rotate` which rotates a bit pattern a given number of places. The function prototype is:

   ```
   unsigned int rotate(unsigned int value, int n)
   ```

   The process of rotation is similar to shifting, except that when a value is rotated to the left the bits that are shifted out of the high order bits are shifted back into the low order bits. Similarly with a right rotation. Left and right shifts are denoted by positive and negative values for `n` respectively.

2. Write a function called `getbits` which delivers the value of the `n`-bit pattern contained in the argument value starting at bit position `p`:

   ```
   unsigned int getbits(unsigned int p, unsigned int n,
                                        unsigned int value)
   ```

3. Write a function that reverses the bit representation of a byte. For example: `10101110` yields `01110101` when reversed.

4. Incorporate the above three functions into the bit vector classes.

18

Further Language Constructs

This is the final chapter, and one in which we introduce four further features of C++. The first construction extends the concept of derivation to include *multiple inheritance* – a derived class inheriting features from more than one base class. The next construction is the *exception mechanism.* This is a relatively recent addition to the language and current compilers may not yet support it. The *linkage specification* permits C++ programs to call functions defined in other languages, notably C. The final feature we review is the *goto statement.* This we have deliberately held until this final chapter to encourage the programmer to develop applications without it, hence reinforcing the idea that we can compose our programming logic around the sequence, selection and control structures of Chapter 6.

18.1 Multiple inheritance

The class hierarchies we have formed are structured as trees in which a derived class has one base class. When introducing the input/output stream library in Chapter 15 we observed how a class may be derived from more than one base class (see Figure 15.1). This we called *multiple inheritance,* and it gives rise to a *type lattice* (or *directed acyclic graph,* DAG) for the class inheritance hierarchy.

While multiple inheritance is not as common as single inheritance, it is useful when it is necessary to introduce a class which combines the behaviour of two or more other classes. For example, an academic institution employs lecturers to teach students. Some senior students are also employed as technical assistants in laboratory practical sessions. A technical assistant is both a student and a lecturer.

Suppose we have a class `Person` describing the general properties of people, including name and social security number:

```
class Person {
  // .....
protected:
  String      theName;
  String      theSSN;
  // .....
};
```

A `Student` is also a `Person`. A `Student` has the same properties as a `Person` and, additionally, the name of the course on which a `Student` is enrolled. A `Lecturer` is a `Person` too. The additional features associated with a `Lecturer` are the job title and salary.

```
class Student : public Person {
  // .....
private:
  String       theCourse;
  // .....
};

class Lecturer : public Person {
  // .....
private:
  String         theJobTitle;
  long           theSalary;
  // .....
};
```

A `TechnicalAssistant` is both a `Student` and a `Lecturer`. We express this by using multiple inheritance to inherit from both classes:

```
class TechnicalAssistant : public Student, public Lecturer {
  // .....
};
```

The class declaration for `TechnicalAssistant` introduces a new class derived from both `Student` and `Lecturer`. Any number of base class names may appear in the comma separated list. No name may be duplicated in the list (see below).

The resulting class hierarchy is given in Figure 18.1. We observe that class `TechnicalAssistant` inherits the properties of class `Person` twice in this graph. The C++ programming language considers this arrangement perfectly valid. In many situations this is not what we require, but be aware that the language considers it to be legal.

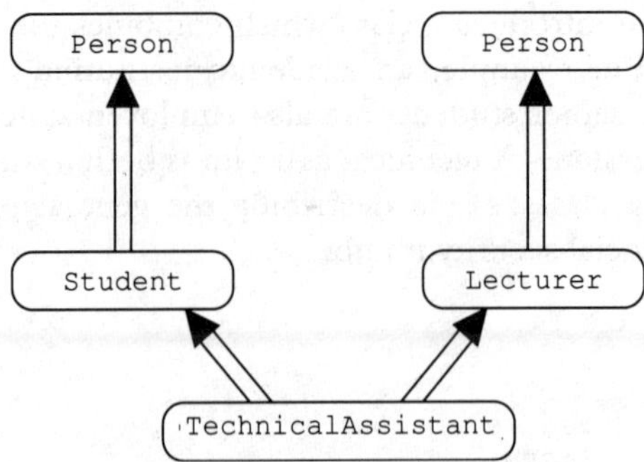

Figure 18.1

In this context, however, we would naturally wish for a `TechnicalAssistant` to inherit the properties of class `Person` once. This would ensure that a `TechnicalAssistant` had one name and one social security number and not two of each. Further, the arrangement would remove ambiguities. If within the class `TechnicalAssistant` we refer to the inherited item `theName` from class `Person`, then is it the `theName` inherited via class `Student` or is it the `theName` inherited through class `Lecturer`?

With multiple inheritance a class inherits from more than one base class. Consider Program 18.1 in which class `Derived` inherits from two base classes `Base1` and `Base2` with, respectively, two inherited data members `b1` and `b2`. Since the derived class is publicly derived from its two bases, the inherited data members are accessible. Hence the program's output is:

```
First: 10, second: 20
```

PROGRAM 18.1

```
#include <iostream.h>

class Base1 {
public:
  Base1(int b) { b1 = b; }
  int     get(void) const { return b1; }
protected:
  int     b1;
};

class Base2 {
public:
  Base2(int b) { b2 = b; }
  int     get(void) const { return b2; }
protected:
  int     b2;
};

class Derived : public Base1, public Base2 {
public:
  Derived(int b1, int b2) : Base1(b1), Base2(b2) {}
  int     first(void) const { return b1; }
  int     second(void) const { return b2; }
};

int main()
{
  Derived d(10, 20);

  cout << "First: " << d.first() << ", second: " << d.second()
    << "\n";
  return (0);
}
```

If each base class had been developed by independent programming teams then there is nothing to stop both base classes referring to their members by the same name, say, `b`. In that case, member functions `first` and `second` of class `Derived`:

```
int first(void) const { return b; }
```

elicit an error from the compiler complaining that the reference to the data member `b` is ambiguous. The compiler is unable to determine whether the `b` used in the return statement is that inherited from `Base1` or from `Base2`.

If we restore the program to its form in Program 18.1 but change function `main` to read:

```
int main()
{
  Derived        d(10, 20);

  cout << "First: " << d.get() << ", second: " << d.get()
    << "\n";
  return (0);
}
```

then an ambiguity reappears since the compiler cannot determine with which `get` function it is dealing. The base class name and the scope resolution operator is required here to remove the ambiguity. Hence, the correct form for `main` is:

```
int main()
{
  Derived        d(10, 20);

  cout << "First: " << d.Base1::get()
       << ", second: " << d.Base2::get() << "\n";
  return (0);
}
```

We observed in the previous section that a class name may appear at most once in a list of base classes. This restriction is required to resolve the kinds of ambiguity previously illustrated. Hence the following is illegal:

```
class Base { ..... protected: int b; };
class Derived : public Base, public Base {    // error
```

because, for example, in a member function of class `Derived` every reference to data member `b` would be ambiguous and incapable of resolution.

A class may, however, be included twice as an indirect base class. This we saw in Figure 18.1. In Program 18.2 the base class `Common` is inherited twice into class `Derived`. The class hierarchy resulting from this program is shown in Figure 18.2.

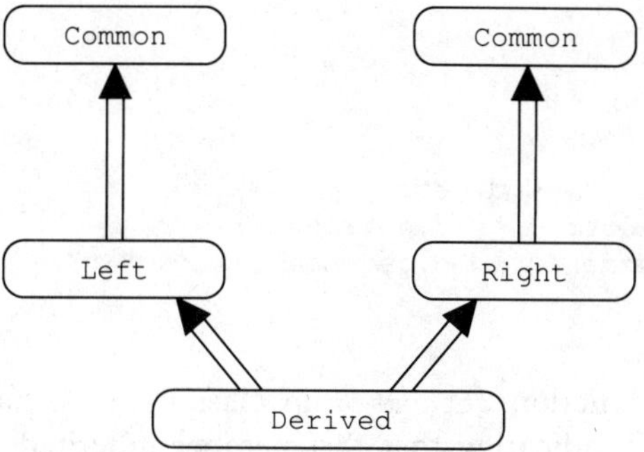

Figure 18.2

PROGRAM 18.2

```
#include <iostream.h>

class Common {
public:
  Common(int x) { common = x; }
  int     get(void) const { return common; }
protected:
  int     common;
};

class Left : public Common {
public:
  Left(int l, int c) : Common(c) { left = l; }
  int     get(void) const { return left; }
protected:
  int     left;
};

class Right : public Common {
public:
  Right(int r, int c) : Common(c) { right = r; }
  int     get(void) const { return right; }
protected:
  int     right;
};

class Derived : public Left, public Right {
public:
  Derived(int c, int l, int r)
  : Left(l, c), Right(r, c) {}
  int     getleft(void) const { return left; }
  int     getright(void) const { return right; }
  int     getcommon(void) const { return Left::common; }
```

```
};

int main()
{
  Derived        d(10, 20, 30);

  cout << "Left: " << d.getleft()
       << ", right: " << d.getright()
       << ", common " << d.getcommon() << "\n";
  return (0);
}
```

Note how member function `getcommon` in class `Derived` had to disambiguate the member `common` by indicating that the member inherited through class `Left` was selected.

Further ambiguities would arise were, for example, class `Common` to be named as a direct base class for `Derived` in addition to being an indirect base class through both `Left` and `Right`. Given the class header:

```
class Derived : public Left, public Right, public Common {
  // .....
};
```

then the resulting class hierarchy would be as shown in Figure 18.3.

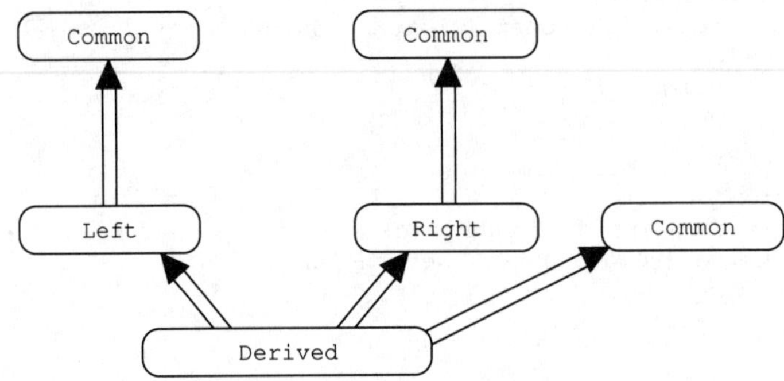

Figure 18.3

In Section 11.5 the type compatibility rule of C++ was defined. Any instance of a derived class may be used in place of a base class. Referring to Figure 18.2, the following is perfectly acceptable:

```
void      f(Common*);     // prototype
Left      left(10, 20); // object
f(&left);                 // ok
```

Because `Derived` contains two `Common` sub-objects, `f` cannot be passed a `Derived` object:

```
Derived  derived(30, 40, 50); // object;
f(&derived);                  // error
```

18.2 Virtual base classes

Figure 18.2 is invariably not what is required. Usually, only one copy of the data members of class `Common` is wanted. The solution is to declare `Common` as a *virtual base class* of both `Left` and `Right`. The definitions for the latter would then look like this:

```
class Left : virtual public Common {
  // .....
};

class Right : public virtual Common {
  // .....
};
```

Note that the order of the reserved keywords `virtual` and `public` is irrelevant.

The class hierarchy for this new arrangement is given in Figure 18.4. Only one copy of the base class `Common` is included in class `Derived`. An instance of class `Derived` has only one member `common`, and removes the ambiguity previously noted. Program 18.3 illustrates this.

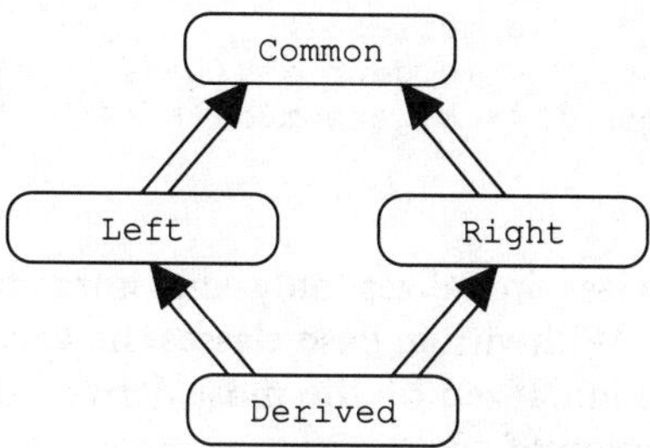

Figure 18.4

PROGRAM 18.3

```
#include <iostream.h>

class Common {
public:
  Common(int x) { common = x; }
  int     get(void) const { return common; }
protected:
  int     common;
};
```

```
class Left : public virtual Common {
public:
  Left(int l, int c) : Common(c) { left = l; }
  int     get(void) const { return left; }
protected:
  int     left;
};

class Right : public virtual Common {
public:
  Right(int r, int c) : Common(c) { right = r; }
  int     get(void) const { return right; }
protected:
  int     right;
};

class Derived : public Left, public Right {
public:
  Derived(int c, int l, int r)
   : Common(c), Left(l, c), Right(r, c) {}
  int     getleft(void) const { return left; }
  int     getright(void) const { return right; }
  int     getcommon(void) const { return common; }
};

int main()
{
  Derived        d(10, 20, 30);

  cout << "Left: " << d.getleft()
       << ", right: " << d.getright()
       << ", common " << d.getcommon() << "\n";
  return (0);
}
```

Normally, a derived class initializes only the immediate base classes in its member initialization list. With virtual base classes, however, it is necessary for the common base class to be initialized by the most derived class. Hence in Program 18.3 we have the initialization of `Common` by `Derived` as in:

```
Derived(int c, int l, int r) : Common(c), ..... { ..... }
```

Explicit initialization of `Common` by `Derived` can be omitted if `Common` has a default constructor.

18.3 Multiple inheritance and virtual functions

Virtual functions and polymorphism operate much as expected. Program 18.4 implements the class hierarchy of Figure 18.2, and introduces the virtual function `whoAmI`. Dynamic binding of the function call is illustrated with the function `polymorphism`. The program delivers the expected output:

```
I am Common
I am Left
I am Right
```

PROGRAM 18.4

```
#include <iostream.h>

class Common {
public:
  Common(int x) { common = x; }
  int                  get(void) const
        { return common; }
  virtual void         whoAmI(void) const
        { cout << "I am Common\n"; }
protected:
  int     common;
};

class Left : public Common {
public:
  Left(int l, int c) : Common(c) { left = l; }
  int              get(void) const
        { return left; }
  void             whoAmI(void) const
        { cout << "I am Left\n"; }
protected:
  int     left;
};

class Right : public Common {
public:
  Right(int r, int c) : Common(c) { right = r; }
  int              get(void) const
        { return right; }
  void             whoAmI(void) const
        { cout << "I am Right\n"; }
protected:
  int     right;
};

class Derived : public Left, public Right {
public:
  Derived(int c, int l, int r)
        : Left(l, c), Right(r, c) {}
  int     getleft(void) const { return left; }
  int     getright(void) const { return right; }
};

int main()
{
  void    polymorphism(Common* cp);    // prototype
```

```
    polymorphism(new Common(10));        // create object on heap ..
    polymorphism(new Left(20, 30));      // and pass pointer
    polymorphism(new Right(40, 50));
    // polymorphism(new Derived(60, 70, 80)); ambiguous
    return (0);
  }

  void      polymorphism(Common* cp)
  {
    cp->whoAmI();
  }
```

Note how the fourth call to function `polymorphism` would cause ambiguity since we cannot dynamically bind from a `Derived*` to a `Common*` as the former has two such bases and a compiler error would be reported.

CASE STUDY 18.1
Sales team

An organization employs a number of staff some of whom are given responsibility for a small team of staff. Each employee has a job title and salary in addition to their normal qualities such as their name, date of birth, etc. Each sales employee keeps a log of their achieved sales and each manager knows which staff they are responsible for. A sales manager has responsibility for a sales team comprising some of the company staff.

This company scenario gives rise to the object model presented in Figure 18.5. Class `Person` represents the general properties of people. Class `Employee` inherits these general properties and additionally includes their job title and salary. A `Sales` employee records the sales achieved in some sales period. A `Manager` is responsible for a group of employees and a `SalesManager` is involved both with sales himself as well as a sales team and is set some sales target for his team.

Class `SalesManager` directly inherits from both class `Sales` and `Manager`. From class `Sales`, a `SalesManager` has a personal sales achievement. From class `Manager` comes the sales team for which he is leader.

The program we develop reads the sales statistics for the company and for each sales manager presents the total sales for that team against the sales target.

The relevant classes are `Manager` and `SalesManager`. These and the application program are listed below.

```
  // ———————- FILE: manager.h ————————

  //
  //  A Manager is an Employee who has responsibility for
  //       a number of associated employees.
  //

  #ifndef MANAGER
    #define MANAGER
```

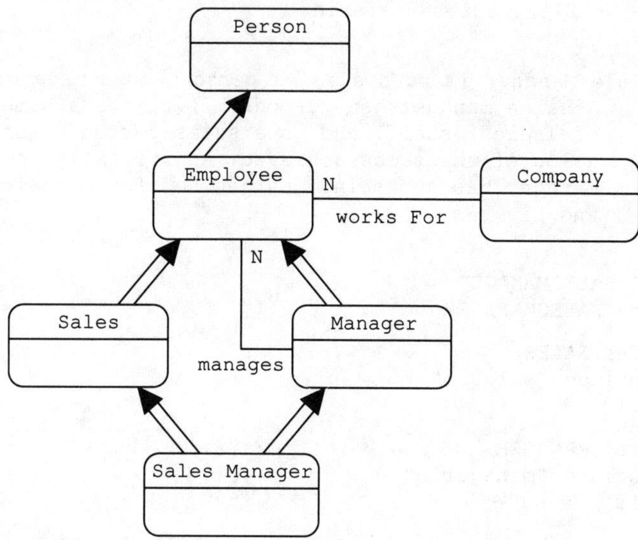

Figure 18.5

```
#ifndef EMPLOYEE
  #include "employee.h"
#endif

#ifndef SORTEDCOLLECTION
  #include "sorcol.h"
#endif

class Manager : virtual public Employee {
public:
  Manager(const Employee& anEmployee, const String& aDivision);

  void assign(const Employee& aMember);

protected:
  SortedCollection<Employee> theManagedEmployees;
  String                     theDivision;
};

inline Manager::Manager(const Employee& anEmployee, const
                                                String& aDivision)
       : Employee(anEmployee),
         theDivision(aDivision)
{}

inline void    Manager::assign(const Employee& aMember)
       { theManagedEmployees.add(aMember); }

#endif    // MANAGER

// ---------- END: manager.h ----------
```

```
// ——————— FILE: salesmanager.h ———————————

//
//  A SalesManager is both a sales person and a manager.
//       A sales manager has responsibility for a number
//       of (sales) staff, and as a sales person also has
//       a log of the sales achieved. Additionally, a sales
//       manager has a combined target set for himself
//       and his team.
//

#ifndef SALESMANAGER
  #define SALESMANAGER

  #ifndef SALES
    #include "sales.h"
  #endif

  #ifndef MANAGER
    #include "manager.h"
  #endif

  class SalesManager : public Sales, public Manager {
  public:
    SalesManager(const String& aName,
                 const String& aJobTitle, ULong aSalary,
                 ULong anAchievedSales, const String& aDivision,
                 ULong aTarget);

    void salesReport(void) const;

  private:
    ULong       theTarget;
  };

  inline SalesManager::SalesManager(const String& aName,
                      const String& aJobTitle, ULong aSalary,
                 ULong anAchievedSales, const String& aDivision,
                 ULong aTarget)
   : Employee(aName, aJobTitle, aSalary),
     Sales(Employee(aName, aJobTitle, aSalary), anAchievedSales),
     Manager(Employee(aName, aJobTitle, aSalary), aDivision),
     theTarget(aTarget)
   {}

#endif   // SALESMANAGER

// ————————- END: salesmanager.h ——————————

// ————————- FILE: salesmanager.cpp ——————————

#include <iostream.h>

#ifndef SALESMANAGER
  #include "salesmanager.h"
#endif

void     SalesManager::salesReport(void) const
```

```
{
  cout << "Division: " << theDivision << "\n";
  cout << "\tManager: " << theName << "\n";
  cout << "\tTarget: " << theTarget << "\n";

  ULong teamTotalSales = this->achievedSales();

  Iterator<Employee>    iter(theManagedEmployees);
  while(iter.isExhausted() == FALSE){
    const Employee& emp = iter.selection();
    teamTotalSales += emp.achievedSales();
    iter.advance();
  }
  cout << "\tTotal sales: " << teamTotalSales << "\n";
}

// ———————- END: salesmanager.cpp ————————

// ———————- FILE: case01.cpp ————————

#include "iostream.h"
#include "fstream.h"

#ifndef COMPANY
  #include "company.h"
#endif

#ifndef SALESMANAGER
  #include "salesmanager.h"
#endif

int main(int argc, char* argv[])
{
  if(argc != 2){
    cerr << "Usage: " << argv[0] << " filename\n";
    return (1);
  }

  ifstream       dataFile(argv[1], ios::in);
  if( ! dataFile){
    cerr << argv[0] << ": cannot open " << argv[1] << "\n";
    return (2);
  }

  String companyName;
  dataFile >> companyName;

  Company        company(companyName);
  String managerName, jobTitle, division;
  ULong          salary, achieved, target;

  while(dataFile >> managerName >> jobTitle >> salary >> achieved
    >> division >> target){
    SalesManager* salesManager = new SalesManager(managerName,
      jobTitle, salary, achieved, division, target);
    company.appoint(*salesManager);
```

```
        String      teamMemberName;
        dataFile >> teamMemberName;

        while(teamMemberName != managerName){
          dataFile >> jobTitle >> salary >> achieved;
          Sales* salesMember = new Sales(Employee(teamMemberName,
            jobTitle, salary), achieved);
          company.appoint(*salesMember);
          salesManager->assign(*salesMember);

          dataFile >> teamMemberName;
        }
      }

      company.salesReport();

      return (0);
    }

    // -------- END: case01.cpp ----------
```

18.4 Exception handling

The class library introduced in Chapter 12 necessarily had to validate data items to ensure the integrity of the structures formed and manipulated. For example, the initial container classes such as `SortedCollection` used a `VVector` for their underlying representation, and the `VVector` class constructor ensures that the required size is not less than one. Similarly, the member function `operator[]` of class `VVector` used for indexing, checks that the supplied index is within bounds.

The author of these classes knew when an error situation had arose but was unable to determine how the application should proceed. Accordingly, the default action was to report an error and terminate the program. Program termination is a somewhat Draconian action. Whilst the author of the class may not know in what context the error has occurred, the author of the application program may know how the program might proceed in such an eventuality.

To support this pattern of events the current language specification supports *exceptions*. An exception is *raised* by the piece of code determining an error situation. An *exception handler* in the application code traps the occurrence of the exception and takes the necessary action.

The exception handling mechanism of C++ has been influenced by an elegant arrangement introduced into the functional programming language ML [Har 86]. A function which identifies that an error has occurred but is unable to determine how to proceed `throws` an exception anticipating that its caller can `catch` the exception with an exception handler and deal gracefully with the problem.

The distinguishing feature of ML's exception handling mechanism adopted by C++ is that an exception is raised by throwing an object of some (user-defined exception) class. The error handler then determines the nature of the exception by effectively examining the type of the object. Further, if information needs to be communicated to the handler from the code throwing the exception, then this too can be transferred by the exception class object.

As a simple illustration, consider a function `sub` which returns the difference of its two integer arguments `p` and `q`, provided `p >= q`; otherwise it throws the exception `Negative`:

```
class Negative {};          // exception class

int sub(int p, int q)
{
  if(p >= q)
    return (p-q);
  throw Negative();         // default constructor
}
```

Function `subtract` provides a handler for exception `Negative`. If the exception is raised when the auxiliary function `sub` is called, then the handler specified in `subtract` returns zero instead:

```
int subtract(int p, int q)
{
  try {
    return sub(p, q);
  }
  catch(Negative){
    return 0;
  }
}
```

Detecting and handling exceptions is expressed with a *try block*, the basic syntax of which is:

```
try {
  // compound statement
}
catch(exception-declaration){
  // compound statement
}
```

The clause `try { ..... }` surrounds that code in which function `subtract` wishes to detect and handle any exceptions. The clause `catch( ..... ) { ..... }` is the exception handler. The *exception declaration* specifies the type for the object which may be raised by an exception. If such an exception does occur then the code for that handler is executed.

More realistically, consider class `VVector` introduced earlier. Errors might occur in a number of places. For example, the constructor expects a non-zero size argument. The indexing function `operator[]` should check for the occurrence of a bounds error. A code fragment for class `VVector` with exception classes `Size` and `Range` is:

```
class VVector {
public:
  class Size {};                  // exception classes
  class Range {};
  VVector(UInt sz = DEFAULTSIZE)
          { if(sz == 0)
              throw Size();
            // .....
          }

  void*          operator[] (UInt index) const
          { if(index >= theSize)
              throw Range();
            // .....
          }

  // .....
private:
  void**  theVVector;   // representation
  UInt    theSize;      // holds the size of the the VVector
};
```

An application program declaring and using `VVectors` can protect itself from errors with the code:

```
void f(int size)
{
  try {
    VVector    table(size);
    // .....
    int item = table[0];
    // .....
  }
  catch(VVector::Size){
    // ..... bad vector size
  }
  catch(VVector::Range){
    // ..... subscript error
  }
}
```

Observe how the `catch` clause can be cascaded to filter out one or more possible exceptions in the order of appearance. Note also that the exception class names for `VVector` have local scope and must be fully qualified in the `catch` clause exception declaration.

The exception declaration in a handler may consist of the keyword `'...'` as used in a function argument declaration (see Section 14.4). Such a declaration specifies a match for any exception thrown.

```
void f(int size)
{
  try {
```

```
    VVector     table(size);
    // .....
    int item = table[0];
    // .....
  }
  catch(...){
    // ..... any exception processed here
  }
}
```

If we also wish to specify particular exceptions, then `catch(...)` must be the last handler in a try block.

A handler may also partly process the exception then re-throw it again for some other handler to continue dealing with it. For example:

```
void f(int size)
{
  try {
    VVector     table(size);
    // .....
    int item = table[0];
    // .....
  }
  catch(...){
    .....        // partly processed here, then
    throw;       // pass to some other handler
  }
}
```

The function calls will continue to unwind seeking a handler to process the exception. Failing that, the program calls the function `terminate` to deal with problems that cannot be resolved with the normal exception handling mechanism.

The exception declaration specifies a type – the type of the exception raised by the `throw` clause. Strictly, the type specifies the type of the object which is actually thrown. Since an object is thrown, we may use it to communicate information back to the handler. For example, we might modify class `Range` to carry the value of the subscript error which caused the problem:

```
class VVector {
  public:
    class Size {};                        // exception classes
    class Range {
    public:
      Range(UInt sub) : theSubscript(sub) {}
      UInt      subscript(void) const { return theSubscript; }
    private:
      UInt      theSubscript;
    };

    VVector(UInt sz = DEFAULTSIZE)
          { if(sz == 0)
                throw Size();
```

```
    // .....
  }

    void*        operator[] (UInt index) const
         { if(index >= theSize)
             throw Range(index);
           // .....
  }

    // .....
  private:
    void**       theVVector; // representation
    UInt         theSize;    // holds the size of the the VVector
  };
```

and:

```
void f(int size)
{
  try {
    VVector     table(size);
    // .....
    int item = table[0];
    // .....
  }
  catch(VVector::Size){                  // exception with no
                                                     information
    // ..... bad vector size
  }
  catch(VVector::Range rangeError){  // exception with
                                                     information
    cerr << "Range error: " << rangeError.subscript() << "\n";
    // .....
  }
}
```

Exercise 6 in Chapter 11 introduced a class hierarchy of triangular figures. Class `Triangle` is at the root and represents a general three-sided figure. The derived class `RightTriangle` specializes this base class to handle all right-angled triangles.

18.5 Linkage specification

Overloading function names gives added convenience to the programmer, placing the burden of resolution on the compilation system. Whilst the compiler is able to resolve overloaded function calls, two or more instances of discrete function definitions with the same name passed to a linker cannot be distinguished. This problem is primarily due to the technology used by linkers.

To circumvent this limitation, C++ compilers encode each function name using additional material from the function's signature. The encoding scheme details are not relevant to the programmer and may differ across systems. They do, however, result in uniqueness of names between functions.

The encoding scheme removes one problem but introduces another. C++ programs will undoubtedly utilize functions from other libraries, notably C libraries. A C function will be compiled into a C++ linkage-compatible form but without name encoding by the C compiler. However, when the C library function is referenced in the C++ program the C++ compiler will encode the name, which the linker will then fail to match with the original C function. For example, the C library function `sqrt` referenced in a C++ program with:

```
double  sqrt(double);
```

will be encoded by the C++ compiler into a name differing from its original, which the linker will report as a linkage error.

A *linkage specification* is used to turn off this effect. For example, for function `sqrt` we would write:

```
extern "C" double sqrt(double);
```

A series of such functions in a header file may be combined with:

```
extern "C" {
     double    sqrt(double);
     double    exp(double);
     // .....
}
```

Of course, if this appeared in `<math.h>` it would confuse the C compiler, hence we must conditionally compile the C++ material using the pre-processor:

```
//   File:     math.h

#ifdef __cplusplus
     extern "C" {
#endif
          double    sqrt(double);
          double    exp(double);
          // .....
#ifdef __cplusplus
     }
     #endif
```

with the predefined pre-processor macro `__cplusplus` used to test for a C++ environment.

18.6 The goto statement

We conclude our discussion of the C++ programming language by introducing the only remaining statement. The *goto statement* permits unconditional transfers of control from one part of a function to another, and follows the syntax:

```
goto label;
```

where *label* is an identifier and `goto` is a reserved keyword. Labels are not declared in the sense of program variables. The label identifier in a `goto` statement must be the same as a named label associated with some statement in the current function. Labels are effectively declared on the statement with which they associate. A labelled statement is preceded by a label identifier immediately followed by a colon symbol, as in:

```
label : statement;
```

When a `goto` statement is executed, control passes immediately to the statement prefixed with the corresponding label. Examples of labelled statements include:

```
sum : a = b + c + d;
bug : cerr << "Execution error\n";
```

Statements may be multiply labelled, permitting one statement to be referenced by different named labels. Thus, we might have:

```
bug : recover : abort : exit(1);
```

The free format of C++ would permit this last example to also appear as:

```
bug :
recover :
abort : exit(1);
```

The `null statement` may be labelled, so that we have:

```
dummy : /* null statement */ ;
```

C++ permits a `goto` statement to transfer control to any other statement within the function in which it is used. However, certain kinds of branching are illegal. For example, transferring control into the middle of a compound statement from outside it, bypassing any initialization of variables declared at the head of the compound statement, results in a compilation error:

```
  // .....
  // .....
  goto middle;
  // .....
  // .....
  {
    int sum = 0, divisor = 1;
    // .....
    // .....
middle :                                  // error
    // .....
  }
```

Other restrictions that should also apply to the use of the `goto` statement include:

- Branching into the 'then' or 'else' parts of an `if` statement from outside the `if` statement.

- Branching into the body of a `switch` statement.
- Branching into the body of an iteration statement.

Indiscriminate use of the `goto` statement must be avoided since it leads to obscure code which can be difficult to maintain. The fact that both the selection and repetition control structures can be emulated using only `if` and `goto` statements does not mean that `goto` should be used as a substitute. The keywords `while`, `for` and `do` signify repetition; `if` and `switch` denote selection. Their appearance in a program immediately indicates the desired control flow. An `if ..... goto` pair fails to convey this same information. By way of comparison, consider Program 18.5 which repeats the processing in Program 6.14. Note how the repetition is now implemented using a combined `if` and `goto`. Further, the tests are conducted with the same pairing. Overall, the program logic is much less obvious.

PROGRAM 18.5

```
//
//  A piece of text consists of a character sequence
//      spanning a number of lines and terminated by a period
//      symbol. Count the number of "words" in the text,
//      where a word is defined as any character string
//      delimited by whitespace (blank, tab or newline)
//      symbols.
//

#include <iostream.h>

const char      PERIOD = '.';
const char      BLANK  = ' ';
const char      TAB    = '\t';
const char      NEWLINE= '\n';

enum Bool { FALSE, TRUE };

int main()
{
  char c;                                 // data character
  int  words = 0;                         // word counter
  Bool inword = FALSE;                    // word indicator

loop:
  cin.get(c);                             // get next character
  if(c == PERIOD)                         // terminator?
    goto finish;                         // yes - complete program

  if(c == BLANK || c == TAB || c == NEWLINE){ // whitespace?
    inword = FALSE;                       // outwith a word
    goto loop;                            // go fetch next character
  }
```

```
    if (inword == FALSE){                   // within a word?
      inword = TRUE;                        // now in a word
      words++;                              // increment counter
    }

    goto loop;                              // cycle for next character

  finish:
    cout << "Number of words is " << words << "\n";
    return (0);
  }
```

The freedom to destroy the program structure makes the `goto` statement a dangerous facility, and hence a topic for advanced study. The `goto` statement should only be used in exceptional circumstances, when the required control flow cannot be reasonably expressed by the primitives introduced in Chapter 6. In practice, this is so rare that the `goto` statement can be virtually ignored. This way, the difficulties associated with its use can be avoided.

18.7 Summary

1. C++ supports multiple inheritance in which a class is derived from one or more base classes. If necessary, virtual base classes ensure that only one copy of a multiply inherited base class is included.

2. Exceptions establish a clear separation of normal code from that associated with error handling. Exceptions provide a means whereby a function, upon identifying an error situation for which it is unable to determine what is the correct course of action, can report this position to the calling function. This commonly occurs with class member functions whose sole responsibility is to implement the class operation, and not directly handle the error.

3. The linkage specification permits C++ programs to exploit functions developed in some other language, notably C. The linkage specification suppresses the name encoding otherwise performed by C++ compilers.

4. The `goto` statement may violate the principles of structured programming. The `goto` statement permits unconditional transfer of control and results in unmanageable code. There are few situations which demand the use of the `goto` statement.

18.8 Exercises

1. In Program 18.4 make the base class `Common` a virtual base class. What additionally has to be specified in the class? Can the fourth call to function polymorphism be resolved? Explain.

2. Revue member functions of the container class library, identifying how exceptions may be raised and, where appropriate, how they should be handled.

3. Reduce the standard control flow primitives (`while`, `if`, etc.) to statements involving labels and `goto` statements.

Appendices

A

Hardware Characteristics

The following table summarizes the hardware properties of the basic data types of a C++ program on two typical configurations:

	INTEL 80 × 86	*DEC VAX**
`char`	8 bits	8 bits
`short`	16 bits	16 bits
`int`	16 bits	32 bits
`long`	32 bits	32 bits
`unsigned`	16 bits	32 bits
`float`	32 bits	32 bits
`double`	64 bits	64 bits

The header `<limits.h>` defines constants for the sizes of the integral values. The values below give minimum magnitudes; greater values may be employed.

`CHAR_BIT`	`8` bits in a `char`
`CHAR_MAX`	`UCHAR_MAX` maximum value of `char`, unsigned or `SCHAR_MAX` or signed representation
`CHAR_MIN`	`0` minimum value of `char`, unsigned or `SCHAR_MIN` or signed representation
`INT_MAX`	`+32767` maximum value of `int`
`INT_MIN`	`-32768` minimum value of `int`
`LONG_MAX`	`+2147483647` maximum value of `long`
`LONG_MIN`	`-2147483648` minimum value of `long`
`SCHAR_MAX`	`+127` maximum value of `signed char`
`SCHAR_MIN`	`-128` minimum value of `signed char`
`SHRT_MAX`	`+32767` maximum value of `short`
`SHRT_MIN`	`-32768` minimum value of `short`
`UCHAR_MAX`	`255` maximum value of `unsigned char`

* VAX is a registered trademark of Digital Equipment Corporation.

`UINT_MAX`	`65535` maximum value of `unsigned int`
`ULONG_MAX`	`4294967295` maximum value of `unsigned long`
`USHRT_MAX`	`65535` maximum value of `unsigned short`

The names in the table below are floating point constants defined in `<float.h>`. The given value represents the permitted minimum value. Implementations will define their own appropriate values.

`DBL_DIG`	`15` decimal digits of precision
`DBL_EPSILON`	`2.2E-16` smallest number `x` such that `x + 1.0 != 1.0`
`DBL_MANT_DIG`	`53` number of digits in the floating point mantissa for base `FLT_RADIX`
`DBL_MAX`	maximum double floating point number
`DBL_MAX_EXP`	`1024` largest integer such that the value of `FLT_RADIX` raised to this integer power then subtract 1 does not exceed `DBL_MAX`
`DBL_MAX_10_EXP`	`308` largest integer such that `10` raised to this power does not exceed `DBL_MAX`
`DBL_MIN`	`2.2E-308` smallest normalized double floating point number
`DBL_MIN_EXP`	`-1021` smallest integer such that the value of `FLT_RADIX` raised to this integer power then subtract 1 is not less than `DBL_MIN`
`DBL_MIN_10_EXP`	`-307` smallest integer such that `10` raised to this power is not less than `DBL_MIN`
`FLT_DIG`	`6` decimal digits of precision
`FLT_EPSILON`	`1.2E-7` smallest number `x` such that `x + 1.0 != 1.0`
`FLT_MANT_DIG`	`24` number of digits in the floating point mantissa for base `FLT_RADIX`
`FLT_MAX`	maximum floating point number
`FLT_MAX_EXP`	`128` largest integer such that the value of `FLT_RADIX` raised to this integer power then subtract 1 does not exceed `FLT_MAX`

`FLT_MAX_10_EXP`	`+38` largest integer such that the value `10` raised to this power does not exceed `FLT_MAX`
`FLT_MIN`	`1.2E-38` smallest normalized floating point number
`FLT_MIN_EXP`	`-125` smallest integer for the exponent part of a floating point number to base `FLT_RADIX`
`FLT_MIN_10_EXP`	`-37` smallest integer for the exponent part of a floating point number to base `10`
`FLT_RADIX`	`2` base to which the exponent part of all floating point numbers are represented
`FLT_ROUNDS`	`1`, `0` or `-1` nature of rounding used by the particular implementation: `1`: round to nearest representable value `0`: truncate toward zero `-1`: no rule applies
`LDBL_DIG`	`19` decimal digits of precision in a long double
`LDBL_EPSILON`	`1.1E-19` smallest number `x` such that `x + 1.0 != 1.0`
`LDBL_MANT_DIG`	`64` number of digits in the floating point mantissa for base `FLT_RADIX`
`LDBL_MAX`	 maximum long double floating point number
`LDBL_MAX_EXP`	`16384` largest integer such that the value of `FLT_RADIX` raised to this integer power then subtract 1 does not exceed `LDBL_MAX`
`LDBL_MAX_10_EXP`	`+4392` largest integer such that `10` raised to this power does not exceed `LDBL_MAX`
`LDBL_MIN`	 smallest normalized long double floating point number
`LDBL_MIN_EXP`	`-16381` smallest integer such that the value of `FLT_RADIX` raised to this integer power then subtract 1 is not less than `LDBL_MIN`
`LDBL_MIN_10_EXP`	`-4391` smallest integer such that `10` raised to this power is not less than `LDBL_MIN`

B

ASCII Character Set

The following table lists the American Standard Code for Information Interchange (ASCII) character codes in hexadecimal, octal and decimal and the associated character symbol. The ASCII code is a 7 bit code with the range 0 to 127 inclusive. Character codes 0 through 31 inclusive, and decimal 127 are the non-printing characters or *control characters*.

ASCII character	*Hexadecimal code*	*Octal code*	*Decimal code*
NUL (CTRL SPACE)	00	000	0
SOH (CTRL A)	01	001	1
STX (CTRL B)	02	002	2
ETX (CTRL C)	03	003	3
EOT (CTRL D)	04	004	4
ENQ (CTRL E)	05	005	5
ACK (CTRL F)	06	006	6
BEL (CTRL G)	07	007	7
BS (CTRL H or BACKSPACE)	08	010	8
HT (CTRL I or TAB)	09	011	9
LF (CTRL J or LINEFEED)	0A	012	10
VT (CTRL K)	0B	013	11
FF (CTRL L)	0C	014	12
CR (CTRL M or RETURN)	0D	015	13
SO (CTRL N)	0E	016	14
SI (CTRL O)	0F	017	15
DLE (CTRL P)	10	020	16
DC1 (CTRL Q)	11	021	17
DC2 (CTRL R)	12	022	18
DC3 (CTRL S)	13	023	19
DC4 (CTRL T)	14	024	20
NAK (CTRL U)	15	025	21
SYN (CTRL V)	16	026	22
ETB (CTRL W)	17	027	23

ASCII character	*Hexadecimal code*	*Octal code*	*Decimal code*
CAN (CTRL X)	18	030	24
EM (CTRL Y)	19	031	25
SUB (CTRL Z)	1A	032	26
ESC (CTRL [or ESC)	1B	033	27
FS (CTRL \)	1C	034	28
GS (CTRL])	1D	035	29
RS (CTRL ^)	1E	036	30
US (CTRL ?)	1F	037	31
(space)	20	040	32
!	21	041	33
"	22	042	34
# (hash symbol)	23	043	35
$	24	044	36
%	25	045	37
& (ampersand)	26	046	38
' (quote)	27	047	39
(	28	050	40
)	29	051	41
* (asterisk)	2A	052	42
+	2B	053	43
, (comma)	2C	054	44
-	2D	055	45
. (period)	2E	056	46
/	2F	057	47
0	30	060	48
1	31	061	49
2	32	062	50
3	33	063	51
4	34	064	52
5	35	065	53
6	36	066	54
7	37	067	55
8	38	070	56
9	39	071	57
: (colon)	3A	072	58
; (semicolon)	3B	073	59
<	3C	074	60
=	3D	075	61
>	3E	076	62
?	3F	077	63

ASCII character	*Hexadecimal code*	*Octal code*	*Decimal code*
@ (at symbol)	40	100	64
A	41	101	65
B	42	102	66
C	43	103	67
D	44	104	68
E	45	105	69
F	46	106	70
G	47	107	71
H	48	110	72
I	49	111	73
J	4A	112	74
K	4B	113	75
L	4C	114	76
M	4D	115	77
N	4E	116	78
O	4F	117	79
P	50	120	80
Q	51	121	81
R	52	122	82
S	53	123	83
T	54	124	84
U	55	125	85
V	56	126	86
W	57	127	87
X	58	130	88
Y	59	131	89
Z	5A	132	90
[	5B	133	91
\ (backslash)	5C	134	92
]	5D	135	93
^ (circumflex)	5E	136	94
_ (underscore)	5F	137	95
` (grave)	60	140	96
a	61	141	97
b	62	142	98
c	63	143	99
d	64	144	100
e	65	145	101
f	66	146	102

ASCII character	*Hexadecimal code*	*Octal code*	*Decimal code*
g	67	147	103
h	68	150	104
i	69	151	105
j	6A	152	106
k	6B	153	107
l	6C	154	108
m	6D	155	109
n	6E	156	110
o	6F	157	111
p	70	160	112
q	71	161	113
r	72	162	114
s	73	163	115
t	74	164	116
u	75	165	117
v	76	166	118
w	77	167	119
x	78	170	120
y	79	171	121
z	7A	172	122
{	7B	173	123
	(stick symbol)	7C	174	124
}	7D	175	125
~ (tilde)	7E	176	126
delete	7F	177	127

C

Reserved Keywords

The following is a list of reserved keywords; identifiers used by the C++ programming language. They may not be used as programmer-defined identifiers.

`asm`	`double`	`new`	`switch`
`auto`	`else`	`operator`	`template`
`break`	`enum`	`private`	`this`
`case`	`extern`	`protected`	`throw`
`catch`	`float`	`public`	`try`
`char`	`for`	`register`	`typedef`
`class`	`friend`	`return`	`union`
`const`	`goto`	`short`	`unsigned`
`continue`	`if`	`signed`	`virtual`
`default`	`inline`	`sizeof`	`void`
`delete`	`int`	`static`	`volatile`
`do`	`long`	`struct`	`while`

D

Identifiers

An *identifier* is created according to the following rule:

> An identifier is a combination of letters and digits, the first of which must be a letter. The underscore symbol (_) is permitted in an identifier and is considered to be a letter.

An identifier may be any length. However, many compilers consider the first 31 characters as significant in an object with *internal linkage*. The 32nd and subsequent characters in an identifier are ignored. Further, identifiers for external objects are processed by systems software other than compilers (such as linking loaders), and may only consider the first 6 characters as significant. These systems may not be case sensitive and fail to distinguish between two identifiers treated as unique by the C++ compiler.

E

Operators

The C++ programming language supports an extensive list of *operators*. The table below provides the full list. The table presents the symbol(s) used to represent the operator, a description of the operator, and the operator associativity. The operators are listed in non-increasing order of precedence. Thus, the operators addition (+) and subtraction (-) have equal precedence, and both have higher precedence than the equality (==) operator. The addition and subtraction operators associate left to right. The precedence and associativity are used to determine how an expression is evaluated. The general rule is that operators with highest precedence are evaluated first. An expression involving operators of equal precedence is evaluated according to the associativity of the operators.

Operator	*Description*	*Associativity*
`::`	Class scope resolution (binary)	Left to right
`::`	Global scope (unary)	Right to left
`()`	Function call	Left to right
`()`	Value construction	Left to right
`[]`	Array element reference	Left to right
`->`	Pointer to class member reference	Left to right
`.`	Class member reference	Left to right
–	Unary minus	Right to left
+	Unary addition	Right to left
`++`	Increment	Right to left
—	Decrement	Right to left
`!`	Logical negation	Right to left
~	One's complement	Right to left
`*`	Pointer dereference (indirection)	Right to left
`&`	Address	Right to left
`sizeof`	Size of an object	Right to left
`(type)`	Type cast (coercion)	Right to left
`new`	Create free store object	Right to left
`delete`	Destroy free store object	Right to left

Operator	*Description*	*Associativity*
`->*`	Pointer to member selector	Left to right
`*`	Pointer to member selector	Left to right
`*`	Multiplication	Left to right
`/`	Division	Left to right
`%`	Modulus	Left to right
`+`	Addition	Left to right
`-`	Subtraction	Left to right
`<<`	Left shift	Left to right
`>>`	Right shift	Left to right
`<`	Less than	Left to right
`<=`	Less than or equal	Left to right
`>`	Greater than	Left to right
`>=`	Greater then or equal	Left to right
`==`	Equality	Left to right
`!=`	Inequality	Left to right
`&`	Bitwise AND	Left to right
`^`	Bitwise XOR	Left to right
`|`	Bitwise OR	Left to right
`&&`	Logical AND	Left to right
`||`	Logical OR	Left to right
`?:`	Conditional expression	Right to left

`=`
`*=  /=  %=`
`+=  -=`
`&=  ^=  |=`
`<<=  >>=`
	Assignment operators	Right to left

`,`	Comma operator	Left to right

F

C++ Library Functions

Many C++ facilities are provided by C/C++ libraries. The facilities are categorized by their functionality and belong to a particular library. The capabilities detailed in this Appendix are partitioned into six groupings:

F.1 Operations on characters
F.2 Operations on strings
F.3 General utilities
F.4 Input/output procedures
F.5 Mathematical functions
F.6 Variable argument lists

To use a function from one of these libraries, the appropriate `#include` command should be used to provide the relevant library declarations. Many functions, particularly those that provide operations on characters, are macros. All of the facilities we discuss are described as if they were functions to permit detailing the number and type of the arguments.

F.1 Character functions

The standard header file `<ctype.h>` contains a set of macros that are used to process single characters. The macros fall into two categories: test a single character, and convert a single character. The macros are made accessible by the pre-processor statement:

```
#include <ctype.h>
```

The macros which test a single character return an `int` value that is non-zero (logical `TRUE`) or zero (logical `FALSE`) according to whether the test succeeds or not. All these functions are distinguished with the prefix `'is'`, for example, `isdigit`. The functions have an argument of type `int`. The macros which perform character translation have the prefix `'to'` (e.g. `toupper`) and return an `int` representation of some `int` character argument.

isalnum

```
int isalnum(c)
```

Return non-zero if `c` represents an alphanumeric character; otherwise returns zero. The alphanumeric characters are any one of `0-9`, `a-z` and `A-Z` inclusive.

isalpha

```
int isalpha(c)
```

Return non-zero if `c` represents an alphabetic character; otherwise returns zero. The alphabetic characters are `a-z` and `A-Z` inclusive.

iscntrl

```
int iscntrl(c)
```

Return non-zero if `c` represents a control character; otherwise returns zero. The control characters are the 'non printing' characters. From the standard ASCII set, the control characters are `0x00` to `0x1F` inclusive and also `0x7F`.

isdigit

```
int isdigit(c)
```

Return non-zero if `c` represents a decimal digit character; otherwise returns zero. The decimal digits include `0` to `9` inclusive.

isgraph

```
int isgraph(c)
```

Return non-zero if `c` represents a graphics character; otherwise returns zero. From the standard ASCII character set, the graphics characters are those with codes `0x21` to `0x7E` inclusive.

islower

```
int islower(c)
```

Return non-zero if `c` represents a lower case alphabetic character; otherwise returns zero. The lower case alphabetic characters include `a-z` inclusive.

isprint

```
int isprint(c)
```

Return non-zero if `c` represents a printable character; otherwise returns zero. From the standard ASCII character set, the printable characters are those with codes `0x20` to `0x7E` inclusive.

ispunct

```
int ispunct(c)
```

Return non-zero if `c` represents a punctuation symbol; otherwise returns zero. The punctuation character as any printable character, except the space character and any character which returns `TRUE` from `isalnum`.

isspace

```
int isspace(c)
```

Return non-zero if `c` represents a whitespace character; otherwise returns zero. The whitespace characters from the standard ASCII character set are horizontal tab (`0x09`), newline (`0x0A`) and space (`0x20`), formfeed (`0x0C`), carriage return (`0x0D`) and vertical tab (`0x0B`).

isupper

```
int isupper(c)
```

Return non-zero if `c` represents an upper case alphabetic character; otherwise returns zero. The upper case characters are `A-Z` inclusive.

isxdigit

```
int isxdigit(c)
```

Return non-zero if `c` represents a hexadecimal digit character; otherwise returns zero. The hexadecimal digits are `0-9`, `a-f` and `A-F` inclusive.

tolower

```
int tolower(c)
```

If `c` represents an upper case alphabetic character, then `tolower` returns the corresponding lower case character; otherwise `c` is returned unchanged.

toupper

```
int toupper(c)
```

If `c` represents a lower case alphabetic character, then `toupper` returns the corresponding uppercase character; otherwise `c` is returned unchanged.

F.2 String processing

A string in C++ is an array of characters terminated by the ASCII NUL character ('\0'). String constants in a program are automatically constructed in this form by the C++ compiler.

The standard header file <string.h> contains a series of external referencing declarations to the string handling functions. Generally, there are two classes of functions. The first category is concerned with varieties of string copying. The functions usually return a character pointer result. When characters are transferred to a destination string no checks are performed to ensure that the destination string is sufficiently large. Possible array overflow can then occur and corrupt other program variables. The second class of functions perform tests and return a non-zero value representing TRUE or 0 for FALSE. Some of the more important functions are presented below.

strcat

```
char* strcat(char* s1, const char* s2)
```

Append the content of the string s2 to the end of the string s1. The first character of s2 overwrites the null character which terminates s1. A pointer to the first character of s1 is returned.

strchr

```
char* strchr(const char* s, int c)
```

The string s is searched for the first occurrence of the character c. If c is found, the function returns a pointer to c in s; otherwise NULL is returned.

strcmp

```
int strcmp(const char* s1, const char* s2)
```

Compares the two strings s1 and s2. If s1 is less than s2 the function returns a negative value. If s1 equals s2, zero is returned. If s1 is greater than s2, a positive value is returned. Two strings are equal if they have the same length and have identical content. String s1 is less than string s2 if (a) their content is identical to some character and then the next character from s1 is less than the next from s2 according to the character set encoding; or (b) string s2 is longer than string s1 and the content of s1 and s2 up to the length of s1 are identical.

strcpy

```
char* strcpy(char* s1, const char* s2)
```

Overwrite the original content of the string `s1` with the content of the string `s2`. A pointer to the first character of `s1` is returned.

strcspn

```
size_t strcspn(const char* s1, const char* s2)
```

Compares string `s1` with string `s2` and returns the length of the initial segment of string `s1` that consists of characters not found in `s2`.

strlen

```
size_t strlen(const char* s)
```

Return the number of characters in the string `s`, not including the terminating null character. The standard header file `<stddef.h>` contains a `typedef` for the type `size_t` specifying some size of unsigned integer object.

strncat

```
char* strncat(char* s1, const char* s2, size_t n)
```

Append the first `n` characters from the string `s2` to the end of the string `s1`. If `s2` contains fewer than `n` characters, only these are appended. A pointer to the first character of `s1` is returned.

strncmp

```
int strncmp(const char* s1, const char* s2, size_t n)
```

Compare up to `n` characters of the two strings `s1` and `s2`. Returns a negative integer if `s1` is less than `s2`; zero if `s1` equals `s2`; and a positive integer if `s1` is greater than `s2` (see `strcmp`). If either string contains fewer than `n` characters, the entire string is used.

strncpy

```
char* strncpy(char* s1, const char* s2, size_t n)
```

Overwrites the original content of string `s1` with the first `n` characters of string `s2`. If `s2` contains fewer than `n` characters, the entire string is used. A pointer to the first character of `s1` is returned.

strpbrk

```
char* strpbrk(const char* s1, const char* s2)
```

Returns a pointer to the first character in `s1` that matches any character in `s2`; otherwise it returns `NULL`.

strrchr

```
char* strrchr(const char* s, int c)
```

The string `s` is searched for the last occurrence of the character `c`. If `c` is found, the function returns a pointer to `c` in `s`; otherwise `NULL` is returned.

The `mem.....` functions manipulate objects as character arrays. Unlike the string functions, these operate on a region of memory and do not stop upon encountering a null character.

memchr

```
void* memchr(const void* r, int c, size_t n)
```

Searches the first `n` characters in region `r` for character `c`. It returns a pointer to the character if it is found; otherwise it returns `NULL`.

memcmp

```
int memcmp(const void* r1, const void* r2, size_t n)
```

Compares the first `n` characters of the region `r1` and `r2` character by character. If a character in `r1` is greater than that of the corresponding character in `r2` then it returns a number greater than zero; if a character in `r1` is less than that of the corresponding character in `r2` then it returns a number less than zero; otherwise it returns zero if both regions are identical.

memcpy

```
void* memcpy(void* r1, const void* r2, size_t n)
```

Copy the first `n` characters from region `r2` into region `r1`. A pointer to the first character of `r1` is returned. The behaviour of `memcpy` is undefined if the two regions overlap.

memmove

```
void* memmove(void* r1, const void* r2, size_t n)
```

Copy the first `n` characters from region `r2` into region `r1`. Unlike `memcpy`, function `memmove` operates correctly even if the two regions overlap. A pointer to the first character of `r1` is returned.

memset

```
void* memset(void* r, int c, size_t n)
```

Fills the first `n` bytes of the region pointed to by `r` with copies of the character `c` and returns a pointer to `r`.

F.3 General utilities

The header file <stdlib.h> declares a number of types and macros and several functions of general applicability. The types and macros are as follows:

MACROS

RAND_MAX	The maximum value returned by the rand function (see below).
EXIT_SUCCESS	Value indicating that a program executed correctly.
EXIT_FAILURE	Value indicating that a program executed incorrectly.

TYPES

div_t	The type of the structure returned by div .
ldiv_t	The type of the structure returned by ldiv .

FUNCTIONS

Some of the more important functions are presented below.

abs

```
int abs(int n)
```

Returns the absolute value (i.e. the distance from zero) of the integer n. The behaviour is undefined if the value cannot be represented; on two's complement machines the most negative number has no positive equivalent.

atof

```
double atof(const char* s)
```

Converts the string referred to by s into a double precision floating number. It is equivalent to the call:

```
strtod(s, (char**)NULL)
```

atoi

```
int atoi(const char* s)
```

Converts the string referred to by s into an integer. It is equivalent to the call:

```
(int) strtol(s, (char**)NULL, 10)
```

atol

```
long int atol(const char* s)
```

Converts the string referred to by `s` into a `long`. It is equivalent to the call:

```
strtol(s, (char**)NULL, 10)
```

bsearch

```
void* bsearch(const void* key, const void* base,
    size_t n, size_t size,
    int (*cmp)(const void* arg1, const void* arg2))
```

Searches the array `base[0], ..... , base[n-1]` for an item that matches `*key`. The items in the array must be in ascending order. `n` is the number of elements in the array and `size` is the size in bytes of an array item. The function `cmp` is used to compare the search key with table entries, and returns negative (zero, positive) if the first argument is less (equal, greater) than the second. `bsearch` returns a pointer to the array element for which there is a match, or `NULL` if none is found.

div

```
div_t div(int num, int den)
```

Divide the numerator `num` by the denominator `den` and return a structure of type `div_t`. This structure consists of two int members named `quot` (the quotient from `num/den`), and `rem` (the remainder from `num/den`).

The quotient is positive if the signs of the arguments are the same; otherwise the sign of the quotient is negative. The sign of the remainder is the same as the sign of the numerator.

exit

```
void exit(int status)
```

Gracefully terminate a program. When called, `exit` performs the following actions: (a) calls all the functions registered through `atexit` (see system documentation) in reverse order; (b) flushes all output stream buffers, closes the streams and removes all temporary files created by `tmpfile`; and (c) returns control to the environment providing an implementation defined `status` value. Successful termination is denoted by the status value zero or `EXIT_SUCCESS`; failure by `EXIT_FAILURE`.

getenv

```
char* getenv(const char* name)
```

The environment itself can make information available to a program. This information is available in an implementation defined environment list of string pairs – a name and its defined value. Function `getenv` searches this list for a name corresponding to the string pointed to by `name` and returns a pointer to the string that defines the corresponding value; otherwise it returns `NULL`.

labs

```
long int labs(long int n)
```

Returns the absolute value of its long integer argument. The behaviour is undefined if the value cannot be represented; on 2's complement machines the most negative number has no positive equivalent.

ldiv

```
ldiv_t ldiv(long int num, long int den)
```

Divides the numerator `num` by the denominator `den` and returns a structure of type `ldiv_t`. This structure consists of two long members named `quot` (the quotient from `num/den`) and `rem` (the remainder).

The quotient is positive if the signs of the arguments are the same; otherwise the sign of the quotient is negative. The sign of the remainder is the same as the sign of the numerator.

qsort

```
void qsort(void* base, size_t n, size_t size,
           int (*cmp)(const void*, const void*))
```

Sorts into ascending order the array `base[0], ..... , base[n-1]` of objects of size `size` bytes. The function `cmp` is used to compare two elements from the array and returns negative (zero, positive) if the first argument is less (equal, greater) than the second.

rand

```
int rand(void)
```

Generate and return a pseudo random integer in the range `0` to `RAND_MAX`.

srand

```
void srand(unsigned int seed)
```

Establish an initial `seed` value for the sequence of pseudo random numbers generated by `rand`. If no call to `srand` is made before using `rand` it is as if the seed were initialized to `1`.

strtod

```
double strtod(const char* s, char** endp)
```

Converts the string pointed to by `s` to a double precision floating point number. Any leading whitespace in the string `s` is ignored. Following the whitespace characters is the character sequence representing the floating point value as defined in Section 3.1. Any unconverted suffix in `s` is pointed to by `*endp` unless `strtod` is called with `endp` as `NULL`.

strtol

```
long int strtol(const char* s, char** endp, int base)
```

Converts the string pointed to by `s` to a long integer. Any leading whitespace in the string `s` is ignored. Following the whitespace characters is the characters sequence representing the long value as defined in Section 3.1. Any unconverted suffix in `s` is pointed to by `*endp` unless `strtol` is called with `endp` as `NULL`.

`base` gives the base of the number being read, from `0` to `36` inclusive. If base is zero, then `strtol` expects a number in the form of a C++ integer constant (leading `0` implies octal, and leading `0x` or `0X` implies hexadecimal). If `base` is between `2` and `36`, conversion is done assuming that base. If the `base` exceeds `10`, then the letters `a-z` and `A-Z` are given the values `10-35` respectively. An explicit base `16` also permits a leading `0x` or `0X`.

strtoul

```
unsigned long strtoul(const char* s, char** endp, int base)
```

Operates as per `strtol` except that the result is unsigned, and that no leading sign is permitted in the string `s`.

system

```
int system(const char* prog)
```

Pass the string `prog` to the environment's command processor for execution. If `prog` is `NULL` then `system` returns zero if a command processor exists, otherwise it returns non-zero. If `prog` is not `NULL`, then `system` returns an implementation dependent value.

F.4 C++ I/O stream library

Chapters 4 and 15 introduced the C++ *iostream library*. The exact content of the iostream library will be defined by the ANSI C++ standardization committee. This appendix presents a reference account of the classes which form the iostream library.

Output with class ostream

Class `ostream` overloads the << operator to support output of the standard types. In each case the operator returns a reference to the `ostream` instance for which it was called so that it may be concatenated.

```
class ostream : public ios {
public:
      ostream&  operator<< (const char*);      // string
      ostream&  operator<< (char);
      ostream&  operator<< (short);
      ostream&  operator<< (int);
      ostream&  operator<< (long);
      ostream&  operator<< (double);
      // .....
};
```

Examples:

```
int  j = 45, k = -123;
float  x = 12.34;
char  c = 'W';
char*  m = "Hello";

cout << '[' << "Some message" << ']';         // [Some message]
cout << '[' << j << ']';                      // [45]
cout << '[' << k << ']';                      // [-123]
cout << '[' << x << ']';                      // [12.34]
cout << '[' << c << ']';                      // [W]
cout << '[' << m << ']';                      // [Hello]
```

Class `ostream` provides a member function `put` to insert a single character on the nominated stream:

```
class ostream : public ios {
public:
      ostream&  put(char);
      // .....
};

cout.put('[').put(c).put(']');                // [W]
```

Input with class istream

Class `istream` overloads the >> operator to support input of the standard types.

The operator returns a reference to the `istream` instance for which it was called so that it may be concatenated.

```
class istream : public ios {
public:
  istream&  operator>> (char*);       // string
  istream&  operator>> (char&);
  istream&  operator>> (short&);
  istream&  operator>> (int&);
  istream&  operator>> (long&);
  istream&  operator>> (double&);
  // .....
};
```

Examples (in the input column a □ symbol represents a blank space):

```
char          ch;
int           i;
double        d;

cin >> ch >> i >> d;
```

Input	Effect
A123□45.67	ch = 'A', i = 123, d = 45.67
A□□123□□45.67	ch = 'A', i = 123, d = 45.67
□ □A □ □123 45.67	ch = 'A', i = 123, d = 45.67

Single characters and strings may also be input with the member function `get`:

```
class istream : public ios {
public:
  istream&  get(char& ch);
  istream&  get(char* line, int limit, char delim = '\n');
  // .....
};
```

Both functions do not treat whitespace characters appearing in the input stream in any special way. The first version of function `get` reads a single character from the input stream, placing it in the `ch` argument. The second form inputs at most `limit-1` characters, storing it in the character array `line`. If, when reading the input, the end-of-file or the delimiter denoted by the third argument is encountered before `limit-1` characters are read, then only that portion of the input is stored in the string. The string argument is properly terminated when the function returns. The delimiter is not included in the string.

Examples:

```
char      ch1, ch2;
char      line[80];
```

```
cin.get(ch1).get(ch2).get(line, 80);
```

Input	Effect
ABCDEF	ch1 = 'A', ch2 = 'B', line = "CDEF"
A□CDEF	ch1 = 'A', ch2 = '□', line = "CDEF"
ABCD□EF	ch1 = 'A', ch2 = 'B', line = "CD□EF"

Formatting with class ios

Class `ios` is the root class of the I/O stream library. An `ios` object connects a stream (either an `istream` or an `ostream`) to an underlying stream buffer used to hold the input or output characters. Class `ios` controls how characters are inserted into and removed from the buffer. Modification of this behaviour is provided by functions which set the appropriate data members, with complementary functions to allow a client to examine these properties. Other interrogative operations are supplied to determine the state of an `ios` object.

```
class ios {
public:
    int  width(void) const;      // get field width
    int  width(int);             // set/get field width
    int  precision(void) const;  // get floating point precision
    int  precision(int);         // set/get floating point precision
    char fill(void) const;       // get fill character
    char fill(char);             // set/get fill character
    // .....
};
```

Examples:

```
cout << '[' << 27 << ']';                  // [27]

cout.width(4);                             // set field width to 4
cout << '[' << 27 << ']';                  // [□□27]

cout.width(4);
cout.fill('*');                            // set fill character to '*'
cout << '[' << 27 << ']';                  // [**27]

cout.width(4);                             // set field width to 4
cout.width(0);                             // reset
cout << '[' << 27 << ']';                  // [27]

cout << '[' << 12.345678 << ']';           // [12.345678]

cout.precision(4);
cout << '[' << 12.345678 << ']';           // [12.3457], rounded
```

Class `ios` introduces a number of data members to control the behaviour of the formatting operations. These members operate as *format state flags*, controlled by the member functions `setf` and `unsetf`. These data and function members are inherited by `iostream` classes such as `ostream` and `istream`. The class `ios` also introduces a number of enumeration constants, symbolically denoting particular formatting values.

```
class ios {
public:
  long setf(long);
  long setf(long, long);
  long unsetf(long);
  // .....

  enum {
    left,              // left adjusted output
    right,             // right adjusted output
    skipws,            // skip whitespace on input
    internal,          // padding after sign or base indicator
    dec,               // decimal conversion
    oct,               // octal conversion
    hex,               // hexadecimal conversion
    showbase,          // use base indicator on output
    showpoint,         // force decimal point (floats)
    uppercase,         // uppercase hexadecimal output
    showpos,           // prepend '+' to positive numbers
    scientific,        // use 1.2345E2 format
    fixed              // use 123.45 format
    // .....
  };
  // .....
};
```

Member function `setf` sets the format state according to its argument(s), returning the previous state. The latter can be used, if required, to reset the original state. The version of `setf` with one argument sets the formatting flags according to its argument value. Previous formatting flags unaffected by the argument remain unchanged. The two argument version of `setf` first resets the format state flags to zero before setting the values according to the first argument. The second argument is necessary to ensure that there are no effects on other parts of the stream state. For example:

```
cout.setf(ios::showbase);
```

shows the numeric base of an integral type. The forms:

```
cout.setf( ....., ios::adjustfield);
cout.setf( ....., ios::basefield);
cout.setf( ....., ios::floatfield);
```

respectively set the formatting states for adjusting the field, for numeric or string output values, and for floating point output values.

```
cout.width(4);
cout.setf(ios::left, ios::adjustfield);      // left justify
cout << '[' << 27 << ']';                    // [27 □ □]
```

```
cout.setf(ios::oct, ios::basefield);          // octal output
cout << '[' << 27 << ']';                     // [33]

cout.setf(ios::showbase);                     // base prefix
cout.setf(ios::hex, ios::basefield);          // hexadecimal
cout << '[' << 27 << ']';                     // [0x1b]

cout.setf(ios::showbase);                     // base prefix
cout.setf(ios::hex, ios::basefield);          // hexadecimal
cout.setf(ios::uppercase);                    // in caps
cout << '[' << 27 << ']';                     // [0X1B]

cout << '[' << 12.3456789 << ']';             // [12.345679]

cout.setf(ios::scientific, ios::floatfield);
cout << '[' << 12.3456789 ']';                // [1.234567e+01]

cout.setf(ios::fixed, ios::floatfield);
cout << '[' << 12.3456789 << ']';             // [12.345679]
```

Manipulators

The header file `<iomanip.h>` supplies a series of *manipulators* which make formatting more convenient than that described above. For example, instead of writing:

```
cout.width(4);                         // set field width to 4
cout << '[' << 27 << ']';              // [□□27]
```

we may present this as:

```
cout << setw(4) << '[' << 27 << ']';
```

The manipulator function `setw` achieves the same as the `ios` member function `width`, but with the added convenience of incorporating directly into the output statement. The standard manipulators are:

```
oct       // use octal notation on input/output
dec       // use decimal notation on input/output
hex       // use hexadecimal notation on input/output

endl      // send '\n' to output then flush
ends      // send '\0' to output then flush
flush     // flush output stream

ws        // eat whitespace on input stream
```

The following manipulators take a single argument. The first four examples have arguments of type `int`. The other two have a `long` argument.

```
setbase          // see ios::setf
setfill          // see ios::fill
setprecision     // see ios::precision
setw             // see ios::width
resetiosflags    // see ios::unsetf
setiosflags      // see ios::setf
```

Examples:

```
cout << setw(4) << setfill('*') << '[' << 27 << ']'; // [**27]

cout << setprecision(4) << '[' << 12.345678 << ']'; // [12.3457]

cout << setbase(8) << '[' << 27 << ']';              // [33]

cout << setiosflags(ios::scientific | ios::floatfield) << '[' <<
                                  12.3456789 << ']'; // [1.234567e+01]
```

Files

The header file `<fstream.h>` introduces a number of classes concerned with file I/O.

Output files are opened by defining an object of class `ofstream`, given the file name as the argument:

```
ofstream  output("results");
```

The `ofstream` class constructor may be given an optional second argument which specifies alternative opening modes:

```
class ofstream : public ostream {
public:
     ofstream(const char*, int = ios::out);
     // .....
};
```

The default value for this second argument denotes that an `ofstream` is opened for writing. Other possible values are defined by an enumeration in class `ios`:

```
class ios {
public:
  // .....
  enum {
    in,           // reading
    out,          // writing
    ate,          // open and seek to end of file
    app,          // append
    trunc,        // empty the file
    nocreate,     // fail if file does not exist
    noreplace     // fail if file exists
  };
    // .....
};
```

Input files are opened by defining an object of class `ifstream`, given the file name as the argument:

```
ifstream  input("data");
```

The `ifstream` class constructor may be given an optional second argument which specifies alternative opening modes:

```
class ifstream : public istream {
public:
  ifstream(const char*, int = ios::in);
  // .....
};
```

The default value for this second argument denotes that an `ifstream` is opened for reading. Other possible values are defined by the enumeration in class `ios`.

Before performing any operations on an `ofstream` or an `ifstream` it is best to ensure that the constructor has succeeded:

```
ofstream  output("results");

if( ! output){
  // ..... error action
}
```

Class `ofstream` is derived from the class `ostream` and hence all the `ostream` operations are applicable to an `ofstream` object. A similar arrangement applies to class `ifstream`.

```
ofstream  output("results");
ifstream  input("data");

input >> day >> month >> year;
output << setw(2) << day << '/' << month << '/' << year;
```

Default constructors for both these classes permit us to define an object which is not attached to a file. The file is subsequently opened with the operation `open` and closed with the operation `close`:

```
ofstream  output;
// .....
output.open("results");
// .....
output.close();
```

Simultaneous input and output on a file is provided by a class `fstream`. Effectively, this class is derived from classes `ostream` and `istream` permitting operations from both classes to be applied to an `fstream` object:

```
fstream   diary("calendar", ios::in | ios::out);
```

Since class `ofstream` is derived from `ostream` we inherit from the latter stream positioning functions. Similarly, class `ifstream` inherits stream positioning functions from class `istream`. For example, from class `ostream` we inherit:

```
class ostream {
public:
  // .....
  ostream&  seekp(long);              // absolute
  ostream&  seekp(long, seek_dir);    // relative
  long      tellp(void);              // current position
  // .....
};
```

The first form of `seekp` positions the output at a given character position in the file. Any subsequent output will start from that position. The second form of `seekp` repositions the output a number of characters relative to the current position. The relative movement is determined by the enumeration `seek_dir`:

```
enum seek_dir { beg, cur, end };
```

For example:

```
ofstream  output("results");

output.seekp(0L, end);                  // go to end
output << "\n";                         // write here
output.seekp(0L, beg);                  // go to beginning
```

Similarly, class `istream` provides member functions `seekg` and `tellg`.

Class `ios` provides a number of member functions for interrogating the state of a stream:

```
class ios {
public:
  // .....
  int  bad(void);              // invalid operation attempted
  int  eof(void);              // end of file encountered
  int  fail(void);             // operation failure
  int  good(void);             // ok to proceed
  // .....
};
```

These member functions are then inherited by the stream classes:

```
ofstream  output("results");

if( output.fail()){
  // ..... open failure
}

while( ! output.eof()){
  // ..... process all of file
}
```

F.5 Mathematical functions

The mathematical functions are declared by the library header file `<math.h>`. For all the functions a *domain* error occurs if an input argument is outwith the domain over which the function is defined (for example, taking the square root of a negative value). If this occurs, `errno` (defined in `<errno.h>`) is set to the constant `EDOM` (defined in `<math.h>`), and the function returns a result that is implementation dependent.

For all functions a *range* error occurs if the result of the function cannot be represented by a `double`. In this case `errno` is set to the constant `ERANGE` (defined in `<math.h>`), and the function returns the value `+HUGE_VAL` (defined in `<math.h>`) with correct sign.

In the following table, arguments `x` and `y` are of type `double`, `n` is of type `int`, and all the functions return a `double`. Trigonometric functions operate with radian values.

`acos(x)`	trigonometric arc cosine of `x`, the result expressed in radians between `0` and π.
`asin(x)`	trigonometric arc sine of `x`, the result expressed in radians between `-π/2` and `π/2`.
`atan(x)`	trigonometric arc tangent of `x`, the result expressed in radians between `-π/2` and `π/2`.
`atan2(x, y)`	trigonometric arc tangent of `x/y`, the result expressed in radians between $-\pi$ and π.
`ceil(x)`	returns the floating point equivalent of the integer value not less than `x`.
`cos(x)`	trigonometric cosine of `x`, where `x` is expressed in radians.
`cosh(x)`	hyperbolic cosine of `x`.
`exp(x)`	exponential of `x`.
`fabs(x)`	absolute value of `x`.
`floor(x)`	returns the floating point equivalent of the largest integer not greater than `x`.
`fmod(x, y)`	floating point remainder of `x/y` with the same sign as `x`. If `y` is zero the result is implementation defined.
`frexp(x, int *exp)`	partitions the double value `x` into its *mantissa* and *exponent* parts. It returns the mantissa `m` such that `0.5 <= m < 1 or m = 0`. The exponent is placed in the area pointed to by `exp`.
`ldexp(x, n)`	computes `x` multiplied by `2` raised to the power `n`.
`log(x)`	natural logarithm.
`log10(x)`	logarithm of `x` to the base `10`.
`modf(x, double *ip)`	splits the argument `x` into its integral and fractional parts (each having the same sign as `x`). It stores the integral part in `*ip` and returns the fractional part.
`pow(x, y)`	computes `x` to the power `y`.
`sin(x)`	trigonometric sine of `x`, where `x` is expressed in radians.
`sinh(x)`	hyperbolic sine of `x`.
`sqrt(x)`	square root of `x`.
`tan(x)`	trigonometric tangent of `x`, where `x` is expressed in radians.
`tanh(x)`	hyperbolic tangent of `x`.

F.6 Variable argument lists

The header file `<stdarg.h>` declares and defines routines that are used to traverse a variable length function argument list. It declares the type `va_list`, and the functions `va_start`, `va_arg` and `va_end`. Generally these operations are implemented by macros.

Before any attempt is made to access a variable argument list, `va_start` must be called. It is defined as:

```
void va_start(va_list ap, lastarg)
```

The macro initializes `ap` for subsequent use by `va_arg` and `va_end`. The second argument is the identifier naming the rightmost parameter of the calling function.

Following initialization, macro `va_arg` can be used to sequentially access the anonymous arguments of the calling function. It is effectively defined as:

```
type va_arg(va_list ap, type)
```

Each call to this macro returns the value of the subsequent argument. The second argument to this macro is the name of the type of the required argument and is the type of the value returned. The macro modifies `ap` for further calls.

The macro:

```
void va_end(va_list ap)
```

must be called once following processing of the variable argument list. This must be done before the calling function returns to ensure proper cleanup of the environment.

Bibliography

[Bar90] *C Problem Solving and Programming*, Kenneth Barclay. Prentice Hall, 1990.

[Boo91] *Object Oriented Design with Applications*, Grady Booch. Benjamin/Cummings, 1991.

[Cat91] *Object Data Management*, Roderic Cattell. Addison Wesley, 1991.

[Dew89] *Programming in C++*, Stephen Dewhurst, Kathy Stark. Prentice Hall, 1989.

[Ell90] *The Annotated C++ Reference Manual*, Margaret Ellis, Bjarne Stroustrup. Addison Wesley, 1990.

[Gol83] *Smalltalk-80 The Language and its Implementation*, A. Goldberg, D. Robson. Addison Wesley, 1983.

[Gor90] *Data Abstraction and Object-Oriented Programming in C++*, Keith Gorlen, Sanford Orlow and Perry Plexico. Wiley, 1990.

[Har88] *The Definition of Standard ML, Version 2*, R. Harper, R. Milner, M. Tofte. ECS-LFCS-88-62. University of Edinburgh.

[Ker88] *The C Programming Language* (second edition), Brian Kernighan, Dennis Ritchie. Prentice Hall, 1988.

[Lin71] *Informal Introduction to Algol 68*, C. H. Lindsey, S. G. van Der Meulen. North Holland, 1971.

[Lip91] *C++ Primer*, Stanley Lippman. Addison Wesley, 1991.

[Pug90] *Skip Lists: A Probabilistic Alternative to Balanced Tree*, William Pugh, CACM, June 1990, Vol. 33, No. 6.

[Rum91] *Object Oriented Modeling and Design*, James Rumbaugh, Michael Blaha, William Premerlani, Frederick Eddy, William Lorensen. Prentice Hall, 1991.

[Str86] *The C++ Programming Language*, Bjarne Stroustrup. Addison Wesley, 1986.

[Str91] *The C++ Programming Language* (second edition), Bjarne Stroustrup. Addison Wesley, 1991.

Index